NEW HAMPSHIRE PRACTICE

WILLS, TRUSTS AND GIFTS
Fourth Edition

Volume 7

WILLIAM V.A. ZORN

Originally authored by

CHARLES DeGRANDPRE

2020 CUMULATIVE SUPPLEMENT

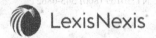 LexisNexis

QUESTIONS ABOUT THIS PUBLICATION?

For questions about the **Editorial Content** appearing in these volumes or reprint permission, please call:

Christine Lee-Pao at .... (848) 702-4541
Email: .... christine.lee-pao@lexisnexis.com
Outside the United States and Canada, please call . . . . (973) 820-2000

For assistance with replacement pages, shipments, billing or other customer service matters, please call:

Customer Services Department at . . . . (800) 833-9844
Outside the United States and Canada, please call . . . . (518) 487-3385
Fax Number . . . . (800) 828-8341
Customer Service Website . . . . http://www.lexisnexis.com/custserv/

For information on other Matthew Bender publications, please call

Your account manager or . . . . (800) 223-1940
Outside the United States and Canada, please call . . . . (937) 247-0293

Library of Congress Card Number: 97-81025

ISBN: 978-0-3271-6284-1 (print)

Cite this publication as:

DeGrandpre, New Hampshire Practice: Wills, Trusts and Gifts, Volume 7 § [sec. no.] (4th Edition, LexisNexis Matthew Bender)

Example:

DeGrandpre, New Hampshire Practice: Wills, Trusts and Gifts, Volume 7 § 3.01 (4th Edition, LexisNexis Matthew Bender)

Because the section you are citing may be revised in a later release, you may wish to photocopy or print out the section for convenient future reference.

Editorial Office
230 Park Ave., 7th Floor, New York, NY 10169 (800) 543-6862
www.lexisnexis.com

MATTHEW◆BENDER

(12/2020–Pub.82049)

Volume 7 Table of Contents

Volume 7 Table of Contents

Volume 7 Table of Contents

Volume 7 Table of Contents

Volume 7 Table of Contents

Volume 7 Table of Contents

Volume 7 Table of Contents

PUBLISHER'S PREFACE

LexisNexis Matthew Bender is pleased to present this 2020 Cumulative Supplement to 7 New Hampshire Practice: Wills, Trusts and Gifts, Fourth Edition. This Cumulative Supplement incorporates case decisions and statutory changes affecting probate practice in New Hampshire since the fourth edition of this publication in 2003. It should be retained for use until the publication of the 2021 Cumulative Supplement.

New sections to the volume and new titles to existing sections are listed in the Table of Contents and in the section analysis of the chapter to which they are added. The numbering scheme for footnotes is designed to assist the user in determining the relationship of new material in this supplement added to existing sections in Volume 7. New footnotes or footnotes for new text are assigned a footnote number that consists of the last footnote number for the preceding extant text and an additional decimal number. Where no instruction is given, new material goes at the end of the respective section or footnote.

Where new text in the supplement is meant to replace or add to existing material in the main volume, a direction line appears in the supplement, immediately after the affected section reference.

PUBLISHER'S PREFACE

I

INTRODUCTION

CHAPTER 1

INTRODUCTION

Page 2: Delete the text of § 1.02 in its entirety and substitute the following:

§ 1.02 Uniform Probate Code

The National Conference of Commissioners on Uniform State Laws in 1969 promulgated a Uniform Act entitled, in short, "The Uniform Probate Code." This Code was approved by the American Bar Association the same year and presented to the states for adoption. To date, some 19 states[1] have adopted all or some portion of the Uniform Probate Code. The Uniform Probate Code has been submitted to the New Hampshire Legislature for adoption on at least two occasions. However, there was substantial opposition to the Code because of the sweeping changes it would make in the basic procedures. As a result, registers of probate, among many, have opposed the bills and the Code has not been enacted in New Hampshire. The adoption movement nationally seems to be stalled since there has been only four adoptions by states since 1979.

Despite its limited acceptance in the states, the Code has a substantial impact on probate law in many states. The Code is considered an authoritative statement of what the law in this area should be. It also is useful for drafting purposes and our New Hampshire legislators have used the law in enacting narrow revisions of the probate statutes.

The complete title of the Uniform Probate Code is "An Act Relating to Affairs of Decedents, Missing Persons, Protected Persons, Minors, Incapacitated Persons and Certain Others." Thus, the Code is designed to be a very broad treatment of this area of the law. The Code is made up of seven articles:

Article I—General Provisions, Definitions and Probate Jurisdiction of Court;

Article II—Intestacy, Wills and Donative Transfers;

Article III—Probate of Wills and Administration;

Article IV—Foreign Personal Representatives; Ancillary Administration;

Article V—Uniform Guardianship and Protective Proceedings Act;

Article VI—Non-Probate Transfers On Death;

Article VII—Trust Administration; and

1

Article VIII—Effective Date and Repealer.

The basic sections relate to the main purpose as described in its long title, but subsequent amendments have included sections designed to be enacted either as part of the Code or as free-standing acts. These other sections include the Uniform Simultaneous Death Act, the Uniform Testamentary Additions to Trusts Act, the Uniform Disclaimer of Property Interests Act, the Uniform Disclaimer of Transfers by Will, Intestacy or Appointment Act, the Uniform Statutory Rule Against Perpetuities, the Uniform International Wills Act, the Uniform Succession Without Administration Act, the Uniform Estate Tax Apportionment Act, the Uniform Guardianship and Protective Proceedings Act, the Uniform Durable Power of Attorney Act, the Uniform Nonprobate Transfers Act, and the Uniform TOD Security Registration Act.

In 1990, Article II of the Code, which was the law of intestacy, wills and donative transfers, was substantially revised, after the completion of a systematic study of the Code conducted by the Joint Editorial Board for the Uniform Probate Code. The revisions were a result of the finding that many changes had occurred in the law and society since the promulgation of the original Code:

> In the twenty or so years between the original promulgation of the Code and the 1990 revisions, several developments occurred that prompted the systematic round of review. Three themes were sounded: (1) the decline of formalism in favor of intent-serving policies; (2) the recognition that will substitutes and other inter-vivos transfers have so proliferated that they now constitute a major, if not the major, form of wealth transmission; (3) the advent of the multiple-marriage society, resulting in a significant fraction of the population being married more than once and having stepchildren and children by previous marriages and in the acceptance of a partnership or marital-sharing theory of marriage.[2]

The 1990 revisions were a response to these themes.

The entire Code is a useful tool in providing alternative approaches to New Hampshire procedure and should be part of any New Hampshire probate practitioner's library.

---

[1] Alaska, Arizona, Colorado, Florida, Hawaii, Idaho, Maine, Massachusetts, Michigan, Minnesota, Montana, Nebraska, New Jersey, New Mexico, North Dakota, Pennsylvania, South Carolina, South Dakota, Utah.

[2] Prefatory Note, Article II, Uniform Probate Code.

CHAPTER 2
WILLS, TRUSTS, GIFTS, AND PROBATE TERMS

Page 5: Delete the text of § 2.01 in its entirety and substitute the following:

§ 2.01   Definitions of Commonly Used Terms

Listed below are some of the standard terms frequently encountered by the estate planner and probate practitioner. This glossary is not intended to be a comprehensive dictionary definition. Its function is to provide the reader with a quick reference or refresher and to point to appropriate places in this text, in a New Hampshire statute, or in Charles DeGrandpre's 10 New Hampshire Practice: Probate and Administration of Estates, Trusts and Guardianships, 4th ed., or where the reader may find more information on the topic.

Accounting. 1. An itemized statement of all sums received by and paid out by the administrator that identifies the source of the funds or the consideration paid. 2. An annual statement of transactions affecting a trustee's estate filed by a testamentary trustee. See DeGrandpre, 10 New Hampshire Practice: Probate and Administration of Estates, Trusts and Guardianships, 4th ed., Chapter 39.

—Settling an Account. The hearing procedure in which a probate judge approves or "allows" an administrator's account. See DeGrandpre, 10 New Hampshire Practice: Probate and Administration of Estates, Trusts and Guardianships, 4th ed., Chapter 39.

Ademption. The real or personal property bequeathed by will that is no longer in existence at the time of the testator's death. The legacy is lost because there is nothing on which the bequest can operate. See Chapter 15, this publication.

Administrator. 1. Any individual authorized by the probate court to administer an estate or execute a will. 2. The court-appointed personal representative of a person who died without a will. See DeGrandpre, 10 New Hampshire Practice: Probate and Administration of Estates, Trusts and Guardianships, 4th ed., Chapters 24, 25.

—Administrator, d.b.n. (*de bonis non*). A successor administrator appointed by the probate court to take over the administration of an estate only partially settled by a prior administrator. See DeGrandpre, 10 New Hampshire Practice: Probate and Administration of Estates, Trusts and Guardianships, 4th ed., Chapter 29.

—Administrator, w.w.a. (*with the will annexed*). An administrator appointed by the court when the testator fails to nominate an executor or when the person nominated is unable or unwilling to act as executor. See DeGrandpre, 10 New Hampshire Practice: Probate and Administration of Estates, Trusts and Guardianships, 4th ed., Chapter 29.

3

Advancement. The doctrine that a transfer of property to a child made by an intestate decedent prior to his death is presumed an advancement, and the value of that property is deducted from that child's share upon the distribution of the decedent's estate. This doctrine only applies to intestacy. See Chapter 17, this publication.

After Acquired Property. Any estate, right, or interest in real property acquired by the testator after making his will passes by will if it appears that this is the testator's intention. See R.S.A. 551:7 and Chapter 16, this publication.

Agent. A person who is granted authority to act for a principal under a power of attorney. *See* R.S.A. 564-E:102 and Chapter 42, this publication.

Anatomical Gift. An *inter vivos* or testamentary gift by any individual of sound mind and at least 18 years of age of all or any part of his body, the gift to take effect upon death. See R.S.A. 291-A:2 and Chapter 37, this publication.

Appointee. The persons to whom the property interests are appointed by the donee. See Chapter 19, this publication.

Appointment. The act of the probate court which appoints the person nominated by the testator to be his executor. The person nominated in a will has no authority until he has been appointed by the probate court. See Chapter 18, this publication.

Attestation. A mental act where one takes note that the signature on a will exists as a fact. See R.S.A. 551:2 and Chapter 6, this publication.

Beneficiary. (1) One who will benefit from a transfer of property. The transfer may be in the form of will, trust, or gift. (2) The person for whose benefit the property is held. See Chapters 16, 26, this publication.

Bequest. A gift by will of personal property. Compare "devise" which is a gift of realty. See Chapter 16, this publication.

Class Gift. A bequest made to a class of beneficiaries that is reasonably definable. The intent of the testator as to the meaning to be given to the class of beneficiaries controls. See Chapter 16, this publication.

Clean Hands. A defense in which a person, who has been injured or prejudiced by the act of a person seeking a constructive trust, asks for equitable relief, must come with clean hands. See Chapter 30, this publication.

Codicil. An amendment to a will. The word "will" includes codicils. A codicil must be executed with the same formalities as a will. The will and the codicil together constitute one instrument. See R.S.A. 21:22 and Chapter 11, this publication.

Common Law Marriage. The arrangement between a man and a woman who cohabit together without the legal requisites for a marriage. In New Hampshire, such a cohabitation arrangement is recognized as a marriage for inheritance purposes in very limited circumstances. See R.S.A. 457:39 and DeGrandpre, 11 New Hampshire Practice: Probate and Administration of Estates, Trusts and Guardianships, 4th ed., Chapter 52.

Conservator. A person appointed by the probate court to manage the affairs of another who is not necessarily mentally incompetent. The conservator controls the estate of the ward and not his person. A conservator may be appointed in a voluntary guardianship. See DeGrandpre, 11 New Hampshire Practice: Probate and Administration of Estates, Trusts and Guardianships, 4th ed., Chapter 74.

Construction of Wills. The process in which a will is given meaning so that the testator's plan will be effectuated, and the estate will pass to the proper persons as outlined in the testamentary document. See Chapter 13, this publication.

Cy Pres. A common law equitable rule which provides that a court, when necessary, may revise the terms of a charitable trust due to changed conditions, since the trust was created to achieve the intended benefits to the public and prevent failure of a trust. The court will substitute another charitable object which will best approximate the original intent of the settlor. See Chapter 32, this publication.

Descent and Distribution. The law relating to the inheritance rights of relatives of a decedent, also referred to as intestacy. See R.S.A. 561 and DeGrandpre, 11 New Hampshire Practice: Probate and Administration of Estates, Trusts and Guardianships, 4th ed.

Devise. The gift of bequest of a decedent's real estate under a will. The term is often used interchangeably with legacy and loosely used to define any testamentary gift, whether of real or personal property. See Chapter 16 and DeGrandpre, 10 New Hampshire Practice: Probate and Administration of Estates, Trusts and Guardianships, 4th ed., Chapter 37.

—Devisee. A person given an interest in real property under a will. See DeGrandpre, 10 New Hampshire Practice: Probate and Administration of Estates, Trusts and Guardianships, 4th ed., Chapter 37.

—General Devise. A passing of real property to another under a will without a specific reference to the real property. See DeGrandpre, 10 New Hampshire Practice: Probate and Administration of Estates, Trusts and Guardianships, 4th ed., Chapter 37.

—Specific Devise. A gift by will of a specific piece of real property that is so described as to distinguish it from other real property. See DeGrandpre, 10 New Hampshire Practice: Probate and Administration of Estates, Trusts and Guardianships, 4th ed., Chapter 37.

Disclaimer. A renunciation of, waiver of, or formal refusal to accept a title, interest, claim, trust or estate, or any part thereof. This term can also mean written instrument by which a disclaimer is formally effected. See Chapter 20, this publication.

Donative Intent. The manifest intention of the donor by any words or acts to give and an unconditional delivery of the thing given necessary for a noted gift. See Chapter 34, this publication.

Elective Share. The right of a surviving spouse to take a statutory share in lieu of the share given under the will of a deceased spouse. See R.S.A. 560:10, 14 and DeGrandpre, 11 New Hampshire Practice: Probate and Administration of Estates, Trusts and Guardianships, 4th ed., Chapter 52.

Escheat. (1) The accruing to the state of property of a decedent dying without heirs. (2) Any unclaimed property that, after the passage of a specific period of time, is presumed abandoned and accrues to the state. See R.S.A. 471-C, R.S.A. 561:8, 10–12b and DeGrandpre, Volumes 10 and 11, New Hampshire Practice: Probate and Administration of Estates, Trusts and Guardianships, 4th ed., Chapters 37, 54.

Estate. All of an individual's property, real and personal, including any rights and interests that person may have in any property. See DeGrandpre, 10 New Hampshire Practice: Probate and Administration of Estates, Trusts and Guardianships, 4th ed., Chapter 18 et seq.

Executor. The personal representative of a person who died leaving a will. See Chapter 18 and DeGrandpre, 10 New Hampshire Practice: Probate and Administration of Estates, Trusts and Guardianships, 4th ed., Chapters 25, 29.

—Executor *De Son Tort (of his wrong).* A person who wrongfully takes possession and controls a decedent's property and is held to the duties of an administrator. See DeGrandpre, 10 New Hampshire Practice: Probate and Administration of Estates, Trusts and Guardianships, 4th ed., Chapter 29.

Fertile Octagenarian Rule. The conclusive, common law presumption that a person of any age and of either sex can have children. See Chapter 32, this publication.

Fraud. The willful deception by a beneficiary as to the character or contents of the instrument or as to the extrinsic facts that are material to the disposition of the testator's property which will cause the will to be invalid. See Chapter 8, this publication.

Fraud on the Spouse's Share. A prohibition against a spouse's conveyance of assets to others prior to death so as to decrease the spouse's statutory share, when the conveyance is made with the intent to defraud the spouse. See DeGrandpre, 11 New Hampshire Practice: Probate and Administration of Estates, Trusts and Guardianships, 4th ed., Chapter 52.

Future Interest. A presently existing property interest which gives legal rights in the future to its owner. Further, interests can either be retained by the transferor or created in a transferee. See Chapter 16, this publication.

Gifts.

—*Causa Mortis* (gifts in expectation of death). A gift made by the donor under the apprehension of death, revocable during the lifetime of the donor, and which will revert to him in case he shall survive the donee or shall be delivered from the peril of death in which it is made. See Chapter 35, this publication.

—*Inter Vivos.* A voluntary, unconditional transfer of property by one to another without any consideration or compensation, which passes title of the property to the donee and is not revocable by the donor. See Chapter 34, this publication.

Grantor. See "settlor." The person who causes the trust to come into existence while the trustee is the person who is the holder of the title of the property. See Chapter 26, this publication.

Guardian. A person invested by the probate court with the power and duty of taking care of the person and/or property of another who is considered incapable of managing his affairs due to some defect of understanding. See DeGrandpre, 11 New Hampshire Practice: Probate and Administration of Estates, Trusts and Guardianships, 4th ed., Chapter 70 et seq.

Heir. The term "heir," "heirs-at-law" and "next-of-kin" have been deleted from New Hampshire statutes and in their stead, the term "issue" is employed. In common parlance, an "heir-at-law" is one who would succeed to part or all of an estate under the statute of descent and distribution in the absence of a will. See Chapter 16, this publication.

Implied Trust. A trust whereby the intent of a property owner is implied or is of no concern. See Chapter 30, this publication.

Constructive Trust. A remedial device created by courts of equity by which property is taken from one who has possession wrongfully and is given to another. It is not based on the intent of the parties, but it is implied, or imposed, by law to prevent unjust enrichment. Not a true trust. See Chapter 30, this publication.

—Resulting Trust. A remedial device of the court. An implied trust that is based upon the assumed intent of the property owner. A resulting trust arises where a person enables or causes a disposition of property under circumstances that raise an inference that he does not intend the title holder to have the beneficial interest therein. A resulting trust is not a true trust. See Chapter 30, this publication.

Insolvent Estate. An estate where it appears that the assets are insufficient to pay all debts, expenses and taxes due from the estate. It is not necessary that the estate actually be insolvent to be administered as an insolvent estate. An estate which is insolvent is said to be administered in the insolvency course. See DeGrandpre, 11 New Hampshire Practice: Probate and Administration of Estates, Trusts and Guardianships, 4th ed., Chapter 49.

In Terrorem **Clause.** A provision in a will that a bequest to a beneficiary shall be void if the beneficiary disputes or contests the will. See Chapter 17, this publication.

Intestacy. The law governing the distribution of property upon the death of a decedent who dies without a will, or who dies with a will but without disposing of all of his property. In New Hampshire, this law is called the Statute of Descent and Distribution. See DeGrandpre, 11 New Hampshire Practice: Probate and Administration of Estates, Trusts and Guardianships, 4th ed., Chapter 54.

Incorporation by Reference. The rule which validates a will that incorporates by reference another document or paper not executed with the requisite formalities of the Statute of Wills. The document or paper must be in existence when the will is made and must be sufficiently identified in the will. See Chapter 9, this publication.

Inventory. An itemized account or listing of the assets in the decedent's estate filed with the probate court by the administrator. The inventory contains a description of all real estate, a schedule of all goods, chattel, stocks, bonds, other effects of the deceased, all notes, bank deposits, interest owed and other written evidences of debt, i.e., all property in which the decedent had an interest. See DeGrandpre, 10 New Hampshire Practice: Probate and Administration of Estates, Trusts and Guardianships, 4th ed., Chapter 34.

Issue. Any person who is either a child, grandchild, or other lawful, lineal descendant of the decedent. Issue may include, under some circumstances, adopted children or other descendants. See Chapter 16, this publication.

—Blood Issue. Lineal descendants of a decedent who are of the decedent's bloodline. The term excludes adopted children. See Chapter 16, this publication.

—Adopted Children. An adopted child is considered the same as a natural child and enjoys the same rights of inheritance. Once adoption is final, the adopted child generally loses all rights of inheritance from his natural parents. See R.S.A. 170-B:20 and Chapter 16, this publication.

—Stepchildren. The children of a decedent's spouse born of a prior marriage. Only when the testator clearly intends that a stepchild be deemed to be a natural child will the term "issue" include step-children. Otherwise, "issue" refers to a relationship by blood and not by marriage, so the stepchild would not inherit property. Step-children have no rights of inheritance from a stepparent under the laws of descent and distribution. See R.S.A. 561 and Chapter 16, this publication.

—Illegitimate Children. Children born out of wedlock. The term "issue" does not include illegitimate children. Illegitimate children are now called "children born of unwed parents." A child born of unwed parents inherits through his mother as if born in lawful wedlock. An illegitimate child has inheritance rights only with respect to the intestacy of the natural father. See R.S.A. 561:4 and Chapter 16, this publication.

—Legitimate Children. Children born in wedlock. The parents' marital status at the time the child is born controls. See Chapter 16, this publication.

—Legitimated Children. Blood issue of a parent born out of wedlock but later legally recognized by the parent as legitimate issue of the parent. See Chapter 16, this publication.

Lapse. A legacy that lapses or becomes extinguished by the death of a legatee during the lifetime of a testator. The "anti-lapse statute" prevents a legacy from lapsing if a legatee or devisee dies with heirs in the descending line. The bequest passes to the heirs. See R.S.A. 551:12 and Chapter 16, this publication.

Legacy. 1. Strictly, a gift or bequest of personal property under a will. 2. Legacy may be deemed to include real estate if the will establishes that as the testator's intent. See Chapter 16, this publication and DeGrandpre, 10 New Hampshire Practice: Probate and Administration of Estates, Trusts and Guardianships, 4th ed., Chapter 37.

—**Demonstrative Legacy.** A bequest of a certain sum of money that is paid out of a specific fund in existence at the time of the testator's death. See Chapter 16, this publication and DeGrandpre, 10 New Hampshire Practice: Probate and Administration of Estates, Trusts and Guardianships, 4th ed., Chapter 37.

—**General Legacy.** A bequest or gift under a will that comes out of the general assets of the testator's estate. The item or the fund from which it comes is not identified. See Chapter 16, this publication and DeGrandpre, 10 New Hampshire Practice: Probate and Administration of Estates, Trusts and Guardianships, 4th ed., Chapter 37.

—**Legatees.** One who takes an interest in personal property under a will. See Chapter 16, this publication and DeGrandpre, 10 New Hampshire Practice: Probate and Administration of Estates, Trusts and Guardianships, 4th ed., Chapter 37.

—**Pecuniary Legacy.** A bequest of a sum of money or an annuity. See Chapter 16 and DeGrandpre, 10 New Hampshire Practice: Probate and Administration of Estates, Trusts and Guardianships, 4th ed., Chapter 37.

—**Specific Legacy.** A gift by will of a specific thing or of some portion of the testator's estate described so as to distinguish it from other articles of the same nature. See Chapter 16, this publication and DeGrandpre, 10 New Hampshire Practice: Probate and Administration of Estates, Trusts and Guardianships, 4th ed., Chapter 37.

Letters of Administration. A certificate of formal notice of the probate court's appointment of an administrator to act on behalf of an estate. This notice is also known as a certificate of appointment. See DeGrandpre, 10 New Hampshire Practice: Probate and Administration of Estates, Trusts and Guardianships, 4th ed., Chapter 24.

License. The permission of a probate court to conduct a sale. See DeGrandpre, 10 New Hampshire Practice: Probate and Administration of Estates, Trusts and Guardianships, 4th ed., Chapter 35.

Living Will. A document by which a person articulates his desire and direction that measures to prolong his life be withheld or discontinued in circumstances where there is no hope of recovery. See R.S.A. 137-H and Chapter 39, this publication.

Lost Person. A person who has left home, has not been heard of, or from, directly or indirectly for one year, and is believed to be dead. See R.S.A. 553:18 and DeGrandpre, 10 New Hampshire Practice: Probate and Administration of Estates, Trusts and Guardianships, 4th ed., Chapter 22.

Minor. A person under the age of 18. Unless a minor is married, he or she may not make a will. See Chapter 16, this publication.

Mistake.

—Of Fact. A mistake by a testator as to the extent of his property, its location, or the exact proportions in which it is distributed. A will cannot be set aside as invalid if the testator is of sound mind and under no undue influence. See Chapter 8, this publication.

—Of Law. A mistake by a testator concerning the legal effect of the language used in his will. Short of unconscionability, a will is valid even if the testator mistook the legal effect of the language used, or that he acted upon the mistaken advice of counsel, provided the advice was given in an honest belief that it was sound. See Chapter 8, this publication.

Next-of-Kin. See "heir," this chapter.

Non-Claim Statute. The statute of limitations requiring that a demand by a claimant be made of an administrator within a certain time period, and requiring that an action to collect the claim be filed within a certain time period, or the claim is barred. See R.S.A. 556:1 and DeGrandpre, 10 New Hampshire Practice: Probate and Administration of Estates, Trusts and Guardianships, 4th ed., Chapter 41.

Oral Contract to Make a Will. A decedent's oral promise to bequeath personal property, devise land, or leave a portion or all of his estate to another, in return for adequate consideration from the promisee. See Chapter 24, this publication.

Personal Representative. A person to whom the administration of an estate or the execution of a will has been granted by the probate court. The term includes executors and administrators. The Uniform Probate Code favors this term, but it is not commonly used in New Hampshire. See DeGrandpre, 10 New Hampshire Practice: Probate and Administration of Estates, Trusts and Guardianships, 4th ed., Chapter 24 et seq.

Power of Appointment. A power of appointment is a future interest created by a testator in another which enables a testator to control the future devolution of his property while retaining a certain amount of flexibility. See Chapter 19, this publication.

—Donee. The person in whom a power of appointment is created or reserved. See Chapter 19, this publication.

—Donor. The person who creates or reserves the power of appointment. See Chapter 19, this publication.

—Object of the Power. Those persons among whom the donee is given the power to appoint the property that is subject to the power. See Chapter 19, this publication.

—Takers in Default of Appointment. Persons who receive subject property if the donee of a power of attorney either fails to exercise a power or fails to exercise it effectively. See Chapter 19, this publication.

Principal. A person who executes a power of attorney delegating specified duties to a known agent. See R.S.A. 564-E:102 and DeGrandpre, 11 New Hampshire Practice: Probate and Administration of Estates, Trusts and Guardianships, 4th ed., Chapter 74.

Private Claim. A debt due from the estate to its administrator. See DeGrandpre, 10 New Hampshire Practice: Probate and Administration of Estates, Trusts and Guardianships, 4th ed., Chapter 39.

Probate. 1. The process of proving the document offered as a decedent's last will and testament before the court. 2. The entire body of law relating to the distribution of property upon a person's death. See DeGrandpre, 10 New Hampshire Practice: Probate and Administration of Estates, Trusts and Guardianships, 4th ed., Chapters 5, 23.

Probate Bond. A surety instrument that a fiduciary posts, in a specified amount, with the probate court in a probate proceeding, by which the surety promises to indemnify the estate for improper actions by the fiduciary. See DeGrandpre, 10 New Hampshire Practice: Probate and Administration of Estates, Trusts and Guardianships, 4th ed., Chapter 28.

Probate Law. The areas of law commonly handled by a probate court, including distributions of estates, conservatorships, guardianships, testamentary trusts, adoptions, termination of parental rights, change of name, permission to marry, etc. See DeGrandpre, 10 New Hampshire Practice: Probate and Administration of Estates, Trusts and Guardianships, 4th ed., Chapters 3, 4, 5.

Proof in Common Form. A method of proving a will in an uncontested probate proceeding that does not require the oral testimony of all witnesses to the will as to its proper execution. See DeGrandpre, 10 New Hampshire Practice: Probate and Administration of Estates, Trusts and Guardianships, 4th ed., Chapter 14.

Proof in Solemn Form. A method of proving a will that requires public notice and examination of all witnesses to a will. It is a more elaborate procedure than proof in common form. See DeGrandpre, 10 New Hampshire Practice: Probate and Administration of Estates, Trusts and Guardianships, 4th ed., Chapter 44.

Property. Any interest in property owned by a decedent. See Chapter 16, this publication.

—Personal Property. A decedent's tangible and intangible property, rights, and interests, other than real property. See DeGrandpre, 10 New Hampshire Practice: Probate and Administration of Estates, Trusts and Guardianships, 4th ed., Chapter 33 et seq.

—Real Property. A decedent's real estate. See DeGrandpre, 10 New Hampshire Practice: Probate and Administration of Estates, Trusts and Guardianships, 4th ed., Chapter 35.

Tangible Personal Property. A decedent's goods and chattels. The term does not include intangible personal property such as stocks, bonds, mutual funds, or cash accounts. See DeGrandpre, 10 New Hampshire Practice: Probate and Administration of Estates, Trusts and Guardianships, 4th ed., Chapter 39.

Pour-over Clause. A clause in a will which permits the testator's assets to be "poured-over" or transferred to an existing revocable or *inter vivos* trust. See Chapter 16, this publication.

Precatory Language. An expression of the settlor's "hope," "wish," or "recommendation." See Chapter 28, this publication.

Pretermitted Child. Any child born after the death of the testator and every child or issue of a child of the deceased not named or referred to in his will who is not a devisee or legatee. Such a child is entitled to the same portion of the estate, real and personal, as he would be if the deceased were intestate. See R.S.A. 551:10 and Chapter 14, this publication.

Purchase Money Resulting Trust. A trust is presumed whereby one person supplies the consideration for the purchase of property, but title is taken in the name of another. See Chapter 30, this publication.

Quantum Meruit. In probate, a recovery for reasonable value of services performed in consideration of a promise by the decedent to leave the promisee all or a portion of his estate. See Chapter 24, this publication.

Renunciation. An act by a beneficiary to prevent the passage of title to himself of property bequeathed or devised to him after the death of the testator. See Disclaimer *above* and Chapter 20, this publication.

Residuary Clause. A clause in a will which disposes the part of property that remains after satisfying the bequests and devises. See Chapter 19, this publication.

Revival. The regained validity of an earlier will where a later will revoking the earlier will is itself revoked. In New Hampshire, the revocation of a second will does not revive the first will without evidence that such was the intention of the testator. See Chapter 12, this publication.

Revocation.

—Dependent Relevant Revocation. An attempted revocation, in whole or in part, of a will by a testator. The testator is assumed to have made a revocation on the condition that the attempted revocation was successful. See Chapter 12, this publication.

—Express Revocation. An action of a testator to invalidate his will. A revocation is accomplished by either a subsequent writing or by a physical act which invalidates the will. See R.S.A. 551:13 and Chapter 12, this publication.

—Implied Revocation. An invalidation of a will by a change in circumstances of the testator, or his family, devisees, legatees, or estate, occurring after the making of the will. In New Hampshire, implied revocation is restricted to very few instances. See R.S.A. 551:14 and Chapter 12, this publication.

Rule Against Perpetuities. A rule restricting the amount of time in the future during which an individual may impose restrictions on property. See Chapter 32, this publication.

Settlor. The person who causes the trust to come into existence, while the trustee is the person who is the holder of the title of the property. See "grantor" *above* and Chapter 26, this publication.

Simultaneous Death. Where there is no sufficient evidence that two or more persons have died otherwise than simultaneously. See R.S.A. 563:1 and Chapter 44, this publication.

Statute of Frauds. A statutory rule requiring that the disposition of land by will or by trust must be in writing, except for trusts arising or resulting by implication of law. See R.S.A. 477:17 and Chapter 30, this publication.

Statute of Uses. The statute that effectively converts a conveyance into full legal and equitable title in the beneficiary without the beneficiary being required to take any action. See Chapter 29, this publication.

Survival of Action. The law relating to when an action, pending or not yet pending, by or against a decedent at his death, may be initiated or continued after the decedent's death. See R.S.A. 508, 556 and DeGrandpre, 10 New Hampshire Practice: Probate and Administration of Estates, Trusts and Guardianships, 4th ed., Chapter 46.

Testamentary Capacity. The required mental capacity necessary for an individual to have the ability to make a will. In New Hampshire, a person must be "of sane mind" to make a will. See R.S.A. 551:1, 2 and Chapter 8, this publication.

Trust. A fiduciary relationship with respect to property in which one person ("trustee") is the holder of the title to property, subject to an equitable obligation to use the property for the benefit of another. See Chapter 26, this publication.

—Express Trust. A trust that comes into being because the person having the power to create it expresses an intent to have the trust created and complies with the requisite formalities for establishing the trust. Such trusts are distinguished from implied trusts which arise by implication of law. See Chapter 28, this publication.

—Inter Vivos Trust. An express trust, either revocable or irrevocable, established by the settlor during his life. It is often referred to as a "living trust" or a "revocable trust." See Chapters 26, 31, this publication, and DeGrandpre, 11 New Hampshire Practice: Probate and Administration of Estates, Trusts and Guardianships, 4th ed., Chapter 65.

—Revocable Trust. An *inter vivos* trust over which the grantor retains the power to revoke or terminate. See DeGrandpre, 11 New Hampshire Practice: Probate and Administration of Estates, Trusts and Guardianships, 4th ed., Chapter 65.

—Testamentary Trust. An express trust created by will that comes into existence upon the death of the testator and must meet the requirements of the Statute of Wills. It is subject to the primary jurisdiction of the Probate Court. See Chapters 26, 31, this publication, and DeGrandpre, 11 New Hampshire Practice: Probate and Administration of Estates, Trusts and Guardianships, 4th ed., Chapter 64.

—Voluntary Trust. A voluntary trust is an express trust created by the settlor in which he makes himself the trustee for the benefit of another if the requirements for a valid *inter vivos* trust are met. See Chapter 31, this publication.

—**Charitable Trust.** A charitable trust is an express trust, either testamentary or *inter vivos*, in which the trustee holds the property for charitable purposes. Charitable trusts are sometimes referred to as public trusts or charities. See Chapter 31, this publication.

—**Discretionary Trust.** A discretionary trust is a trust in which the trustee has the discretion to pay or not to pay both the income and/or the principal to the trust beneficiary and contains provisions against alienation by the beneficiary or attachment by creditors. See Chapter 31, this publication.

—**Insurance Trust.** An express *inter vivos* trust in which the corpus is an insurance policy, usually on the life of the settlor, and the trust is the beneficiary of the policy. See Chapter 31, this publication.

—**Private Trust.** A private trust is an express trust of real or personal property in which the beneficiaries are individuals or noncharitable organizations. See Chapter 31, this publication.

—**Spendthrift Trust.** An express trust in which the trust instrument provides that the interest of the beneficiary is neither alienable nor subject to the claims of creditors. See Chapter 31, this publication.

—**Support Trust.** A support trust is a trust in which it is provided that the trustee shall pay or apply only so much of the income and the principal, or either, as is necessary for the education or support of the beneficiary. See Chapter 31, this publication.

Trustee. The fiduciary who holds title to the property subject to an equitable interest of the beneficiary. See Chapter 26, this publication.

Trust Property (Res). The property held by the trustee which must be described with definiteness. Other terms used interchangeably with trust property are: "corpus," "principal," "trust estate," or "trust res." A trust cannot be created unless there is trust property—an interest capable of ownership and transferability. See Chapter 26, this publication.

Undue Influence. The actions of a third party who stands to benefit under the will which improperly influences the testator's free will and which renders the instrument something other than an expression of the wishes and determination of the testator. The influence must amount to force and coercion, not influence of affection and attachment. Undue influence will void the will. See Chapter 8, this publication.

Uniform Testamentary Additions to Trusts Act. The act that validates a devise or bequest made by a will to the trustees of a trust established or to be established by the testator, so long as the trust is identified in the testator's will and the trust is set forth in a written instrument executed before or concurrently with the execution of the testator's will. See R.S.A. 563-A and Chapters 10, 26, this publication.

Uniform Transfers to Minors Act. The act which provides that a valid gift can be made to a minor by a transfer to a custodian for the benefit of a minor and by registering the property in the name of the custodian "as custodian for the minor." See R.S.A. 463-A and Chapter 36, this publication.

Voluntary Administration. A simplified form of administration designed for small estates. See DeGrandpre, 10 New Hampshire Practice: Probate and Administration of Estates, Trusts and Guardianships, 4th ed., Chapter 19.

Wait and See Rule. A court may determine the validity of the contingent future interest on the date the contingency actually occurs rather than at the date the interest is created. See Chapter 32, this publication.

Ward. A person who, due to some defect of understanding, is considered incapable of administering his own affairs and over whom or over whose property a guardian is appointed. See DeGrandpre, 11 New Hampshire Practice: Probate and Administration of Estates, Trusts and Guardianships, 4th ed., Chapter 70 et seq.

Will. A will is the instrument made by a person of sane mind over the age of 18, unless married under that age, in order to devise and dispose of their real and personal property according to their intentions. It must be in writing, signed by the testator and properly attested to and subscribed by two or more witnesses in conformity with the requirements of the Statue of Wills. See R.S.A. 21:22 and Chapter 5, this publication.

—Alien's Will. A will made by a foreign born person who does not qualify as a citizen of the United States, but who is a resident of New Hampshire. An alien may take, purchase, hold, convey, or devise real estate, and such property may descend in the same manner as if he were a citizen. See R.S.A. 477:20 and Chapter 5, this publication.

—Foreign Will. A will that is executed in accordance with the attestation and execution requirements of another state which seeks to operate upon property located in New Hampshire. Once a duly authenticated copy of the will is proved and allowed by a court in another jurisdiction to be filed in the probate courts of New Hampshire, it has the same effect as if executed in conformity with the laws of New Hampshire. See R.S.A. 552:13 and Chapter 6, this publication.

—Holographic Will. A will that is handwritten and signed by the testator. New Hampshire does not recognize holographic wills unless the requirements of the Statute of Wills are met. See Chapter 5, this publication.

—Joint Will. A will in which two or more persons execute the same instrument as their respective will. New Hampshire has no statute to validate or judicial authority to recognize a joint will. See Chapter 5, this publication.

—Lost Will. A will the original of which cannot be located. In New Hampshire, a lost will may, upon proper proof, be admitted to probate. The proponent of the lost will must sufficiently prove the contents and its due execution. See Chapter 6, this publication.

15

—**Mutual Will.** A will that is essentially identical to a separate instrument that arises as the result of an agreement between two testators. A reciprocal will. See Chapter 5, this publication.

—**Nuncupative Will.** A "non-written" will, i.e., an oral will. Generally, New Hampshire does not recognize a nuncupative will. See R.S.A. 551:15, 16 for a narrow exception and Chapter 5, this publication.

—**Reciprocal Will.** A will that is essentially identical to a separate instrument that arises as the result of an agreement between two testators. A mutual will. See Chapter 5, this publication.

—**Self-Proving Will.** A will acknowledged by the testator before a notary public or a justice of the peace making it unnecessary for a witness of the will to testify as to its validity in court. See R.S.A. 551:2-a and Chapter 6, this publication.

—**Soldier's and Sailor's Will.** A will made by a soldier or sailor without the requisite formalities to dispose of personal property. See R.S.A. 551:15 and Chapter 5, this publication.

Will Contest. Litigation challenging the validity of a will for any reason. See DeGrandpre, 10 New Hampshire Practice: Probate and Administration of Estates, Trusts and Guardianships, 4th ed., Chapter 44.

Will Substitute. A testamentary-like device that operates to convey property of one person upon death to another without compliance with the requirements of the Statute of Wills. See Chapter 22, this publication.

CHAPTER 4
ROLE OF ATTORNEY IN DRAFTING WILL

§ 4.01　Risks of Improperly Drafted Wills

Page 30: Add the following paragraph at the end of the text to this section:

The New Hampshire Bar Association has adopted Ethics Committee Opinion No. 2008-09/1, dated May 13, 2009, entitled *Drafting Lawyer Acting as Fiduciary for Client*, which establishes guidelines for attorneys drafting wills in which the attorney drafting the will is nominated to act as fiduciary, either as executor or as trustee. This ethics opinion should be reviewed to assure compliance with it as an attorney drafts a will in such circumstances covered by the opinion. The committee's opinion is attached in the Appendix to this volume as Form 71.

Library References

Aucutt, "*Creed or Code: The Calling of the Counselor in Advising Families,*" 36

ACTEC Law Journal 4, page 669 (2001).

§ 4.03 Attorney as Beneficiary in Will Which Attorney Drafted

Page 31: Delete the quoted content from Rule 1.8(c) after the first paragraph and substitute the following:

Rule 1.8(c). A lawyer shall not solicit any substantial gift from a client, including a testamentary gift, or prepare on behalf of a client an instrument giving the lawyer or a person related to the lawyer any substantial gift unless the lawyer or other recipient of the gift is related to the client.

§ 4.05 Action By Beneficiary Where Will Not Executed

Page 36: Delete the last paragraph of this section and substitute the following:

In *Estate of Agnew v. Ross*,[20] the Supreme Court of Pennsylvania held that, in order to maintain an action against the drafting attorney, the plaintiff must be named as a beneficiary in an executed document, and since the intended beneficiaries were not named in the will, the action against the attorney failed.

[20] 152 A.3d 247 (Pa. 2017).

§ 4.06 Potential Conflicts of Interest in Representing Both Spouses for Drafting Wills

Page 36: Add the following at the end of the text to this section:

For a discussion of the ethical guidelines that apply when an attorney is asked to represent two clients jointly in the preparation of estate planning documents, see New Hampshire Bar Association Ethics Committee Opinion, #2014–2015/10.

CHAPTER 5
TYPES OF WILLS

§ 5.01 Introduction; Writing Requirement

Page 37: Delete the text of this section in its entirety and substitute the following:

R.S.A. 551:1 gives to all persons over the age of 18 years, and married persons under that age, of sane mind, the right to devise and dispose by will of their real and personal property, or any right or interest they may have in such property. The will must be in writing, signed by the testator or by some person at his or her express direction in his or her presence, and properly attested to and subscribed by two or more witnesses. R.S.A. 21:22, part of the principles of statutory construction of the Revised Statutes, provides that the legislature's use of the word *will* in the statutes shall include codicils.

§ 5.02   Holographic Wills; Attestation Requirements

Page 38: Replace the second paragraph of this section with the following:

Because there is a widespread perception that such handwritten wills are valid, such wills occasionally turn up but, unless executed in a state where such wills are valid, they are universally denied probate for failing to meet the statutory requirements.[2]

[2] In the Matter of Rice, 118 N.H. 528, 390 A.2d 1146 (1978).

§ 5.05   Joint, Mutual or Reciprocal Wills

Page 43: Insert the following at the end of the text to this section:

In *In re Estate of Brown*,[17.1] the Tennessee Supreme Court held that where a husband and his wife executed mutual wills pursuant to a contract not to revoke and after the husband's death his wife executed a new will with terms different from those required in the contract the mutual promise not to revoke was sufficient consideration.

[17.1] 402 S.W.3d 193 (Tenn. 2013).

§ 5.06   Aliens' Wills

Page 45: Replace the fourth sentence of the second paragraph of this section with the following:

However, the treaty must establish the parties' intent to confer the rights of inheritance upon nonresident alien decedents and if it fails to do so, the treaty will not be effective to grant inheritance rights to nonresident aliens of that country.[29]

[29] Lazarou v. Maroros, 101 N.H. 383, 143 A.2d 669 (1958).

§ 5.07   International Wills

Page 47: Insert the following at the end of the text to this section:

Form 67 is a complete form for an international will meeting the requirements of the Uniform International Wills Act and of the Washington Convention of 1973.

CHAPTER 6

FORMALITIES OF EXECUTION

§ 6.02   Statutory Requirements—In General

Page 52: Add the following at the end of this section:

There has been a developing trend in American law as a growing number of American states have begun to reverse traditional rules requiring strict compliance with execution requirements and rules disallowing reformation as to mistakes in the contents of wills. This trend is based upon not only state legislative changes, but upon the new Restatement (Third) of Property: Wills and Other Donative Transfers (1999). A leading authority in this area, Professor John H. Langbein, Associate Reporter for the Third Restatement, has discussed this trend in an excellent article entitled "Curing Execution Errors and Mistaken Terms in Wills."[18.1] Furthermore, Section 2-203 of the Uniform Probate Code has provided since 1990 that a will with execution errors will be treated "as if it had been executed in compliance with [the statutory requirements] if the proponent . . . establishes by clear and convincing evidence that the decedent intended the document" as his or her will.

"In recent years, the definition of the term 'will' has changed dramatically. The type of writing necessary to create a valid will is evolving, and courts are moving away from adherence to strict compliance. Probate courts across the country, faced with everything from DVDs to post-it-notes, are admitting to probate these nontraditional 'documents' as writings intended as wills."[18.2]

The continuing heated issue whether compliance with the Will's Act is strictly required or whether substantial compliance or harmless error may be sufficient to cure a will that does not comply with the formalities of the Will's Act is discussed in an article entitled "*Wills Act Compliance—Strict Compliance vs. Substantial Compliance/Harmless Error: Flawed Narrative = Flawed Analysis?*" by Peter T. Wendel.[18.3]

[18.1] Probate & Property Magazine, Jan./Feb. 2004, at 28.

[18.2] LaRatta and Osorio, "*What's in a Name? Writings Intended as Wills,*" 28 Probate and Property 3, page 47 (2014).

[18.3] 31 Probate & Property Magazine, at 23 (May/June 2017).

[2] Signing

Page 54: Insert the following after the third paragraph of the text:

In the case of *In re Estate of Catherine Fischer,*[32.1] the court had before it the issue of whether the witness signed in the presence of the testator. The court citing to *Healey v. Bartlett,*[32.2] found that the witnesses had not signed the will in the presence of the testator where the facts showed that the bed-ridden testator signed the will at the request of her attorney at her bedside. Later in the presence of the witnesses, the attorney asked the testatrix, among other things, if she had read the will, if she understood the will, if it disposed her property in the manner she wished, and if she wished the will to be signed that day and if she wanted the witnesses to act as witnesses, to all of which she answered in the affirmative. However, it appeared that the witnesses did not sign the will in the room in which the testatrix lay in bed; rather, they signed the will on the porch outside:

The petitioner bore the burden of proving that the witnesses signed the will in the testatrix's presence. Yet there was no evidence in the record that, but for the testatrix's physical infirmities, she could have 'readily . . . seen and heard' what the witnesses were doing, had she been so disposed.[32.3]

Nor was there evidence that the witnesses were 'so near' to the testatrix that she was conscious of where they were and what they were doing when they signed the will.[32.4] On this record, we are unable to defer to the probate court's finding that the witnesses signed the will in the testatrix's presence.[32.5]

[32.1] 152 N.H. 669 (2005).

[32.2] 73 N.H. 110, 111 (1904).

[32.3] Healey v. Bartlett, 73 N.H. 110, 112 (1904).

[32.4] Healey v. Bartlett, 73 N.H. 110, 111 (1904).

[32.5] See R.S.A. 567-A:4.

Page 55: Insert the following at the end of the text to this section:

A testator's signature on a self-proving affidavit does not cure the lack of a signature on the will even though the testator had initialed page 1 of a 2-page will. The court held that the will was not signed by the testator because the self-proving affidavit is a separate document that is not part of the will.[36.1]

A will is not valid when the testator signed a self-proving affidavit but did not sign the will itself.[36.2]

[36.1] In re Estate of Chastain, 401 S.W.3d 612 (Tenn. 2012).

[36.2] In re Estate of Chastain, 401 S.W.3d 612 (Tenn. 2012).

[4] **Witnesses**

Page 58: Delete the sixth paragraph of this subsection and substitute with the following:

In *Hodgman v. Kittredge*,[59] it was held that a valid and beneficial devise or legacy to the wife of a subscribing witness rendered the husband incompetent as a witness and the entire will was invalid because under common law a spouse could not testify against the other in any cause in which either was interested. However, *Stewart v. Harriman*[59.1] held that a witness is not rendered incompetent if their spouse is the executor of a will simply by such executor's receipt of ordinary fees and commissions received for the performance of their duties as executor. Moreover, in the later case of *Cochran v. Brown*,[60] it was held that the wife of an executor who served as a witness to a will under which her executor husband received a bequest of the residue of the estate was not incompetent and was considered a credible witness. Generally, it has been held in recent cases that attesting witnesses are considered competent and therefore credible even though they may receive some indirect benefit under the will.[61] Despite these cases, the better practice is to obtain as witnesses to a will persons who are entirely unrelated to the matter and who are young enough to be likely available to testify as to the proper execution of the will at the testator's death.

[59] 67 N.H. 254, 32 A. 158 (1892).

[59.1] 56 N.H. 25.

[60] 76 N.H. 9, 78 A. 1072 (1911).

[61] Leonard v. Stanton, 93 N.H. 113, 36 A.2d 271 (1944); In re Amor's Estate, 99 N.H. 417, 112 A.2d 665 (1955).

[5] Uniform Probate Code Provision

Page 60: Delete the last blocked paragraph of this section and insert the following in its place:

A will referring, at the time of its execution, to a writing that has yet to be prepared does not incorporate such by reference. A testator cannot reserve to himself the power to modify a will by written instrument subsequently prepared and not executed in a manner required by law. Therefore, while the doctrine of incorporation of documents by reference in a will is recognized in New Hampshire, the documents referred to must be in existence when the will itself is executed.[61.1] Such document may have no significance apart from its effect on the dispositions made by the will.

[61.1] Kellom v. Beverstock, 100 N.H. 329, 126 A.2d 127 (1956).

§ 6.04 Lost Wills

Page 62: In the first paragraph of this section, replace the fourth sentence with the following:

The proponent of the lost will must sufficiently prove the contents of the will and its due execution, as well as demonstrate that the testator did not intend to revoke the lost will.[71]

[71] Atkinson, Wills, § 97 (2d ed. 1953).

Page 62: Add the following text after the first paragraph of this section:

In *In re Estate of King*,[73.1] an earlier will was lost while in the possession of the testator. A later original codicil was found which republished the will and the proponents for probating the lost will argued that the later codicil which republished the will was sufficient to prove the last will. However, the Supreme Court held that:

> When a testator executes both a will and a codicil adopting a minor change to that will, and then destroys that will, it is clear that the testator's intent is to revoke the entire testamentary scheme. . . . In this case, the 1997 codicil made only a few minor amendments and was not sufficiently complete as a testamentary document to stand alone without the original will. Thus, the revocation of the 1994 will would have also revoked the 1997 codicil.[73.2]

The Massachusetts Supreme Judicial Court in *In re Estate of Beauregard*[73.3] held that presumption of revocation that arises when a will last known to be in the possession of the testator and cannot be found after the testator's death, can be rebutted by evidence requiring only a standard of a preponderance of the evidence, rejecting imposing a higher burden to rebut the presumption. *See also*, Restatement (Third) of Property (Wills and Other Donative Transfers) Section 4.1.

[73.1] 149 N.H. 226 (2003).

[73.2] *In re* Estate of King, 149 N.H. 226, 231 (2003).

[73.3] 921 N.E.2d 954 (Mass. 2010).

CHAPTER 8

TESTAMENTARY CAPACITY, UNDUE INFLUENCE, FRAUD AND MISTAKE

A. TESTAMENTARY CAPACITY

§ 8.01   In General

Library References

Page 80: Add the following to the Library References already in the text:

Blackadar, Christine M.V. and Parker B. Potter, Jr., *Alzheimer's Disease and Testamentary Capacity: The Effects of a New Diagnosis on an Age-Old Problem*, NHBJ (September 1998).

Nelson A. Raust, *Ethical Challenges in Representing Elderly Clients*, 46 NHBJ 28 (Spring 2005).

Sarah Moore, J.D., *Alzheimer's Disease as Affecting Testamentary Capacity*, 47 ALR 5th 523 (1997).

Mazoff, "*A Common Thread to Weave a Patchwork: Advocating for Testamentary Exception Rules*," Phoenix L. Rev. 729 (2010).

§ 8.02   Estate Planning for Incompetent Persons

Page 80: Replace the second paragraph, the enumerated list thereunder, and the third paragraph with the following:

Only a guardian of the incompetent person, duly appointed by the probate court, may petition the probate court for authorization to "plan for the testamentary distribution of the ward's estate."[5] The guardian's petition must include the following information:

(a) A description of the proposed action;

(b) The anticipated results including any income, estate, or inheritance tax savings;

(c) The ward's wishes, if known;

(d) The ward's financial condition, including present and anticipated future expenses for maintenance, support, and medical care, debts, and support obligations;

(e) The ward's medical condition;

(f) The ward's prior estate planning action, including significant lifetime gifts, will, beneficiary designations, joint ownership, or trusts;

(g) The ward's family situation, including the family members who would inherit from the ward if the ward dies intestate;

(h) Whether the gift is intended to reduce the ward's assets or income in order to qualify for governmental benefits;

(i) The ward's housing situation during the 12 months prior to the filing of the petition; and

(j) A description of the care and services that the ward requires and is currently receiving.[6]

Notice of the petition shall be given "to all interested parties, including the ward, the intended donees or beneficiaries of the contemplated estate plan, family members who would inherit from the ward if the ward died intestate, beneficiaries under current estate planning documents or contracts, the attorney for the ward, and such other parties as the court directs."[7]

[5] R.S.A. 464–A:26–a, III.

[6] R.S.A. 464–A:26–a, III.

[7] R.S.A. 464–A:26–a, IV.

Page 82: Add the following at the end of this section:

The growing longevity of Americans has caused a rise in the number of cases involving older clients with diminishing capacity. This has caused practitioners to struggle with the issues surrounding situations where the client gradually loses capacity instead of suddenly moving from a competent state to an incompetent state. An article in the *Journal of the American College of Trusts and Estates Council*, entitled "The New Wrinkled Faces of Capacity: The Older Client With Diminishing Capacity," Vol. 30, p. 301 (2005), is a good review of the issues confronting practitioners with such clients.[8.1]

[8.1] A. Frank Jones & Bernard A. Crooks, authors.

§ 8.04 Standards for Determination of Testamentary Capacity

Page 84: Replace:

[27] 141 N.H. 658 (1997).

Page 85: Replace:

[28] *In re* Estate of Washburn, 141 N.H. 658, 660 (1997).

Page 85: Replace:

[29] *In re* Estate of Washburn, 141 N.H. 658, 661 (1997).

Page 85: Replace:

[30] *In re* Estate of Washburn, 141 N.H. 658, 662 (1997).

§ 8.05 Presumptions and Burden of Proof

Page 87: Replace:

[44] 141 N.H. 658 (1997).

Page 89: Add the following at the end of § 8.07:

§ 8.07A   Premortem Will Contest of Capacity

There is a growing trend in the states to enact statutory procedures to allow testators or grantors of trusts during their lifetimes to initiate a court proceeding to rule on the validity of their wills and trusts. These states presently include Alaska, Arkansas, Delaware, Nevada, North Dakota and Ohio.[46.1]

An interesting article on the pros and cons of pre-death will contests can be found in Volume 27, No. 2 of Probate & Property in an article entitled "Before the Party's Over—The Arguments Pro and Against Pre-Death Will Contests" by Skidmore & Morris. The authors conclude that before the growing trend in the states to allow pre-will contests is accepted, "the probate litigation bar should have a serious conversation about what the problems the new laws are intended to address and whether the potential benefits out-weigh the apparent disadvantages."

New Hampshire has joined this trend by the enactment of R.S.A. 552:18, entitled Proof of Will During Life. A person residing in the state or owning property in the state may commence a judicial proceeding to determine the validity of his or her will, subject only to the subsequent modification or revocation of the will. The statute also contains an extended list of interested persons who must be notified of the proceeding, including the petitioner's spouse, legatees and devisees under the terms of the will, and persons who would take the individual's property if he or she had died on the date of filing the petition.[46.2] The proof required shall be the usual burden of proof as provided as if proving a will in solemn form. The statute particularly provides that a person acting as an individual's guardian, conservator or attorney in fact is not allowed to commence proceedings on behalf of the individual.[46.3]

[46.1] *"Financing Your Future: A Will and a Way,"* Wall Street Journal, March 21, 2011.

[46.2] R.S.A. 552:18 III.

[46.3] R.S.A. 552:18 I.

B.   UNDUE INFLUENCE

§ 8.10   Presumptions and Burden of Proof

Page 91: Add the following at the end of the text to this section:

In the absence of a fiduciary relationship, preponderance of the evidence is sufficient to prove undue influence.[61.1]

In *Burkhalter v. Burkhalter,*[61.2] the Iowa Supreme Court, in a dispute involving a modification of an irrevocable trust, extensively discussed the amount of evidence required to prove undue influence on a testator. While applying the preponderance of the evidence standard, the court also acknowledged the existing requirement that trust provisions must "clearly" be the result of undue influence and stated that such a requirement is not inconsistent with the preponderance standard.

[61.1] Caraveo v. Perez (*In re* Estate of Bethurem), 129 Nev. 869, 313 P.3d 237 (2013).

[61.2] 841 N.W.2d 93 (Iowa 2013).

§ 8.11 Evidence

Page 93: Add the following text at the end of this section:

Some commentators have identified certain variables found in many undue influence cases:

> Although many pathways lead to undue influence, a simple model can be constructed to understand its genesis by considering three classes of variables:
>
> (1) predisposing factors,
>
> (2) vulnerability enhancers, and
>
> (3) execution variables.

Simply put, certain characteristics make an individual susceptible to being manipulated (predisposing factors), that if nurtured "properly" (vulnerability enhancers) are likely to produce the desired outcome (execution variables). To understand the development of undue influence, how these factors operate, interact, and overlap must be considered.[74.1]

Predisposing factors include: (1) death of a spouse; (2) depression; (3) isolation; (4) social attention; (5) anxiousness; (6) dependency; (7) diminished mental capacity; and (8) undetected pathology.[74.2]

[74.1] Turkat, *Psychological Aspects of Undue Influence*, Probate & Property Magazine, Jan./Feb. 2003, at 36, 37.

[74.2] Turkat, *Psychological Aspects of Undue Influence*, Probate & Property Magazine, Jan./Feb. 2003, at 37, 38.

§ 8.12 Particular Cases

[2] Cases Finding Undue Influence

Page 97: Add the following at the end of the text to this subsection:

> (7) *Webber Revocable Living Trust* and *In re Estate of Webber.*[81.1] In this very important case, the New Hampshire Circuit Court found that a police officer who befriended the testator had entered into a confidential relationship with her and exerted undue influence on her late in her life causing her to write a will principally benefitting himself. Because the opinion is so important, and cannot be readily found, the author has added it to the list of forms in this publication. See Form 72.

[81.1] Seventh Circuit Court, Probate Division Strafford County #318-2013-EQ-00694 and #318-2012-ET-01509 (2016).

D. MISTAKE

§ 8.15   In General

Page 100: Add the following paragraph at the end of the text to this section:

There has been a developing trend in American law as a growing number of American states have begun to reverse traditional rules requiring strict compliance with execution requirements and rules disallowing reformation as to mistakes in the contents of wills. This trend is based upon not only state legislative changes, but upon the new Restatement (Third) of Property: Wills and Other Donative Transfers (1999). A leading authority in this area, Professor John H. Langbein, Associate Reporter for the Third Restatement, has discussed this trend in an excellent article entitled "Curing Execution Errors and Mistaken Terms in Wills."[92.1] Furthermore, Section 2-203 of the Uniform Probate Code has provided since 1990 that a will with execution errors will be treated "as if it had been executed in compliance with [the statutory requirements] if the proponent . . . establishes by clear and convincing evidence that the decedent intended the document" as his or her will.

[92.1] Probate & Property Magazine, Jan./Feb. 2004, at 28.

CHAPTER 9

INCORPORATION BY REFERENCE

§ 9.02   Conditions of Application—In General

[1]   Non-Existence of Document Referenced in Will

Page 106: Add the following at the end of this section:

In *In re Estate of King*,[16] the Supreme Court held that a codicil which makes only minor changes to a will and which specifically republishes it was not sufficient to incorporate by reference a lost will because such a codicil is not "an independent testamentary instrument equivalent to the will that it amends."[17]

[16] 149 N.H. 226 (2003).

[17] *In re* Estate of King, 149 N.H. 226, 232 (2003).

CHAPTER 11

CODICILS

§ 11.02   Execution and Proof

Page 113: Add the following at the end of the text to this section:

Some practitioners[5.1] argue against the use of codicils except for very minor modifications, citing two cases[5.2] which, the author argues, demonstrate the potential perils of codicils. Rather, it is argued that the entire will should be republished with the changes included in the body of the new document.

[5.1] Pruett, *"Tales from the Dark Side: Drafting Issues from the Fiduciaries' Perspective,"* 35 ACTEC Journal 331 (2009).

[5.2] Honeycutt v. Honeycutt, 284 Ga. 42, 663 S.E.2d 232 (2008); Dyess v. Brewton, 284 Ga. 583, 669 S.E.2d 145 (2008).

§ 11.03   Construction and Effect

Page 114: Add the following at the end of the text to this section:

In *In re Estate of King*,[12] a codicil making minor changes to a will is not sufficient alone to prove a lost will even though the codicil specifically republishes the will:

> New Hampshire, along with the majority of other jurisdictions, has adopted the . . . view that the codicil and will together function as a single testamentary instrument. . . . In determining whether the revocation of the will revokes the codicil, the general rule in these jurisdictions is:
>
> > [W]here a codicil is of such a character that it may stand independently of the will, the revocation of the will does not affect the codicil. If, however, a codicil is not so complete a testamentary instrument as to stand alone, the revocation of the will to which it is appurtenant automatically revokes it. [79 Am. Jur. 2d *Wills* § 476 (2002)].
>
> We agree with the rule. Although the petitioner's suggested bright-line rule would simplify probate procedures, we fear that it may contravene the testator's intent. When a testator executes both a will and codicil adopting a minor change to that will, and then destroys that will, it is clear that the testator's intent is to revoke his entire testamentary scheme. The rule proposed by the petitioner would dictate a contrary result. Moreover, the petitioner's rule forces a testator who has drafted numerous minor codicils to destroy every one of these codicils, in addition to the original will, to accomplish a revocation.[13]

[12] 149 N.H. 226 (2003).

[13] *In re* Estate of King, 149 N.H. 226, 231 (2003).

CHAPTER 12
REVOCATION AND REVIVAL

§ 12.01   Express Revocation—In General

Page 118: In the carryover text of the first paragraph, replace the sentence after n. 3 with the following:

The oral declarations of the testator as to whether or not a revocation was intended are admissible on the issue of revocation, with such question of revocation being one of fact for a jury.[4]

[4] Managle v. Parker, 75 N.H. 139, 71 A. 637 (1908).

Page 118: Replace:

[6] 141 N.H. 628, 690 A.2d 1011 (1997).

[2] By Physical Act

Page 120: Replace n. 19 with the following:

[19] Gardiner v. Gardiner, 65 N.H. 230, 232, 19 A. 651, 653 (1889).

Page 121: Add the following before the last paragraph of this subsection:

The Ohio Court of Appeals has held that where a testator marked an "X" through substantial portions of the will, including a general bequest of money, and wrote other writings and multiple signatures on the will between and around the typewritten words to the will, but left her original signature untouched, the will was not revoked.[20.1]

[20.1] Horst v. Horst, 184 Ohio App. 3d 281 (Ohio Ct. App. Montgomery County 2009).

Page 122: Add the following at the end of the text to this section:

Physical acts by the testator on a photocopy of the will, including crossing out phrases and hand written additions which were initialed by the testator, did not revoke the will.[22.1]

[22.1] *In re* Estate of Sullivan, 868 N.W.2d 750 (Minn. Ct. App. 2015).

[3] Presumption of Revocation

Page 122: Add the following paragraphs at the end of this subsection:

An important recent case concerning the application of presumption of revocation is *In re Estate of King*.[29.1]

The New Hampshire Supreme Court overruled the probate court which had found that the proponents of the will had failed to meet their burden of overcoming the presumption of revocation in a situation where the decedent and his wife had a stormy marriage and the original will was last in the defendant's possession but could not be found at his death. The Supreme Court found that the trial court had misinterpreted the presumption of revocation and ruled that there was evidence that the testator had not intended to revoke his will, pointing out that presumptions only take the place of evidence if there is no evidence, but if there is evidence, then the presumption vanishes:

> In this case, the presumption vanishes because there was evidence to the contrary. The existence of the 1997 codicil and copy of the 1994 will alone was legally sufficient to rebut the presumption . . . . Under New Hampshire law . . . evidence need only support an inference against revocation to rebut the presumption . . . . The fact that Douglas' attorney retained a copy of the will along with a codicil supports such an inference in two ways. First, if Douglas wished to revoke his entire testamentary scheme by destroying his original will, it is likely that he would have contacted Peterson and had the copy and codicil destroyed as well. Second, the fact that Douglas had only a copy of the will at the consultation with Peterson supports an inference that he had lost the original will before the execution of the codicil. Thus, the evidence was sufficient to overcome the presumption of revocation.[29.2]

The Court went on to find that once the proponent overcomes the presumption of revocation, the trial court "must decide whether the proponent has proven by a preponderance of the whole evidence that the will was more likely lost than destroyed"[29.3] and the probate court had erred since it had instead improperly placed the burden upon the proponent to establish what had happened to the will.

Upon remand to the probate court following the appeal to the Supreme Court, in the *Estate of King*, the probate court found that the decedent died intestate because the petitioner failed to prove by a preponderance of the evidence that the decedent's will was more likely lost than destroyed. It is then headed by up to the Supreme Court and in an opinion issued September 9, 2004, the Supreme Court upheld the probate court's determination.[29.4] The Supreme Court found that it would not disturb the trial court's findings and therefore upheld the trial court's finding that the estate of the decedent passed by intestacy:

> We acknowledge that the facts in this case do not overwhelmingly dictate a particular result. Nevertheless, because a reasonable person could decide as did the probate court based upon the evidence, we defer to the probate court's findings . . . . Accordingly, based upon a review of the record, we hold that the probate court's findings that the petitioner failed to establish by a preponderance of the evidence that the will was more likely lost than destroyed is not plainly erroneous and could easily be made.[29.5]

The Court went on to hold, however, that the petitioners opposing the probate of the will were not entitled to attorney's fees because the Court concluded that "the respondents challenged the will for their own benefit and not for that of either the estate or the court."[29.6]

[29.1] 149 N.H. 226 (2003).

[29.2] *In re* Estate of King, 149 N.H. 226, 232–233 (2003).

[29.3] *In re* Estate of King, 149 N.H. 226, 233 (2003).

[29.4] *In re* Estate of King, 151 N.H. 425, 857 A.2d 1257 (2004).

[29.5] *In re* Estate of King, 151 N.H. 425, 857 A.2d 1257 (2004).

[29.6] *In re* Estate of King, 151 N.H. 425, 857 A.2d 1257 (2004).

§ 12.02   Implied Revocation

Page 123: In the third paragraph of this section, replace the first sentence with the following:

If the testator remarries his former spouse, the previously revoked will is revived, but only if such will or provisions are revoked solely by operation of R.S.A. 513:13, III.[32]

[32] Law 1999, 148.

Page 123: Insert the following after the fourth paragraph of this section:

Effective January 1, 2004, implied revocation of testamentary dispositions by divorce was extended to include the disposition of property held in revocable trusts by decedents, pursuant to the enactment of R.S.A. 551:13, III:

> If after executing a trust instrument in which a sole grantor reserves a power to alter, amend, revoke or terminate the provisions of the trust, the grantor is divorced or the marriage is annulled, the divorce or annulment revokes any disposition or appointment of property made by the trust to the former spouse, any provision conferring a general or special power of appointment to the former spouse, and any nomination of the former spouse as trustee, unless the trust expressly provides otherwise. Property prevented from passing to a former spouse because of revocation by divorce or annulment passes as if the former spouse and all heirs in the descending line of such former spouse who are not also heirs at law of the decedent failed to survive the decedent, and other provisions conferring some power or office on the former spouse are interpreted as if the spouse and all heirs in the descending line of such former spouse who are not also heirs at law of the decedent failed to survive the decedent. Any devise or distribution to any such heirs in the descending line of such former spouse that is contingent upon such spouse predeceasing the grantor is revoked by this section, unless the trust expressly provides otherwise. If provisions are revoked solely by this paragraph, they are revived by the grantor's remarriage to the former spouse. A decree of separation which does not terminate the status of husband and wife is not a divorce for the purposes of this paragraph. No change of circumstances other than as described in this paragraph revokes a trust.

Page 124: In the second sentence of the seventh paragraph of this section, replace the word "No" with "Nor".

Page 125: Insert the following as the last paragraphs of this section:

In the case of *In re Estate of Sharek*,[47.1] the former wife of the decedent and the named executrix in his will petitioned for estate administration. The Hillsborough County Probate Court initially ordered that the wife was the sole residuary beneficiary, but reconsidered, reversed itself, and suspended the wife's appointment pending the petition for appointment filed by the appellee, the decedent's brother-in-law. The wife appealed the probate court's decision that R.S.A. Section 551:13(11) (2007) applied and revoked her interest under the decedent's will.

On appeal, the New Hampshire Supreme Court affirmed the decision of the probate court. It held that a retrospective application of Section 551:13(11) was permissible because the wife's expectation of taking under the decedent's will was merely that, an expectation. It was not a vested right. As for the testator, his "right" to name a residuary beneficiary was no more vested than a devisee's or legatee's expectation of taking under a will. Thus, there was no impediment to retrospective application of Section 551:13.

[47.1] 156 N.H. 28, 930 A.2d 388 (2007).

§ 12.03   Dependent Relative Revocation

Page 126: Replace n. 50 with the following:

[50] Gardiner v. Gardiner, 65 N.H. 230, 232, 19 A. 651, 653 (1889).

Page 127: Add the following to the library references:

Library References

Storrow, "*Dependent Relative Revocation: Presumption or Probability?*," 48 Real Property, Trust and Estate Journal 3, page 497 (2014).

CHAPTER 13

CONSTRUCTION OF WILLS

§ 13.04   Primary Principle of Construction

Page 135: Replace n. 21 with the following:

[21] Osgood v. Vivada, 94 N.H. 222, 50 A.2d 227 (1946); Stearns v. Matthews, 94 N.H. 435, 55 A.2d 78 (1947); Amoskeag Trust Co. v. Haskell, 96 N.H. 89, 70 A.2d 210 (1950), *reh'g denied*, 96 N.H. 89, 71 A.2d 408; Fiske v. Warner, 99 N.H. 236, 109 A.2d 37 (1954); In re Lathrop's Estate, 100 N.H. 393, 128 A.2d 199 (1957); In the Matter of Shirley Estate, 117 N.H. 922, 379 A. 2d 1261 (1977); In re Estate of Sayewich, 120 N.H. 237, 413 A.2d 581 (1980).

Page 136: Replace n. 31 with the following:

[31] Stevens v. Underhill, 67 N.H. 68, 36 A. 370 (1883); Jones v. Bennett, 78 N.H. 224, 99 A. 18 (1916); Amoskeag Trust Co. v. Haskell, 96 N.H. 89, 70 A.2d 210 (1950), *reh'g denied*, 96 N.H. 89, 71 A.2d 408; Fletcher v. Cotton, 81 N.H. 243, 123 A. 889 (1924).

§ 13.05   Presumptions—In General

[4]   Presumption Against Partial Intestacy

Page 139: In the first paragraph of this subsection, insert the following after n. 47:

Rather, the inclusion of detailed residue clauses clearly intended to dispose of any remainder of an estate are further evidence of an intention to avoid the application of intestacy laws.[47.1]

[47.1] White v. Corinthian Lodge, F. & A.M. 100 N.H. 138, 143 (1956); Cotter v. Cotter, 103 N.H. 551, 554 (1961).

Page 141: Replace n. 56 with the following:

[56] Burpee v. Pickard, 94 N.H. 307, 52 A.2d 286 (1947).

§ 13.06   Construction of Particular Language

Page 142: Insert the following at the end of the third full paragraph of this section, after n. 65:

The Court has also taken into consideration the experience of the drafter of a will in determining whether the usage of terms of art such as "issue" were intended to be given their legal effect.[65.1]

[65.1] Amoskeag Trust Co. v. Preston, 107 N.H. 330, 335 (1966).

CHAPTER 14

PRETERMITTED CHILDREN

§ 14.01   Background on Disinheriting Children

Page 150: Insert the following at the end of the text of this section, after n. 9:

Relatedly, a reference to a child need not be direct. Rather, it is sufficient if a child is referenced indirectly so as to indicate that the deceased had the child in mind when he made the will.[9.1]

[9.1] *In re* Estate of Osgood, 122 N.H. 961, 965 (1982).

§ 14.02   Application of R.S.A. 551:10—In General

Library References

Page 152: Add the following to the library references at the end of this section:

See Adam J. Hirsch, *"Airbrushed Heir: The Problem of Children Omitted from Wills,"* 50 Real Property, Trust and Estate Law Journal 2, page 175 (2015). This extensive article examines the two theories underlining the rules regarding pretermitted children: mistaken omission and failure to account for change of circumstances.

[3]   Child or Issue Not Referred to in Will

Page 158: Replace:

[45] 141 N.H. 628, 690 A.2d 1011 (1997).

Page 159: Delete the last line of this section and substitute the following:

In re Estate of Treloar[45.1] addressed the issue whether the grandchild of the testator, whose parent was deceased was sufficiently referred to under the statute where the daughter's surviving husband (referred to as "son-in-law") was appointed the executor was a sufficient reference to the claimant, the court carefully distinguishing *In re Estate of Laura*. The court held that it was not, stating that *In re Estate of Laura* was an exception to its general rule and applied "only when the 'testator has a predeceased child who is neither named, referred to, nor a devisee or a legatee under the testator's will' and the will names 'the next degree of issue in the line of descent.' "[45.2] Thus, in *Treloar*, the claimants qualified as pretermitted children since they were not referenced in the will.

[45.1] 151 N.H. 460 (2004).

[45.2] 151 N.H. 460, 464 (2004).

[4] Child or Issue Not a Devisee or a Legatee

Page 159: Insert the following as the final paragraph of this section:

In *Robbins v. Johnson*,[46.1] the Supreme Court had before it the applicability of the pretermitted heir statute to the provisions of an inter vivos trust, in a situation where the pretermitted child had been allowed to take against the estate of the decedent, but the child also sought to take its share of the decedent's assets held in the name of the decedent's inter vivos trust. The Supreme Court declined to apply the statute which specifically refers only to wills to assets held in trust, noting that:

> trusts are not the only type of so-called will substitute by which individuals pass property at death. Other will substitutes include payable on death accounts, transfer on death accounts, life insurance proceeds to a named beneficiary, and pension funds. We believe that the legislature should decide whether, as a matter of policy, it wishes to extend the pretermitted heir statute to will substitutes, such as the trust at issue. Absent clear indication from the legislature that this is its intention, we decline to apply the [pretermitted heir] statute to the trust.[46.2]

[46.1] 147 N.H. 44 (2001).

[46.2] Robbins v. Johnson, 147 N.H. 44, 46 (2001).

§ 14.04 Admissibility of Extrinsic Evidence

Page 160: Add the following to the text at the end of the section:

In *In re Estate of Came*,[51.1] a divided Supreme Court rejected as inadmissible "extrinsic evidence," the provisions of a non pour-over, free standing trust created before the will but which referred to the child who claimed to be pretermitted in the will, the court stating that "the respondent and executor will not be allowed to prevent application of the pretermission statute by introducing extrinsic evidence, such as the trust document, in order to show the intent of the testator that the petitioner was not out of this testator's mind, as the court's 'task is not to investigate the circumstances to divine the intent of the testator; rather it is to review the language contained within the four corners of the will for a determination of whether the testator named or referred to [the petitioner].' "

This exacting rule was reaffirmed in 2004 in *In re Estate of Treloar*,[51.2] when the court declined "the petitioner's invitation to overrule *In re Estate of Came*,[51.3] absent any argument that *Came* has 'come to be seen so clearly as error that its enforcement was for that very reason doomed.' "[51.4] The *Treloar* case involved a situation where the alleged predeceased children were not named in the will, although their mother's spouse (their step-father) was named as executor. The court held that "such references are insufficient. They do not clearly evidence the testator's intent to disinherit either [the mother] or her issue [the claimant here]."[51.5]

[51.1] 129 N.H. 544 (1987).

[51.2] 151 N.H. 460 (2004).

[51.3] 129 N.H. 544 (1987).

[51.4] *In re* Estate of Treloar, 151 N.H. 460, 463 (2004).

[51.5] *In re* Estate of Treloar, 151 N.H. 460, 464 (2004).

CHAPTER 15

ADEMPTION

§ 15.01　General Principles

Page 165: In the carryover paragraph of this section, insert the following after the second sentence, after ". . . is a specific legacy.":

Because special advantages accrue to specific devisees, courts are not inclined to construe a devise as specific unless it is the clear intention of the testator.[1.1]

[1.1] King v. Onthank, 152 N.H. 16, 18 (2004).

§ 15.02　Application of the Doctrine—Disposition of the Property Devised or Bequeathed

Page 167: Add the following at the end of the text to this section:

Where a testator transferred property specifically devised in a will to a family partnership, the doctrine of ademption applies.[9.1]

[9.1] Matter of Braunstein, 125 A.D.3d 1267, 4 N.Y.S.3d 663 (2015).

[1]　Change in Nature of the Property Devised or Bequeathed

Page 167: Add the following after the first full paragraph of this section:

In *In re Estate of Donovan*,[11.1] the New Hampshire Supreme Court stated that New Hampshire followed the general rule that "[it] is well-settled that if, after a testator has executed his will in which he makes a specific bequest of corporate stock, the testator sells the stock and does not acquire other stock, an ademption occurs and a legatee has no valid claim on the proceeds on the sale," citing to Ademption of a Specific Legacy of Corporate Stock or Other Corporate Securities, 61 A.L.R. 2d 449 (1958).

[11.1] 162 N.H. 1, 20 A.3d 989 (2011).

Page 167: Delete the last sentence and footnote of the second paragraph of the text and add the following new paragraphs in its place:

"It is the prevailing rule that in the absence of a contrary intent, increasing the number of corporate shares of a bequest of stock dividends, splits, etc., does work in ademption of the bequest and the legatee is entitled to the increased number of shares."[16]

In New Hampshire, two cases decided the same year have dealt with this issue. In *In re Doonan Estate*,[16.1] the court rejected any use of a formulaic rule as to whether the bequest of the stock was to be considered as 'specific' or 'general.' Rather, the testator's intention is the cardinal rule and in the *Doonan Estate* case, the court found that the facts seemed to indicate that the residuary legatee (to whom the stock splits would go if not to the specific legatee) was the primary focus of the testator's munificence.

However, in the later case of *In re Harvey Estate*,[16.2] decided the same year, the court ruled that the specific legatee took later stock splits: "In the last analysis, the problem is not solved solely by classifying the bequest, but is determined by the intent of the testator," citing to the *Doonan* case. However, in the *Harvey* case, the court found that the testator's intention was clear and established the prevailing rule as follows:

"We hold that in the absence of action by the testator indicating a desire to reduce the bequest the additional shares resulting from the split should be transferred to the trustee. This result is reinforced by preference indicated in the will for this bequest over the residuary bequest **but absence of this factor would not change the result** (Emphasis added)."[16.3]

[16] 80 Am. Jur. 2d. Wills § 1594 (1975). *See also* Annotation, "*Change In Stock Structure or Split or Substitution of Stock of Corporation, As Affecting Bequest of Stock*," 46 A.L.R. 3rd (1972).

[16.1] 110 N.H. 157 (1970).

[16.2] 110 N.H. 484 (1970).

[16.3] 110 N.H. 484, 487–488 (1970).

CHAPTER 16

LEGACIES AND DEVISES

A. PRINCIPLES OF CONSTRUCTION

§ 16.01   Construction of *Issue*—In General

[1]   Adopted Children

Page 180: In the last paragraph, replace the second sentence as follows::

R.S.A. 170–B:25, V provides in language the earlier adoption statute did not contain that "Upon the issuance of a final decree of adoption, all reciprocal rights of inheritance between the adoptee and the adoptive parents and their respective collateral or lineal relatives shall contemporaneously begin."

§ 16.02   Construction of *Heirs* and *Next-of-Kin*

Page 184: Replace "Jenkins v. Jenkins" with "Simes v Ward et al.".

Page 184: Replace n. 22 with the following:

   [22] 78 N.H 533 (1918).

Page 184: Replace "supreme court" with "Supreme Court".

Page 185: Replace "extraneous" with "outside".

Page 186: Insert the following as the last paragraphs of this section:

When a child is conceived through artificial insemination that occurs *after* the death of the father who provided the sperm, can the child be viewed as "surviving issue" under New Hampshire's intestacy statute, N.H. Rev. Stat. Ann. Section 561:1 (2007)? The New Hampshire Supreme Court said "no" in the case of *Eng Khabbaz v. Commissioner & Social Security Administration.*[31.1]

Here are the facts: After the father of a child was diagnosed with a terminal illness, he began to bank his sperm so that his wife could conceive a child through artificial insemination. The child was so conceived after the father's death. When the wife sought Social Security survivor's benefits for the child, benefits were denied based on a finding that the child could not inherit from the father under N.H. Rev. Stat. Ann. Section 561:1. The wife argued that the child was a surviving issue of the father under the meaning of the intestacy statute. The United States District Court for the District of New Hampshire certified a question to the New Hampshire Supreme Court asking whether a child conceived after her father's death via artificial insemination was eligible to inherit from her father as his surviving issue under the New Hampshire intestacy law.

The high court held that the plain meaning of the word "surviving" was

36

remaining alive or in existence. To remain alive or in existence after her father passed away, the child would necessarily have had to have been "alive" or "in existence" at the time of his death. The child was conceived more than a year after the father's death. It followed, therefore, that no posthumously-conceived child was a "surviving issue" within the plain meaning of the intestacy statute. The court declined to rely on public policy considerations to reach a different outcome, as such matters of public policy are reserved for the legislature.

The entire issue of the legal recognition of posthumously conceived children is beginning to receive a lot of attention. See the excellent article by Kathryn Venturatos Lorio entitled, *Conceiving the Inconceivable: Legal Recognition of the Posthumously Conceived Child.*[31.2]

[31.1] 155 N.H. 798, 930 A.2d 1180 (2007).

[31.2] 34 ACTEC Journal 3, page 154 (Winter 2008).

[1] Uniform Probate Code Provision

Page 186: Replace n. 32 with the following:

[32] U.P.C. § 1-201(20).

B. BENEFICIARIES GENERALLY

§ 16.03 Disinheritance of Beneficiaries

Page 188: Insert the following at the end of this section:

In the case of *In re Estate of Bourassa,*[35.1] petitioner, the decedent's live-in companion, sought a spousal share of the decedent's estate under RSA 561:1 (2007) because the decedent's will had made no provision for the petitioner. The Rockingham County Probate Court found that petitioner was not the decedent's common law spouse under RSA 457:39, and she appealed.

The Supreme Court held that the trial court properly found that the couple never acknowledged each other as husband and wife. Witnesses, including former employees, the decedent's siblings and a business associate, testified that the decedent never held out petitioner as his wife. Two of the decedent's daughters testified that petitioner had said that she would never be "anybody's common law," and the decedent's executor testified that petitioner said that she would never be anyone's wife. Petitioner had corrected a newspaper reporter who described the couple as married, and she mentioned the decedent as her "significant other" in unrelated litigation. The couple had separate bank accounts and health insurance and had titled their real property and their vehicles separately. Three months before his death, the decedent left a box for "spouse" blank when completing a chiropractor's intake form. The Supreme Court affirmed the judgment.

See the article by Dayan which analyzes the flaws in our current system relating to child disinheritance and recommends a solution, *"The Kids Aren't Alright: An Examination of Some of the Flaws in American Law Regarding Child Disinheritance, the Reasons That Children Should Be Protected, and a Recommendation for the United States to Learn From the Australian Model That Protects Children*

Against Disinheritance," 17 Cardozo J. Int'l & Comp. L. 375 (2009).

[35.1] 157 N.H. 356, 949 A.2d 704 (2008).

Page 188: Add the following at the end of § 16.03:

§ 16.03A   Children Born by Biotechnological Means

Complex issues relating to the inheritance rights of children born through *in vitro* fertilization or other biotechnological means has begun to spawn many entirely new issues relating to inheritance rights. Practitioners are referred to the comprehensive article entitled "*Heirs in the Freezer—Bronze Age Biology Confronts Biotechnology,*" 36 ACTEC Journal, Vol. 36, No. 1, Summer 2010, page 179.

See also Williams, "*Over My Dead Body: The Legal Nightmare and Medical Phenomenon of Posthumous Conception Through Postmortem Sperm Retrieval,*" 34 Campbell L. Rev. 181 (2011).

In *Burns v. Astrue,*[36.1] the Utah Supreme Court held that a sperm storage agreement executed by the husband that required that after his death his stored sperm be donated to his wife did not show his consent to be the parent of a child conceived by the wife using the deposited sperm. The court ruled that the mere act of preserving sperm does not show such a consent.

Library References

Carpenter, "*Sex Post Facto: Advising Clients Regarding Posthumous Conception,*" 38 ACTEC Law Journal 2&3, page 187 (2012).

[36.1] 2012 UT 71, 289 P.3d 551.

§ 16.13   Receipt of Property by Persons Guilty of Unlawful Killing

Page 209: Add the following at the end of the text to this section:

See Konsdorf and Prulhiere, "*Killing Your Chances of Inheriting: The Problem with the Application of the Slayer Statute to Cases of Assisted Suicide,*" 39 ACTEC Law Journal 3, page 399 (2013).

Page 213: Add the following new section after § 16.13:

§ 16.13A   Laughing Heir

A laughing heir has been defined as "an heir distant enough to feel no grief when a relative dies and leaves an inheritance (generally viewed as a windfall) to the heir."[119.1]

An interesting article, "The Laughing Heir" What's so Funny?, points out that many state jurisdictions do not limit succession by collaterals, which allows distant heirs to inherit.[119.2]

[119.1] Black's Law Dictionary 742 (8th ed. 2004).

[119.2] 48 Real Property, Trust and Estate Law Journal 2, page 321 (2013).

C. DEVISES OF REAL PROPERTY

§ 16.15 Devises of Life Estates and Remainders

Page 216: Add the following at the end of the first paragraph:

The Georgia Supreme Court in *Anderson v. Anderson*[123.1] held that where a parent devised real estate to a child in the first sentence, and in the second sentence stated that "this land to go to the surviving heir or heirs" of the child created a life estate in the land in the child, with a remainder to the child heirs.

[123.1] 791 S.E.2d 40 (Ga. 2016).

E. SURVIVORSHIP AND LAPSE OF LEGACIES AND DEVISES

§ 16.31 Class Gifts

Page 237: Add the following at the end of the text to this section:

Castillo v. Ott[198.1] holds that a class gift is not subject to the anti-lapse statute.

[198.1] ___ Ohio App. ___, 2015-Ohio-905, 28 N.E.3d 157 (6th Dist.).

CHAPTER 17

PARTICULAR WILL CLAUSES

§ 17.01 Clauses Providing for Deduction of Advancements

Page 249: In footnotes 1 and 2, replace "Dickson" with "Dixon".

§ 17.02 In Terrorem Clauses

Page 251: Replace "Burtman v. Batman" with "Burtman v. Butman".

Page 253: Add the following at the end of the text to this section:

In a strict interpretation of a no-contest clause, the California Intermediate Appellate Court has held that a beneficiary's pleading in response to a petition for instructions by the fiduciary violated a no-contest clause in his parent's trust because the beneficiary's claim indirectly contested the validity of the trust and an amendment to it in an attempt to receive an increased share of the trust.[16.1]

Recently, there has been more activity regarding in terrorem clauses. In *Shelton v. Tamposi*,[16.2] the Rockingham County Probate Court applied the rule in *Burtman* to a trust's no contest provision to disqualify a trust beneficiary from sharing in a multi-million dollar trust because the court had found that she had violated the trust's in terrorem provision. Subsequently, the Legislature enacted RSA 551:22 and RSA 564-B:10-1004 which specifically enforce no contest provisions in both trusts and wills. The two statutes mirror one another, and define what a no contest provision is and provide detailed provisions for the enforcement of such provisions.[16.3]

In the *Tamposi* case, on appeal to the New Hampshire Supreme Court, the Court ruled that the petitioner, trustee of the trust that contained the in terrorem provision, did not have standing to contest on appeal the trial court's ruling on the in terrorem clause. The Court pointed out that the beneficiary herself had a personal interest sufficient to enable her to appeal on this issue but had failed to do so.[16.4]

In *In re Estate of Stan*,[16.5] the court held that a challenge to the appointment of a personal representative did not trigger an in terrorem clause.

See "The Use of Declaratory Judgments to Test the Enforceability of No-Contest Clauses."[16.6] Joseph J. Viviano argues for the use of a declaratory judgment action to ascertain whether probable cause exists before contesting a trust that includes a no-contest clause.

[16.1] Cook v. Cook, 177 Cal. App. 4th 1436, 99 Cal. Rptr. 3d 913 (Cal. App. 2d Dist. 2009). In two recent probate court decisions, the Rockingham County Probate Court and the Hillsborough County Probate Court each enforced an in terrorem or no-contest clause to disinherit beneficiaries who contested a will or trust. *See* Tamposi v. Tamposi, Jr. et al., Hillsborough County Probate Court, Case No. 36-207-EQ-02109 and Hoeg et al. v. Hoeg, Rockingham County Probate Court, Case No. 318-209-EQ-01346.

[16.2] 2010 N.H. Super. LEXIS 78 (2010).

[16.3] *See "New Laws on In Terrorem ("No-Contest") Clauses in Wills and Trusts—Closing the Loopholes"* by Catalfino and DeGrandpre, to be published in the Fall of 2011 edition of the New Hampshire Bar Journal.

[16.4] Shelton v. Tamposi, 164 N.H. 490, 62 A.3d 741 (2013).

[16.5] 301 Mich. App. 435, 839 N.W.2d 498 (2013).

[16.6] 50 Real Property, Trust and Estate Law Journal 1, page 75 (2015).

§ 17.04 Funeral and Burial Provisions

Page 255: Insert the following at the end of this section:

Effective January 1, 2000, the legislature enacted R.S.A. 290 regarding the control of the body of a deceased person. The statute essentially provides a prioritized list of next-of-kin of the decedent who shall have custody and control of the decedent's body.[26] Custody and control is defined to mean "the right to make all decisions, consistent with applicable laws, regarding the handling of a dead body, including but not limited to possession, at-need funeral arrangements, final disposition, and disinterment."[27]

R.S.A. 290:16, IV establishes the priority of next-of-kin having custody and control:

(a) The spouse.

(b) An adult son or daughter.

(c) A parent.

(d) An adult brother or sister.

(e) An adult grandchild.

(f) An adult niece or nephew who is the child of a brother or sister.

  (g) A maternal grandparent.

  (h) A paternal grandparent.

  (i) An adult aunt or uncle.

  (j) An adult first cousin.

  (k) Any other adult relative in descending order of blood relationship.

[26] R.S.A. 290:16.

[27] R.S.A. 290:16, II.

CHAPTER 18

NOMINATION OF EXECUTORS AND GUARDIANS

A. EXECUTORS

§ 18.02 Appointment—In General

Page 259: Add after footnote 6:

Should the probate court refuse to appoint the executor, the court will next look to the widow, next of kin, or such other suitable person as they may nominate.[6.1]

[6.1] R.S.A. 553:2, I.

[1] Minors

Page 259: Add before footnote 7:

Upon the appointment of a minor who has come of age, the administration before granted shall be revoked unless it was granted to a co-executor, in which case the minor shall be a joint executor.

[2] Corporations

Page 259: Replace the second paragraph with the following:

Until 1994, New Hampshire did not extend to banks and corporations not incorporated in New Hampshire the right to act as fiduciary.[8] As a result, it had been common practice in New Hampshire for an officer of an out-of-state bank to be named as the fiduciary in lieu of the foreign bank itself. However, the Supreme Court obliquely criticized this practice. In 1994, R.S.A. 390:13 was revised to provide that foreign trust companies or other institutions with fiduciary powers may be appointed as trustee or executor in New Hampshire, providing that the state in which the trust company or bank has its principal place of business allows trust companies, banks, or similar corporations incorporated under the laws of New Hampshire to be appointed in that state.[9] This statutory authority permitting

41

a foreign institution to be appointed as trustee or executor was repealed in 2015. No legislation granting such power has subsequently been passed.

[8] Bank of New Hampshire v. Tilton, 82 N.H. 81, 129 A. 492 (1925); *see* In re Farnsworth's Estate, 109 N.H. 15, 241 A.2d 204 (1968).

[9] R.S.A. 390:13, II.

[10–12] [Reserved]

§ 18.03   Uniform Probate Code Provision

Page 261: Replace n. 19 with the following:

[19] U.P.C. § 1-201(b).

B.   GUARDIANS

§ 18.07   Nomination of Guardian in Anticipation of Subsequent Mental or Physical Disability

Page 263: Replace the first paragraph of section with the following:

R.S.A. 464–A:10, IV enables a competent adult to nominate a guardian of his or her person or estate in the future event of his or her subsequent mental or physical disability or incompetence. This nomination may include either a guardian of the person or of the property, or both. One or more persons may be nominated, and one or more substitutes may be nominated. Any person may be nominated as guardian, including banks or trust companies, other than a public guardianship and protection program.[31.1] An individual may specify a person who he or she wishes to exclude from consideration as guardian. The nomination must be in writing and must conform to the execution requirements for deeds, pursuant to the requirements of R.S.A. 477:9.

[31.1] Developmental Disabilities Advocacy Center, Inc. v. Melton 521 F.Supp. 365 (1981).

Page 264: Insert the following as the last paragraphs of this section:

In the case of *Guardianship of E.L.*,[34] a guardian was appointed (pursuant to N.H. Rev. Stat. Ann. Section 464-A:4(1)) for an incarcerated ward who had been diagnosed as suffering from psychotic features of a bipolar disorder. After ten years, the ward petitioned to terminate the guardianship. The Merrimack County Probate Court denied the petition, and the ward appealed. The ward had been convicted of sexually assaulting his wife. A guardian was appointed to ensure that he took his medication and followed medical advice. After a hearing on the ward's petition, the trial court found that he remained unable to make his own medical decisions and that no less restrictive alternative to guardianship existed.

Affirming the decision of the lower court, the Supreme Court held that the evidence established that the ward had limited insight into his mental illness, intended to stop taking his medications, and, without medication, would pose a danger to himself and others. Based on the evidence, the trial court could reasonably find that he was compliant with his medications only because of the guardianship, not because he appreciated the need for them. In addition, a power of attorney was not a sufficient "less restrictive" form of intervention, because the ward could cancel it.

In *Guardianship of R.A.*,[35] a probate court properly held that a guardian had authority to admit a ward to a hospital under N.H. Rev. Stat. Ann. Section 464-A:25(l)(a) (2005) as nothing in the statute conditioned the guardian's authority upon court review every five years.

There, the petitioner-ward challenged a decision of the Coos County Probate Court, which authorized his guardian to admit him to New Hampshire Hospital and require him to take his medication. Before the New Hampshire Supreme Court, the ward argued that the guardian did not have authority to admit him to the hospital or consent to his medication on the ground that guardianship authority terminated when the court review mandated by Section 464-A:25(l)(c) (2005) did not occur.

The Supreme Court held that nothing in the subparagraph conditioned the guardian's authority to admit the ward into the hospital upon court review every five years. In addition, the issue of whether the guardian's authority to consent to medical treatment had expired was moot because Section 464-A:25(l)(c) had been amended to change the period to review a guardian's authority to consent to a ward's medical care from every five years to every year. Thus, even if the probate court assumed that the guardian's authority to consent to medical treatment expired every five years because the probate court had not reviewed it, that conclusion had little bearing on the authority of guardians under the amended statute.

Finally, in the case of *In re Christopher K.*,[36] following a hearing in the Hillsborough County Probate Court, the admittee was involuntarily admitted to a state hospital for a period not to exceed three years "with a conditional discharge as soon as appropriate." At some point, he was conditionally discharged. According to the court-appointed psychiatrist, at the time of the conditional discharge, he had mental health problems. Thereafter, his conditional discharge was revoked because of his noncompliance with taking medication, threatening and/or assaulting behavior, and drug use that exacerbated his mental illness. Later, he was again conditionally discharged. Eventually, a petition to renew that conditional discharge was filed. The probate court then renewed the conditional discharge for a period of three years.

On appeal, the Supreme Court found that his constitutional rights regarding substantive due process were not violated by the three-year extension of the period of Conditional discharge. The relevant statute was narrowly drawn so that the period for conditional discharge could be extended because he was refusing to take his medication, making him a danger to himself and others, which was proven by clear and convincing evidence. The probate court's judgment was affirmed.

[34] 154 N.H. 292, 911 A.2d 35 (2007).

[35] 920 A.2d 1213 (2007).

[36] 923 A.2d 187 (2007).

CHAPTER 19
POWERS OF APPOINTMENT

§ 19.01 Introduction

Page 266: Insert the following at the end of the text to this section:

A brief overview of New Hampshire's law of Powers of Appointment can be found in an article by Nina Dow, entitled "More Power to You; A Quick Look at Powers of Appointment and Powers of Attorney."[0.1]

[0.1] NH Bar News, July 19, 2017, page 29.

§ 19.02 Definitions

Page 266: Replace "growth" with "gross".

Page 267: Replace n. 6 with the following:

[6] R.S.A. 566:1–a.

Page 267: Delete paragraphs after footnote 6 until end of section and reserve the footnote.

§ 19.03 Purpose

Page 268: Add the following at the end of the text to this section:

An extensive article exploring the use of powers or appointment can be found in Volume 47, Number 3, *The Real Property, Trust & Estate Law Journal* (2013) at page 529. The article by Blattmachr, Kamin & Bergman entitled "Estate Planning's Most Powerful Tool: Powers of Appointment Refreshed, Redefined, and Reexamined" advocates for the thoughtful, but frequent, for post-death contingencies. The authors at page 557 particularly emphasize the use of powers of appointment in trust decanting:

> [p]owers of appointment have a newly discovered—or rediscovered— aspect, as applied to the increasingly popular tool known as trust decanting. Decanting generally refers to the transfer of assets from an existing trust to a different trust instrument, and has gained heightened prominence as a means of accomplishing tax planning, making adminis- trative updates to old trusts, and, where appropriate, modifying the substantive terms of previously drafted trust documents to respond to changing conditions.

§ 19.08 Exercise of the Power—In General

Page 274: Add the following at the end of the text to this section:

In *In re Estate of Shepherd*,[40.1] the Wisconsin Appellate Court allowed extrinsic evidence to be admitted to determine whether the will exercised a power of appointment where the will was ambiguous. The court held that the testimony of the drafting attorney that the omission of a direct reference to the power was a drafting error was admissible.

Whether or not a power of attorney is properly exercised when the power requires a specific exercise has created disputes. An article by Kenneth Kingma entitled *"Using Equity to Aid the Exercise of a Power of Appointment That Fails to Specifically Refer to the Power"*[40.2] explores the use of equitable powers to avoid rigid compliance with the specific reference requirement.

[40.1] 344 Wis. 2d 440, 823 N.W.2d 523, 2012 WI App 116.

[40.2] 51 Real Property, Trust and Estate Law Journal 3, page 457 (2017).

CHAPTER 20

RENUNCIATION AND DISCLAIMER

A. UNIFORM DISCLAIMER OF PROPERTY INTERESTS ACT AS ADOPTED BY NEW HAMPSHIRE

§ 20.01 Generally: Power of Attorney Under New Hampshire Statute

Page 284: Add the following at the end of the text to this section:

An exploration of the use of disclaimers under the New Hampshire Uniform Act in the real estate law context can be found in the note by Goodwin & Wells entitled *"Qualified Disclaimers: A Trap for the Unwary Real Estate Lawyer,"* New Hampshire Bar News, May 17, 2003, page 19.

§ 20.08 Waiver and Bar

Page 293: In the last paragraph of this section, replace the first sentence with the following:
Under federal tax rules, any acceptance of any type of benefit from the property will disqualify the disclaimer from favorable tax treatment.[41]

[41] I.R.C. § 2518.

§ 20.09 Binding Effect of Disclaimers and Written Waivers

Page 293: Add the following at the end of the text to this section:

The Supreme Court of Vermont has held that a disclaimer cannot be revoked because it was based on a mistake of law, but that it may be revoked if it was procured through the exercise of undue influence.[44.1]

[44.1] Carvalho v. Estate of Carvalho, 186 Vt. 112, 978 A.2d 455, 2009 VT 60 (2009).

CHAPTER 22
WILL SUBSTITUTES

§ 22.01   Introduction

Page 302: Add the following at the end of the text to this section:

Professor John Langbein has commented that the "deepest trend now affecting the day-to-day realty of gratuitous transfers in the United States is the nonprobate revolution, by which I mean the burgeoning use of will substitutes to transfer property on death."[3.1]

[3.1] 38 ACTEC Law Journal 1, page 10 (2012).

§ 22.03   Jointly Held Real Property

Page 304: Add text after the last sentence of § 22.03:

The unique and paradoxical nature of joint tenancies is explored in the article by Orth, 46 Real Prop. Tr. & Est. L. J. 483 (2012).

[2]   Creating Joint Tenancies

Page 305: After § 22.03[2] delete entire § 22.03[3] (Tax Consequences) in text:

§ 22.04   Jointly Held Personal Property

Page 306: Delete the sentence after footnote 31 and reserve the footnote.

§ 22.05   Bank Accounts—In General

[1]   Joint Accounts

Page 309: Replace the first paragraph and list with the following:

In 1953, the legislature moved to end the muddle and confusion that surrounded joint bank accounts by enacting R.S.A. 384:28. In 2016 the 4 legislature repealed R.S.A 384:28 and replaced it with R.S.A 383-B:4-405 which provides

> The statute provides that when any account is established in any bank in New Hampshire in the names of two persons, payable to either of such persons and payable to the survivor of them, the account upon the death of either of said persons becomes the property of the survivor, free of claims of the donor co-depositor's heirs. The statute applies irrespective of whether:

> A person or persons may establish a deposit account at a state or foreign depository bank doing business in this state pursuant to a written agreement. The written agreement shall govern the rights of any person who is named as an owner of the account. In the absence of a written

agreement, if 2 or more persons are named on a deposit account as owners, the account shall be payable to any owner, and in the event of death, to the survivor or survivors of them. The survivors shall be entitled to ownership of the account whether or not (i) the funds deposited were the property of only one or some of the owners, (ii) at the time of the making of such deposits there was any intention on the part of the owners making such deposit to vest the other owner or owners with a present interest therein, (iii) only one of the owners during their several lives had the right to withdraw such deposit, or (iv) there was any delivery of any bank book, account book, savings account book, certificate of deposit, or other evidence of such an account, by the owner or owners making such deposit to the other owner or owners. The receipt by an owner of the account of any payment from the account made by the depository bank on the owner's request shall discharge the depository bank from any liability for any payment so made. Nothing in this paragraph shall be construed to prohibit an owner making a deposit or deposits from withdrawing the deposit during his or her lifetime, nor shall the existence of the right to withdraw the deposit during his or her lifetime defeat the rights provided herein for the owner or his or her survivors.[43]

There are no New Hampshire reported cases involving R.S.A 383-B:4-405, but its similarity to its predecessor R.S.A 384:28 would lead practitioners to conclude that relevant case law interpreting R.S.A 384: 28 woul be applicable to R.S.A. 383-B:4-404.

[43] R.S.A. 3383-B:4-405.

[3]   Gifts Inter Vivos of Bank Accounts

Page 315: Insert the following at the end of the text to this section:

In 2015, RSA 364:28, which addressed the transfer of funds on the death of one of two account owners was repealed, causing confusion. Effective August 8, 2016, RSA 383-B:4-405 was enacted to provide that any person can create a deposit account at a state or foreign depository bank doing business in New Hampshire pursuant to a written agreement that governs the rights of all named owners of the account. If there is no written agreement and two or more persons are named as account owners, the account should be payable to any owner, and in the event of a death, to the survivor of them. Survivors shall be entitled to ownership whether or not (1) the funds deposited were the property of one or some of the owners; (2) at the time of making such deposits there was no intentions to give the property to the other owner; (3) only one of the owners has the right to withdraw from the account; or (4) there was any delivery of bank books, account books, savings account books, certificates of deposits, or other evidence of such accounts by the owner making such deposits to the other owner.

IV
TRUSTS

CHAPTER 25
INTRODUCTION

§ 25.01   Scope of the Part

Page 333: Insert the following at the beginning of the text of this section:

The law of trusts in New Hampshire has been greatly modified, revised, and improved by recent legislative activities. Effective October 1, 2004, the New Hampshire Legislature adopted as R.S.A. 564-B the Uniform Trust Code, as modified for New Hampshire.[0.1] This Uniform Trust Code was substantially amended in 2005 and 2006 by a Technical Amendments Act.[0.2] Also in 2006, the court adopted the Trust Modernization and Competitiveness Act which further amended the Uniform Trust Code and trust law provisions in New Hampshire to allow for private trust companies and other forms of modern trust or administration. In addition, the 2006 legislation adopted as R.S.A. 564-C the Uniform Principal and Income Act. The legislature's 2006 changes were to make New Hampshire the leader amongst the states in modern trust law, with the purpose of attracting jobs and business to the state.

Care must be taken by the practitioner to review these laws before proceeding in this area as many parts of the text of Part IV are affected and altered by the provisions of this series of legislation.

[0.1] 2004, 130:1.

[0.2] 2005, 270:1; 2006, 91:1.

CHAPTER 26
GENERAL PRINCIPLES

§ 26.02   Trusts Distinguished From Other Arrangements—In General

[2]   Bank Accounts

Page 337: Delete the sentence after footnote 11.

CHAPTER 27

JURISDICTION OVER TRUSTS

§ 27.01   Jurisdiction of Courts—In General

[1]   Probate Court Jurisdiction

Page 344: Insert the following before footnote 2:

subject to R.S.A. 498:4-a as described below.

Page 344: Insert the following at the end of text of this section:

Regarding the equity jurisdiction of the Probate Court, the reader should be aware that the governor signed into law on May 28, 2008, revisions to RSA 547:3-b. The provision now reads: The probate court shall have the powers of a court of equity in all cases within its subject matter jurisdiction in which there is not a plain, adequate, and complete remedy at law. The court may hear and determine such cases according to the course of equity, and may grant writs of injunction whenever the same are necessary to prevent fraud or injustice.[2.1]

In the case of *In re Guardianship of Dorson*,[2.2] an insurer challenged a judgment of Hillsborough County Probate Court which required the insurer to reimburse an estate for money that a prior guardian had misappropriated. The new guardians asked the probate court to surcharge the prior guardian for all amounts he had improperly withdrawn, including lost income after the parties entered into a partial settlement. The prior guardian was terminated, failed to file an accounting, and left the country with money from the estate's funds that was invested in an annuity. The insurer argued that the estate was entitled only to interest at the statutory rate under RSA 336:1, II (Supp. 2007).

On appeal, the Supreme Court found that the surcharge imposed by the probate court, regardless of whether it took the form of interest or lost appreciation, was part of the debt or loss to the estate and did not constitute prejudgment interest governed by RSA 524:1-a or RSA 524:1-b. The probate court imposed a surcharge that was designed to put the estate in the same position it would have been in had the prior guardian not misappropriated the funds. The probate court did not engage in an unsustainable exercise of discretion by awarding the difference in value of the units of the annuity from the date they were misappropriated to the date that the probate court approved the partial settlement. The Supreme Court affirmed the lower court's judgment.

[2.1] RSA 547:3-b (added May 28, 2008).

[2.2] 156 N.H. 382, 934 A.2d 545 (2007).

[2]   Superior Court Jurisdiction

Page 345: Replace "R.S.A. 543:1" with "R.S.A. 547:3".

Page 345: Insert the following at the end of text of this section:

Regarding the *cypres* doctrine, the reader should be aware that the governor signed into law on May 28, 2008, revisions to RSA 498:4-a. The statute now reads: "the Superior Court shall exercise jurisdiction pursuant to RSA 498:4-a through 498:4-e only where the claims or defenses raised are related to a matter otherwise pending before or within the jurisdiction of the Superior Court. In all other cases involving the doctrine of *Cy Pres*, jurisdiction shall lie in the probate court."[3.1]

[3.1] RSA 498:4-a I (added May 28, 2008).

§ 27.03   Charitable Trusts

Page 347: Replace the content of this section with the following:

The jurisdiction over charitable trusts is shared concurrently by the Probate and Superior Courts. R.S.A. 498:1, 543:1. R.S.A. 543:1 provides that "The probate court shall have concurrent jurisdiction with the superior court in cases involving charitable uses and trusts other than express trusts, as that term is defined in R.S.A. 564–A:1, I." Furthermore, R.S.A. 498:1 provides that:

> The superior court shall have the powers of a court of equity in the following cases: charitable uses; trusts other than express trusts as that term is defined in R.S.A.564–A:1 . . . except that the court of probate shall have exclusive jurisdiction over equitable matters arising under its subject matter jurisdiction authority in R.S.A. 547, R.S.A. 547–C and R.S.A.552–7.

§ 27.04   Governing Law

Page 348: Add after footnote 22:

The mere fact that New Hampshire possesses jurisdiction to probate a decedent's estate does not mean that the jurisdiction is necessarily exclusive, nor does it require the court to exercise its jurisdiction. Rather, a court may decline such jurisdiction if, for example, another court with concurrent jurisdiction may be a more convenient forum to decide the particular matter, or proceedings pertaining to the same matter may be pending in another state.[23]

[23] *In Re* Estate of Mullin, 169 N.H. 632, 637.

CHAPTER 28
CREATION

§ 28.01   Formal Requirements—In General

Page 351: Insert the following at the beginning of the text of this section:

The law of trusts in New Hampshire has been greatly modified, revised, and improved by recent legislative activities. Effective October 1, 2004, the New Hampshire Legislature adopted as R.S.A. 564-B the Uniform Trust Code, as modified for New Hampshire.[0.1] This Uniform Trust Code was substantially amended in 2005 and 2006 by a Technical Amendments Act.[0.2] Also in 2006, the court adopted the Trust Modernization and Competitiveness Act which further amended the Uniform Trust Code and trust law provisions in New Hampshire to allow for private trust companies and other forms of modern trust or administration. In addition, the 2006 legislation adopted as R.S.A. 564-C the Uniform Principal and Income Act. The legislature's 2006 changes were to make New Hampshire the leader amongst the states in modern trust law, with the purpose of attracting jobs and business to the state.

Care must be taken by the practitioner to review these laws before proceeding in this area as many parts of the text of Part IV are affected and altered by the provisions of this series of legislation.

[0.1] 2004, 130:1.

[0.2] 2005, 270:1; 2006, 91:1.

CHAPTER 30

IMPLIED TRUSTS

A. RESULTING TRUSTS

§ 30.04 Trusts Arising From Gratuitous Conveyances

Page 376: Insert the following as the last paragraphs of this section:

The facts of a 2007 decision of the U.S. Bankruptcy Court for the District of New Hampshire illustrate a trust arising from a gratuitous conveyance. In 1989, the debtor in bankruptcy had transferred unimproved land to the transferee and his wife as a wedding present; and the transferee borrowed money to build a house on the property. When the transferee and his wife had financial difficulties, the debtor bought the property at a foreclosure sale and entered into a financing agreement so that the transferee and his wife could remain on the property. In March 2005, the debtor transferred the parcel of land with the residence on it to the transferee. The transferee did not pay any cash at the time of the transfer. (By this time, the transferee had already lived in the residence for 16 years.) The debtor filed for bankruptcy relief 45 days after the March 2005 transfer.

The court held that, based on the evidence and applying New Hampshire law, a resulting trust existed. The debtor acquired title to the property at the foreclosure sale for the benefit of the transferee and held it for him in a resulting trust until the March 2005 transfer. At all times, the parties intended the property for use by the transferee. The transferee remained in continuous possession, using the property as his home, and eventually took over sole financial responsibility for the property. Accordingly, the court would not set aside the March 2005 transfer and entered judgment for the transferee.[13.1]

[13.1] Askenaizer v. May (*In re* Jewett), 2007 BNH 18; 2007 Bankr. LEXIS 1526 (May 2, 2007).

B. CONSTRUCTIVE TRUSTS

§ 30.10   Generally

Page 384: Add the following at the end of the text to this section:

In *In re Estate of Couture*[59.1] is an expansive decision by the New Hampshire Supreme Court. The court upheld the trial court's imposition of a constructive trust on the proceeds paid to the decedent's wife out of an ERISA Benefit Plan. The Supreme Court quoted the *Milne* case to the effect that "the specific instances in which equity imposes a constructive trust are numberless, as numberless as the modes by which property may be obtained through bad faith and unconscientious acts." This case expands the law of constructive trusts to cover many instances of unjust enrichment, as long as the thread of a confidential relationship exists.

[59.1] 166 N.H. 101, 89 A.3d 541 (2014).

§ 30.12   Standard and Burden of Proof

Page 388: Add the following at the end of the text to this section:

In *In re Estate of Couture*,[72.1] the court held that "[t]o support a claim for constructive trust, the moving party must demonstrate by clear and convincing evidence that such action is warranted."

[72.1] 166 N.H. 101, 89 A.3d 541 (2014).

§ 30.13   Pleading

Page 388: Insert the following at the end of the text to this section:

In *In re Estate of Couture*,[76.1] the court held that "the Petitioner had standing to seek a constructive trust because, as one the decedent's heirs, he has a direct legal or equitable interest in the decedent's estate." In this case, the Petitioner was one of the decedent's legal heirs even though the constructive trust, if imposed, would not be for his benefit but for the benefit of the estate of the decedent.

[76.1] 166 N.H. 101, 89 A.3d 541 (2014).

§ 30.14   Grounds for Imposition of a Trust

[3]   Fraud, Duress or Undue Influence

Page 390: Add the following at the end of the text to this section:

In *In re Estate of Couture*,[85.1] the court upheld the trial court's imposition of a constructive trust where because of "the respondent's fraud and deceit, the decedent was not only induced to marry her but also to designate her as a beneficiary of his life insurance policy."

[85.1] 166 N.H. 101, 89 A.3d 541 (2014).

[6] Abuse of a Confidential Relationship

Page 396: Add the following at the end of the text to this section:

In *Elter-Nodvin v. Nodvin*,[116.1] the New Hampshire Supreme Court held that where the parties were in a divorce proceeding a confidential relationship did not exist between husband and wife

> because, notwithstanding the couple's marital plans to provide for one another at death, [the husband's] filing for divorce notified the [wife] petitioner that his plans had changed. At that point, the petitioner's alleged belief that Stephen would continue to act in her best interest by following through with the couple's existing estate plan became unreasonable.

The Court held that the fiduciary duty arising from the marriage relationship did not continue where the husband and wife each hired independent professional counsel to represent them in the contested proceeding and as a result, when the husband requested a divorce, he unequivocally signaled his desire to have the Court redistribute the couple's assets rather than abide by whatever plans were in place prior to the divorce filing. As a consequence, the husband was permitted to change the beneficiaries of life insurance policies during the divorce proceedings.

In *In re Estate of Couture*,[116.2] the New Hampshire Supreme Court made clear that the simple relationship of husband and wife was sufficient to create a confidential relationship the abuse of which would lead to the imposition of a constructive trust.

[116.1] 163 N.H. 678, 48 A.3d 908 (2012).

[116.2] 166 N.H. 101, 89 A.3d 541 (2014).

CHAPTER 31

EXPRESS TRUSTS

§ 31.01 In General

Page 397: Insert the following at the beginning of the text of this section:

The law of trusts in New Hampshire has been greatly modified, revised, and improved by recent legislative activities. Effective October 1, 2004, the New Hampshire Legislature adopted as R.S.A. 564-B the Uniform Trust Code, as modified for New Hampshire.[0.1] This Uniform Trust Code was substantially amended in 2005 and 2006 by a Technical Amendments Act.[0.2] Also in 2006, the court adopted the Trust Modernization and Competitiveness Act which further amended the Uniform Trust Code and trust law provisions in New Hampshire to allow for private trust companies and other forms of modern trust or administration. In addition, the 2006 legislation adopted as R.S.A. 564-C the Uniform

Principal and Income Act. The legislature's 2006 changes were to make New Hampshire the leader amongst the states in modern trust law, with the purpose of attracting jobs and business to the state.

Care must be taken by the practitioner to review these laws before proceeding in this area as many parts of the text of Part IV are affected and altered by the provisions of this series of legislation.

[0.1] 2004, 130:1.

[0.2] 2005, 270:1; 2006, 91.1.

§ 31.02   Types of Express Trusts

[1]   Testamentary Trusts

Page 399: Insert the following as the last paragraph of this subsection:

Whether a trust is a testamentary trust or an inter vivos trust may be irrelevant in some circumstances. In *Robbins v. Johnson*,[8.1] the question was whether the pretermitted heir statute applied to an inter vivos trust and the Supreme Court held that:

> The plaintiffs' focus upon whether the trust is testamentary or inter vivos is misplaced. Even if the trust is deemed inter vivos, it arguably still functions like a will because it provides for the distribution of property after Robbins' death. As the Restatement (Third) of Trusts 25 comment b (Tent. Draft No. 1, 1966) explains: In proper usage today . . . the terms 'testamentary' and 'nontestamentary' (or 'inter vivos') simply describe the means chosen to make disposition of property, not the legal characteristics of the disposition or the nature of the interests created . . . . Issues are obscured and litigation invited by confusing or unsound dicta often found in opinions that attempt to explain why something is or is not a present trust.[8.2]

[8.1] 147 N.H. 44 (2001).

[8.2] Robbins v. Johnson, 147 N.H. 44, 46 (2001).

[2]   Inter Vivos Trusts

Page 400: Insert the following as the final paragraph of this subsection:

Whether a trust is a testamentary trust or an inter vivos trust may be irrelevant in some circumstances. In *Robbins v. Johnson*,[11.1] the question was whether the pretermitted heir statute applied to an inter vivos trust and the Supreme Court held that:

> The plaintiffs' focus upon whether the trust is testamentary or inter vivos is misplaced. Even if the trust is deemed inter vivos, it arguably still functions like a will because it provides for the distribution of property after Robbins' death. As the Restatement (Third) of Trusts 25 comment b (Tent. Draft No. 1, 1966) explains: In proper usage today . . . the terms 'testamentary' and 'nontestamentary' (or 'inter vivos') simply describe the means chosen to make disposition of property, not the legal charac-

teristics of the disposition or the nature of the interests created . . . .
Issues are obscured and litigation invited by confusing or unsound dicta
often found in opinions that attempt to explain why something is or is not
a present trust.[11.2] The

[11.1] 147 N.H. 44 (2001).

[11.2] Robbins v. Johnson, 147 N.H. 44, 46 (2001).

Page 400: Insert the following new subsection after subsection 31.02[2], Inter Vivos Trusts:

[3] Nominee Trusts

A nominee trust, also called a passive trust,

> exists when the trustees have no discretionary duties to perform . . . . The
> key to the nominee nature of a trust is that the beneficiaries are in practical
> control of the trust property . . . . For instance, in *Dwire v. Sullivan*,[11.3]
> we noted that the trust at issue stated explicitly that the trustee 'shall act
> only as an agent of the beneficiaries.'. . . Similarly, in *Roberts v.
> Roberts*,[11.4]

the Massachusetts Supreme Judicial Court ruled that a trust that gave the trustees
'no power to deal in or with the Trust Estate except as directed by the
beneficiaries' was a nominee trust.[11.5]

A trust is not a nominee trust where the trustee is granted discretionary powers
and has imposed upon it numerous active management duties.[11.6]

[11.3] 138 N.H. 428, 430 (1994).

[11.4] 646 N.E.2d 1061, 1062 (Mass. 1995).

[11.5] Robbins v. Johnson, 147 N.H. 44, *concurring opinion*, at 46.

[11.6] Robbins v. Johnson, 147 N.H. 44, 47 (2001).

§ 31.05 Spendthrift Trusts

Page 403: Add the following to the text at the end of the section:

With the adoption of the Uniform Trust Code, effective October 1, 2004, the
New Hampshire law concerning spendthrift trusts was substantially altered.
R.S.A. 564-B:5-503(b) provides that, subject to certain conditions, a beneficiary's
current or future distribution from a trust may be attached by the beneficiary's
child, spouse, former spouse, or creditor who provided services for the protection
of the beneficiary's interest in the trust.

§ 31.07 Support Trusts; Special Needs Trusts

Page 410: Insert the following as the last paragraphs of this section:

Appeal of Lowy[63.1] is another instance where New Hampshire's highest court
recognized a special needs trust. In *Lowy* the petitioner, a Medicaid applicant,
sought review of a decision of the Administrative Appeals Unit (MU) of the
respondent, the New Hampshire Department of Health and Human Services
(DHHS), which upheld a denial of Medicaid eligibility.

The Medicaid applicant was a developmentally disabled man who lived with his parents. Prior to the application for Medicaid benefits, the parents executed an irrevocable trust with the express intent of creating a special needs trust that conformed with 42 U.S.C.S. Section 1396p(d)(4)(A). Thus, the applicant claimed that the assets were to be excluded for purposes of Medicaid resource eligibility. However, the AAU determined that the required payback provision in the trust agreement was unenforceable.

The Supreme Court disagreed and reversed in part, finding that the phrase "to the extent required by law" was only a general requirement to construe the promise in the payback provision in accordance with the law and did not defeat the intent of the applicant's parents to create a special needs trust as the parents expressly stated in the trust document that that was the purpose of the trust. However, the DHHS was not required to verify the purpose, recipient, and amount of the trust distributions which could be counted as income by a less intrusive means than production of the trust document, which would reveal the trust corpus value, based on N.H. Code Admin. R.Ann. He-W 606.78(a)(l)(a) (amended 2006).

The court reversed the portion of the MU'S decision that denied the exclusion of the assets in the applicant's special needs trust as resources for the purposes of Medicaid eligibility. However, the court affirmed the decision insofar as it required the applicant to provide the trust agreement for verification of the purpose, recipient and amount of trust distributions that could be counted as income. The court remanded for further proceedings.

In *Appeal of Huff (N.H. HHS)*,[63.2] the petitioner, a disabled adult, appealed a final decision of the Administrative Appeals Unit (MU) of the respondent, the New Hampshire Department of Health and Human Services, which concluded that special needs trust distributions functioned as income for purposes of Medicaid eligibility for medical assistance under the Aid to the Permanently and Totally Disabled (APTD) program, 42 U.S.C.S. Section 1351, *et seq.*

On review, the Supreme Court vacated the MU'S finding because the hearing officer of the M U failed to determine whether the state had a Medicaid plan in place on January 1, 1972, and whether that plan had been approved pursuant to 42 U.S.C.S. Section 1396a(f). Those determinations presented questions of fact, which the court declined to address in the first instance. It was error for the hearing officer to rely and adjudicate the case based solely on N.H. Code Admin. R. Ann. He.-W 654.04(b)(10) absent a conclusion that New Hampshire was not a state that opted to the provisions of Section 209(b) of the Social Security Act and that N.H. Code Admin. R. Ann. He.-W 654.04 was consistent with federal obligations or that the rule was part of the state's approved Medicaid plan in 1972 by 42 U.S.C.S. Section 1396a. On remand, the AAU was to abide by N.H. Rev. Stat. Ann. Section 161:4(IV) and N.H. Code Admin. R. Ann. He.-W 602.04(a) and ensure compliance with federal and state statutes, rules and regulations, including 42 U.S.C.S. Section 1396a, if the state were found to be a Section 209 state. Accordingly, the court vacated the order of the AAU and remanded the cause for further proceedings before the AAU.

63.1 Appeal of Lowy, 156 N.H. 57, 931 A.2d 552 (2007).

63.2 Appeal of Huff (N.H. HHS), 154 N.H. 414, 910 A.2d 1287 (2006).

§ 31.09   Charitable Trusts

[1]   Definition and Nature

Page 413: Insert the following as the last paragraphs of this section:

In the divorce case of *In re Chamberlin*,**74.1** the petitioner-wife sought a divorce in the Newport Family Division. The trial court found that the corpus of the parties' irrevocable charitable trust was not marital property and that their right to receive interest from the trust, although marital property, was of negligible monetary value. The wife appealed.

The Supreme Court affirmed the lower court's decision. The wife had argued that the trust corpus was marital property. The Supreme Court disagreed, explaining that the corpus of the parties' irrevocable charitable trust was not marital property because they could not invade it. Because the corpus did not belong to either party at the time of the divorce, it was not legal error to exclude it from the marital estate. Assets used to fund the trust ceased belonging to them once the assets were in the trust and beyond the parties' reach, removing the assets from the statutory definition of marital property. The parties' right to receive interest distributions if the corpus exceeded a certain amount was marital property, but it was not an unsustainable exercise of discretion to find the monetary value of this asset was negligible to the husband because the trust had not reached the amount at which interest was distributable, his age was advanced, and his health was poor.

74.1 *In re* Chamberlain, 918 A.2d 1 (2007).

Page 417: Add the following new section at the end of the chapter:

§ 31.10   Asset Protection Trusts

There has been a growing trend in the states to allow donors to create trusts for their own benefit that are protected from future creditors. As of this date, seven states have legislation allowing for such trusts: Oklahoma, Missouri, Alaska, Delaware, Nevada, Rhode Island, and Utah.

Effective September 9, 2008, New Hampshire recognized asset protection trusts. *See* Chapter 564-D of the Revised Statutes Annotated entitled, Qualified Dispositions In Trust Act.

See the extensive article by Christopher Paul entitled *"Innovation or a Race to the Bottom? Trust (Modernization) in New Hampshire,"* 7 Pierce L. Rev. 353 (2009).

CHAPTER 32

THE RULE AGAINST PERPETUITIES

§ 32.03   The New Hampshire Approach to the Rule—In General

[4]   Recent Legislative Activity

Page 430: Delete the single paragraph of this subsection and substitute with the following:

Effective January 1, 2004, the New Hampshire legislature has provided for a modified elimination of the rule against perpetuities as to wills and to trusts. As to wills, R.S.A. 547:3-k provides that the common law rule against perpetuities shall not be applied by the probate court to any disposition of property or interest therein in a will if (1) the instrument making the disposition contains a provision which expressly exempts the instrument from application of the rule; and (2) the trustee or other person to whom the power is properly granted has the power under the governing instrument to sell, mortgage or lease property for any period of time beyond the period that is required for an interest created under the governing instrument to vest in order to be valid under the rule against perpetuities. Thus, for a draftsman, in order to eliminate the application of the rule against perpetuities to a will, the will needs to have a provision expressly exempting the will from the application of the rule.

As to trusts, R.S.A. 564:24 provides for an identical exemption if the trust instrument contains a provision expressly exempting the trust from the application of the rule, etc. The trust provision applies to all trusts including trusts as defined in R.S.A. 564-A:1.

New Hampshire's modified abolition of the rule against perpetuities follows the leads of several states which have abolished the rule in whole or in part. The pressure for abolition of the rule has come from testators (many of whom are self-styled millionaire entrepreneurs) who wish to establish so-called dynasty or perpetual trusts.[56] The state of the law across the country concerning changes in the rule against perpetuities has taken many forms. See the article entitled *Fifty-one Flowers, Current Perpetuities Law in the United States*, by Lynn Foster, Probate & Property, July/August, p. 30 (2008).

Forms: Form 48-A is a clause for use in a will or trust involving the exemption from the application of the rule against perpetuities as provided by the 2004 changes concerning the common law rule against perpetuities.

[56] *Dynasty Trusts and The Rule Against Perpetuities*, 116 Harv. L. Rev. 2588 (2003); *The Rise of The Perpetual Trust*, 50 UCLA C. Rev. 1303 (2003).

CHAPTER 34

GIFTS INTER VIVOS

§ 34.01 Definition and Nature

Page 438: Insert the following as the last paragraphs of this section:

In a child support case, the Supreme Court held that because the state's statutory definition of "gross income" (for computing child support payments) did not include gifts, the trial court erred when it included gifts which the mother regularly received from her own family in its calculation of child support.[6.1]

In *Fulton,* the respondent-mother sought to modify the petitioner-father's child support obligation. The father then filed a cross-petition to modify child support and visitation, The Strafford Superior Court entered orders regarding the visitation and support of the parties' minor children. The mother appealed.

The mother argued that the father's increased salary, and one child's reaching the age of majority, were substantial changes warranting modification of child support. The father sought modification of support based upon his increased commuting costs and the mother's changed financial situation. The high court held, *inter alia,* that because gifts were not included in N.H. Rev. Stat. Ann. Section 458-C:2(IV)'s definition of "gross income," the trial court erred in including gifts the mother regularly received from her family in her gross income when it calculated child support. The Supreme Court reversed the order modifying child support, and the case was remanded for further proceedings.

A gift made with the "understanding" for its use does not create a conditional gift, rather such language was held to be "precatory" by the Mississippi Supreme Court and, thus, the will gave the beneficiary a fee simple ownership of the property.[6.2]

[6.1] *In re* Fulton, 154 N.H. 264 (2006).

[6.2] Nichols v. Phillips (*In re* Estate of Brill), 76 So. 3d 695 (Miss. 2011).

§ 34.04 Donative Intent

Page 441: Insert the following paragraph as the last paragraph of this section:

A revocable inter vivos trust is not invalid as an incomplete donative transfer.[22.1]

In *Colon v. Raymond,*[22.2] the New Hampshire Supreme Court held that "the burden of proving that a transfer of property is a gift is on the grantee or the party who asserts that a gift has been made." The Court then went on to rule that the presumption of gift of transfers between close family members does not extend to gifts to in-laws.

[22.1] Robbins v. Johnson, 147 N.H. 44 (2001).

§ 34.09   Gifts of Ward's Property by Guardian

Page 449: Delete the third paragraph of this section and substitute with the following:

R.S.A. 464-A:26-a, III requires that the petition of the guardian to the court shall include the following information:

(a) A description of the proposed action;

(b) The anticipated results including any income, estate, or inheritance tax savings, and, if the gift is being made in order to qualify the ward for Medicaid, any resulting period of Medicaid disqualification;

(c) The ward's wishes, if known;

(d) The ward's financial condition, including present and anticipated future expenses for maintenance, support, and medical care, debts, and support obligations;

(e) The ward's medical condition;

(f) The ward's prior estate planning action, including significant life-time gifts, will, beneficiary designations, joint ownership, or trusts;

(g) The ward's family situation, including the family members who would inherit from the ward if the ward dies intestate;

(h) Whether the gift is intended to reduce the ward's assets or income in order to qualify the ward for Medicaid or other governmental benefits;

(i) The ward's housing situation during the 12 months prior to the filing of the petition; and

(j) A description of the care and services that the ward requires and is currently receiving.

Before authorizing the guardian to make lifetime gifts, the court must find by a preponderance of the evidence that the proposed gifts and/or testamentary plan are consistent with the ward's wishes or, based on circumstances as they then exist, that

(a) The testamentary distribution of the ward's estate will minimize taxation and/or facilitate distribution of the ward's estate to family, friends, or charities who would be likely recipients of gifts from the ward;

(b) The proposed gift is not likely to adversely affect the ward's housing options, access to care and services, or general welfare;

(c) The proposed gift does not create a foreseeable risk that the ward will be deprived of sufficient assets to cover his or her needs during any period of Medicaid ineligibility that would result from the proposed gift; and

(d) The proposed gift is not likely to result in premature or unnecessary nursing home placement or institutionalization of the ward, or compromise the ward's access to care or services in the least restrictive setting in which his or her needs can be met.

VI. The probate court, prior to authorizing a lifetime gift, shall appoint a guardian ad litem if the proposed gift benefits the guardian personally or otherwise creates a potential conflict of interest between the ward's interests and the guardian's personal interests.

VII. The department of health and human services, county attorney, and the department of justice shall be notified and shall have the opportunity to address the court in any proceeding under this section if the court has concerns relative to:

(a) The impact on the ward of any period of Medicaid ineligibility that would result from the proposed gift; or

(b) Whether the ward has been the victim of a crime or has been or is at risk of being abused, neglected, or exploited within the meaning of R.S.A. 161-F:43.[66]

In the case of *In re Guardianship of Luong*,[66.1] the petitioner-guardians proposed a final estate plan for a ward, which the Hillsborough County Probate Court rejected. The probate court adopted an alternative estate plan drafted by a court-appointed referee, and the guardians appealed to the Supreme Court.

The ward was in a persistent vegetative state. She also had a minor child. The court first held that RSA 464-A:26-a (2004) placed the burden of drafting a ward's estate plan, if one was to be drafted, upon the guardian. The probate court's equity authority under RSA 547:3-b (2007) could not be exercised in circumvention of the express language of RSA 464-A:26-a. Accordingly, the probate court could not appoint a referee to independently draft an estate plan; thus, it erred in adopting the estate plan drafted by the referee.

Next, the probate court properly rejected the guardians' final estate plan, which included large gifts and bequests to the ward's parents and siblings. Although the guardians had presented evidence that the estate plan was consistent with Vietnamese traditions, witnesses testified that: (1) the ward's daughter was the most important person in her life, which was consistent with evidence from the daughter's father, her guardian; (2) the ward had designated the daughter as her sole beneficiary of her life insurance policy; and (3) she had done so because she wanted everything she had to go to her daughter.

The Supreme Court affirmed the probate court's rejection of the guardians' final estate plan. It reversed the probate court's adoption of the estate plan drafted by the referee and remanded the case.

[66] R.S.A. 464-A:26-a, V.

[66.1] 157 N.H. 429, 951 A.2d 136 (2008).

CHAPTER 36

UNIFORM TRANSFERS TO MINORS ACT

§ 36.05   Transfers to Custodian

Page 461: Delete that portion of the text which follows "(3)" and substitute the following:

(3) The transfer is less than or equal to ten thousand dollars ($10,000) in value; otherwise a guardianship over the estate of the minor shall be required by the probate court pursuant to R.S.A. 463, unless otherwise ordered by the court.

This is a substantial change from the narrow provisions of the Uniform Gift to Minors' Act and should be very helpful in connection with the administration of estates where gifts to minors are made that, in the absence of the provisions of the new Act, would require the appointment of a guardian of a minor in order to meet the requirements of the probate court.

Where a minor whose estate is not under legal guardianship shall be entitled to receive from any administrator, trustee, etc., any distribution of personal property by will or intestate succession, the administrator, executor, or trustee may make such distribution to the person nominated as such minor's guardian for the benefit of such minor under either R.S.A. 463-A or under another state's Uniform Transfers to Minors' Act.[8.1]

[8.1] R.S.A. 561:20.

CHAPTER 39

LIVING WILLS

§ 39.01   Background on Refusal of Medical Treatment and Living Wills

Page 471: Insert the following at the beginning of this section:

Effective January 1, 2006, new legislation completely revises the law of living wills, medical powers of attorney, and do-not-resuscitate orders to make it easier for people to plan for and make known their end-of-life decisions.[0.1]

> The directives allow people to dictate what care they wish to accept or reject in a medical emergency or if they're near death and can't speak for themselves. They could, for example, say whether they want to receive food and water through tubes if they're unable to swallow—an issue that

affected the brain-damaged Florida woman, Terri Schiavo, who died after the courts ordered her feeding tube removed based on her husband's assertion she would not want to live that way.

The law clarifies and updates the forms, which allow people to legally appoint another person to make health care decisions on their behalf.

It also makes it easier to prepare the documents by allowing people to sign in the presence of two witnesses or have a notary or a justice of the peace serve as a witness. Under the old law, the documents had to be notarized. People who would benefit from the person's estate can not serve as witnesses.

The law also establishes rules for medical orders barring the use of cardiopulmonary resuscitation to revive someone. Hospitals, nursing homes, and other medical facilities currently handle do-not-resuscitate orders based on their own policies. The law formalizes the process.

It also gives the power to doctors and nurse practitioners to make the decision if the person's agent cannot be immediately contacted if CPR would unnecessarily harm the person. The person can revoke the order at any time.

Doctors must make a diligent effort to reach an agent before issuing a do-not-resuscitate order on their own.

Care must be taken by the practitioner to review this law before proceeding in this area as many parts of the text are affected and altered by the provisions of this legislation.

[0.1] *Union Leader*, June 20, 2006, p. B3.

CHAPTER 40
DURABLE POWERS OF ATTORNEY FOR HEALTH CARE

The New Hampshire law regarding advanced directives concerning health care decision making was completely revised, effective January 1, 2007. RSA 137-J followed a long process of study and considerable debate. Therefore, the text of this section should be taken for historical background purposes only.

The reader is directed to an excellent article by Attorneys LaFrance and Leaver entitled *Advance Directives Revisited, Health Care Decision-Making Legislation Approved*, in the 48 New Hampshire Bar Journal 1, page 29, (Spring 2007).

§ 40.01 Nature and Purpose

Page 481: Insert the following before the text of this section:

Effective January 1, 2006, new legislation completely revises the law of living wills, medical powers of attorney, and do-not-resuscitate orders to make it easier for people to plan for and make known their end-of-life decisions.[0.1]

The directives allow people to dictate what care they wish to accept or reject in a medical emergency or if they're near death and can't speak for themselves. They could, for example, say whether they want to receive food and water through tubes if they're unable to swallow—an issue that affected the brain-damaged Florida woman, Terri Schiavo, who died after the courts ordered her feeding tube removed based on her husband's assertion she would not want to live that way.

The law clarifies and updates the forms, which allow people to legally appoint another person to make health care decisions on their behalf.

It also makes it easier to prepare the documents by allowing people to sign in the presence of two witnesses or have a notary or a justice of the peace serve as a witness. Under the old law, the documents had to be notarized. People who would benefit from the person's estate can not serve as witnesses.

The law also establishes rules for medical orders barring the use of cardiopulmonary resuscitation to revive someone. Hospitals, nursing homes, and other medical facilities currently handle do-not-resuscitate orders based on their own policies. The law formalizes the process.

It also gives the power to doctors and nurse practitioners to make the decision if the person's agent can not be immediately contacted if CPR would unnecessarily harm the person. The person can revoke the order at any time.

Doctors must make a diligent effort to reach an agent before issuing a do-not-resuscitate order on their own.

Care must be taken by the practitioner to review this law before proceeding in this area as many parts of the text are affected and altered by the provisions of this legislation.

[0.1] *Union Leader*, June 20, 2006, p. B3.

Page 482: Insert the following after the third paragraph of this section:

Although the form provided by the statute for a durable power of attorney for health care provides specifically that the agent is authorized "to make any and all health care decisions for me" it is not absolutely clear whether the New Hampshire durable power of attorney for health care authorizes placement of the principal in a nursing home facility over the objection of family members of the agent or of the agent himself.

CHAPTER 41

DO NOT RESUSCITATE ORDERS

§ 41.01 Introduction

Page 489: Insert the following before the text of this section:

Effective January 1, 2006, a new legislation completely revises the law of living wills, medical powers of attorney, and do-not-resuscitate orders to make it easier for people to plan for and make known their end-of-life decisions.[0.1]

The directives allow people to dictate what care they wish to accept or reject in a medical emergency or if they're near death and can't speak for themselves. They could, for example, say whether they want to receive food and water through tubes if they're unable to swallow—an issue that affected the brain-damaged Florida woman, Terri Schiavo, who died after the courts ordered her feeding tube removed based on her husband's assertion she would not want to live that way.

The law clarifies and updates the forms, which allow people to legally appoint another person to make health care decisions on their behalf.

It also makes it easier to prepare the documents by allowing people to sign in the presence of two witnesses or have a notary or a justice of the peace serve as a witness. Under the old law, the documents had to be notarized. People who would benefit from the person's estate can not serve as witnesses.

The law also establishes rules for medical orders barring the use of cardiopulmonary resuscitation to revive someone. Hospitals, nursing homes, and other medical facilities currently handle do-not-resuscitate orders based on their own policies. The law formalizes the process.

It also gives the power to doctors and nurse practitioners to make the decision if the person's agent can not be immediately contacted if CPR would unnecessarily harm the person. The person can revoke the order at any time.

Doctors must make a diligent effort to reach an agent before issuing a do-not-resuscitate order on their own.

Care must be taken by the practitioner to review this law before proceeding in this area as many parts of the text are affected and altered by the provisions of this legislation.

[0.1] *Union Leader,* June 20, 2006, p. B3.

CHAPTER 42

POWERS OF ATTORNEY FOR FINANCIAL AFFAIRS

Page 497: Replace §§ 42.01 through 42.04 as follows:

§ 42.01　General Power of Attorney—In General

Any person may appoint another to act as his agent under the general principles of agency law.[1] The person making the appointment is denominated the principal and the holder of the power is denominated the agent.[2] There is no particular or prescribed form by which a person may appoint another to act as his agent. However, every power of attorney to convey real estate must be signed and acknowledged.[3] Such written power of attorney may be recorded as required for a deed and a copy of the record used as evidence whenever a copy of the deed so made is admissible.[4]

One who is a holder of a general power of attorney is a fiduciary as to his principal.[5] As such, when dealing with the principal's finances, the holder of the power of attorney is subject to strict fiduciary accounting rules as to the principal's financial assets and may be liable for interest on any funds misappropriated from the principal.[6]

Different governmental departments of the State of New Hampshire have established rules for the appointment of agents by persons dealing with the governmental agency, which vary greatly in form. See, for example, Form 778, "Authorized Representative Declaration" of the Division of Human Services.[7]

Forms in Appendix of Forms and Checklists

Form 60 is the statutory form power of attorney as set forth in R.S.A. 564-E:301.

[1]　Death, Disability or Incompetence of Principal

A general power of attorney is revoked or terminated by the death or incompetency of the principal unless the power is coupled with an interest.[8] However, a general power of attorney is not revoked or terminated by the death, disability, or incompetence of the principal "as to the agent or other person that, without actual knowledge of the incapacity, acts in good faith under the power of attorney."[9] Any action taken under such a power, "unless otherwise invalid or unenforceable, binds the principal and the principal's successors in interest."[10]

[2]　Safe Deposit Boxes; Bank Accounts

A power of attorney authorizing access to a safe deposit box survives the death of the principal and the holder of the power of attorney may have continued access after the death of the principal to the safe deposit box.[14] Furthermore, a bank may continue to honor a power of attorney over a bank account until it receives written notice or is on actual notice of the death of the principal.[15]

[1] Restatement (Second) of Agency, § 1(1) (1958).

[2] Restatement (Second) of Agency, § 1(2) and (3) (1958).

[3] R.S.A. 477:9.

[4] R.S.A. 477:9.

[5] *In re* Estate of Ward, 129 N.H. 4, 523 A.2d 28 (1986).

[6] *In re* Estate of Ward, 129 N.H. 4, 523 A.2d 28 (1986).

[7] https://www.dhhs.nh.gov/dfa/documents/dfa-778.pdf.

[8] Avis Lane, 10 N.H. 156 (1839); *In re* Estate of Kelly, 130 N.H. 773, 779 (1988); R.S.A. 564-E:110(a).

[9] R.S.A. 564-E:110(e).

[10] R.S.A. 564-E:110(e).

[11–13] Reserved.

[14] R.S.A. 383-B:5-501(g).

[15] R.S.A. 383-B:4-401(a).

§ 42.02 Durable Power of Attorney That Survives Disability or Incompetency

In 1977, New Hampshire created a new type of power of attorney, which was designated by statute as a "special" or "limited" power of attorney.[16] The statute was amended to cure certain problems with the statute as written. The power of attorney that survives the disability or incompetency of the testator is now referred to as a durable power of attorney.[17] This terminology is similar to that used in other states.

Effective January 1, 2018, a power of attorney created under the Uniform Power of Attorney Act (R.S.A. Chapter 564-E) is durable unless it expressly provides that it is terminated by the incapacity of the principal.[18] By use of a durable power of attorney, great flexibility can be achieved in connection with planning for the handling of a person's property, particularly as to elderly persons. For example, an elderly person may execute a special power of attorney giving the agent the power to transfer, upon the person's incompetence, assets of the person to a previously established revocable trust. In this manner, suitable provision can be made to manage the estate of an incompetent person without the necessity of resorting to the more burdensome and expensive procedure of a guardianship. It is recommended that a durable power of attorney be considered in all cases in which elderly clients are represented.

Library References

For designating an agent under a power of attorney for healthcare, *see* Ruth Ansell, *Powers of Attorney: Who Do You Trust?* 38 N.H.B.J. 6 (1997).

[1] Limitations on Agent

Because of the continuing abuses by agents holding durable powers of attorney to treat property of the principal as their own or to otherwise act improperly under the power granted to the agent by the principal, the legislature has continued to attempt to strengthen provisions relating to durable powers of attorney by placing limitations on the power of the agent to act, particularly in making gifts of the principal's property. Effective January 1, 2018, an attorney-in-fact is not authorized to make gifts pursuant to the durable power of attorney, to the attorney-in-fact or to others unless (1) the power of attorney explicitly authorizes such gifts, and (2) a proposed gift would not leave the principal without sufficient assets or income to provide for the principal's care without relying on Medicaid, or public assistance or charity, unless the gift is approved in advance by the court.[19]

The legislature went on further to provide that an attorney-in-fact cannot make a gift to himself or herself of property belonging to the principal unless the terms of the power of attorney explicitly provides for the authority to make gifts to the attorney-in-fact, or the gift is approved in advance by the court.[20]

If it is desired by the principal that gifts to the attorney-in-fact are to be empowered, care must be taken by the draftsman to provide in the power of attorney a very clear authorization to do so in compliance with the statute. In such case, the provision to make gifts to the agent should include a limitation to a maximum of the greater of $5,000 or 5% of the aggregate value of the estate during any calendar year to avoid the creation of a general power of appointment in the agent which would be subject to taxation under the Internal Revenue Code.

To further strengthen these new provisions, the powers of the superior and probate courts in the matters of reviewing gifts made by an agent of the principal's property has been broadened to include the power to issue injunctions.[21] Furthermore, the appropriate court is given specific power in its proceedings under R.S.A. 564-E:116(g) to determine if particular gifts or other transactions are authorized. In determining the authority of an agent to make a gift, the court shall consider:

(1) Evidence of the principal's intent;

(2) The principal's personal history of making or joining in the making of lifetime gifts;

(3) The principal's estate plan;

(4) The principal's foreseeable obligations and maintenance needs and the impact of the proposed gift on the principal's housing options, access to care and services, and general welfare;

(5) The income, gift, estate or inheritance tax consequences of the transaction;

(6) Whether the proposed gift creates a foreseeable risk that the principal will be deprived of sufficient assets to cover his or her needs during any period of Medicaid ineligibility that would result from the proposed gift; and

(7) Whether the proposed gift is likely to result in premature or unnecessary nursing home placement or institutionalization of the principal, or compromise the principal's access to care or services in the least restrictive setting in which his or her needs can be met.[21.1]

[16] Laws 1977, ch. 453:1.

[17] R.S.A. 564-E:104.

[18] R.S.A. 564-E:104.

[19] R.S.A. 564-E:201(a)(2).

[20] R.S.A. 564-E:201(b).

[21] R.S.A. 564-E:116.

[21.1] R.S.A. 564-E:217(b).

[2] Fiduciary Relationship

Because of the risk that agents (who can be unsophisticated lay people), often times do not appreciate the unique nature of the fiduciary relationship created by the power, it is wise practice to provide the agent with a letter of instructions concerning the proper use of the power of attorney. See the Appendix for Form 62, a letter of instructions to an agent under a durable power of attorney.

Forms in Appendix of Forms and Checklists

Form 61 is a form of a durable power of attorney for financial affairs, which complies with the requirements of the statute. This form also contains a provision by which the agent is given the power to transfer, upon the principal's incompetence, assets of the principal to a revocable trust previously established by the principal. This provision is very important for flexibility in handling the assets of an incompetent person.

Form 61 also empowers the agent to make gifts to the natural objects of the principal's bounty, with a limitation on such transfers to the agent to a maximum of the greater of $5,000 or 5 percent of the aggregate value of the estate during any calendar year. This limitation is made to negate the creation of a general power of appointment in the agent, which would be subject to taxation under the Internal Revenue Code.

Form 62 is a form of a letter of instructions designed to be given to an agent to advise him of his fiduciary relationship to the principal and instructing him about the proper use of the power of attorney.

[3] Death, Disability or Incompetence of Principal

A durable power of attorney is revoked or terminated by the death of the principal unless the exception for persons in military service contained in R.S.A. 564-E:106(c)(2) applies. Moreover, the Uniform Power of Attorney Act provides that a general power of attorney is not revoked or terminated by the death, disability, or incompetence of the principal "as to the agent or other person that, without actual knowledge of the incapacity, acts in good faith under the power of attorney."[21.2]

[4] Appointment of Guardian or Conservator

If a guardian or conservator is subsequently appointed for the principal, then the agent must account to the guardian or conservator as well as to the principal during the continuance of his appointment.[22] The guardian or conservator, upon his appointment, is specifically empowered to revoke, suspend, or terminate all or any part of any such special power of attorney.[23]

[5] Foreign Powers of Attorney

Effective January 1, 2018, the Uniform Power of Attorney Act sets forth in

R.S.A. 564-E:106(c) that "a power of attorney executed other than in [New Hampshire] is valid in [New Hampshire] if, when the power of attorney was executed, the execution complied with: (1) the law of the jurisdiction that determines the meaning and effect of the power of attorney pursuant to RSA 564-E:107; or (2) the requirements for a military power of attorney pursuant to 10 U.S.C. section 1044b, as amended."

[6]   Required Notices to Principal and Agent

The Uniform Power of Attorney Act provides detailed specification of required language concerning notices to the principal and to the agent that must be included in all powers of attorney and signed by the principal at the time of the execution of the power (R.S.A. 564-E:105(a)) and by the agent "prior to exercising the power granted under the general power of attorney" (R.S.A. 564-E:113(a)). The statute has been strengthened to provide that the agent "shall have no authority to act as an agent unless the person has signed (other than by electronic signature) and affixed to the general power of attorney an acknowledgment . . ."[24]

> **Notice to the Principal:** As the "Principal," you are using this Power of Attorney to grant power to another person (called the "Agent") to make decisions, including, but not limited to, decisions concerning your money, property, or both, and to use your money, property, or both on your behalf. If this Power of Attorney does not limit the powers that you give to your Agent, your Agent will have broad and sweeping powers to sell or otherwise dispose of your property, and to spend your money without advance notice to you or approval by you. Unless you have expressly provided otherwise in this Power of Attorney, your Agent will have these powers before you become incapacitated, and unless you have expressly provided otherwise in this Power of Attorney, your Agent will continue to have these powers after you become incapacitated. You have the right to retain this Power of Attorney and to release it later or to request that another person retain this Power of Attorney on your behalf and release it only if one or more conditions specified in advance by you are satisfied. You have the right to revoke or take back this Power of Attorney at any time, so long as you are of sound mind. If there is anything about this Power of Attorney that you do not understand, you should seek professional advice.

*   *   *   *   *

> **Notice to Agent:** You will have no authority to act as agent under this Power of Attorney until you sign and affix this acknowledgment to the Power of Attorney.
>
> I, _____, have read the attached power of attorney and am the person identified as the agent for the principal. I hereby acknowledge that when I act as agent I am given power under the power of attorney to make decisions about money, property, or both belonging to the principal, and

to spend the principal's money, property, or both on the principal's behalf, in accordance with the terms of the power of attorney. When acting as agent, I have duties (called "fiduciary duties") to act in the principal's best interest, to act in good faith, and to act only within the scope of authority granted in the power of attorney, as well as other duties imposed by law to the extent not provided otherwise in the power of attorney. As an agent, I am not entitled to use the money or property for my own benefit or to make gifts to myself or others unless the power of attorney specifically gives me the authority to do so. As an agent, my authority under the power of attorney will end when the principal dies and I will not have authority to manage or dispose of any property or administer the estate of the principal. If I violate a fiduciary duty under the power of attorney, I may be liable for damages and may be subject to criminal prosecution. If there is anything about this power of attorney, or my duties under it, that I do not understand, I understand that I should seek professional advice.

[21.2] R.S.A. 564-E:110(e).

[22] R.S.A. 564-E:108(b).

[23] R.S.A. 564-E:108(b)(3).

[24] R.S.A. 564-E:113(a).

§ 42.03 Judicial Supervision of Agent Under Durable Power

R.S.A. 564-E:116 provides that a petition may be filed in the superior or probate courts "to determine whether a power of attorney is in effect, to determine whether a power of attorney has terminated, to determine whether an agent's authority has terminated, to determine whether a particular gift is authorized as provided in subsection [R.S.A. 564-E:116(g)], to determine whether a particular transaction is authorized, to construe a power of attorney or to review the agent's conduct, and to grant appropriate relief."

R.S.A. 564-E:116 provides that the petition contemplated under the statute may be filed by any of the following persons:

(1) the principal;

(2) the agent;

(3) a guardian, conservator, or other fiduciary acting for the principal;

(4) a person authorized to make health-care decisions for the principal;

(5) the principal's spouse, parent, or descendant;

(6) a person who would take property of the principal under the laws of intestate succession if the principal were to die at the time the petition is filed, whether or not the principal has a will;

(7) a person named as a beneficiary to receive any property, benefit, or contractual right on the principal's death or as a beneficiary of a trust created by or for the principal that has a financial interest in the principal's estate; or

(8) the department of justice, the department of health and human services, the county attorney, or any other governmental agency having regulatory authority to protect the welfare of the principal.

In a proceeding under this section commenced by the filing of a petition by a person other than the agent, the court may order the agent to pay reasonable attorney's fees to the petitioner if the court determines that the agent has clearly violated his fiduciary duties under the power of attorney or has failed without any reasonable cause or justification to submit accounts or reports after written request.[25]

R.S.A. 564-E:116(f) provides that "unless good cause is shown, court hearings conducted on a petition filed under this section shall be closed to the general public." *Chapman v. Douglas,*[26] makes clear, however, that a court may order a hearing open to the press where there is compelling reason shown to support the good cause test. In the *Chapman* case, the defendant was a public figure, both on the state and national level, and the allegations against him were serious. The Supreme Court held that these factors were enough to support a finding that proceedings should be open to the public.

This statutory provision creates a needed and useful safeguard to potential abuses by the holders of powers of attorney, particularly where the power of attorney is a durable power of attorney and the principal becomes incompetent.

In addition to the civil powers of the probate and superior courts, an agent who misuses a power of attorney by improperly making gifts to himself can be found guilty of theft. *State v. Gabusi.*[29]

Library References

For financial exploitation of a principal by an agent under a power of attorney, *see* Castelli, *Patient Abuse: Protecting the Patient from the Caregiver,* 39 N.H.B.J. 59, 61–62 (1998).

[25] R.S.A. 564-E:116(e).
[26] 146 N.H. 209; 772 A.2d 318 (2001).
[27–28] Reserved.
[29] 149 N.H. 327 (2003).

§ 42.04   Uniform Acts and the Uniform Probate Code

The Uniform Durable Powers of Attorney Act (1977)was adopted in at least twenty-nine jurisdictions. A later act, entitled Uniform Statutory Form Power of Attorney Act (1988), described a form of statutory power of attorney and was designed to be used in conjunction with the earlier act or with a state's own power of attorney statute.

The 1977 Act was part of the Uniform Probate Code as Section 5-5012505. New Hampshire did not adopt either Act, but the draftsmen of the New Hampshire statute obviously used the 1977 Uniform Act as a reference because of the similarities in some of the provisions of the two statutes.

The Uniform Law Commission approved the Uniform Power of Attorney Act

(UPOAA), which replaces the earlier Uniform Durable Power of Attorney Act, the Uniform Statutory Form Power of Attorney Act, and Article V, Part 5 of the Uniform Probate Code. This new Uniform Act has been adopted in many states, and it is predicted that it will be adopted by many other states as understanding of its advantages spreads.[31]

The New Hampshire Legislature enacted the provisions of UPOAA effective on January 1, 2018.

[30] Reserved.

[31] Haddleton, *"The Durable Power of Attorney Is On the Way,"* Probate & Property, May/June 2010, page 50.

CHAPTER 43

ANTENUPTIAL AGREEMENTS

§ 43.03   Divorce and Separation

[3]   Fairness Standard

Page 515: Delete the last sentence of this subsection and substitute with the following:

Cases involving prenuptial agreements are often very fact specific. For example, in *Yannalfo v. Yannalfo*,[32] the issue was whether an agreement was invalid because of duress. The facts showed that the party seeking to void the agreement relied upon the fact that the agreement was presented to her approximately one day before the wedding. The Supreme Court upheld the agreement stating that in the particular circumstances there involved, no duress had been shown. In contrast, in *In re Estate of John Albert Hollett*,[33] the Court had before it a prenuptial agreement which was sought to be set aside because of duress. The Court stated that "under the heightened security afforded to prenuptial agreements, the timing of the agreement is of paramount importance in assessing whether it was voluntary."[34]

Unlike the *Yannalfo* case, the prenuptial agreement in *Hollett* involved many millions of dollars and was an entire agreement between the parties affecting all of their assets. The agreement was presented to the wife less than forty-eight hours before the scheduled wedding. The wife obtained the advice of an attorney and signed the agreement on the morning of their wedding. The parties were married for eleven years until the husband's death. The surviving spouse sued to invalidate the prenuptial agreement. The Court first held that a claim of duress is essentially a claim if the agreement was not signed voluntarily. The Court went on to hold that under "the heightened scrutiny afforded to prenuptial agreements, the timing of the agreement is of paramount importance in assessing whether it was voluntary . . . . Fairness demands that the party presented with the agreement have 'an opportunity to seek independent advice and a reasonable time to reflect on the proposed terms.' "[35] The Supreme Court overturned the enforcement of the agreement by the lower court because it concluded "as a matter of law that her [the wife's] signing of the agreement was involuntary under the heightened standard applied to prenuptial agreements."[36]

[32] 147 N.H. 597 (2002).

[33] 150 N.H. 39; 834 A.2d 348 (2003).

[34] *In re* Estate of John Albert Hollett, 834 A.2d. 352 (2003).

[35] *In re* Estate of John Albert Hollett, 834 A.2d. 352 (2003).

[36] *In re* Estate of John Albert Hollett, 834 A.2d. 352, 354 (2003).

§ 43.04   Forms and Terms of the Agreement

Page 515: Rename footnote 32 of this section to footnote 37:

CHAPTER 44

UNIFORM SIMULTANEOUS DEATH ACT

§ 44.02   Provisions of the Act

Page 520: Add the following at the end of the text to this section:

Effective January 1, 2006, R.S.A. 563:5, V, provides that an individual, whose death is not established and who is absent for a continuous period of four (4) years, during which time the individual has not been heard from, and whose absence is not satisfactorily explained after diligent search and inquiry, shall be presumed to be dead. The statute specifically goes on to provide that "the individual's death is presumed to have occurred **at the end of the period**, unless there was sufficient evidence for determining that death occurred earlier."

APPENDIX OF FORMS AND CHECKLISTS

Page 526: Substitute this form for Form 1 in the text:

FORM 1   Client Questionnaire

CONFIDENTIAL CLIENT DATA REQUEST

Please complete this form prior to the scheduled conference. We understand and appreciate that everyone's schedule is busy, so please do the best that you can when completing this information. **Please be assured that this information will be maintained in strict confidence in full compliance with our Privacy Policy.**

NOTE: Most clients come to us by referral, we like to acknowledge those sources. Please let us know who referred you to this firm.

Referred by: _____

DATE: _____

I. FAMILY AND OCCUPATIONAL DATA: Please complete the following family data as it may be applicable to you:

Client No. 1: _____

        First   Middle Initial   Last

Date of Birth: _____ S.S. # _____ Citizenship: _____

Home Address: _____

        Street   City   State   Zip

Mailing Address: _____

(if different)   P.O. Box or other info   City   State   Zip

Home Tel. # _____ Cell # _____

E-Mail: _____ Fax # _____

Name of Employer: _____

Business Address: _____

Occupation: _____ Work Tel. # _____

While married, have you ever lived in a community property state (AK, AZ, CA, ID, LA, NV, NM, TX, WA, or WI)? _____

Client No. 2 (spouse): _____

               First   Middle Initial   Last

Date of Birth: _____ S.S. # _____ Citizenship: _____

Home Tel. # _____ Cell # _____

E-Mail: _____ Fax # _____

Name of Employer: _____

Business Address: _____

Occupation: _____ Work Tel. # _____

While married, have you ever lived in a community property state (AK, AZ, CA, ID, LA, NV, NM, TX, WA, or WI)? _____
_____

NOTE: If you are benefiting individuals <u>other</u> than children (i.e. grandchildren, nieces, nephews, etc.), edit this section as appropriate or add a separate sheet providing similar information for each beneficiary, including the beneficiary's relationship to you:

Children: *(Check here _____ if you have attached separate sheets if more space was needed)*

(1) Legal Name: _____

Date of Birth: _____ S.S. # _____ Citizenship: _____
                                (optional)

Status: _____ Occupation: _____
      Married / Divorced / Single / Student

Address: _____

Home Tel. # _____ Cell # _____

Their children and ages: _____ Age _____
                          _____ Age _____

Are there any special issues or problems relating to this child?   **Y/N**
_____

(2) Legal Name: _____

Date of Birth: _____ S.S. # _____ Citizenship: _____
                                (optional)

Status: _____ Occupation: _____
      Married / Divorced / Single / Student

Address: _____

Home Tel. # _____ Cell # _____

Their children and ages: _____ Age _____

_____ Age _____

Are there any special issues or problems relating to this child?   **Y/N**

_____

(3) Legal Name: _____

Date of Birth: _____ S.S. # _____ Citizenship: _____

(optional)

Status: _____ Occupation: _____

Married / Divorced / Single / Student

Address: _____

Home Tel. # _____ Cell # _____

Their children and ages: _____ Age _____

_____ Age _____

Are there any special issues or problems relating to this child?   **Y/N**

_____

(4) Legal Name: _____

Date of Birth: _____ S.S. # _____ Citizenship: _____

(optional)

Status: _____ Occupation: _____

Married / Divorced / Single / Student

Address: _____

Home Tel.# _____ Cell # _____

Their children and ages: _____ Age _____

_____ Age _____

Are there any special issues or problems relating to this child?   **Y/N**

_____

1. Do you have any deceased children? _____

2. Did any deceased child leave children or grandchildren now living? __

3. Are any of your children adopted? _____

4. Were you or your spouse married before? Husband ( ) Wife ( )

If so, to whom and when? _____

5. Were any children born of these prior marriages/relationships? _____

6. How were these marriages terminated? _____

    If by divorce, please attach a copy of your divorce decree or bring it with you to the initial conference.

7. Do you or your estate (or your spouse or his/her estate) have any outstanding obligations benefiting a former spouse or children? _____

    If so, please provide details. _____

8. Have you and your spouse entered into a Prenuptial Agreement? _____

    If so, please attach a copy or bring it with you to the initial conference.

9. Do you have any children by other persons? _____

10. Is anyone else dependent on you for support?

14. How would you describe your health? Are there any problems we should be aware of?
    Client No. 1 _____
    Client No. 2 _____

II. FINANCIAL DATA:

1. ADVISORS (Optional)

Some of the people you will need to contact are listed below:

Other Attorney (if any):
Name: _____
Address: _____
_____
Phone: _____

Financial/Insurance Advisor:
Name: _____
Address: _____
_____
Phone: _____

Accountant:
Name: _____
Address: _____
_____
Phone: _____

Financial/Insurance Advisor:
Name: _____
Address: _____
_____
Phone: _____

Primary Physician (Client 1):
Name: _____
Address: _____
_____
Phone: _____

Primary Physician (Client 2):
Name: _____
Address: _____
_____
Phone: _____

2. INSURANCE COVERAGE
A. LIFE INSURANCE

Insurance Carrier	Owner	Beneficiary	Face Amount	Policy #	Policy Location
_____	_____	_____	$_____	_____	_____
_____	_____	_____	$_____	_____	_____
_____	_____	_____	$_____	_____	_____

B. LONG-TERM CARE INSURANCE

Insurance Carrier	Benefit Amount	Policy Located At:
_____	$_____	_____
_____	$_____	_____

C. DISABILITY INSURANCE

Insurance Carrier	Benefit Amount	Policy Located At:
_____	$_____	_____
_____	$_____	_____

D. HEALTH INSURANCE (optional)

Insurance Carrier: _____   Insurance Carrier: _____
Address: _____   Address: _____
Phone: _____   Phone: _____

Type: _____   Type: _____
Insurance #: _____   Insurance #: _____

III. REAL ESTATE:[1]

	Address	County/State	Approx. Value	Mortgage Amount
(1)	_____	_____	_____	_____
(2)	_____	_____	_____	_____

[1] Please provide us with copies of recent homeowner's insurance bills and mortgage statement on each listed property. If available, please also bring your deeds to the conference. If not available, we can obtain your deeds from the registry.

IV. ASSET PROFILE:

Please attach a copy of your personal financial statement or complete the following ASSET PROFILE using approximate amounts, but valuing your assets at their fair market value.

Item	Client No. 1	Client No. 2	Joint	Indebtedness
Checking Accounts	$_____	$_____	$_____	$_____
Savings Accounts	$_____	$_____	$_____	$_____
Investment Accounts	$_____	$_____	$_____	$_____
Home Residence	$_____	$_____	$_____	$_____
2nd Home	$_____	$_____	$_____	$_____
Land Holdings	$_____	$_____	$_____	$_____
Personal Property	$_____	$_____	$_____	$_____
IRA/401(k)	$_____	$_____	$_____	$_____
Other Retirement	$_____	$_____	$_____	$_____
Business	$_____	$_____	$_____	$_____
Life Insurance	$_____	$_____	$_____	$_____
Other	$_____	$_____	$_____	$_____
TOTALS	$_____	$_____	$_____	$_____

Further Explanation: _____

Current Income	SALARY	INTEREST	DIVIDENDS	OTHER
Client No. 1:				
Client No. 2:				

V. BUSINESS DATA:

1. Do you operate a business or have an ownership interest in a business? If so, describe briefly.

   Client No. 1: _____

   Client No. 2: _____

   A. Is this business a sub-chapter S corporation? _____

   B. Is there any by-law or stock agreement governing or restricting in any way the sale or transfer of the shares in this business? _____

VI. PRESENT ESTATE PLANNING POSITION:

1. Do you presently have a will (or other estate planning documents)?

   Client No. 1: _____ Client No. 2: _____

   Name/Address of attorney: _____

   Please attach a copy or bring it with you to the initial conference.

2. Have you made taxable gifts and filed gift tax returns in past years?
   Gift _____ Year _____
   If possible, please provide a copy of your latest gift tax return, if any.

3. Have you created or do you presently benefit from any trusts?
   _____
   Please attached a copy of the trust or bring it with you to the initial conference.

4. Do you expect to receive any substantial inheritances? _____
   If so, please provide some detail (we will discuss this in more detail at our initial conference).

VII. BURIAL INSTRUCTIONS:

Do you have specific burial instructions that you want to be carried out? If so, please describe: _____

_____

VIII. COMMENTS

_____

_____

IX. ISSUES TO CONSIDER PRIOR TO THE FIRST MEETING

During our meeting we will be discussing a number of issues relating to your estate plan. We will most certainly have a thorough and complete discussion, however, if you would like to prepare in advance for this meeting, we suggest that you consider the following issues:

1. Who is best suited to deal with your financial issues, if or when you are disabled?

    Primary: _____

    Contingent: _____

2. Who is best suited to deal with your health care issues, if or when you are disabled?

    Primary: _____

    Contingent: _____

3. Who or whom is best suited to serve as the guardian of your children?

    Primary: _____

    Contingent: _____

4. Are there specific issues that you would like to address during our first meeting?

    _____

    _____

X. ADDITIONAL ITEMS TO BRING TO YOUR FIRST MEETING

At our first meeting, it may be helpful (but not absolutely necessary) to have available to us the following information:

- Copies of deeds to any real estate that you hold.
- Recent mortgage statements/bills relating to real estate that you own.
- Copies of recent homeowner's insurance statements/bills relating to real estate that you own.
- Copies of previous estate planning documents, if any.

Page 539: Substitute this form for Form 4 in the text:

FORM 4   Simple Will

LAST WILL
OF

_____

I, _____, of _____, County of _____, State of New Hampshire, do make this will and hereby revoke all other wills and codicils previously made by me.

1.   <u>DEBTS, EXPENSES AND TAXES</u>. I direct that all my legal debts, funeral expenses and expenses of administration be paid as soon after my death as practical. I further direct that all such debts and expenses, as well as all estate, inheritance, transfer, legacy or succession taxes (state and federal), and any interest or penalties thereon which may be assessed or imposed with respect to my estate, or any part thereof, wheresoever situated, whether or not passing under my will, including the taxable value of all policies of insurance on my life and all transfers, powers, rights or interests includible in my estate for purposes of such taxes and duties, shall be paid out of my residuary estate as an expense of administration and without apportionment, and shall not be prorated or charged against any of the other gifts in this will or against property not passing under this will.

2.   <u>REAL ESTATE</u>. I give and devise to _____ absolutely, all of my right, title and interest, whatever it may be, in the real estate used as our home property or properties at the time of my death.

3.   <u>TANGIBLE PERSONAL PROPERTY</u>. I give and bequeath to _____ absolutely, all of my tangible personal property and household effects owned by me at the time of my death, including furniture, clothing, jewelry, silver, books, pictures, china, automobiles and their equipment, other vehicles and their equipment, and other articles of personal and household use or ornament.

I express the hope that said beneficiaries will dispose of said tangible personal property and household effects according to my wishes, however my wishes may be made known to them, but I expressly declare that I do not intend to create any trust in law or in equity with respect to said tangible personal property.

If a division of the property under this bequest is required among the beneficiaries, such division shall be made by the beneficiaries, in appropriate shares, as they may amicably agree. I prefer that said beneficiaries shall agree upon the manner in which said property is to be divided, but should they not agree among themselves as to the division thereof within ninety (90) days after my death, I give my executor full power and authority to divide said property among said beneficiaries, in appropriate shares, and his determination with respect thereto shall, insofar as permitted by law, be binding and conclusive upon such beneficiaries.

4.   <u>RESIDUARY ESTATE</u>. All the rest, residue and remainder of my estate, of whatever kind or nature, wherever found and however acquired, including any property over which I have a power of appointment, I give, devise and bequeath to _____ if _____ he/she survives me.

If _____ shall not survive me, then I give, devise and bequeath my residuary estate to my issue who so survive me, such issue to take <u>per stirpes</u>.

5.   <u>ADMINISTRATIVE POWERS</u>. My executor hereinafter named, and any other administrator, executor, or trustee administering my estate shall have all of the powers granted to trustees by New Hampshire common law and statutory authority (including, but not limited to, the Uniform Trustees' Powers Act, R.S.A. 564-A, and the Uniform Trust Code, R.S.A. 564-B, as they may be amended from time to time), without restrictions. Where the context of this statute requires, the word "executor" or "administrator" shall be substituted for the word "trustee" and the word "estate" shall be substituted for the word "trust."

6.   <u>SURVIVAL REQUIREMENT</u>. No person shall be deemed to have survived me, or any other person or event under the terms of this will, unless such person survives the end of the period commencing with the close of the calendar day of my death, the death of such other person or on which such event occurs, and ending with the close of the thirtieth (30th) calendar day thereafter.

7.   <u>EXECUTORS</u>. I nominate my _____, _____, of _____, _____ as executor under this will.

If my said _____ should be unable or unwilling to serve in this capacity for any reason, then I nominate my _____, _____, of _____, _____ as successor.

It is my desire that the executor and the designated alternate shall be allowed to serve with the minimum bond required by the Probate Court.

8.   <u>EXPRESS INTENT</u>. Except as otherwise expressly provided by this will, I intentionally make no provision for the benefit of any child of mine, nor the issue of any child of mine, whether now alive, now deceased, or hereafter born or deceased.

9.   <u>DEFINITIONS</u>. Whenever used in this will the words "child," "children," or "issue" are intended to include not only persons who are descendants by blood, but also persons, and issue of persons, who have been adopted according to law prior to their attaining the age of eighteen (18) years.

Masculine, feminine, and neuter pronouns shall each include all genders, and the singular shall include the plural, and vice versa, where the context or facts so admit.

The captions and paragraph headings of this will are inserted only as a matter of convenience and for reference, and in no way define, limit or describe the scope or intent of this will, nor in any way affect this will.

IN WITNESS WHEREOF, I hereunto set my hand and, in the presence of two (2) witnesses, declare this to be my will, on _____, 2009. For identification, I have signed each of the _____ (_____) pages of this will.

_____

Signed and declared by the said _____ as and for his will, in the presence of us, who, at his request, in his presence, and in the presence of each other, hereunto subscribe our names as witnesses.

_____ residing at _____

_____ residing at _____

ACKNOWLEDGEMENT AND AFFIDAVIT FOR
SELF-PROVING WILL PURSUANT TO R.S.A. 551:2-a

THE STATE OF NEW HAMPSHIRE
COUNTY OF _____, SS.

The foregoing instrument was acknowledged before me this _____, 2009, by _____, the testator; _____ and _____, the witnesses, who under oath do swear as follows:

1. The testator signed the instrument as his will or expressly directed another to sign for him.

2. This was the testator's free and voluntary act for the purposes expressed in the will.

3. Each witness signed at the request of the testator, in his presence, and in the presence of the other witness.

4. To the best of my knowledge, at the time of the signing the testator was at least 18 years of age, or if under 18 years was a married person, and was of sane mind and under no constraint or undue influence.

_____
Notary Public/Justice of the Peace
My Commission Expires:
(Seal)

Page 543: Substitute this form for Form 5 in the text:

FORM 5   Self-Proving Will
LAST WILL
OF
———————————————————

I, _____, of _____, County of _____, State of New Hampshire, do make this will and hereby revoke all other wills and codicils previously made by me.

1.   <u>DEBTS AND EXPENSES</u>. I direct that all my legal debts, funeral expenses and expenses of administration be paid as soon after my death as practical. I further direct that all such debts and expenses shall be paid as an expense of administration and without apportionment out of my residuary estate passing into _____ and in the manner prescribed by the provisions of said REVOCABLE TRUST.

2.   <u>REST AND RESIDUE</u>. I give, devise and bequeath all the rest, residue and remainder of my estate, of whatever kind or nature, wherever found and however acquired, including any property over which I have a power of appointment, to that person who, at the time of my death, is serving as trustee under a certain instrument of revocable trust executed by me concurrently herewith and entitled _____, and I direct that said residuary estate shall be held and administered in accordance with the terms of _____.

3.   <u>ADMINISTRATIVE POWERS</u>.

A.   My executor hereinafter named, and any other administrator, executor, or trustee administering my estate shall have all of the powers granted to trustees by New Hampshire common law and statutory authority (including, but not limited to, the Uniform Trustees' Powers Act, R.S.A. 564-A, and the Uniform Trust Code, R.S.A. 564-B, as they may be amended from time to time), without restrictions. Where the context of this statute requires, the word "executor" or "administrator" shall be substituted for the word "trustee" and the word "estate" shall be substituted for the word "trust."

B.   All estate, inheritance, transfer, legacy or succession taxes (state or federal), and any interest or penalties thereon (but excluding any additional tax imposed by Section 2032A or 2057 of the Internal Revenue Code of 1986, or any provision successor thereto, or any generation-skipping transfer tax imposed under Chapter 13 of the Internal Revenue Code of 1986, or any provision successor thereto) paid to any domestic or foreign taxing authority with respect to all property taxable by reason of my death, whether such taxes be payable by my estate or any recipient of any such property and whether or not such property passes under this will or under _____, shall be charged against and paid without apportionment out of that portion of my residuary estate passing into _____ and in the manner prescribed by the provisions of _____.

1.   My executor shall have full power and authority to make any and all

estate, inheritance and income tax elections available to my executor, including specifically (a) the dates and methods which shall be selected for the valuation of property in my gross estate for federal and state estate and inheritance tax purposes and the payment of all such taxes, and (b) whether a deduction shall be taken as an income tax deduction or an estate tax deduction. My executor's decisions with respect to all elections shall be binding and conclusive upon all concerned. No compensating adjustments between income and principal or in the amount of any bequest or devise in this will shall be made as a result of any such decision.

OR

1.   My executor, in his sole, exclusive and unrestricted discretion, shall have full power and authority to determine to elect (under Section 2056(b)(7) of the Internal Revenue Code of 1986, or any provision successor thereto, as amended) to qualify all or a specific portion of the trust referred to herein for the federal estate tax marital deduction. I suggest, but do not direct, that in exercising such discretion, my executor attempt to minimize (or eliminate, if possible) the federal and state estate, inheritance or other death taxes payable by my estate at the time of my death. However, my executor should also consider the effect of his election upon the federal and state estate, inheritance or other death taxes which will be payable by my spouse's estate at my spouse's death, particularly if my spouse dies before this election must be made. The decision of my executor with respect to the exercise of the election shall be final and conclusive upon all persons whose interests in my estate are directly or indirectly affected by the election.

My executor shall have the power to join with my spouse in the filing of any tax returns for any year or years for which I have not filed such return or returns prior to my death and to pay all or such ratable share of any taxes (together with any interest and penalties thereon) as my executor shall deem proper. I further authorize and empower my executor to consent that any gifts made by my spouse prior to my death be treated as made one-half (1/2) by me for the purposes of any gift tax laws and returns.

2.   If my probate estate shall not have sufficient liquid assets to satisfy such taxes, and any interest and penalties thereon, as my executor, after consultation with the trustee of _____, shall determine, my executor shall request payment of said taxes from _____ by making, signing and delivering to the trustee of said trust a certificate stating (a) the total amount required of the trustee for the purpose of making the payments involved, (b) the government (state or federal), the authority or agency or department thereof, to whom such payments are to be made, and (c) the amount to be paid and the nature of the payment to be made to each of the same.

3. My executor is empowered to consult with the trustee of _____ and to take whatever actions seem necessary to carry these directions into effect.

4. My executor shall have full power and authority to allocate the generation-skipping transfer tax exemption allowed under Section 2631 of the Internal Revenue Code of 1986, or any provision successor thereto, to any property with respect to which I am the transferor, including inter vivos and testamentary transfers, whether or not such property passes under this will, as my executor deems appropriate. My executor may make such allocation in whole or in part to any trust, or trust share, established by me, or by my spouse, if said spouse predeceased me, with respect to which I am treated as the transferor for generation-skipping transfer tax purposes. Notwithstanding R.S.A. 564-A:3, II, or any provision successor thereto, my executor's decision with respect to such allocation shall be binding and conclusive upon all concerned if made in good faith with reasonable intent to lessen or eliminate the impact of estate or generation-skipping transfer taxes, whether or not such allocation is successful in achieving the results sought and without regard to its effect on beneficiaries in the same or different generations.

5. My executor shall have the full power and authority to execute qualified disclaimers under Section 2518 of the Internal Revenue Code of 1986, or any provision successor thereto, and those in accordance with the law applicable to the state where I am domiciled at the time of my death.

C. In order to facilitate administration of my estate plan, I give to my executor full power to make sales to the trustee from time to time serving under _____; to make and receive loans and/or advances to or from said trust, said sales and said loans and/or said advances to be made on such terms as my executor and said trustee shall think proper, and I direct that all judgments, decisions, and actions so taken shall be final and binding upon all persons if made reasonably and in good faith; even though the person serving as trustee under _____ shall be the same as the fiduciary under this will.

D. If my probate estate shall not have sufficient liquid assets to satisfy my legal debts, funeral expenses and expenses of administration, as my executor, after consultation with the trustee of _____, shall determine, my executor shall request payment of any, or all, of said debts and expenses from _____ by making, signing and delivering to the trustee of said trust a certificate stating (a) the total amount required of the trustee for the purpose of making the payments involved, (b) the persons or creditors to whom such payments are to be made, and (c) the amount to be paid and the nature of the payment to be made to each of the same.

E. No executor hereunder ever shall be liable for involuntary losses or for any loss or damage except such as is caused by his own individual bad faith; my executor may, from time to time, consult and employ counsel with respect to the meaning, construction and operation of this will, particularly with respect to the apportionments, allocations, distributions and disbursements hereunder described; my executor may act on the advice of counsel without incurring liability on account of any such actions.

F. The provisions of this paragraph shall not be construed as affecting the authority of my executor, in his discretion, either to pay, settle or compromise any taxes not presently due, or to delay payment, settlement or compromise thereof until such time as he and/or my trustee shall determine.

G. In connection with the allowance of all accounts of all fiduciaries appointed under this will or under any other instrument executed by me, I request the court having jurisdiction to dispense with all requirements for the appointment of anyone to represent the interests of minors or persons unborn or unascertained.

4. <u>EXECUTORS</u>. I nominate my spouse, _____, as executrix under this will.

If my said spouse should be unable or unwilling to serve in this capacity for any reason, then I nominate _____ as successor executor.

If _____ should be unable or unwilling to serve in this capacity for any reason, then I nominate _____ as successor executor.

It is my desire that my said spouse and the designated alternates shall be allowed to serve with the minimum bond required by the Probate Court.

5. <u>GUARDIANS</u>. If my spouse, _____, survives me, I nominate her to be guardian of the person and property of each of my children who shall be a minor at the time of my death (and I request the Court having jurisdiction thereof to make appointment accordingly).

If my said spouse does not survive me or should be unable or unwilling to act in this capacity for any reason, then I nominate my _____, _____, of _____, _____ to serve as successor guardian.

It is my desire that my said spouse and the designated alternate shall be allowed to serve with the minimum bond required by the Probate Court.

6. <u>EXPRESS INTENT</u>. Except as otherwise expressly provided by this will and under _____, I intentionally make no provision for the benefit of any child of mine, nor the issue of any child of mine, whether now alive, now deceased, or hereafter born or deceased.

7. <u>NON-RECIPROCAL WILLS</u>. Although it is my understanding that my spouse, _____, is or may be executing a last will at or about the time of the execution of this, my last will, it is not my or our intention that such wills be construed or deemed mutual, reciprocal or dependent one upon the other, nor are such wills executed pursuant to a contract.

8. <u>DEFINITIONS</u>. Whenever used in this will the words "child," "children," or "issue" are intended to include not only persons who are descendants by blood, but also persons, and issue of persons, who have been adopted according to law prior to their attaining the age of eighteen (18) years.

Masculine, feminine and neuter pronouns shall each include all genders, and the singular shall include the plural, and vice versa, where the context or facts so admit.

The captions and paragraph headings of this will are inserted only as a matter of convenience and for reference, and in no way define, limit or describe the scope or intent of this will, nor in any way affect this will.

IN WITNESS WHEREOF, I hereunto set my hand and, in the presence of two (2) witnesses, declare this to be my will, on _____, 2009. For identification, I have signed each of the _____ (_____) pages of this will.

_____

_____

Signed and declared by the said _____ as and for his will, in the presence of us, who at his request, in his presence, and in the presence of each other, hereunto subscribe our names as witnesses.

_____ residing at _____

_____ residing at _____

ACKNOWLEDGMENT AND AFFIDAVIT FOR
SELF-PROVING WILL PURSUANT TO R.S.A. 551:2-a

THE STATE OF NEW HAMPSHIRE
COUNTY OF _____, SS.

The foregoing instrument was acknowledged before me on _____, 2019, by _____, the testator; _____ and _____, the witnesses, who under oath do swear as follows:

1. The testator signed the instrument as his will or expressly directed another to sign for him.

2. This was the testator's free and voluntary act for the purposes expressed in the will.

3. Each witness signed at the request of the testator, in his presence, and in the presence of the other witness.

4. To the best of my knowledge, at the time of the signing the testator was at least 18 years of age, or if under 18 years was a married person, and was of sane mind and under no constraint or undue influence.

_____
Notary Public/Justice of the Peace
My Commission Expires:
(Seal)

Page 563: Substitute this form for Form 21 in the text:

FORM 21   In Terrorem Clause—Will

<u>CONTEST OF THIS WILL [OR MY SPOUSE'S WILL,] OR MY TRUST
AGREEMENTS [OR MY SPOUSE'S TRUST AGREEMENTS]</u>. Notwithstanding any provision herein to the contrary, if any beneficiary under this will, in good faith or otherwise, shall, directly or indirectly, institute, conduct, or in any manner whatsoever take part in or aid in any proceedings to contest the validity of my will [or my spouse's will], or any codicil thereto, or contest the validity of any trust created by me [or my spouse], or any amendment thereto, or impair, invalidate, set aside or vary the terms of any such instrument as amended at the time of my death [or my spouse's death], or challenge the actions of the executor of my estate [or my spouse's estate] in the performance of their duties under such will or any codicil thereto, or challenge the actions of any trustee or other fiduciary of any trust created by me [or my spouse] in the performance of the trustee's or other fiduciary's duties as described in such trust, or pursue any other act or proceeding to frustrate or defeat my intent [or my spouse's intent, as applicable,] as described in such instrument, or shall induce any other person to pursue any such action, then, in such event, the provision herein made for the benefit of such person or persons, and his, her, or their issue, shall thereupon be revoked. Such person or persons, and his, her, or their issue, shall thereafter be excluded from any participation in my estate, whether under this will or through the laws of intestacy, and shall cease to have any right or title to such estate and the share to which such person or person or issue would have been entitled shall thereafter be administered as if such person or persons had predeceased me without leaving living issue.

Provided, however, in the case of an action brought solely to challenge the acts of an executor, trustee, or other fiduciary, then this provision shall be unenforceable to the extent such executor, trustee, or other fiduciary is found to have committed a breach of its fiduciary duty or a breach of trust.

Nothing contained herein shall be construed to prevent the executor of my will, [the executor of my spouse's will,] or the trustee or any other fiduciary of any trust created by me or my spouse, or their successors, from instituting or bringing any action, suit, or proceeding for the construction or interpretation of the provisions of any such instrument. Nor shall the provisions hereunder be construed to prevent any beneficiary from disclosing relevant information in a proceeding for the administration of my estate, my spouse's estate, or the administration of any trust created by me [or my spouse].

<u>Note: Language enclosed in brackets is added where client is married</u>.

Page 578: Substitute this form for Form 35 in the text:

FORM 35   Revocable Trust with a Marital Bequest and Family Trust

THE _____ REVOCABLE TRUST OF _____

TRUST AGREEMENT, made on _____, 2011, between _____, residing in _____, New Hampshire (hereinafter called the "Grantor"), and _____, residing in _____, New Hampshire (hereinafter called the "Trustee").

At the time of the signing of this trust, the Grantor's spouse is _____, and the Grantor's children are _____, _____ and _____.

1.   TRUST PROPERTY. All property transferred and delivered to the Trustee, which the Trustee may, at any time, hold or acquire, including cash, securities, or other property, shall be referred to collectively as the "trust estate" and held and administered and disposed of by the Trustee for the uses and purposes, and upon the terms and conditions, herein set forth.

2.   DISPOSITIVE PROVISIONS: LIFETIME. The Trustee shall hold, manage, invest and reinvest the trust estate, and shall collect the income thereof and dispose of the net income and principal as follows:

A.   Pay such parts of the income, if any, and such parts of the principal of this trust to, or for the benefit of, the Grantor as the Grantor directs from time to time for the Grantor's support in reasonable comfort, education (including college, graduate, and professional education), and maintenance in health (including medical, dental, hospital, nursing and nursing home expenses). Any income accrued or accumulated at the time of the Grantor's death shall be paid and transferred to principal, to be administered according to the terms hereinafter provided.

B.   In addition, during the lifetime of the Grantor, if the Grantor becomes so incapacitated that the Grantor cannot exercise the Grantor's rights under sub-paragraph 2.A. above, and there are sufficient assets in this trust to do so, the Trustee is authorized to pay such parts of the income, if any, and such parts of the principal of this trust to, or for the benefit of, the Grantor, the Grantor's spouse and the Grantor's children as it deems advisable for their support in reasonable comfort, education (including college, graduate, and professional education), and maintenance in health (including medical, dental, hospital, nursing and nursing home expenses), taking into consideration the amount of their income from sources other than this trust.

It is the Grantor's intention that the support in reasonable comfort, education (including college, graduate, and professional education), and maintenance in health (including medical, dental, hospital, nursing and nursing home expenses) of the Grantor and the Grantor's spouse shall be of primary concern, and the Trustee shall exercise its discretion in using principal for the Grantor and the Grantor's spouse, considering all other

91

beneficiaries to be secondary and without liability to any other beneficiary for the use of principal for the Grantor and the Grantor's spouse.

C.   Further, the Trustee is authorized to give, transfer or convey any of the trust estate to charities and persons of the Grantor's natural affection to whom the Grantor would normally consider making such gifts, transfers or conveyances, whether outright or in trust, having in mind the ultimate objective of such gifts, transfers or conveyances is either (i) the qualification for state or federal medical, welfare or other assistance programs for the Grantor's or the Grantor's spouse's benefit, or (ii) the reduction of the state and federal estate, inheritance, transfer, legacy and succession taxes and any interest and penalties thereon imposed by reason of the Grantor's death or the Grantor's spouse's death.

3.   DISPOSITIVE PROVISIONS: AFTER DEATH. Upon the death of the Grantor, the Trustee shall thereafter apply and distribute the trust estate as follows:

A.   The Trustee shall distribute the following items from the trust estate, outright and free of trust, to those of the following named beneficiaries who survive the Grantor:

1. _____ to _____;

2. _____ to _____;

3. _____ to _____; and

4. _____ to _____.

B.   After the distributions, if any, in sub-paragraph 3.A. above, if the Grantor's spouse, _____, survives the Grantor, the Trustee shall distribute to the Grantor's said spouse, outright and free of trust, all **remaining** items of tangible personal property and household effects which are then part of the trust estate, including furniture, clothing, jewelry, silver, books, pictures, china, automobiles and their equipment, other vehicles and their equipment, and other articles of personal and household use or ornament.

If the Grantor's said spouse shall not survive the Grantor, said tangible personal property and household effects shall be distributed, outright and free of trust, to the Grantor's issue who so survive the Grantor, such issue to take *per stirpes*.

The Grantor expresses the hope that said beneficiaries will dispose of said tangible personal property and household effects according to the Grantor's wishes, however said wishes may be made known to them.

If a division of the property under this distribution is required among the beneficiaries, such division shall be made by the beneficiaries, in appropriate shares, as they may amicably agree.

The Grantor prefers that said beneficiaries shall agree upon the manner in which said property is to be divided, but should they not agree among themselves as to the division thereof within ninety (90) days after the Grantor's death, the Trustee shall have full power and authority to divide said property among said beneficiaries, in appropriate shares, and its determination with respect thereto shall, insofar as permitted by law, be binding and conclusive upon such beneficiaries.

C. After the distributions, if any, in sub-paragraphs 3.A. and 3.B. above, the Trustee shall distribute the following sums, outright and free of trust, to those of the following named beneficiaries who survive the Grantor:

1. _____ DOLLARS ($_____) to _____;

2. _____ DOLLARS ($_____) to _____;

3. _____ DOLLARS ($_____) to _____; and

4. _____ DOLLARS ($_____) to _____;

D. After the distributions, if any, in sub-paragraphs 3.A., 3.B. and 3.C above, if the Grantor's spouse, _____, survives the Grantor, the Trustee shall divide the remaining trust estate into two parts, one to be known as the "Marital Bequest," and the other as the "Family Trust."

1. <u>Marital Bequest</u>. The Trustee shall distribute to the Grantor's spouse, outright and free of trust, an amount equal to the maximum allowable federal estate tax marital deduction as calculated by law in effect at the time of the Grantor's death, diminished by the value for federal estate tax purposes of all items in the Grantor's gross estate which qualify for said deduction and which pass or have passed to the Grantor's spouse under the Grantor's will, by survivorship in joint tenancy or tenancy by the entirety property, by life insurance settlement, by operation of law or otherwise than under this paragraph.

Provided, however, that if the amount of the maximum allowable federal estate tax marital deduction in the Grantor's estate is greater than the amount needed to reduce the federal estate tax to zero, after considering the available unified tax credit (the applicable credit amount or applicable exclusion amount) and state death tax credit or deduction allowable in determining such tax (provided that the state death tax credit or deduction shall be taken into account only to the extent that doing so would not result in an increase in state death taxes which would otherwise be payable), then the amount shall be equal only to that portion of such marital deduction that is needed to reduce the federal estate tax on the Grantor's estate to zero.

The amount distributed to the Grantor's spouse shall be known as the Marital Bequest.

93

2. For the purpose of determining the amount to be transferred into the Marital Bequest, values shall be those which are finally determined for federal estate tax purposes. Elections made by the Grantor's executor with respect to taking certain deductions for income tax purposes rather than for estate tax purposes shall determine the aforesaid values and the amount to constitute the Marital Bequest. The words "which pass" or "has passed" shall have the same meaning as under the Internal Revenue Code for marital deduction purposes.

3. In making allocation or distribution to the Marital Bequest the Trustee is authorized to satisfy the Marital Bequest in cash or in kind, or in combination of both, provided that all assets placed in the Marital Bequest shall be valued for the purpose of being placed in the Marital Bequest at their fair market value as determined as of the dates of respective distributions to the Marital Bequest, which dates shall be the dates on which the Trustee makes specific allocation on its books of account (if such assets are in negotiable form), or when delivery is made in proper form for transfer, or a deed is executed (if real estate), and the aggregate fair market value thereof shall be no less than the amount required to completely fund the Marital Bequest. The Trustee is further authorized to estimate the size of the Marital Bequest and to transfer said funds, subject, however, to any adjustments which may be required upon final determination of the federal estate tax on the Grantor's estate.

4. No debts, funeral expenses, expenses of administration of the Grantor's estate, inheritance, estate, transfer, legacy or succession taxes (state and federal), and any interest or penalties thereon shall be apportioned against or paid from the Marital Bequest, except to the extent the assets of both the Grantor's estate and the Family Trust are insufficient for this purpose.

5. If the Grantor's spouse or the Grantor's spouse's executor disclaims said spouse's interest in and power over any property of the Marital Bequest, then the Trustee shall pay the disclaimed trust assets over to the Family Trust and thereafter said assets shall be administered as part thereof.

6. If the Grantor or the executor of the Grantor's estate or any other individual (including any individual who shall transfer property in trust hereunder or the executor or administrator of the estate of such individual), deems it necessary to allocate any portion of the trust estate to a separate trust share which will allow such assets to qualify for a state marital deduction pursuant to any applicable provision of state law, then notwithstanding anything to the contrary contained in this agreement, the Trustee is authorized to establish a separate Marital QTIP Trust, the terms of which will qualify for the state marital

deduction, to hold the property received in trust hereunder as it, in its sole, absolute, and uncontrolled discretion, shall deem advisable; provided, however, that the amount set aside in the state Marital QTIP Trust shall be equal only to that portion of such marital deduction that is needed to reduce the state estate tax on the Grantor's estate to zero.

E.   Family Trust. The Family Trust shall consist of all of the remainder of the trust estate which has not been heretofore previously allocated and shall be held and administered and disposed of by the Trustee as follows:

1.   If the Grantor's spouse, _____, survives the Grantor, then, during said spouse's lifetime, the Trustee may pay over to the Grantor's spouse or may use, apply or expend for said spouse's direct or indirect benefit, so much or all of the income of the trust hereby created and so much or all of the principal of said trust as the Trustee may deem proper or necessary for the Grantor's said spouse's support in reasonable comfort, education (including college, graduate, and professional education), and maintenance in health (including medical, dental, hospital, nursing and nursing home expenses).

   a.   The Trustee may also pay over to or use, apply or expend for the direct or indirect benefit of the Grantor's children who are from time to time living during said period, or pay to the Grantor's spouse for their benefit, so much or all of the income or principal of the trust hereby created as the Trustee may deem proper or necessary for their support in reasonable comfort, education (including college, graduate, and professional education), and maintenance in health (including medical, dental, hospital, nursing and nursing home expenses).

   b.   It is the Grantor's intention that the support in reasonable comfort, education (including college, graduate, and professional education), and maintenance in health (including medical, dental, hospital, nursing and nursing home expenses) of the Grantor's spouse shall be of primary concern, and the Trustee shall exercise its discretion in using principal for the Grantor's spouse, considering all other beneficiaries to this trust to be secondary and without liability to any other beneficiary for the use of principal for the Grantor's spouse.

   c.   In addition, the Grantor's spouse shall have the absolute right once during each and every calendar year, between December 1 and December 31 inclusive, to withdraw any amount from the principal of the Family Trust, in cash or in kind. The maximum amount that may be withdrawn annually by said spouse under this sub-paragraph, however, shall not exceed the maximum amount over which an individual may have a power of withdrawal without its lapse in such year being deemed to be a release of such power under Section 2514(e) of the Code. Such right to withdraw shall be non-cumulative.

d. The Grantor's spouse shall have a limited power of appointment over said spouse's entire interest in the principal and accumulated income of the Family Trust, in favor of the Grantor's issue, in such shares, proportion, manner and amount, whether outright, in trust, or otherwise, as the Grantor's spouse, by said spouse's last will, duly proved and allowed, or, if no probate administration of said spouse's estate is required, then as filed with the Probate Court, may appoint; provided, however, that this limited power of appointment is specifically referred to by the terms of said will; and provided, further, that in no event shall said limited power of appointment be exercisable in favor of the Grantor's said spouse, said spouse's estate, said spouse's creditors, or the creditors of said spouse's estate.

Such property remaining in the Family Trust on the death of the Grantor's spouse which has not been appointed by said spouse's last will, in accordance with the power hereinabove vested in Grantor's spouse, shall be administered in accordance with the provisions described hereinbelow.

2. Upon the death of the Grantor's spouse, or upon the Grantor's death if the Grantor's spouse does not survive the Grantor, the Trustee shall apportion the unappointed balance of the principal and accumulated income of the trust estate, or the remaining principal and accumulated income of said trust estate, as the case may be, into equal shares as follows:

one (1) such share to each of the Grantor's living children, and

one (1) such share to each family group composed of the living issue of any child of the Grantor who is then deceased.

Said equal shares shall then be held and administered and disposed of as follows:

a. In the case of each share apportioned to a living child of the Grantor, the Trustee may, in each and every year beginning with the date of said apportionment, pay over to said child or use, apply or expend for said child's direct or indirect benefit, so much or all of the net income of said share and so much or all of the principal of said share as the Trustee may, in its sole, absolute, and uncontrolled discretion, deem wise and safely consistent with said child's support in reasonable comfort, education (including college, graduate, and professional education), and maintenance in health (including medical, dental, hospital, nursing and nursing home expenses).

    i.   Whenever, at or after said time of apportionment, said child shall have attained the age of thirty (30) years, he shall have the right to request in writing and to receive one-third (1/3) of the balance of his share; and

    ii.   Whenever, at or after said time of apportionment, said child shall have attained the age of thirty-five (35) years, he shall have the right to request in writing and to receive an additional one-half (1/2) of the balance of his share; and

    iii.   Whenever, at or after said time of apportionment, said child shall have attained the age of forty (40) years, he shall have the right to request in writing and to receive the entire balance of his share, at which time his trust shall terminate.

    iv.   It is the Grantor's belief that, in some circumstances, it may be beneficial for said child to leave the management of his trust share in the hands of the Trustee.

        Therefore, said child may elect to leave his trust share, or any portion thereof, in the hands of the Trustee, as a separate fund, to be held and administered and disposed of as said child shall direct.

    v.   The share held by the Trustee for the benefit of a child as described above shall, from the time of the death of the child after the time above set for apportionment into shares, be administered for the benefit of the child's issue in the manner described below.

b.   In the case of each share apportioned to the living issue of a deceased child of the Grantors, said share shall be administered for the benefit as a family group of such of the issue of said deceased child as from time to time shall be living.

    The Trustee may pay over to the issue, or may use, apply or expend for their direct or indirect benefit, so much of the income and principal of the trust estate, at such times and in such proportions as the Trustee may determine, in its sole, absolute, and uncontrolled discretion, for support in reasonable comfort, education, (including college, graduate, and professional education), and maintenance in health (including medical, dental, hospital, nursing and nursing home expenses).

    The Trustee may make such payments, use, application, expenditure or accumulation of the income and principal thereof as it shall think proper for the direct or indirect benefit of the members of said family group without being required to observe any precept or rule of equality of enjoyment as between said members.

Final distribution shall be made of whatever shall remain of said share, *per stirpes*, among said living issue and free and clear of all trusts, at a time to be chosen by the Trustee, in the Trustee's sole, absolute, and uncontrolled discretion, but not later than the youngest then living child of the Grantor's deceased child attaining the age of thirty (30) years.

    c. If at any time before the final distribution of any of the trust shares hereinabove described (after taking into consideration all provisions thereof), there shall be no person in existence who is eligible to have the benefit of the trust of such share, then the share in question shall be reapportioned in equal shares among the other shares of the trust estate apportioned pursuant to sub-paragraph 3.___.___. above, and each equal share shall continue to be held and administered in trust, or distributed free and clear of all trusts, as the case may be, to or for the benefit of persons then and thereafter living, in accordance with the fortunes of the share to which said reapportionment is made.

  3. If, at any time before the final distribution of all of the trust shares hereinabove described, there shall be no person in existence who is eligible to have the benefit of any trust shares, the Trustee shall divide all of the trust estate then remaining into two (2) equal parts which shall be distributed, outright and free of trust, as follows:

    a. One (1) part to those persons then living who would have taken the Grantor's estate, and in such shares thereof as they would have taken, had the Grantor then died intestate, domiciled in New Hampshire; and

    b. One (1) part to those persons then living who would have taken the Grantor's spouse's estate, and in such shares thereof as they would have taken, had Grantor's spouse then died intestate, domiciled in New Hampshire.

  F. If the Grantor's residential real estate is held in the trust estate and used by the Grantor's said spouse as a residence, then, during said spouse's lifetime, said spouse shall be permitted exclusive use and occupancy of said residential real estate.

Also, the Grantor's said spouse may, during said spouse's lifetime, in writing, delivered to the Trustee, request the Trustee to sell said residential real estate and to provide a substitute residence, of approximately equal or lesser value to the residence then occupied by the Grantor's said spouse.

Upon receipt of such written request, the Trustee shall then have full power and authority to make reasonable efforts to obtain such substitute residence and to sell the residential real estate then occupied by the Grantor's said spouse.

The costs of selling said residential real estate, of obtaining such substitute residence and of moving the Grantor's said spouse and said spouse's belongings out of said spouse's then occupied residence and into said substitute residence may, in the Trustee's sole, absolute, and uncontrolled discretion, be borne by the trust share to which such real estate has been allocated, to the extent there shall be sufficiently liquid assets to satisfy same.

The Trustee shall have full power and authority to execute any and all documents necessary to carry out the foregoing purpose.

The Trustee shall not be responsible, directly or indirectly, for the success, failure or ultimate satisfaction of the Grantor's said spouse in connection therewith.

The costs and expenses of maintenance and repairs to keep such residential real estate in the same condition it is in at the commencement of said use (reasonable wear and tear excepted), real estate taxes and other normal costs of maintenance and upkeep of said residential real estate, including fire and casualty insurance, may, in the Trustee's sole, absolute, and uncontrolled discretion, be borne by the trust share to which such real estate has been allocated, to the extent there shall be sufficiently liquid assets to satisfy same.

References in this paragraph to a "residence" shall include without limitation any variant of ownership of residential real property, including so-called cooperatives and condominiums, and payment of a refundable or nonrefundable admissions fee for a residential care facility.

G. Notwithstanding any provision hereinabove to the contrary, the Trustee shall not make any distribution of the Marital Bequest, or of income or principal from the Family Trust, to the Grantor's spouse, _____, if the Grantor's said spouse waives testate distribution of the Grantor's will and claims a statutory share of the Grantor's estate under R.S.A. 560:10, or any provisions successor thereto. In such event, the trust estate benefiting the Grantor's spouse shall be administered as if the Grantor's spouse were not then living.

H. The provisions contained hereinabove which require the Trustee to apportion the trust estate into shares and parts of shares are for purposes of computation only and shall not be construed to require the Trustee to make physical segregation of one share or a part of a share from the others, although the Trustee shall have full right to make such segregation if it thinks it better to do so.

Notwithstanding said provisions, the Trustee shall have the full right to regard the trust estate as one undivided estate for purposes of management and investment.

I. If the Grantor or the executor of the Grantor's estate or any other individual (including any individual who shall transfer property in trust hereunder or the executor or administrator of the estate of such individual), has allocated any portion or all of any Generation Skipping Transfer ("GST") exemption provided by Section 2631(a) of the Internal Revenue Code to any property to be held in trust hereunder, then notwithstanding anything to the contrary contained in this agreement, the Trustee is authorized to establish such number of separate trusts, with identical terms, to hold the property received in trust hereunder as it, in its sole, absolute, and uncontrolled discretion, shall deem advisable, bearing in mind the allocation of the said GST exemption and the desirability that any trust to which all or any portion of the said GST exemption is allocated shall, if practical, have an inclusion ratio of zero.

Further, the Trustee is authorized to allocate such trusts among the trust shares hereinabove created in order to minimize (or eliminate, if possible) any GST tax.

4. TRUSTEE'S POWERS. In the administration of the trust estate, the Trustee shall have all of the powers granted to trustees by New Hampshire common law and statutory authority (including, but not limited to, the Uniform Trustees' Powers Act, R.S.A. 564-A, and the Uniform Trust Code, R.S.A. 564-B, as they may be amended from time to time), without restrictions.

In addition to such power, and not in limitation thereof, the Trustee shall have the following powers, all of which shall be exercised in a fiduciary capacity and for the benefit of the beneficiaries:

A. During the lifetime of the Grantor, the Trustee may retain as an investment, unless and until the Grantor by a writing delivered to the Trustee shall otherwise direct, all of the securities and other property originally assigned, transferred, or delivered to the Trustee hereunder or at any time forming a part of the trust estate, whether or not such securities or other property be of the character authorized by the laws of the State of New Hampshire for the investment of trust funds.

Upon the death or incapacity of the Grantor, the Trustee is authorized to purchase, sell, lease, or alter any investment by buy or sell orders transmitted by it, whether by telephone call, electronic facsimile transmission, computer message or other current non-written method of business communication.

B. To buy, sell and trade in securities of any nature, [on margin], and for such purpose to maintain and operate [margin] accounts with brokers, and to pledge any securities held or purchased by it with such brokers as security for loans and advances made to the Trustee.

C. *[For Corporate Trustees]* To retain the property of the trust estate in the same investments as when received by it or to vary and transpose such investments and to invest and reinvest the property of the trust estate in such manner and in such securities or other property (including common trust funds or similar funds for the participation of trusts of which _____ is trustee and including securities of _____ and any successor thereto) as it in its uncontrolled discretion shall deem best without accountability for any loss for so doing and without liability for depreciation occasioned by so doing even though the property so retained or the investments so made may not be of the character permitted for the investment of trust funds under the laws of the State of New Hampshire or any other state or federal law.

D. To take and hold title to real estate, and to convey any interest in real estate and improvements thereon held in trust, and no purchaser or third party shall be bound to inquire whether the Trustee has said power or is properly exercising said power, or see to the application of any trust asset paid to the Trustee for a conveyance thereof.

E. To have all of the necessary banking powers to open, close, and manage financial accounts, including but not limited to, checking accounts, savings accounts, financial accounts and other related financial instruments and to conduct all necessary financial business in reference to the management of the financial assets of the trust.

F. To rent a safe deposit box and to retain such assets in said box as the Trustee, in its sole, absolute, and uncontrolled discretion, determines appropriate.

G. To borrow money, with or without security, and mortgage or pledge trust property for a period within or extending beyond the duration of the trust.

H. To loan funds to the Grantor's estate upon such terms and conditions as to interest rates, maturities, and security as the Trustee shall determine.

I. To make payments, transfers or conveyances, to the extent possible, to the estate of the Grantor (after exhaustion of the assets of the Grantor's estate) to satisfy legacies, bequests or devises, if any, made under the Grantor's will or included in the Grantor's estate for other purposes, if the Grantor's estate shall be insufficient to satisfy such legacies, bequests or devises.

J. To invest in common trust funds.

K. To select property, in its sole, absolute, and uncontrolled discretion, to be allocated to any trust hereunder or to be distributed in satisfaction of any gift provided for herein without respect to the income tax basis of such property, and the Trustee is specifically excused from any duty of impartiality with respect to the income tax basis of such property.

In the event that residential real estate is held in the trust estate, the Trustee may allocate said residential real estate to any trust created hereunder, to be held and administered and disposed of pursuant to the provisions thereof.

L. To coordinate the filing of any information returns required under Section 6018 of the Internal Revenue Code in cooperation with the executor of the Grantor's estate, if any.

M. To establish passwords for electronic accounts and to have access to and modify any existing password established by the Grantor or a predecessor Trustee for any assets in the trust estate.

N. If at any time during the Grantor's lifetime, there is delivered to the Trustee other than the Grantor, if any, or, if none, then to the successor Trustee, a written opinion, signed by a licensed physician, stating that the Grantor has become incompetent or incapacitated, then from and after the delivery of such written opinion the Trustee other than the Grantor, or the successor Trustee, as the case may be, shall have those powers and authorities with respect to the trust estate given to the Trustee in this trust agreement.

O. If, after the death of the Grantor and the Grantor's spouse, _____, as it may be amended from time to time, is still in existence and the terms of any trust established by said trust are substantially similar to the terms of any trust established by this, _____, the Trustee is authorized and empowered to consolidate such trust with such similar trust established by _____ and to administer them as one trust, unless such consolidation shall be contrary to law or inconsistent with the terms of any instrument supplemental hereto.

P. Regardless of the extent of the authority that the Trustee holds to currently distribute income and/or principal of the trust estate to one or more beneficiaries of the trust, the Trustee shall have full power and authority, to be exercised in its sole, absolute, and uncontrolled discretion, to appoint any or all assets held in this trust estate to any other trust or trusts created under will, deed or otherwise, for the benefit of one or more of the beneficiaries hereunder.

This authority shall be subject to the limitations set forth in R.S.A. 564-B:4-418, as amended from time to time, provided that such appointment clause shall be null and void in the event there is a determination that the application of such clause shall result in the inclusion of any of the trust estate in the Grantor's gross estate under any provision of the Internal Revenue Code, including but not limited to Sections 2041 and 2042, which would not otherwise be includable in the Grantor's gross estate.

Provided further, however, that if this Trust qualifies as a "trust instrument" under the Qualified Dispositions in Trust Act, R.S.A. 564-D, as amended from time to time, then the Trustee may only appoint the assets of the trust estate to a new trust which will continue to qualify as a "trust instrument" under such Act and will provide similar protections to the assets held in this trust estate.

Q. If, at any time before the final distribution of the principal of any trust share hereinabove described, the value of the principal of said trust share shall be equal to, or less than, ONE HUNDRED THOUSAND DOLLARS ($100,000), then the Trustee may, in its sole discretion, terminate said trust share and distribute the principal of said trust share, and any accumulated and undistributed income thereof, outright and free of trust, to those persons then entitled to benefit from said trust share, and in the proportions in which they are then entitled to benefit from said trust share, notwithstanding any provisions of this trust to the contrary.

R. To exercise all the powers, authorities and discretions herein conferred, after the termination of the trust hereunder, until the complete distribution of the trust estate.

5. ADDITIONAL PROPERTY. The Grantor, or the Grantor's spouse may, by will, trust or during their lifetimes, from time to time, transfer and deliver to the Trustee cash, securities, and other property acceptable to the Trustee, in addition to the property presently transferred and delivered, and such cash, securities, and other property shall be held, administered, and disposed of by the Trustee in accordance with the provisions of this agreement without the execution of any further instrument or declaration.

6. REPORTING BY TRUSTEE.

A. At any time and from time to time, the Grantor shall have the power, by written instrument signed and acknowledged by the Grantor and delivered to the Trustee, to settle the report of the Trustee with respect to principal or income, or with respect to both principal and income, and to release and discharge the Trustee of and from any and every claim, demand, accountability, and liability of every nature, arising from any matter or thing done or omitted to be done, in connection with this agreement or any trust hereby created, during the period in respect of which the report of the Trustee shall have been so settled.

Every such settlement, release, and discharge shall be conclusive and binding upon, and shall be an absolute protection to the Trustee against all claims of any income beneficiaries, remaindermen, or other persons who might then or thereafter have or claim any interest under this agreement, and no such income beneficiary, remainderman, or other person shall have any right of accounting, reporting, any claim, or any cause of action against the Trustee arising from any matter or thing done or omitted to be done in connection with this agreement or any trust hereby created, during any period in respect of which the report of the Trustee shall have been so settled.

B. After the death or incapacity of the Grantor, the Trustee may, at the Trustee's sole, absolute, and uncontrolled discretion, and shall, to the extent required by the Uniform Trust Code, R.S.A. 564-B, as it may be amended from time to time, render a Trustee's report as described in the Uniform Trust Code, as it may be amended from time to time, at such intervals as the Trustee may choose or at such times as required by the Uniform Trust Code.

C. A recipient of such a report (or, if under guardianship or conservatorship, then by the Guardian or Conservator, or, if deceased, then by the Executor or Administrator), may, by a written instrument, assent to the report of the Trustee with respect to principal or to income, or with respect to both principal and income.

The assent of the recipient of such report (or, if under guardianship or conservatorship, then by the Guardian or Conservator, or, if deceased, then by the Executor or Administrator) shall make such report binding and conclusive upon all persons then having or who may thereafter have any interest, vested or contingent, in the income or principal of the trust estate and such assent shall forever release and discharge the Trustee of and from any and every claim, demand, accountability, and liability of every nature, arising from any matter or thing done or omitted to be done, in connection with this agreement or any trust hereby created, during the period in respect of which the report of the Trustee shall have been so settled.

D. The failure of any person to object in writing to the Trustee to such a report within thirty (30) days after the delivery of the same to such person hereunder shall be final and binding to the same extent as the written assent hereinabove provided.

E. Any person entitled to such a report, accounting, information, notice and the like (or, if under guardianship or conservatorship, then by the Guardian or Conservator, or, if deceased, then by the Executor or Administrator) may by a written instrument signed and acknowledged by him or her or them, as the case may be, and delivered to the Trustee, waive the right to said Trustee's report or to other information otherwise required to be furnished under the Uniform Trust Code, as it may be amended from time to time.

7. <u>SUCCESSOR TRUSTEE</u>. The following provisions shall govern the addition, removal and succession of the Trustee:

A. The Grantor may, during Grantor's lifetime, add any additional Trustee, or remove any Trustee hereunder and appoint a successor Trustee.

B. If _____ shall be unable or unwilling to serve in the capacity of Trustee for any reason, then the Grantor's spouse, _____, and _____, shall serve in _____ stead.

    1. If the Grantor's said spouse shall be unable or unwilling to serve in the capacity of Trustee for any reason, then _____ shall serve in _____ stead.

    2. If _____ shall be unable or unwilling to serve in the capacity of Trustee for any reason, then _____ shall serve in _____ stead.

       If _____ shall be unable or unwilling to serve in the capacity of Trustee for any reason, then _____ shall serve in _____ stead.

    3. In the event there shall be no successor Trustee who shall be able or willing to serve in the capacity of Trustee, then a majority of the beneficiaries to whom or for whose use the current net income of the trust estate is at the time authorized or required to be paid or applied, either,

       a. acting individually, if then eighteen (18) years of age, or,

       b. by his or her natural parent, or natural guardian, or Court appointed guardian or Court appointed conservator, if then under guardianship or conservatorship,

    shall appoint a successor Trustee.

C. In the event that any beneficiary of the trust, other than the Grantor, shall serve in the capacity of co-Trustee, then the discretionary powers to determine whether income or principal is to be distributed to said beneficiary or to any person to whom said beneficiary owes an obligation of support shall be exercisable only by the remaining Trustee.

It is the Grantor's intention by this sub-paragraph to prohibit said beneficiary from benefiting himself or herself as beneficiary in any way by the exercise of such discretionary powers vested in the Trustee as a group.

D. In the event that any beneficiary of the trust, other than the Grantor or the Grantor's spouse, shall serve in the capacity of sole Trustee and the Trustee has discretionary powers to distribute income or principal to himself, herself, or to any person to whom he or she owes an obligation of support, then such distributions of income or principal shall be exercisable by the sole Trustee.

The maximum amount that may be withdrawn annually by each such beneficiary under this sub-paragraph, however, shall not exceed the maximum amount over which an individual may have a power of withdrawal without its lapse in such year being deemed to be a release of such power under Section 2514(e) of the Internal Revenue Code.

E.   No successor Trustee shall be liable or responsible in any way for any actions or defaults of any predecessor Trustee, nor for any loss or expense from or occasioned by anything done or neglected to be done by any predecessor Trustee. Any successor Trustee shall have, from and after its appointment or succession to office hereunder and without any assignment or other action by any person, all the rights, interests, and powers, including discretionary rights and powers, which are by the provisions of this trust agreement granted to and vested in the Trustee named herein.

8.   <u>FIDUCIARIES</u>. No person dealing with the Trustee shall be responsible for the application of any money, securities, or other property paid or delivered, and the receipt of the Trustee shall be a full discharge; and no person dealing with the Trustee, and no issuer, transfer agent, or other agent of any issuer of any securities shall be under any obligation to ascertain or inquire into the power of the Trustee to purchase, sell, exchange, transfer, mortgage, pledge, create a security interest in, lease, distribute, or otherwise dispose of or deal with any money, securities, or other property.

The Trustee shall not at any time be held liable for any action taken or not taken, including any action intended to lessen or eliminate the impact of estate or generation-skipping transfer taxes with respect to any generation or beneficiary, whether or not such action is successful in achieving the results sought and without regard to its effect on other beneficiaries in the same or different generations, or for any loss or depreciation in the value of any property in any trust created herein, whether due to an error of judgment or otherwise, where the Trustee has exercised good faith and ordinary diligence in the exercise of its duties.

The Trustee shall receive reasonable compensation for its services in the administration of the trusts created herein, including reimbursement for amounts reasonably expended for bookkeeping services, investment services and advice, and other professional or para-professional services. In addition to the compensation herein provided, the Trustee shall receive reasonable compensation for any legal services provided for the benefit of the trust estate, such as handling any litigation involving the trust, preparing state or federal income tax returns, and transferring any real estate.

9.   <u>PERPETUITIES</u>. All trusts established under this instrument shall be exempt from the application of the rule against perpetuities. This provision is

intended to comply with R.S.A. 564:24, and accordingly, the Grantor specifically authorizes the Trustee to sell, mortgage or lease property for any period of time beyond the period that is required for an interest created under this instrument to vest in order to be valid under the rule against perpetuities, as measured by the period defined hereinabove.

The trusts created hereunder shall be perpetual to the fullest extent permitted by the governing law. If any trust created hereunder is deemed to be subject to the law of a jurisdiction (including, but only to the extent applicable to real property) that has a rule against perpetuities or similar rule which limits the period during which property can be held in trust, then such trust (other than a trust created by the exercise of a power of appointment conferred hereunder which exercise commences a new rule against perpetuities period under the law of such jurisdiction) shall terminate in all events upon the expiration of the longest period that property may be held in trust under this trust agreement under the law of such jurisdiction (including any applicable period in gross, such as 21 years, 90 years or 110 years); provided, however, that if the jurisdiction has a rule against perpetuities or similar rule which applies only to certain types of property, such as real property, the provisions of this paragraph shall apply only to such property. If under the law of such jurisdiction the longest period that property may be held in trust may be determined (or alternatively determined) with reference to the death of the last survivor of a group of individuals in being upon the date of this trust agreement, those individuals shall consist of all of the descendants of the Grantor's parents who were in being on the date of this trust agreement. Upon termination of a trust pursuant to the provisions of this paragraph, the trust property shall be transferred, conveyed and paid over to the persons then entitled to receive or have the benefit of the income from the trust in the proportions in which they are entitled thereto, or if their interests are indefinite, then in equal shares.

10.   SPENDTHRIFT PROVISION. Except as herein otherwise provided, the interest of any beneficiary hereunder, either as to income or principal, shall not be anticipated, alienated or in any other manner assigned or pledged or promised by such beneficiary, and shall not be reached by, or be subject to, any legal, equitable or other process, including any bankruptcy or divorce proceeding, or be subject to the interference or control of creditors or others in any way or manner, and all payments to, or the interest of, any beneficiary shall be free from the control or claim of any parent or spouse or former spouse or any other third party. Moreover, no power of appointment or power of withdrawal shall be subject to involuntary exercise. Provided, however, this spendthrift provision shall not restrict the exercise of a disclaimer or the exercise of a power of appointment or withdrawal right granted by this trust agreement. This provision is intended to be a material provision of this trust and any other trust established hereunder.

11.   TAX PROVISION. The trust estate shall not be charged with the payment of any estate, inheritance, legacy, death taxes or duties of any nature (state or federal), or any interest or penalty thereon, except to the extent that the

other assets in the Grantor's estate (excluding any assets which may be exempted from the payment of such taxes by the last will of the Grantor) shall be insufficient to discharge such taxes, interest or penalties or shall be insufficiently liquid to satisfy the same. The Trustee may rely conclusively upon written certification from the executor of the Grantor's estate, or if no probate administration of the Grantor's estate is required under applicable law, upon request of the person or persons nominated as executor under the Grantor's will or upon any other evidence, as to the existence of such insufficiency and the amount thereof; provided, however, that the Trustee shall not pay any additional tax imposed under Section 2032A or 2057 of the Internal Revenue Code or any generation-skipping transfer taxes imposed under Chapter 13 of the Internal Revenue Code imposed by reason of the Grantor's death.

If the Trustee shall be required to pay any such taxes, they shall be charged against the principal of the trust estate as an expense without apportionment.

Provided, that in the event that no probate administration of the Grantor's estate is required under applicable law, the Trustee shall have all the powers and authority given the executor under the Grantor's will in relation to such taxes, including all elections and allocation of the generation-skipping transfer tax exemption under Section 2631 of the Internal Revenue Code.

12. <u>DEBTS AND EXPENSES</u>. The trust estate shall not be charged with the payment of legal debts of the Grantor's estate, funeral expenses or expenses of administration of the Grantor's estate except to the extent that the other assets in the Grantor's estate shall be insufficient to discharge such debts and expenses, or shall be insufficiently liquid to satisfy the same. The Trustee may rely conclusively upon written certification from the executor of the Grantor's estate, or if no probate administration of the Grantor's estate is required under applicable law, upon request of the person or persons nominated as executor under the Grantor's will, or upon any other evidence, as to the existence of such insufficiency and the amount thereof. If the Trustee shall be required to pay any such debts and expenses, the same shall be treated as debts and expenses of the trust estate (to the extent the assets of the Grantor's estate are insufficient to satisfy the same) or as loans to the Grantor's estate (to the extent the liquid assets of the Grantor's estate are insufficient to satisfy the same) if any such debts and expenses are deducted for federal estate tax purposes in computing the value of the Grantor's taxable estate under Section 2053 of the Internal Revenue Code.

If any such debts and expenses are either not so deducted or deductible under Section 2053 of the Internal Revenue Code, however, the same shall be charged against the principal of the trust estate as an expense without apportionment.

This provision shall confer no rights upon anyone except the executor of the Grantor's estate.

13. <u>SURVIVAL REQUIREMENT</u>. No person shall be deemed to have survived the Grantor, or any other person or event under the terms of this trust, unless such person survives the end of the period commencing with the close of

the calendar day of the Grantor's death, the death of such other person or on which such event occurs, and ending with the close of the thirtieth (30th) calendar day thereafter.

14.   <u>DISTRIBUTIONS TO MINORS</u>. In any case where property or funds become distributable to a minor, then the Trustee shall have the additional power to distribute the same in any one or more of the following ways: (1) by distribution directly to the minor; (2) by distribution to the legal guardian of the minor; (3) by distribution to a parent, relative or friend of the minor for the minor's support in reasonable comfort, education and maintenance in health; (4) by applying the same directly for the minor's support in reasonable comfort, education and maintenance in health; (5) by depositing the same in a bank account in the name of the minor or by transferring property to or purchasing property in the name of a custodian for his or her benefit under a Uniform Law relating to transfers or gifts to minors; or (6) by holding the same hereunder in trust or in custody for the minor's support in reasonable comfort, education and maintenance in health and by distributing the remainder thereof to the minor upon coming of age or otherwise to the minor's estate in case of the death of the minor. The receipt of the person to whom property or funds are actually distributed in accordance with any of the foregoing provisions shall fully discharge the Trustee from further accountability therefor.

15.   <u>GOVERNING LAW AND SITUS</u>. The Grantor declares that this agreement and the trust created hereby shall be construed and administered under the laws of the State of New Hampshire, that the validity and effect of this agreement and of this trust shall be determined in accordance with the laws of that State.

Further, the trust shall be under the jurisdiction of the courts of the State of New Hampshire and the Trustee shall voluntarily enter a general appearance in any legal action relating to an accounting of the trust or a declaratory judgment interpreting this trust agreement. The Trustee shall not be chargeable in any court other than one of the courts of that State.

[INSERT IF TRUSTEE HAS AUTHORITY TO CHANGE SITUS]

However, the Trustee, at any time and from time to time, in its discretion, may, (1) remove all or part of the trust estate and hold and administer the same in any other jurisdiction where the Trustee shall be then located, (2) change the situs of administration of any trust from one jurisdiction to another jurisdiction; and (3) elect that the law of such other jurisdiction shall thereafter govern the trust to such extent as may be necessary and appropriate, and to amend the administrative provisions of the trust as the Trustee deems appropriate to ensure compliance and compatibility with such law, whereupon the courts of such other jurisdiction shall have the power to effectuate the purposes of this trust agreement to such extent. The determination of the Trustee as to any such removal of assets or change of situs or governing law shall be conclusive and binding on all persons interested in such trust.

16.   <u>AMENDMENT AND REVOCATION</u>. The Grantor reserves the right at any time or from time to time without the consent of any person and without notice to any person other than the Trustee to revoke or modify the trust hereby created, in whole or in part, to change the beneficiaries hereof, or to withdraw the whole or any part of the trust estate by filing notice of such revocation, modification, change, or withdrawal with the Trustee; provided, however, that the terms of this agreement may not be modified by the Grantor in such manner as to increase the obligations or alter the rates of the commissions of the Trustee without its written consent.

17.   <u>DEFINITIONS</u>. Whenever used in this trust agreement, the words "child," "children," or "issue" are intended to include not only persons who are descendants by blood, but also persons and issue of persons who have been adopted according to law prior to their attaining the age of eighteen (18) years.

References to the "Internal Revenue Code" or "Code" or to provisions thereof are to the Internal Revenue Code of 1986, as amended at the time in question. References to the "Treasury Regulations," "Regulations" and "Regs." are to the Treasury Regulations under the Code. If, by the time in question, a particular provision of the Code has been renumbered, or the Code has been superseded by a subsequent federal tax law, the reference shall be deemed to be to the renumbered provision or the corresponding provision of the subsequent law, unless to do so would clearly be contrary to the Grantor's intent as expressed in this trust agreement, and a similar rule shall apply to references to the Regulations.

References to "R.S.A." are to the New Hampshire Revised Statutes Annotated, as amended at the time in question. If, by the time in question, a particular provision of the Statute has been renumbered, or the Statute has been superseded by subsequent law, the reference shall be deemed to be to the renumbered provision or the corresponding provision of the subsequent law, unless to do so would clearly be contrary to the Grantor's intent as expressed in this trust agreement.

Masculine, feminine and neuter pronouns shall each include all genders, and the singular shall include the plural and vice versa, where the context or facts so admit.

The captions and paragraph headings of this trust agreement are inserted only as a matter of convenience and for reference and in no way define, limit or describe the scope or intent of this agreement, nor in any way affect this agreement.

18.   <u>EXECUTION</u>. This trust agreement, and any amendments hereto, shall be effective when executed by the Grantor, notwithstanding that the signature of the Trustee is provided for, the Trustee's signature being intended to denote the acceptance of the Trustee to serve in that capacity only.

This trust agreement may be executed in any number of counterparts with the same effect as if all of the parties had signed the same document. All counterparts shall be construed together and shall constitute one agreement.

_____   _____
Witness   Grantor

_____   _____
Witness   Trustee

STATE OF NEW HAMPSHIRE
COUNTY OF _____

The foregoing instrument was acknowledged before me on _____, 2011, by _____.

_____
Notary Public/Justice of the Peace
My Commission Expires:
(Seal)

Page 600: Substitute this form for Form 36 in the text:

FORM 36   Revocable Qualified Terminable Interest Property (QTIP Trust)

THE _____ REVOCABLE TRUST OF _____

TRUST AGREEMENT, made on _____, 2011, between _____, residing in _____, New Hampshire (hereinafter called the "Grantor"), and _____, residing in _____, New Hampshire (hereinafter called the "Trustee").

At the time of the signing of this trust, the Grantor's spouse is _____, and the Grantor's children are _____, _____ and _____.

1.   TRUST PROPERTY. All property transferred and delivered to the Trustee, which the Trustee may, at any time, hold or acquire, including cash, securities, or other property, shall be referred to collectively as the "trust estate" and held and administered and disposed of by the Trustee for the uses and purposes, and upon the terms and conditions, herein set forth.

2.   DISPOSITIVE PROVISIONS: LIFETIME. The Trustee shall hold, manage, invest and reinvest the trust estate, and shall collect the income thereof and dispose of the net income and principal as follows:

A. Pay such parts of the income, if any, and such parts of the principal of this trust to, or for the benefit of, the Grantor as the Grantor directs from time to time for the Grantor's support in reasonable comfort, education (including college, graduate, and professional education), and maintenance in health (including medical, dental, hospital, nursing and nursing home expenses). Any income accrued or accumulated at the time of the Grantor's death shall be paid and transferred to principal, to be administered according to the terms hereinafter provided.

B. In addition, during the lifetime of the Grantor, if the Grantor becomes so incapacitated that the Grantor cannot exercise the Grantor's rights under sub-paragraph 2.A. above, and there are sufficient assets in this trust to do so, the Trustee is authorized to pay such parts of the income, if any, and such parts of the principal of this trust to, or for the benefit of, the Grantor and the Grantor's spouse as it deems advisable for their support in reasonable comfort, education (including college, graduate, and professional education), and maintenance in health (including medical, dental, hospital, nursing and nursing home expenses), taking into consideration the amount of their income from sources other than this trust.

It is the Grantor's intention that the support in reasonable comfort, education (including college, graduate, and professional education), and maintenance in health (including medical, dental, hospital, nursing and nursing home expenses) of the Grantor and the Grantor's spouse shall be of primary concern, and the Trustee shall exercise its discretion in using principal for the Grantor and the Grantor's spouse, considering all other beneficiaries to be secondary and without liability to any other beneficiary for the use of principal for the Grantor and the Grantor's spouse.

C. Further, the Trustee is authorized to give, transfer or convey any of the trust estate to charities and persons of the Grantor's natural affection to whom the Grantor would normally consider making such gifts, transfers or conveyances, whether outright or in trust, having in mind the ultimate objective of such gifts, transfers or conveyances is either (i) the qualification for state or federal medical, welfare or other assistance programs for the Grantor's or the Grantor's spouse's benefit, or (ii) the reduction of the state and federal estate, inheritance, transfer, legacy and succession taxes and any interest and penalties thereon imposed by reason of the Grantor's death or the Grantor's spouse's death.

3. <u>DISPOSITIVE PROVISIONS: AFTER DEATH</u>. Upon the death of the Grantor, the Trustee shall thereafter apply and distribute the trust estate as follows:

A. The Trustee shall distribute the following items from the trust estate, outright and free of trust, to those of the following named beneficiaries who survive the Grantor:

1. _____ to _____;

2. _____ to _____;

3. _____ to _____; and

4. _____ to _____.

B. After the distributions, if any, in sub-paragraph 3.A. above, if the Grantor's spouse, _____, survives the Grantor, the Trustee shall distribute to the Grantor's said spouse, outright and free of trust, all **remaining** items of tangible personal property and household effects which are then part of the trust estate, including furniture, clothing, jewelry, silver, books, pictures, china, automobiles and their equipment, other vehicles and their equipment, and other articles of personal and household use or ornament.

If the Grantor's said spouse shall not survive the Grantor, said tangible personal property and household effects shall be distributed, outright and free of trust, to the Grantor's issue who so survive the Grantor, such issue to take *per stirpes.*

The Grantor expresses the hope that said beneficiaries will dispose of said tangible personal property and household effects according to the Grantor's wishes, however said wishes may be made known to them.

If a division of the property under this distribution is required among the beneficiaries, such division shall be made by the beneficiaries, in appropriate shares, as they may amicably agree.

The Grantor prefers that said beneficiaries shall agree upon the manner in which said property is to be divided, but should they not agree among themselves as to the division thereof within ninety (90) days after the Grantor's death, the Trustee shall have full power and authority to divide said property among said beneficiaries, in appropriate shares, and its determination with respect thereto shall, insofar as permitted by law, be binding and conclusive upon such beneficiaries.

C. After the distributions, if any, in sub-paragraphs 3.A. and 3.B. above, the Trustee shall distribute the following sums, outright and free of trust, to those of the following named beneficiaries who survive the Grantor:

1. _____ DOLLARS ($_____) to _____;

2. _____ DOLLARS ($_____) to _____;

3. _____ DOLLARS ($_____) to _____; and

4. _____ DOLLARS ($_____) to _____;

D. After the distributions, if any, in sub-paragraphs 3.A., 3.B. and 3.C. above, if the Grantor's spouse, _____, _____, survives the Grantor, the Trustee shall divide the remaining trust estate into two parts, one to be known as the "Marital QTIP Trust" and the other as the "Family Trust."

1. The Marital QTIP Trust shall consist of an amount equal to the maximum allowable federal estate tax marital deduction as calculated by law in effect at the time of the Grantor's death, diminished by the value for federal estate tax purposes of all items in the Grantor's gross estate which qualify for said deduction and which pass or have passed to the Grantor's spouse under the Grantor's will, by survivorship in joint tenancy or tenancy by the entirety property, by life insurance settlement, by operation of law or otherwise.

Provided, however, that if the amount of the maximum allowable federal estate tax marital deduction in the Grantor's estate is greater than the amount needed to reduce the federal estate tax to zero, after considering the available unified tax credit (the applicable credit amount or applicable exclusion amount) and state death tax credit or deduction allowable in determining such tax (provided that the state death tax credit or deduction shall be taken into account only to the extent that doing so would not result in an increase in state death taxes which would otherwise be payable), then the amount set aside in the Marital QTIP Trust shall be equal only to that portion of such marital deduction that is needed to reduce the federal estate tax on the Grantor's estate to zero.

2. For the purpose of determining the amount to be transferred into the Marital QTIP Trust, values shall be those which are finally determined for

federal estate tax purposes. Elections made by the Grantor's executor with respect to taking certain deductions for income tax purposes rather than for estate tax purposes shall determine the aforesaid values and the amount to constitute the Marital QTIP Trust. The words "which pass" or "has passed" shall have the same meaning as under the Internal Revenue Code for marital deduction purposes and no assets shall be transferred to the Marital QTIP Trust that do not qualify for the marital deduction.

3. In making allocation or distribution to the Marital QTIP Trust the Trustee is authorized to satisfy the Marital QTIP Trust in cash or in kind, or in combination of both, provided that all assets placed in the Marital QTIP Trust shall be valued for the purpose of being placed in the Marital QTIP Trust at their fair market value as determined as of the dates of respective distributions to the Marital QTIP Trust, which dates shall be the dates on which the Trustee makes specific allocation on its books of account (if such assets are in negotiable form), or when delivery is made in proper form for transfer, or a deed is executed (if real estate), and the aggregate fair market value thereof shall be no less than the amount required to completely fund the Marital QTIP Trust. The Trustee is further authorized to estimate the size of the Marital QTIP Trust and to fund the trust, subject, however, to any adjustments which may be required upon final determination of the federal estate tax on the Grantor's estate.

4. No debts, funeral expenses, expenses of administration of the Grantor's estate, inheritance, estate, transfer, legacy or succession taxes (state and federal), and any interest or penalties thereon shall be apportioned against or paid from the Marital QTIP Trust, except to the extent the assets of both the Grantor's estate and the Family Trust are insufficient for this purpose.

5. If the Grantor's spouse or the Grantor's spouse's executor disclaims said spouse's interest in and power over any property of the Marital QTIP, then the Trustee shall pay the disclaimed trust assets over to the Family Trust and thereafter said assets shall be administered as part thereof.

6. If the Grantor or the executor of the Grantor's estate or any other individual (including any individual who shall transfer property in trust hereunder or the executor or administrator of the estate of such individual), deems it necessary to allocate any portion of the trust estate to a separate trust share which will allow such assets to qualify for a state marital deduction pursuant to any applicable provision of state law, then notwithstanding anything to the contrary contained in this agreement, the Trustee is authorized to establish a separate Marital QTIP Trust, the terms of which will qualify for the state marital deduction, to hold the property received in trust hereunder as it, in its sole, absolute, and uncontrolled discretion, shall deem advisable; provided, however, that the amount set aside in the state Marital QTIP Trust shall be equal only to that portion of

such marital deduction that is needed to reduce the state estate tax on the Grantor's estate to zero.

E.   Marital QTIP Trust. The Marital QTIP Trust shall be held and administered and disposed of as follows:

1.   The Trustee shall pay over to the Grantor's spouse all of the net income of this Marital QTIP Trust, including all of the income of any retirement plan payable to this Marital QTIP Trust, during said spouse's life, at least annually, but at more frequent intervals if the Grantor's spouse shall, in writing, direct.

   The Grantor's spouse may at any time by written notice, require the Trustee either to make any nonproductive property of this Trust productive or to convert such nonproductive property to productive property within a reasonable time.

   Also, the Trustee may pay over to the Grantor's spouse whatever part or parts of the principal as the Trustee may deem proper or necessary for said spouse's support in reasonable comfort, education (including college, graduate, and professional education), and maintenance in health (including medical, dental, hospital, nursing and nursing home expenses).

2.   In addition, the Grantor's spouse shall have the absolute right once during each and every calendar year, between December 1 and December 31 inclusive, to withdraw from the principal of the Marital QTIP Trust any amount, in cash or in kind. The maximum amount that may be withdrawn annually by said spouse under this sub-paragraph, however, shall not exceed the maximum amount over which an individual may have a power of withdrawal without its lapse in such year being deemed to be a release of such power under Section 2514(e) of the Internal Revenue Code. Such right to withdraw shall be non-cumulative.

3.   Upon the death of the Grantor's spouse, the Trustee shall pay and transfer all income accrued but undistributed at the date of death of the Grantor's spouse to principal, to be administered according to the terms hereinafter provided.

The Trustee shall then dispose of the then remaining principal as follows:

a.   The Trustee shall first pay, out of the principal of the trust estate, the full amount by which estate, inheritance, transfer, legacy or succession taxes (federal and state), and including penalties or interest thereon, imposed by reason of the Grantor's spouse's death, are increased as a result of the inclusion of this Marital QTIP Trust in the Grantor's spouse's estate for such tax purposes.

   The final determination of the amount due hereunder shall be based upon the values as finally determined for federal estate tax purposes in the Grantor's spouse's estate.

The Grantor's spouse may waive said spouse's estate's right to payment under this sub-paragraph by making specific reference in said spouse's will to the right to payment hereby given to said spouse's estate.

b. The Trustee shall then pay over the principal, if any, remaining at the Grantor's spouse's death and after the payment required under sub-paragraph 3.____.____.a. has been made, to the Family Trust and thereafter said additional principal shall be administered as part thereof.

F. Family Trust. The Family Trust shall consist of all of the remainder of the trust estate which has not been heretofore previously allocated and shall be held and administered and disposed of by the Trustee as follows:

1. If the Grantor's spouse, _____, survives the Grantor, then, during said spouse's lifetime, the Trustee may pay over to said spouse or may use, apply or expend for said spouse's direct or indirect benefit, so much or all of the income of the trust hereby created and so much or all of the principal of said trust as the Trustee may deem proper or necessary for said spouse's support in reasonable comfort, education (including college, graduate, and professional education), and maintenance in health (including medical, dental, hospital, nursing and nursing home expenses).

    a. The Trustee may also pay over to or use, apply or expend for the direct or indirect benefit of the Grantor's children who are from time to time living during said period, or pay to the Grantor's spouse for their benefit, so much or all of the income or principal of the trust hereby created as the Trustee may deem proper or necessary for their support in reasonable comfort, education (including college, graduate, and professional education), and maintenance in health (including medical, dental, hospital, nursing and nursing home expenses).

    b. In addition, after the Marital QTIP Trust has been exhausted, the Grantor's spouse shall have the absolute right once during each and every calendar year, between December 1 and December 31 inclusive, to withdraw any amount from the principal of the Family Trust, in cash or in kind. The maximum amount that may be withdrawn annually by said spouse under this sub-paragraph, however, shall not exceed the maximum amount over which an individual may have a power of withdrawal without its lapse in such year being deemed to be a release of such power under Section 2514(e) of the Internal Revenue Code. Such right to withdraw shall be non-cumulative.

    c. If it becomes necessary for the Trustee to make any payments to or for the benefit of the Grantor's spouse from the principal of the Marital QTIP Trust hereinbefore established, or from the principal of the Family Trust, the Trustee is directed, when it is practicable to do so, to make such payments of principal, if any, from the principal of the Marital QTIP Trust before making any payment from the principal of the Family Trust.

However, it is the Grantor's intention that the support in reasonable comfort, education (including college, graduate, and professional education), and maintenance in health (including medical, dental, hospital, nursing and nursing home expenses) of the Grantor's spouse shall be of primary concern, and the Trustee shall exercise its discretion in using principal for the Grantor's spouse, considering all other beneficiaries to this trust to be secondary and without liability to any other beneficiary for the use of principal for the Grantor's spouse.

2. Upon the death of the Grantor's spouse, or upon the Grantor's death if the Grantor's spouse does not survive the Grantor, the Trustee shall apportion the balance of the principal and accumulated income of the trust estate into equal shares as follows:

one (1) such share to each of the Grantor's living children, and
one (1) such share to each family group composed of the living issue of any child of the Grantor who is then deceased.

Said equal shares shall then be held and administered and disposed of as follows:

a. In the case of each share apportioned to a living child of the Grantor, the Trustee may, in each and every year beginning with the date of said apportionment, pay over to said child or use, apply or expend for said child's direct or indirect benefit, so much or all of the net income of said share and so much or all of the principal of said share as the Trustee may, in its sole, absolute, and uncontrolled discretion, deem wise and safely consistent with said child's support in reasonable comfort, education (including college, graduate, and professional education), and maintenance in health (including medical, dental, hospital, nursing and nursing home expenses).

   i. Whenever, at or after said time of apportionment, said child shall have attained the age of thirty (30) years, he shall have the right to request in writing and to receive one-third (1/3) of the balance of his share; and

   ii. Whenever, at or after said time of apportionment, said child shall have attained the age of thirty-five (35) years, he shall have the right to request in writing and to receive an additional one-half (1/2) of the balance of his share; and

   iii. Whenever, at or after said time of apportionment, said child shall have attained the age of forty (40) years, he shall have the right to request in writing and to receive the entire balance of his share, at which time his trust shall terminate.

iv. It is the Grantor's belief that, in some circumstances, it may be beneficial for said child to leave the management of his trust share in the hands of the Trustee.

Therefore, said child may elect to leave his trust share, or any portion thereof, in the hands of the Trustee, as a separate fund, to be held and administered and disposed of as said child shall direct.

v. The share held by the Trustee for the benefit of a child as described above shall, from the time of the death of said child after the time above set for apportionment into shares, be administered for the benefit of said child's issue in the manner described below.

b. In the case of each share apportioned to the living issue of a deceased child of the Grantor, said share shall be administered for the benefit as a family group of such of the issue of said deceased child as from time to time shall be living.

The Trustee may pay over to the issue, or may use, apply or expend for their direct or indirect benefit, so much of the income and principal of the trust estate, at such times and in such proportions as the Trustee may determine, in its sole, absolute, and uncontrolled discretion, for support in reasonable comfort, education, (including college, graduate, and professional education), and maintenance in health (including medical, dental, hospital, nursing and nursing home expenses).

The Trustee may make such payments, use, application, expenditure or accumulation of the income and principal thereof as it shall think proper for the direct or indirect benefit of the members of said family group without being required to observe any precept or rule of equality of enjoyment as between said members.

Final distribution shall be made of whatever shall remain of said share, *per stirpes*, among said living issue and free and clear of all trusts, at a time to be chosen by the Trustee, in the Trustee's sole, absolute, and uncontrolled discretion, but not later than the youngest then living child of the Grantor's deceased child attaining the age of thirty (30) years.

c. If at any time before the final distribution of any of the trust shares described above (after taking into consideration all provisions thereof), there shall be no person in existence who is eligible to have the benefit of the trust of such share, then the share in question shall be reapportioned in equal shares among the other shares of the trust estate apportioned pursuant to sub-paragraph 3.___.___. above, and each equal share shall continue to be held and administered in trust, or distributed free and clear of all trusts, as the case may be, to or for the benefit of persons then and thereafter living, in accordance with the fortunes of the share to which said reapportionment is made.

3. If, at any time before the final distribution of all of the trust shares described above, there shall be no person in existence who is eligible to have the benefit of any trust shares, the Trustee shall divide all of the trust estate then remaining into two (2) equal parts which shall be distributed, outright and free of trust, as follows:

   a. One (1) part to those persons then living who would have taken the Grantor's estate, and in such shares thereof as they would have taken, had the Grantor then died intestate, domiciled in New Hampshire; and

   b. One (1) part to those persons then living who would have taken the Grantor's spouse's estate, and in such shares thereof as they would have taken, had the Grantor's spouse then died intestate, domiciled in New Hampshire.

G. If the Grantor's residential real estate is held in the trust estate and used by the Grantor's said spouse as a residence, then, during said spouse's lifetime, said spouse shall be permitted exclusive use and occupancy of said residential real estate.

Also, the Grantor's said spouse may, during said spouse's lifetime, in writing, delivered to the Trustee, request the Trustee to sell said residential real estate and to provide a substitute residence, of approximately equal or lesser value to the residence then occupied by the Grantor's said spouse.

Upon receipt of such written request, the Trustee shall then have full power and authority to make reasonable efforts to obtain such substitute residence and to sell the residential real estate then occupied by the Grantor's said spouse.

The costs of selling said residential real estate, of obtaining such substitute residence and of moving the Grantor's said spouse and said spouse's belongings out of said spouse's then occupied residence and into said substitute residence may, in the Trustee's sole, absolute, and uncontrolled discretion, be borne by the trust share to which such real estate has been allocated, to the extent there shall be sufficiently liquid assets to satisfy same.

The Trustee shall have full power and authority to execute any and all documents necessary to carry out the foregoing purpose.

The Trustee shall not be responsible, directly or indirectly, for the success, failure or ultimate satisfaction of the Grantor's said spouse in connection therewith.

The costs and expenses of maintenance and repairs to keep such residential real estate in the same condition it is in at the commencement of said use (reasonable wear and tear excepted), real estate taxes and other normal costs of maintenance and upkeep of said residential real estate, including fire and casualty insurance, may, in the Trustee's sole, absolute, and uncontrolled discretion, be borne by the trust share to which such real estate has been allocated, to the extent there shall be sufficiently liquid assets to satisfy same.

References in this paragraph to a "residence" shall include without limitation any variant of ownership of residential real property, including so-called cooperatives and condominiums, and payment of a refundable or nonrefundable admissions fee for a residential care facility.

H. Notwithstanding any provision to the contrary, the Trustee shall not make any distribution of the Marital QTIP Trust, or of income or principal from the Family Trust, to the Grantor's spouse, _____, if the Grantor's said spouse waives testate distribution of the Grantor's will and claims a statutory share of the Grantor's estate under R.S.A. 560:10, or any provisions successor thereto. In such event, the trust estate benefiting the Grantor's spouse shall be administered as if the Grantor's spouse were not then living.

I. The provisions contained herein which require the Trustee to apportion the trust estate into shares and parts of shares are for purposes of computation only and shall not be construed to require the Trustee to make physical segregation of one share or a part of a share from the others, although the Trustee shall have full right to make such segregation if it thinks it better to do so.

Notwithstanding said provisions, the Trustee shall have the full right to regard the trust estate as one undivided estate for purposes of management and investment.

J. If the Grantor or the executor of the Grantor's estate or any other individual (including any individual who shall transfer property in trust hereunder or the executor or administrator of the estate of such individual), has allocated any portion or all of any Generation Skipping Transfer ("GST") exemption provided by Section 2631(a) of the Internal Revenue Code to any property to be held in trust hereunder, then notwithstanding anything to the contrary contained in this agreement, the Trustee is authorized to establish such number of separate trusts, with identical terms, to hold the property received in trust hereunder as it, in its sole, absolute, and uncontrolled discretion, shall deem advisable, bearing in mind the allocation of the said GST exemption and the desirability that any trust to which all or any portion of the said GST exemption is allocated shall, if practical, have an inclusion ratio of zero.

Further, the Trustee is authorized to allocate such trusts among the trust shares herein created in order to minimize (or eliminate, if possible) any GST tax.

4.   TRUSTEE'S POWERS. In the administration of the trust estate, the Trustee shall have all of the powers granted to trustees by New Hampshire common law and statutory authority (including, but not limited to, the Uniform Trustees' Powers Act, R.S.A. 564-A, and the Uniform Trust Code, R.S.A. 564-B, as they may be amended from time to time), without restrictions.

In addition to such power, and not in limitation thereof, the Trustee shall have the following powers, all of which shall be exercised in a fiduciary capacity and for the benefit of the beneficiaries:

A. During the lifetime of the Grantor, the Trustee may retain as an investment, unless and until the Grantor by a writing delivered to the Trustee shall otherwise direct, all of the securities and other property originally assigned, transferred, or delivered to the Trustee hereunder or at any time forming a part of the trust estate, whether or not such securities or other property be of the character authorized by the laws of the State of New Hampshire for the investment of trust funds.

Upon the death or incapacity of the Grantor, the Trustee is authorized to purchase, sell, lease, or alter any investment by buy or sell orders transmitted by it, whether by telephone call, electronic facsimile trans-mission, computer message or other current non-written method of business communication.

B. To buy, sell and trade in securities of any nature, [on margin], and for such purpose to maintain and operate [margin] accounts with brokers, and to pledge any securities held or purchased by it with such brokers as security for loans and advances made to the Trustee.

C. *[For Corporate Trustees]* To retain the property of the trust estate in the same investments as when received by it or to vary and transpose such investments and to invest and reinvest the property of the trust estate in such manner and in such securities or other property (including common trust funds or similar funds for the participation of trusts of which _____ is trustee and including securities of _____ and any successor thereto) as it in its uncontrolled discretion shall deem best without accountability for any loss for so doing and without liability for depreciation occasioned by so doing even though the property so retained or the investments so made may not be of the character permitted for the investment of trust funds under the laws of the State of New Hampshire or any other state or federal law.

D. To take and hold title to real estate, and to convey any interest in real estate and improvements thereon held in trust, and no purchaser or third party shall be bound to inquire whether the Trustee has said power or is properly exercising said power, or see to the application of any trust asset paid to the Trustee for a conveyance thereof.

E. To have all of the necessary banking powers to open, close, and manage financial accounts, including but not limited to, checking accounts, savings accounts, financial accounts and other related financial instruments and to conduct all necessary financial business in reference to the management of the financial assets of the trust.

F. To rent a safe deposit box and to retain such assets in said box as the Trustee, in its sole, absolute, and uncontrolled discretion, determines appropriate.

G. To borrow money, with or without security, and mortgage or pledge trust property for a period within or extending beyond the duration of the trust.

H. To loan funds to the Grantor's estate upon such terms and conditions as to interest rates, maturities, and security as the Trustee shall determine.

I. To make payments, transfers or conveyances, to the extent possible, to the estate of the Grantor (after exhaustion of the assets of the Grantor's estate) to satisfy legacies, bequests or devises, if any, made under the Grantor's will or included in the Grantor's estate for other purposes, if the Grantor's estate shall be insufficient to satisfy such legacies, bequests or devises.

J. To invest in common trust funds.

K. To select property, in its sole, absolute, and uncontrolled discretion, to be allocated to any trust hereunder or to be distributed in satisfaction of any gift provided for herein without respect to the income tax basis of such property, and the Trustee is specifically excused from any duty of impartiality with respect to the income tax basis of such property.

In the event that residential real estate is held in the trust estate, the Trustee may allocate said residential real estate to any trust created hereunder, to be held and administered and disposed of pursuant to the provisions thereof.

L. To coordinate the filing of any information returns required under Section 6018 of the Internal Revenue Code in cooperation with the executor of the Grantor's estate, if any.

M. To establish passwords for electronic accounts and to have access to and modify any existing password established by the Grantor or a predecessor Trustee for any assets in the trust estate.

123

N. If at any time during the Grantor's lifetime, there is delivered to the Trustee other than the Grantor, if any, or, if none, then to the successor Trustee, a written opinion, signed by a licensed physician, stating that the Grantor has become incompetent or incapacitated, then from and after the delivery of such written opinion the Trustee other than the Grantor, or the successor Trustee, as the case may be, shall have those powers and authorities with respect to the trust estate given to the Trustee in this trust agreement.

O. If, after the death of the Grantor and the Grantor's spouse, _____, as it may be amended from time to time, is still in existence and the terms of any trust established by said trust are substantially similar to the terms of any trust established by this, _____, the Trustee is authorized and empowered to consolidate such trust with such similar trust established by _____ and to administer them as one trust, unless such consolidation shall be contrary to law or inconsistent with the terms of any instrument supplemental hereto.

P. Regardless of the extent of the authority that the Trustee holds to currently distribute income and/or principal of the trust estate to one or more beneficiaries of the trust, the Trustee shall have full power and authority, to be exercised in its sole, absolute, and uncontrolled discretion, to appoint any or all assets held in this trust estate to any other trust or trusts created under will, deed or otherwise, for the benefit of one or more of the beneficiaries hereunder.

This authority shall be subject to the limitations set forth in R.S.A. 564-B:4-418, as amended from time to time, provided that such appointment clause shall be null and void in the event there is a determination that the application of such clause shall result in the inclusion of any of the trust estate in the Grantor's gross estate under any provision of the Internal Revenue Code, including but not limited to Sections 2041 and 2042, which would not otherwise be includable in the Grantor's gross estate.

Provided further, however, that if this Trust qualifies as a "trust instrument" under the Qualified Dispositions in Trust Act, R.S.A. 564-D, as amended from time to time, then the Trustee may only appoint the assets of the trust estate to a new trust which will continue to qualify as a "trust instrument" under such Act and will provide similar protections to the assets held in this trust estate.

Q. If, at any time before the final distribution of the principal of any trust share hereinabove described, the value of the principal of said trust share shall be equal to, or less than, ONE HUNDRED THOUSAND DOLLARS ($100,000), then the Trustee may, in its sole discretion, terminate said trust share and distribute the principal of said trust share, and any accumulated and undistributed income thereof, outright and free of trust, to those persons then entitled to benefit from said trust share, and in the proportions in which they are then entitled to benefit from said trust share, notwithstanding any provisions of this trust to the contrary.

R. To exercise all the powers, authorities and discretions herein conferred, after the termination of the trust hereunder, until the complete distribution of the trust estate.

5. ADDITIONAL PROPERTY. The Grantor, or the Grantor's spouse may, by will, trust or during their lifetimes, from time to time, transfer and deliver to the Trustee cash, securities, and other property acceptable to the Trustee, in addition to the property presently transferred and delivered, and such cash, securities, and other property shall be held, administered, and disposed of by the Trustee in accordance with the provisions of this agreement without the execution of any further instrument or declaration.

6. REPORTING BY TRUSTEE.

A. At any time and from time to time, the Grantor shall have the power, by written instrument signed and acknowledged by the Grantor and delivered to the Trustee, to settle the report of the Trustee with respect to principal or income, or with respect to both principal and income, and to release and discharge the Trustee of and from any and every claim, demand, accountability, and liability of every nature, arising from any matter or thing done or omitted to be done, in connection with this agreement or any trust hereby created, during the period in respect of which the report of the Trustee shall have been so settled.

Every such settlement, release, and discharge shall be conclusive and binding upon, and shall be an absolute protection to the Trustee against all claims of any income beneficiaries, remaindermen, or other persons who might then or thereafter have or claim any interest under this agreement, and no such income beneficiary, remainderman, or other person shall have any right of accounting, reporting, any claim, or any cause of action against the Trustee arising from any matter or thing done or omitted to be done in connection with this agreement or any trust hereby created, during any period in respect of which the report of the Trustee shall have been so settled.

B. After the death or incapacity of the Grantor, the Trustee may, at the Trustee's sole, absolute, and uncontrolled discretion, and shall, to the extent required by the Uniform Trust Code, R.S.A. 564-B, as it may be amended from time to time, render a Trustee's report as described in the Uniform Trust Code, as it may be amended from time to time, at such intervals as the Trustee may choose or at such times as required by the Uniform Trust Code.

C. A recipient of such a report (or, if under guardianship or conservatorship, then by the Guardian or Conservator, or, if deceased, then by the Executor or Administrator), may, by a written instrument, assent to the report of the Trustee with respect to principal or to income, or with respect to both principal and income.

The assent of the recipient of such report (or, if under guardianship or conservatorship, then by the Guardian or Conservator, or, if deceased, then by the Executor or Administrator) shall make such report binding and conclusive upon all persons then having or who may thereafter have any interest, vested or contingent, in the income or principal of the trust estate and such assent shall forever release and discharge the Trustee of and from any and every claim, demand, accountability, and liability of every nature, arising from any matter or thing done or omitted to be done, in connection with this agreement or any trust hereby created, during the period in respect of which the report of the Trustee shall have been so settled.

D. The failure of any person to object in writing to the Trustee to such a report within thirty (30) days after the delivery of the same to such person hereunder shall be final and binding to the same extent as the written assent hereinabove provided.

E. Any person entitled to such a report, accounting, information, notice and the like (or, if under guardianship or conservatorship, then by the Guardian or Conservator, or, if deceased, then by the Executor or Administrator) may by a written instrument signed and acknowledged by him or her or them, as the case may be, and delivered to the Trustee, waive the right to said Trustee's report or to other information otherwise required to be furnished under the Uniform Trust Code, as it may be amended from time to time.

7.   SUCCESSOR TRUSTEE. The following provisions shall govern the addition, removal and succession of the Trustee:

A. The Grantor may, during the Grantor's lifetime, add any additional Trustee, or remove any Trustee hereunder and appoint a successor Trustee.

B. If _____ shall be unable or unwilling to serve in the capacity of Trustee for any reason, then the Grantor's spouse, _____, and _____ shall serve in _____ stead.

1. If the Grantor's said spouse shall be unable or unwilling to serve in the capacity of Trustee for any reason, then _____ shall serve in _____ stead.

2. If _____ shall be unable or unwilling to serve in the capacity of Trustee for any reason, then _____ shall serve in _____ stead.

If _____ shall be unable or unwilling to serve in the capacity of Trustee for any reason, then _____ shall serve in _____ as its successor Trustee, any _____ stead.

C. In the event there shall be no successor Trustee who shall be able or willing to serve in the capacity of Trustee, then a majority of the beneficiaries to whom or for whose use the current net income of the trust estate is at the time authorized or required to be paid or applied, either,

1. acting individually, if then eighteen (18) years of age, or,

2. by his or her natural parent, or natural guardian, or Court appointed guardian or Court appointed conservator, if then under guardianship or conservatorship,

shall appoint a successor Trustee.

D. In the event that any beneficiary of the trust, other than the Grantor, shall serve in the capacity of co-Trustee, then the discretionary powers to determine whether income or principal is to be distributed to said beneficiary or to any person to whom said beneficiary owes an obligation of support shall be exercisable only by the remaining Trustee.

It is the Grantor's intention by this sub-paragraph to prohibit said beneficiary from benefiting himself or herself as beneficiary in any way by the exercise of such discretionary powers vested in the Trustee as a group.

E. In the event that any beneficiary of the trust, other than the Grantor or the Grantor's spouse, shall serve in the capacity of sole Trustee and the Trustee has discretionary powers to distribute income or principal to himself, herself, or to any person to whom he or she owes an obligation of support, then such distributions of income or principal shall be exercisable by the sole Trustee. The maximum amount that may be withdrawn annually by each such beneficiary under this sub-paragraph, however, shall not exceed the maximum amount over which an individual may have a power of withdrawal without its lapse in such year being deemed to be a release of such power under Section 2514(e) of the Internal Revenue Code.

F. In the event that an attorney, an accountant, a certified financial planner or a corporation or financial institution shall be serving as Trustee hereunder, a majority of the beneficiaries to whom or for whose use the current net income of the trust estate is at the time authorized or required to be paid or applied and who shall at the time be at least eighteen (18) years of age may by a written instrument signed and acknowledged by them and delivered to such attorney, accountant, certified financial planner or corporation or financial institution remove said Trustee and, subject to the successor trustee appointments herein, appoint as its successor Trustee, any attorney, accountant, certified financial planner or corporation or financial institution having a trust department capable of rendering financial advice concerning the investments of the trust estate.

G.   No successor Trustee shall be liable or responsible in any way for any actions or defaults of any predecessor Trustee, nor for any loss or expense from or occasioned by anything done or neglected to be done by any predecessor Trustee. Any successor Trustee shall have, from and after its appointment or succession to office hereunder and without any assignment or other action by any person, all the rights, interests, and powers, including discretionary rights and powers, which are by the provisions of this trust agreement granted to and vested in the Trustee named herein.

8.   <u>FIDUCIARIES</u>. No person dealing with the Trustee shall be responsible for the application of any money, securities, or other property paid or delivered, and the receipt of the Trustee shall be a full discharge; and no person dealing with the Trustee, and no issuer, transfer agent, or other agent of any issuer of any securities shall be under any obligation to ascertain or inquire into the power of the Trustee to purchase, sell, exchange, transfer, mortgage, pledge, create a security interest in, lease, distribute, or otherwise dispose of or deal with any money, securities, or other property.

The Trustee shall not at any time be held liable for any action taken or not taken, including any action intended to lessen or eliminate the impact of estate or generation-skipping transfer taxes with respect to any generation or beneficiary, whether or not such action is successful in achieving the results sought and without regard to its effect on other beneficiaries in the same or different generations, or for any loss or depreciation in the value of any property in any trust created herein, whether due to an error of judgment or otherwise, where the Trustee has exercised good faith and ordinary diligence in the exercise of its duties.

The Trustee shall receive reasonable compensation for its services in the administration of the trusts created herein, including reimbursement for amounts reasonably expended for bookkeeping services, investment services and advice, and other professional or para-professional services. In addition to the compensation herein provided, the Trustee shall receive reasonable compensation for any legal services provided for the benefit of the trust estate, such as handling any litigation involving the trust, preparing state or federal income tax returns, and transferring any real estate.

9.   <u>PERPETUITIES</u>. All trusts established under this instrument shall be exempt from the application of the rule against perpetuities. This provision is intended to comply with R.S.A. 564:24, and accordingly, the Grantor specifically authorizes the Trustee to sell, mortgage or lease property for any period of time

beyond the period that is required for an interest created under this instrument to vest in order to be valid under the rule against perpetuities, as measured by the period defined above.

The trusts created hereunder shall be perpetual to the fullest extent permitted by the governing law. If any trust created hereunder is deemed to be subject to the law of a jurisdiction (including, but only to the extent applicable to real property) that has a rule against perpetuities or similar rule which limits the period during which property can be held in trust, then such trust (other than a trust created by the exercise of a power of appointment conferred hereunder which exercise commences a new rule against perpetuities period under the law of such jurisdiction) shall terminate in all events upon the expiration of the longest period that property may be held in trust under this trust agreement under the law of such jurisdiction (including any applicable period in gross, such as 21 years, 90 years or 110 years); provided, however, that if the jurisdiction has a rule against perpetuities or similar rule which applies only to certain types of property, such as real property, the provisions of this paragraph shall apply only to such property. If under the law of such jurisdiction the longest period that property may be held in trust may be determined (or alternatively determined) with reference to the death of the last survivor of a group of individuals in being upon the date of this trust agreement, those individuals shall consist of all of the descendants of the Grantor's parents who were in being on the date of this trust agreement. Upon termination of a trust pursuant to the provisions of this paragraph, the trust property shall be transferred, conveyed and paid over to the persons then entitled to receive or have the benefit of the income from the trust in the proportions in which they are entitled thereto, or if their interests are indefinite, then in equal shares.

10.   SPENDTHRIFT PROVISION. Except as herein otherwise provided, the interest of any beneficiary hereunder, either as to income or principal, shall not be anticipated, alienated or in any other manner assigned or pledged or promised by such beneficiary, and shall not be reached by, or be subject to, any legal, equitable or other process, including any bankruptcy or divorce proceeding, or be subject to the interference or control of creditors or others in any way or manner, and all payments to, or the interest of, any beneficiary shall be free from the control or claim of any parent or spouse or former spouse or any other third party. Moreover, no power of appointment or power of withdrawal shall be subject to involuntary exercise. Provided, however, this spendthrift provision shall not restrict the exercise of a disclaimer or the exercise of a power of appointment or withdrawal right granted by this trust agreement. This provision is intended to be a material provision of this trust and any other trust established hereunder.

11.   TAX PROVISION. The trust estate shall not be charged with the payment of any estate, inheritance, legacy, death taxes or duties of any nature (state or federal), or any interest or penalty thereon, except to the extent that the other assets in the Grantor's estate (excluding any assets which may be exempted from the payment of such taxes by the last will of the Grantor) shall be insufficient

to discharge such taxes, interest or penalties or shall be insufficiently liquid to satisfy the same. The Trustee may rely conclusively upon written certification from the executor of the Grantor's estate, or if no probate administration of the Grantor's estate is required under applicable law, upon request of the person or persons nominated as executor under the Grantor's will or upon any other evidence, as to the existence of such insufficiency and the amount thereof; provided, however, that the Trustee shall not pay any additional tax imposed under Section 2032A or 2057 of the Internal Revenue Code or any generation-skipping transfer taxes imposed under Chapter 13 of the Internal Revenue Code imposed by reason of the Grantor's death.

If the Trustee shall be required to pay any such taxes, they shall be charged against the principal of the trust estate as an expense without apportionment.

Provided, that in the event that no probate administration of the Grantor's estate is required under applicable law, the Trustee shall have all the powers and authority given the executor under the Grantor's will in relation to such taxes, including all elections and allocation of the generation-skipping transfer tax exemption under Section 2631 of the Internal Revenue Code.

12.   <u>DEBTS AND EXPENSES</u>. The trust estate shall not be charged with the payment of legal debts of the Grantor's estate, funeral expenses or expenses of administration of the Grantor's estate except to the extent that the other assets in the Grantor's estate shall be insufficient to discharge such debts and expenses, or shall be insufficiently liquid to satisfy the same. The Trustee may rely conclusively upon written certification from the executor of the Grantor's estate, or if no probate administration of the Grantor's estate is required under applicable law, upon request of the person or persons nominated as executor under the Grantor's will, or upon any other evidence, as to the existence of such insufficiency and the amount thereof. If the Trustee shall be required to pay any such debts and expenses, the same shall be treated as debts and expenses of the trust estate (to the extent the assets of the Grantor's estate are insufficient to satisfy the same) or as loans to the Grantor's estate (to the extent the liquid assets of the Grantor's estate are insufficient to satisfy the same) if any such debts and expenses are deducted for federal estate tax purposes in computing the value of the Grantor's taxable estate under Section 2053 of the Internal Revenue Code.

If any such debts and expenses are either not so deducted or deductible under Section 2053 of the Internal Revenue Code, however, the same shall be charged against the principal of the trust estate as an expense without apportionment.

This provision shall confer no rights upon anyone except the executor of the Grantor's estate.

13.   <u>SURVIVAL REQUIREMENT</u>. No person shall be deemed to have survived the Grantor, or any other person or event under the terms of this trust, unless such person survives the end of the period commencing with the close of the calendar day of the Grantor's death, the death of such other person or on which such event occurs, and ending with the close of the thirtieth (30th) calendar day thereafter.

DO NOT USE THIS EXTRA PROVISION UNLESS SPECIFICALLY DIRECTED TO DO SO:

Provided, however, if the Grantor's spouse should die within said thirty (30) day period or in a common disaster with the Grantor or under such circumstances that there is not sufficient evidence that they died otherwise than simultaneously, it shall be presumed for all purposes of this trust that the Grantor was survived by _____ spouse.

14. <u>DISTRIBUTIONS TO MINORS</u>. In any case where property or funds become distributable to a minor, then the Trustee shall have the additional power to distribute the same in any one or more of the following ways: (1) by distribution directly to the minor; (2) by distribution to the legal guardian of the minor; (3) by distribution to a parent, relative or friend of the minor for the minor's support in reasonable comfort, education and maintenance in health; (4) by applying the same directly for the minor's support in reasonable comfort, education and maintenance in health; (5) by depositing the same in a bank account in the name of the minor or by transferring property to or purchasing property in the name of a custodian for his or her benefit under a Uniform Law relating to transfers or gifts to minors; or (6) by holding the same hereunder in trust or in custody for the minor's support in reasonable comfort, education and maintenance in health and by distributing the remainder thereof to the minor upon coming of age or otherwise to the minor's estate in case of the death of the minor. The receipt of the person to whom property or funds are actually distributed in accordance with any of the foregoing provisions shall fully discharge the Trustee from further accountability therefor.

15. <u>GOVERNING LAW AND SITUS</u>. The Grantor declares that this agreement and the trust created hereby shall be construed and administered under the laws of the State of New Hampshire, that the validity and effect of this agreement and of this trust shall be determined in accordance with the laws of that State.

Further, the trust shall be under the jurisdiction of the courts of the State of New Hampshire and the Trustee shall voluntarily enter a general appearance in any legal action relating to an accounting of the trust or a declaratory judgment interpreting this trust agreement. The Trustee shall not be chargeable in any court other than one of the courts of that State.

[INSERT IF TRUSTEE HAS AUTHORITY TO CHANGE SITUS]

However, the Trustee, at any time and from time to time, in its discretion, may, (1) remove all or part of the trust estate and hold and administer the same in any other jurisdiction where the Trustee shall be then located, (2) change the situs of administration of any trust from one jurisdiction to another jurisdiction; and (3) elect that the law of such other jurisdiction shall thereafter govern the trust to such extent as may be necessary and appropriate, and to amend the administrative provisions of the trust as the Trustee deems appropriate to ensure compliance and compatibility with such law,

whereupon the courts of such other jurisdiction shall have the power to effectuate the purposes of this trust agreement to such extent. The determination of the Trustee as to any such removal of assets or change of situs or governing law shall be conclusive and binding on all persons interested in such trust.

16.   <u>AMENDMENT AND REVOCATION</u>. The Grantor reserves the right at any time or from time to time without the consent of any person and without notice to any person other than the Trustee to revoke or modify the trust hereby created, in whole or in part, to change the beneficiaries hereof, or to withdraw the whole or any part of the trust estate by filing notice of such revocation, modification, change, or withdrawal with the Trustee; provided, however, that the terms of this agreement may not be modified by the Grantor in such manner as to increase the obligations or alter the rates of the commissions of the Trustee without its written consent.

17.   <u>DEFINITIONS</u>. Whenever used in this trust agreement, the words "child," "children," or "issue" are intended to include not only persons who are descendants by blood, but also persons and issue of persons who have been adopted according to law prior to their attaining the age of eighteen (18) years.

References to the "Internal Revenue Code" or "Code" or to provisions thereof are to the Internal Revenue Code of 1986, as amended at the time in question. References to the "Treasury Regulations," "Regulations" and "Regs." are to the Treasury Regulations under the Code. If, by the time in question, a particular provision of the Code has been renumbered, or the Code has been superseded by a subsequent federal tax law, the reference shall be deemed to be to the renumbered provision or the corresponding provision of the subsequent law, unless to do so would clearly be contrary to the Grantor's intent as expressed in this trust agreement, and a similar rule shall apply to references to the Regulations.

References to "R.S.A." are to the New Hampshire Revised Statutes Annotated, as amended at the time in question. If, by the time in question, a particular provision of the Statute has been renumbered, or the Statute has been superseded by subsequent law, the reference shall be deemed to be to the renumbered provision or the corresponding provision of the subsequent law, unless to do so would clearly be contrary to the Grantor's intent as expressed in this trust agreement.

Masculine, feminine and neuter pronouns shall each include all genders, and the singular shall include the plural and vice versa, where the context or facts so admit.

The captions and paragraph headings of this trust agreement are inserted only as a matter of convenience and for reference and in no way define, limit or describe the scope or intent of this agreement, nor in any way affect this agreement.

18.   <u>EXECUTION</u>. This trust agreement, and any amendments hereto, shall

be effective when executed by the Grantor, notwithstanding that the signature of the Trustee is provided for, the Trustee's signature being intended to denote the acceptance of the Trustee to serve in that capacity only.

This trust agreement may be executed in any number of counterparts with the same effect as if all of the parties had signed the same document. All counterparts shall be construed together and shall constitute one agreement.

_____   _____
Witness   Grantor

_____   _____
Witness   Trustee

STATE OF NEW HAMPSHIRE
COUNTY OF _____

The foregoing instrument was acknowledged before me on _____, 2011, by _____.

Notary Public/Justice of the Peace
My Commission Expires:
(Seal)

Page 622: Substitute this form for Form 37 in the text:

FORM 37 Revocable Trust with a Marital Power of Appointment Trust and Family Trust

_____

REVOCABLE TRUST OF 2005

TRUST AGREEMENT, made on _____, 2005, between, residing in _____, New Hampshire (hereinafter called the "Grantor"), and _____, residing in _____, New Hampshire (hereinafter called the "Trustee").

At the time of the signing of this trust, the Grantor's spouse is, and the Grantor's children are _____, and _____.

1. <u>TRUST PROPERTY</u>. All property transferred and delivered to the Trustee, which the Trustee may, at any time, hold or acquire, including cash, securities, or other property, shall be referred to collectively as the "trust estate" and held and administered and disposed of by the Trustee for the uses and purposes, and upon the terms and conditions, herein set forth.

2. <u>DISPOSITIVE PROVISIONS: LIFETIME</u>. The Trustee shall hold, manage, invest and reinvest the trust estate, and shall collect the income thereof and dispose of the net income and principal as follows:

   A. Pay such parts of the income, if any, and such parts of the principal of this trust to, or for the benefit of, the Grantor as the Grantor directs from time to time for the Grantor's support in reasonable comfort, education (including college and professional education), and maintenance in health (including medical, dental, hospital, nursing and nursing home expenses). Any income accrued or accumulated at the time of the Grantor's death shall be paid and transferred to principal, to be administered according to the terms hereinafter provided.

   B. In addition, during the lifetime of the Grantor, if the Grantor becomes so incapacitated that Grantor cannot exercise Grantor's rights under subparagraph 2.A. above, and there are sufficient assets in this trust to do so, the Trustee is authorized to pay such parts of the income, if any, and such parts of the principal of this trust to, or for the benefit of, the Grantor, the Grantor's spouse and the Grantor's children as it deems advisable for their support in reasonable comfort, education (including college and professional education), and maintenance in health (including medical, dental, hospital, nursing and nursing home expenses), taking into consideration the amount of their income from sources other than this trust.

     It is the Grantor's intention that the support in reasonable comfort, education (including college and professional education), and maintenance in health (including medical, dental, hospital, nursing and nursing home expenses) of the Grantor and the Grantor's spouse shall be of primary concern, and the Trustee shall exercise its discretion in using principal for the Grantor and the Grantor's spouse, considering all other beneficiaries to be secondary and without liability to any other beneficiary for the use of principal for the Grantor and the Grantor's spouse.

C.   Further, the Trustee is authorized to give, transfer or convey any of the trust estate to persons of the Grantor's natural affection to whom the Grantor would normally consider making such gifts, transfers or conveyances, whether outright or in trust, having in mind the ultimate objective of such gifts, transfers or conveyances is the qualification for state or federal medical, welfare or other assistance programs for the Grantor's or the Grantor's spouse's benefit and the reduction of the state and federal estate, inheritance, transfer, legacy and succession taxes and any interest and penalties thereon imposed by reason of the Grantor's death or the Grantor's spouse's death.

3.   DISPOSITIVE PROVISIONS: AFTER-DEATH. Upon the death of the Grantor, the Trustee shall thereafter apply and distribute the trust estate as follows:

A.   If the Grantor's spouse, _____, survives the Grantor, the Trustee shall distribute to the Grantor's said spouse, outright and free of trust, all of the tangible personal property and household effects which are then part of the trust estate, including furniture, clothing, jewelry, silver, books, pictures, china, automobiles and their equipment, other vehicles and their equipment, and other articles of personal and household use or ornament.

If the Grantor's said spouse shall not survive the Grantor, said tangible personal property and household effects shall be distributed, outright and free of trust, to the Grantor's issue who so survive the Grantor, such issue to take per stirpes.

The Grantor expresses the hope that said beneficiaries will dispose of said tangible personal property and household effects according to the Grantor's wishes, however said wishes may be made known to them.

If a division of the property under this distribution is required among the beneficiaries, such division shall be made by the beneficiaries, in appropriate shares, as they may amicably agree.

The Grantor prefers that said beneficiaries shall agree upon the manner in which said property is to be divided, but should they not agree among themselves as to the division thereof within ninety (90) days after the Grantor's death, the Trustee shall have full power and authority to divide said property among said beneficiaries, in appropriate shares, and its determination with respect thereto shall, insofar as permitted by law, be binding and conclusive upon such beneficiaries.

135

B. If the Grantor's spouse, _____, survives the Grantor, the Trustee shall divide the remaining trust estate into two parts, one to be known as the "Marital Trust" and the other as the "Family Trust."

1. The Marital Trust shall consist of an amount equal to the maximum allowable federal estate tax marital deduction as calculated by law in effect at the time of the Grantor's death, diminished by the value for federal estate tax purposes of all items in the Grantor's gross estate which qualify for said deduction and which pass or have passed to the Grantor's spouse under the Grantor's will, by survivorship in joint tenancy or tenancy by the entirety property, by life insurance settlement, by operation of law or otherwise.

    Provided, however, that if the amount of the maximum allowable federal estate tax marital deduction in the Grantor's estate is greater than the amount needed to reduce the federal estate tax to zero, after considering the available unified tax credit (the applicable credit amount or applicable exclusion amount) and state death tax credit or deduction allowable in determining such tax (provided that the state death tax credit or deduction shall be taken into account only to the extent that doing so would not result in an increase in state death taxes which would otherwise be payable), then the amount set aside in the Marital Trust shall be equal only to that portion of such marital deduction that is needed to reduce the federal estate tax on the Grantor's estate to zero.

2. For the purpose of determining the amount to be transferred into the Marital Trust, values shall be those which are finally determined for federal estate tax purposes. Elections made by the Grantor's executor with respect to taking certain deductions for income tax purposes rather than for estate tax purposes shall determine the aforesaid values and the amount to constitute the Marital Trust. The words "which pass" or "has passed" shall have the same meaning as under the Internal Revenue Code for marital deduction purposes and no assets shall be transferred to the Marital Trust that do not qualify for the marital deduction.

3. In making allocation or distribution to the Marital Trust the Trustee is authorized to satisfy the Marital Trust in cash or in kind, or in combination of both, provided that all assets placed in the Marital Trust shall be valued for the purpose of being placed in the Marital Trust at their fair market value as determined as of the dates of respective distributions to the Marital Trust, which dates shall be the dates on which the Trustee makes specific allocation on its books of account (if such assets are in negotiable form), or when delivery is made in proper form for transfer, or a deed is executed, if real estate, and the aggregate fair market value thereof shall be no less than the amount required to

completely fund the Marital Trust. The Trustee is further authorized to estimate the size of the Marital Trust and to fund the trust, subject, however, to any adjustments which may be required upon final determination of the federal estate tax on the Grantor's estate.

4. No debts, funeral expenses, expenses of administration of the Grantor's estate, inheritance, estate, transfer, legacy or succession taxes (state and federal), and any interest or penalties thereon shall be apportioned against or paid from the Marital Trust, except to the extent the assets of both the Grantor's estate and the Family Trust are insufficient for this purpose.

5. The Grantor's spouse may disclaim any part or all of this Marital Trust. Any interest disclaimed by the Grantor's said spouse shall be paid over and added to the Family Trust and thereafter shall be administered as part thereof.

6. If the Grantor or the executor of the Grantor's estate or any other individual (including any individual who shall transfer property in trust hereunder or the executor or administrator of the estate of such individual), deems it necessary to allocate any portion of the trust estate to a separate trust share which will allow such assets to qualify for a state marital deduction pursuant to any applicable provision of state law, then notwithstanding anything to the contrary contained in this agreement, the Trustee is authorized to establish a separate Marital QTIP Trust, the terms of which will qualify for the state marital deduction, to hold the property received in trust hereunder as it, in its sole discretion, shall deem advisable; provided, however, that the amount set aside in the state Marital QTIP Trust shall be equal only to that portion of such marital deduction that is needed to reduce the state estate tax on the Grantor's estate to zero.

C. Marital Trust. The Marital Trust shall be held and administered and disposed of as follows:

1. The Trustee shall pay over to the Grantor's spouse during said spouse's life, all of the net income of this Marital Trust, said payments to be made at least annually, but at more frequent intervals if the Grantor's spouse shall, in writing, direct.

Also, the Trustee may pay over to the Grantor's spouse whatever part or parts of the principal as the Trustee may deem proper or necessary for Grantor's spouse's support in reasonable comfort, education (including college and professional education), and maintenance in health (including medical, dental, hospital, nursing and nursing home expenses).

2. In addition, in the event of the incapacity of the Grantor's spouse, the

Trustee may make said payments of income and/or make payments of principal for said spouse's direct benefit.

3. The Trustee shall distribute to or for the benefit of the Grantor's spouse, from time to time, so much or all of the principal of the Marital Trust as Grantor's spouse may request in writing, delivered to the Trustee.

4. The Grantor's spouse shall have full power of appointment over said spouse's entire interest in this Marital Trust, free of all trusts and exercisable by Grantor's spouse alone, by said spouse's will, duly proved and allowed, either in favor of Grantor's spouse's estate or of others, or in favor of Grantor's spouse's estate and of others, as Grantor's spouse shall choose; provided, however, that said full power of appointment shall be exercisable by the Grantor's spouse by reference in said spouse's will to said full power of appointment hereby created.

5. Such property remaining in the Marital Trust on the death of the Grantor's spouse the accrued but undistributed income and the principal and which has not been appointed by Grantor's spouse's will, in accordance with the power hereinabove vested in Grantor's spouse, shall be paid over and added to the Family Trust and thereafter shall be administered as part thereof.

D. <u>Family Trust</u>. The Family Trust shall consist of all of the remainder of the trust estate which has not been heretofore previously allocated and shall be held and administered and disposed of by the Trustee as follows:

1. If the Grantor's spouse, _____, survives the Grantor, then, during said spouse's lifetime, the Trustee may pay over to Grantor's spouse or may use, apply or expend for said spouse's direct or indirect benefit, so much or all of the income of the trust hereby created and so much or all of the principal of said trust as the Trustee may deem proper or necessary for Grantor's spouse's support in reasonable comfort, education (including college and professional education), and maintenance in health (including medical, dental, hospital, nursing and nursing home expenses); provided, however, that in exercising its discretion the Trustee shall take into account other resources of the Grantor's spouse.

a. The Trustee may also pay over to or use, apply or expend for the direct or indirect benefit of the Grantor's children who are from time to time living during said period, or pay to the Grantor's spouse for their benefit, so much or all of the income or principal of the trust hereby created as the Trustee may deem proper or necessary for their support in reasonable comfort, education (including college and professional education), and maintenance in health (including medical, dental, hospital, nursing and nursing home expenses).

b. If it becomes necessary for the Trustee to make any payments to or for the benefit of the Grantor's spouse from the principal of the Marital Trust hereinbefore established, or from the principal of the Family Trust, the Trustee is directed, when it is practicable to do so, to make such payments of principal, if any, from the principal of the Marital Trust before making any payment from the principal of the Family Trust.

However, it is the Grantor's intention that the support in reasonable comfort, education (including college and professional education), and maintenance in health (including medical, dental, hospital, nursing and nursing home expenses) of the Grantor's spouse shall be of primary concern, and the Trustee shall exercise its discretion in using principal for the Grantor's spouse, considering all other beneficiaries to this trust to be secondary and without liability to any other beneficiary for the use of principal for the Grantor's spouse.

2. Upon the death of the Grantor's spouse, or upon the Grantor's death if the Grantor's spouse does not survive Grantor, the Trustee shall apportion the balance of the principal and accumulated income of the trust estate into equal shares as follows:

one (1) such share to each of the Grantor's living children, and

one (1) such share to each family group composed of the living issue of any child of the Grantor who is then deceased.

Said equal shares shall then be held and administered and disposed of as follows:

a. In the case of each share apportioned to a living child of the Grantor, the Trustee may, in each and every year beginning with the date of said apportionment, pay over to said child or use, apply or expend for said child's direct or indirect benefit, so much or all of the net income of said share and so much or all of the principal of said share as the Trustee may, in its sole and uncontrolled discretion, deem wise and safely consistent with said child's support in reasonable comfort, education (including college and professional education), and maintenance in health (including medical, dental, hospital, nursing and nursing home expenses).

i. Whenever, at or after said time of apportionment, said child shall have attained the age of thirty (30) years, he shall have the right to request in writing and to receive one-third (1/3) of the principal of his share; and

ii. Whenever, at or after said time of apportionment, said child shall have attained the age of thirty-five (35) years, he shall have the right to request in writing and to receive an additional one-half (1/2) of the balance of the principal of his share; and

iii. Whenever, at or after said time of apportionment, said child shall have attained the age of forty (40) years, he shall have the right to request in writing and to receive the entire balance of the principal and undistributed income of his share, at which time his trust shall terminate.

iv. It is the Grantor's belief that, in some circumstances, it may be beneficial for said child to leave the management of his trust share in the hands of the Trustee.

Therefore, said child may elect to leave his trust share, or any portion thereof, in the hands of the Trustee, as a separate fund, to be held and administered and disposed of as said child shall direct.

v. The share held by the Trustee for the benefit of a child as hereinabove described shall, from the time of the death of the child after the time hereinabove set for apportionment into shares, be administered for the benefit of the child's issue in the manner herein described in sub-paragraph 3.___.2.b., except that the period of twenty-one (21) years therein specified shall, for the purposes of this subparagraph, be taken to run from the date of the child's death.

b. In the case of each share apportioned to the living issue of a deceased child of the Grantor, said share shall be administered for the benefit as a family group of such of the issue of said deceased child as from time to time shall be living.

The Trustee may make such payments, use, application, expenditure or accumulation of the income and principal thereof as it shall think proper for the direct or indirect benefit of the members of said family group without being required to observe any precept or rule of equality of enjoyment as between said members.

Final distribution shall be made of whatever shall remain of said share, per stirpes, among said living issue and free and clear of all trusts, at a time to be chosen by the Trustee, but not later than twenty-one (21) years after the date hereinabove set for said apportionment.

c. If at any time before the final distribution of any of the trust shares herein above described (after taking into consideration all provisions thereof), there shall be no person in existence who is eligible to have the benefit of the trust of such share, then the share in question shall be reapportioned in equal shares among the other shares of the trust estate apportioned pursuant to sub-paragraph 3.D.2. above, and each equal share shall continue to be held and administered in trust or distributed free and clear of all trusts, as the case may be, to or for the benefit of persons then and thereafter living, in accordance with the fortunes of the share to which said reapportionment is made.

3. If, at any time before the final distribution of all of the trust shares hereinabove described, there shall be no person in existence who is eligible to have the benefit of any trust shares, the Trustee shall divide all of the trust estate then remaining into two (2) equal parts which shall be distributed, outright and free of trust, as follows:

   a. One (1) part to those persons then living who would have taken the Grantor's estate, and in such shares thereof as they would have taken, had the Grantor then died intestate, domiciled in New Hampshire; and

   b. One (1) part to those persons then living who would have taken the Grantor's spouse's estate, and in such shares thereof as they would have taken, had Grantor's spouse then died intestate, domiciled in New Hampshire.

E. If the Grantor's residential real estate is held in the trust estate and used by the Grantor's said spouse as a residence, then, during said spouse's lifetime, said spouse shall be permitted exclusive use and occupancy of said residential real estate.

Also, the Grantor's said spouse may, during said spouse's lifetime, in writing, delivered to the Trustee, request the Trustee to sell said residential real estate and to provide a substitute residence, of approximately equal or lesser value to the residence then occupied by the Grantor's said spouse.

Upon receipt of such written request, the Trustee shall then have full power and authority to make reasonable efforts to obtain such substitute residence and to sell the residential real estate then occupied by the Grantor's said spouse.

The costs of selling said residential real estate, of obtaining such substitute residence and of moving the Grantor's said spouse and said spouse's belongings out of said spouse's then occupied residence and into said substitute residence may, in the Trustee's sole discretion, be borne by the trust share to which such real estate has been allocated, to the extent there shall be sufficiently liquid assets to satisfy same.

The Trustee shall have full power and authority to execute any and all documents necessary to carry out the foregoing purpose.

The Trustee shall not be responsible, directly or indirectly, for the success, failure or ultimate satisfaction of the Grantor's said spouse in connection therewith.

The costs and expenses of maintenance and repairs to keep such residential real estate in the same condition it is in at the commencement of said use (reasonable wear and tear excepted), real estate taxes and other normal costs of maintenance and upkeep of said residential real estate, including fire and casualty insurance, may, in the Trustee's sole discretion, be borne by the trust share to which such real estate has been allocated, to the extent there shall be sufficiently liquid assets to satisfy same.

F. Notwithstanding any provision hereinabove to the contrary, the Trustee shall not make any distribution of the Marital Trust, or of income or principal from the Family Trust, to the Grantor's spouse, _____, if the Grantor's said spouse waives testate distribution of the Grantor's will and claims a statutory share of the Grantor's estate under R.S.A. 560:10, or any provisions successor thereto. In such event, the trust estate benefiting the Grantor's spouse shall be administered as if the Grantor's spouse were not then living.

G. The provisions contained hereinabove which require the Trustee to apportion the trust estate into shares and parts of shares are for purposes of computation only and shall not be construed to require the Trustee to make physical segregation of one share or a part of a share from the others, although the Trustee shall have full right to make such segregation if it thinks it better to do so.

Notwithstanding said provisions, the Trustee shall have the full right to regard the trust estate as one undivided estate for purposes of management and investment.

H. If the Grantor or the executor of the Grantor's estate or any other individual (including any individual who shall transfer property in trust hereunder or the executor or administrator of the estate of such individual), has allocated any portion or all of any Generation Skipping Transfer ("GST") exemption provided by Section 2631(a) of the Internal Revenue Code of 1986, as amended, (and any corresponding sections of any future Internal Revenue Code) to any property to be held in trust hereunder, then notwithstanding anything to the contrary contained in this agreement, the Trustee is authorized to establish such number of separate trusts, with identical terms, to hold the property received in trust hereunder as it, in its sole discretion, shall deem advisable, bearing in mind the allocation of the said GST exemption and the desirability that any trust to which all or any portion of the said GST exemption is allocated shall, if practical, have an inclusion ratio of zero.

Further, the Trustee is authorized to allocate such trusts among the trust shares hereinabove created in order to minimize (or eliminate, if possible) any GST tax.

4.   TRUSTEE'S POWERS DURING GRANTOR'S LIFETIME. In the administration of the trust estate, the Trustee shall have all of the powers granted to trustees under Uniform Trustees' Powers Act, R.S.A. 564-A and the Uniform Trust Code, R.S.A. 564-B, as they may be amended from time to time, without restrictions, when their exercise is not inconsistent with the following powers which the Trustee shall have during the lifetime of the Grantor:

A.   The Trustee shall retain as an investment, unless and until the Grantor by a writing delivered to the Trustee shall otherwise direct, all of the securities and other property originally assigned, transferred, or delivered to the Trustee hereunder or at any time forming a part of the trust estate, whether or not such securities or other property be of the character authorized by the laws of the State of New Hampshire for the investment of trust funds.

B.   The Trustee shall purchase, sell, lease, or alter any investment held under this agreement, only in accordance with directions received by it from the Grantor, whether in writing, by telephone call, electronic facsimile transmission, computer message or other current non-written method of business communication, whether or not the investment shall be of the character authorized by the laws of the State of New Hampshire for investment of trust funds. Without intending in any way to limit the powers conferred upon the Trustee by this paragraph, the Trustee is specifically authorized and empowered to retain as investments of the trust estate, or, upon receiving a direction in writing from the Grantor so to do, to invest the whole or any part of the trust estate in common or preferred stocks, or both, of any one or more corporations, or in any non-income-producing securities or other property, or in any so-called wasting investments.

C.   The Trustee is authorized to buy, sell and trade in securities of any nature, on margin, and for such purpose to maintain and operate margin accounts with brokers, and to pledge any securities held or purchased by it with such brokers as security for loans and advances made to the Trustee.

D.   Provided only that it shall have attempted in good faith to comply with directions received by it from the Grantor, the Trustee shall not be responsible or liable in any way for any action taken with respect to any investment of the trust estate, or for any loss or depreciation resulting from the purchase, retention, sale, exchange, lease, or alteration of any investment, or from any want of diversification of the investments of the trust estate, and shall have no duty to advise anyone with respect to the desirability of any such action. The Trustee shall be entitled to assume that the Grantor is still living until it shall have received notice in writing of the Grantor's death.

E. If at any time during the Grantor's lifetime, the Grantor shall deliver to the Trustee a notice in writing signed by the Grantor stating in substance that the Grantor relinquishes the powers hereinabove reserved by the Grantor, then such powers shall cease and terminate, and from and after the delivery of such notice the Trustee shall have those powers with respect to the trust estate given to it under Paragraph 5.

F. If at any time during the Grantor's lifetime, there is delivered to the Trustee other than the Grantor, if any, or, if none, then to the successor Trustee, a written opinion, signed by a licensed physician, stating that the Grantor has become incompetent or incapacitated, then from and after the delivery of such written opinion the Trustee other than the Grantor, or the successor Trustee, as the case may be, shall have those powers and authorities with respect to the trust estate given to it under Paragraph 2. and Paragraph 5.

G. To exercise all the powers, authorities and discretions herein conferred, after the termination of the trust hereunder, until the complete distribution of the trust estate.

H. The Trustee shall have the power and authority to take and hold title to real estate, and to convey any interest in real estate and improvements thereon held in trust, and no purchaser or third party shall be bound to inquire whether the Trustee has said power or is properly exercising said power, or see to the application of any trust asset paid to the Trustee for a conveyance thereof.

I. The Trustee shall have all the necessary banking powers to open and manage financial accounts, including but not limited to, checking accounts, savings accounts, financial accounts and other related financial instruments and to conduct all necessary financial business in reference to the management of the financial assets of the trust.

5. TRUSTEE'S POWERS AFTER GRANTOR'S INCAPACITY OR DEATH. In the administration of the trust estate, the Trustee shall have all of the powers granted to trustees under the Uniform Trustees' Powers Act, R.S.A. 564-A and the Uniform Trust Code, R.S.A. 564-B, as they may be amended from time to time, without restrictions, either after the death or incapacity of the Grantor, or after delivery of the notice referred to in either subparagraph 4.E. or 4.F. above.

In addition to such powers and not in limitation thereof, the Trustee shall have the following powers:

A. To loan funds to the Grantor's estate upon such terms and conditions as to interest rates, maturities, and security as the Trustee shall determine.

B. To make payments, transfers or conveyances, to the extent possible, to the estate of the Grantor (after exhaustion of the assets of the Grantor's estate) to satisfy legacies, bequests or devises, if any, made under the Grantor's will or included in the Grantor's estate for other purposes, if the Grantor's estate shall be insufficient to satisfy such legacies, bequests or devises.

C. To invest in common trust funds.

D. To buy, sell and trade in securities of any nature, on margin, and for such purpose to maintain and operate margin accounts with brokers, and to pledge any securities held or purchased by it with such brokers as security for loans and advances made to the Trustee.

E. To purchase, sell, lease, or alter any investment by buy or sell orders transmitted by it, whether by telephone call, electronic facsimile transmission, computer message or other current non-written method of business communication.

F. To select property, in its absolute discretion, to be allocated to any trust hereunder or to be distributed in satisfaction of any gift provided for herein without respect to the income tax basis of such property, and the Trustee is specifically excused from any duty of impartiality with respect to the income tax basis of such property.

In the event that residential real estate is held in the trust estate, the Trustee may allocate said residential real estate to any trust created hereunder, to be held and administered and disposed of pursuant to the provisions thereof.

G. If, after the death of the Grantor and the Grantor's spouse, _____, THE _____ REVOCABLE TRUST OF 2005, as it may be amended from time to time, is still in existence and the terms of any trust established by said trust are substantially similar to the terms of any trust established by this, THE _____ REVOCABLE TRUST OF 2005, the Trustee is authorized and empowered to consolidate such trust with such similar trust established by THE _____ REVOCABLE TRUST OF 2005 and to administer them as one trust, unless such consolidation shall be contrary to law or inconsistent with the terms of any instrument supplemental hereto.

H. To exercise all the powers, authorities and discretions herein conferred, after the termination of the trust hereunder, until the complete distribution of the trust estate.

I. If, at any time before the final distribution of the principal of either the Marital Trust or the Family Trust hereinabove described, the value of the principal of said trust estate shall be equal to, or less than, ONE HUNDRED THOUSAND DOLLARS ($100,000), then the Trustee may, in its sole discretion, terminate said trust and distribute the principal of said trust, and any accumulated and undistributed income thereof, outright and free of trust, to those persons then entitled to benefit from said trust, and in the proportions in which they are then entitled to benefit from said trust, notwithstanding any provisions of this trust to the contrary.

6. ADDITIONAL PROPERTY. The Grantor, or the Grantor's spouse may, by will, trust or during their lifetimes, from time to time, transfer and deliver to the Trustee cash, securities, and other property acceptable to the Trustee, in addition to the property presently transferred and delivered, and such cash, securities, and other property shall be held, administered, and disposed of by the Trustee in accordance with the provisions of this agreement without the execution of any further instrument or declaration.

7. ACCOUNTING BY TRUSTEE.

A. At any time and from time to time, the Grantor shall have the power, by written instrument signed and acknowledged by the Grantor and delivered to the Trustee, to settle the account of the Trustee with respect to principal or income, or with respect to both principal and income, and to release and discharge the Trustee of and from any and every claim, demand, accountability, and liability of every nature, arising from any matter or thing done or omitted to be done, in connection with this agreement or any trust hereby created, during the period in respect of which the account of the Trustee shall have been so settled.

Every such settlement, release, and discharge shall be conclusive and binding upon, and shall be an absolute protection to the Trustee against all claims of any income beneficiaries, remaindermen, or other persons who might then or thereafter have or claim any interest under this agreement, and no such income beneficiary, remainderman, or other person shall have any right of accounting, any claim, or any cause of action against the Trustee arising from any matter or thing done or omitted to be done in connection with this agreement or any trust hereby created, during any period in respect of which the account of the Trustee shall have been so settled.

B. At any time and from time to time after the death or incapacity of the Grantor, the beneficiary or all of the beneficiaries to whom or to whose use the current net income of the trust estate is at the time authorized or required to be paid or applied and who shall at the time be at least eighteen (18) years of age may, by a written instrument signed and acknowledged by him or them, as the case may be, and delivered to the Trustee, similarly settle the account of the Trustee with respect to principal or to income, or with respect to both principal and income, and release and discharge the Trustee of and from any and every claim, demand, accountability, and liability of every nature, arising from any matter or thing done or omitted to be done, in connection with this agreement or any trust hereby created, during the period in respect of which the account of the Trustee shall have been so settled.

Any such settlement, excepting only for actions of the Trustee which are found by a court of competent jurisdiction to be willfully or intentionally fraudulent, shall have the same effect in respect of the period covered by the account so settled (which period may cover any time prior to as well as after the death or incapacity of the Grantor) as would a settlement made by the Grantor in respect of a period prior to the Grantor's death or incapacity as hereinabove provided.

C. The failure of any person to object in writing to the Trustee to such an account within thirty (30) days after the delivery of the same to such person hereunder shall be final and binding to the same extent as the written approval hereinabove provided.

8. <u>SUCCESSOR TRUSTEE</u>. The following provisions shall govern the addition, removal and succession of the Trustee:

A. The Grantor may, during Grantor's lifetime, add any additional Trustee, or remove any Trustee hereunder and appoint a successor Trustee.

B. If _____ shall be unable or unwilling to serve in the capacity of Trustee for any reason, then the Grantor's spouse, _____, and _____, shall serve in _____ stead.

1. If the Grantor's said spouse shall be unable or unwilling to serve in the capacity of Trustee for any reason, then _____ shall serve in _____ stead.

2. If _____ shall be unable or unwilling to serve in the capacity of Trustee for any reason, then _____ shall serve in _____ stead.

If _____ shall be unable or unwilling to serve in the capacity of Trustee for any reason, then _____ shall serve in _____ stead.

3. In the event there shall be no successor Trustee who shall be able or willing to serve in the capacity of Trustee, then a majority of the beneficiaries to whom or for whose use the current net income of the trust estate is at the time authorized or required to be paid or applied, either,

a. acting individually, if then eighteen (18) years of age, or,

b. by his or her natural parent, or natural guardian, or Court appointed guardian or Court appointed conservator, if then under guardianship or conservatorship, shall appoint a successor Trustee.

C.   In the event that any beneficiary of the trust, other than the Grantor, shall serve in the capacity of co-Trustee, then the discretionary powers to determine whether income or principal is to be distributed to said beneficiary or to any person to whom said beneficiary owes an obligation of support shall be exercisable only by the remaining Trustee.

It is the Grantor's intention by this sub-paragraph to prohibit said beneficiary from benefiting himself or herself as beneficiary in any way by the exercise of such discretionary powers vested in the Trustee as a group.

D.   In the event that any beneficiary of the trust, other than the Grantor, shall serve in the capacity of sole Trustee and the Trustee has discretionary powers to distribute income or principal to himself, herself, or to any person to whom he or she owes an obligation of support, then such distributions of income or principal shall be exercisable by the sole Trustee. The maximum amount that may be withdrawn annually by each such beneficiary under this sub-paragraph, however, shall not exceed the maximum amount over which an individual may have a power of withdrawal without its lapse in such year being deemed to be a release of such power under Section 2514(e) of the Internal Revenue Code of 1986, as amended and any corresponding Sections of any future Internal Revenue Code.

E.   No successor Trustee shall be liable or responsible in any way for any actions or defaults of any predecessor Trustee, nor for any loss or expense from or occasioned by anything done or neglected to be done by any predecessor Trustee. Any successor Trustee shall have, from and after its appointment or succession to office hereunder and without any assignment or other action by any person, all the rights, interests, and powers, including discretionary rights and powers, which are by the provisions of this trust agreement granted to and vested in the Trustee named herein.

9.   FIDUCIARIES. No person dealing with the Trustee shall be responsible for the application of any money, securities, or other property paid or delivered, and the receipt of the Trustee shall be a full discharge; and no person dealing with the Trustee, and no issuer, transfer agent, or other agent of any issuer of any securities shall be under any obligation to ascertain or inquire into the power of the Trustee to purchase, sell, exchange, transfer, mortgage, pledge, create a security interest in, lease, distribute, or otherwise dispose of or deal with any money, securities, or other property.

The Trustee shall not at any time be held liable for any action taken or not taken, including any action intended to lessen or eliminate the impact of estate or generation-skipping transfer taxes with respect to any generation or beneficiary, whether or not such action is successful in achieving the results sought and without regard to its effect on other beneficiaries in the same or different generations, or for any loss or depreciation in the value of any property in any trust created herein, whether due to an error of judgment or otherwise, where the Trustee has exercised good faith and ordinary diligence in the exercise of its duties.

The Trustee shall receive reasonable compensation for its services in the administration of the trusts created herein, including reimbursement for amounts reasonably expended for bookkeeping services, investment services and advice, and other professional or para-professional services. In addition to the compensation herein provided, the Trustee shall receive reasonable compensation for any legal services provided for the benefit of the trust estate, such as handling any litigation involving the trust, preparing state or federal income tax returns, and transferring any real estate.

10.   <u>PERPETUITIES</u>. All trusts established under this instrument shall be exempt from the application of the rule against perpetuities. This provision is intended to comply with New Hampshire R.S.A. 564:24, and accordingly, the Grantor specifically authorizes the Trustee to sell, mortgage or lease property for any period of time beyond the period that is required for an interest created under this instrument to vest in order to be valid under the rule against perpetuities, as measured by the period defined hereinabove.

The trusts created hereunder shall be perpetual to the fullest extent permitted by the governing law. If any trust created hereunder is deemed to be subject to the law of a jurisdiction (including, but only to the extent applicable to real property) that has a rule against perpetuities or similar rule which limits the period during which property can be held in trust, then such trust (other than a trust created by the exercise of a power of appointment conferred hereunder which exercise commences a new rule against perpetuities period under the law of such jurisdiction) shall terminate in all events upon the expiration of the longest period that property may be held in trust under this trust agreement under the law of such jurisdiction (including any applicable period in gross, such as 21 years, 90 years or 110 years); provided, however, that if the jurisdiction has a rule against perpetuities or similar rule which applies only to certain types of property, such as real property, the provisions of this paragraph shall apply only to such property. If under the law of such jurisdiction the longest period that property may be held in trust may be determined (or alternatively determined) with reference to the death of the last survivor of a group of individuals in being upon the date of this trust agreement, those individuals shall consist of all of the descendants of the Grantor's parents who were in being on the date of this trust agreement. Upon termination of a trust pursuant to the provisions of this paragraph, the trust property shall be transferred, conveyed and paid over to the persons then entitled to receive or have the benefit of the income from the trust in the proportions in which they are entitled thereto, or if their interests are indefinite, then in equal shares.

11.   <u>SPENDTHRIFT PROVISION</u>. Except as herein otherwise provided, the interest of any beneficiary hereunder, either as to income or principal, shall not be anticipated, alienated or in any other manner assigned or pledged or promised by

such beneficiary, and shall not be reached by, or be subject to, any legal, equitable or other process, including any bankruptcy or divorce proceeding, or be subject to the interference or control of creditors or others in any way or manner, and all payments to, or the interest of, any beneficiary shall be free from the control or claim of any parent or spouse or former spouse or any other third party. Moreover, no power of appointment or power of withdrawal shall be subject to involuntary exercise. Provided, however, this spendthrift provision shall not restrict the exercise of a disclaimer or the exercise of a power of appointment or withdrawal right granted by this trust agreement.

12.   TAX PROVISION. The trust estate shall not be charged with the payment of any estate, inheritance, legacy, death taxes or duties of any nature (state or federal), or any interest or penalty thereon, except to the extent that the other assets in the Grantor's estate (excluding any assets which may be exempted from the payment of such taxes by the last will of the Grantor) shall be insufficient to discharge such taxes, interest or penalties or shall be insufficiently liquid to satisfy the same. The Trustee may rely conclusively upon written certification from the executor of the Grantor's estate, or if no probate administration of the Grantor's estate is required under applicable law, upon request of the person or persons nominated as executor under the Grantor's will or upon any other evidence, as to the existence of such insufficiency and the amount thereof; provided, however, that the Trustee shall not pay any additional tax imposed under Section 2032A or 2057 of the Internal Revenue Code of 1986, or any provision successor thereto, or any generation-skipping transfer taxes imposed under Chapter 13 of the Internal Revenue Code of 1986, or any provision successor thereto, imposed by reason of the Grantor's death.

If the Trustee shall be required to pay any such taxes, they shall be charged against the principal of the trust estate as an expense without apportionment.

Provided, that in the event that no probate administration of the Grantor's estate is required under applicable law, the Trustee shall have all the powers and authority given the executor under the Grantor's will in relation to such taxes, including all elections and allocation of the generation-skipping transfer tax exemption under Section 2631 of the Internal Revenue Code of 1986, or any provision successor thereto.

13.   DEBTS AND EXPENSES. The trust estate shall not be charged with the payment of legal debts of the Grantor's estate, funeral expenses or expenses of administration of the Grantor's estate except to the extent that the other assets in the Grantor's estate shall be insufficient to discharge such debts and expenses, or shall be insufficiently liquid to satisfy the same. The Trustee may rely conclusively upon written certification from the executor of the Grantor's estate, or if no probate administration of the Grantor's estate is required under applicable law, upon request of the person or persons nominated as executor under the Grantor's will, or upon any other evidence, as to the existence of such insufficiency and the amount thereof. If the Trustee shall be required to pay any such debts and expenses, the same shall be treated as debts and expenses of the trust estate (to the

extent the assets of the Grantor's estate are insufficient to satisfy the same) or as loans to the Grantor's estate (to the extent the liquid assets of the Grantor's estate are insufficient to satisfy the same) if any such debts and expenses are deducted for federal estate tax purposes in computing the value of the Grantor's taxable estate under Section 2053 of the Internal Revenue Code of 1986, or any provision successor thereto.

If any such debts and expenses are either not so deducted or deductible under Section 2053 of the Internal Revenue Code of 1986, or any provision successor thereto, however, the same shall be charged against the principal of the trust estate as an expense without apportionment.

This provision shall confer no rights upon anyone except the executor of the Grantor's estate.

14.   SURVIVAL REQUIREMENT. No person shall be deemed to have survived the Grantor, or any other person or event under the terms of this trust, unless such person survives the end of the period commencing with the close of the calendar day of the Grantor's death, the death of such other person or on which such event occurs, and ending with the close of the thirtieth (30th) calendar day thereafter.

15.   DISTRIBUTIONS TO MINORS. In any case where property or funds become distributable to a minor, then the Trustee shall have the additional power to distribute the same in any one or more of the following ways: (1) by distribution directly to the minor; (2) by distribution to the legal guardian of the minor; (3) by distribution to a parent, relative or friend of the minor for the minor's support in reasonable comfort, education and maintenance in health; (4) by applying the same directly for the minor's support in reasonable comfort, education and maintenance in health; (5) by depositing the same in a bank account in the name of the minor or by transferring property to or purchasing property in the name of a custodian for his or her benefit under a Uniform Law relating to transfers or gifts to minors; or (6) by holding the same hereunder in trust or in custody for the minor's support in reasonable comfort, education and maintenance in health and by distributing the remainder thereof to the minor upon coming of age or otherwise to the minor's estate in case of the death of the minor. The receipt of the person to whom property or funds are actually distributed in accordance with any of the foregoing provisions shall fully discharge the Trustee from further accountability therefor.

16.   GOVERNING LAW AND SITUS. The Grantor declares that this agreement and the trust created hereby shall be construed and administered under the laws of the State of New Hampshire, that the validity and effect of this agreement and of this trust shall be determined in accordance with the laws of that State and that the Trustee shall not be chargeable in any court other than one of the courts of that State.

Further, the trust shall be under the jurisdiction of the courts of the State of New Hampshire and the Trustee shall voluntarily enter a general appearance in any legal action relating to an accounting of the trust or a declaratory judgment interpreting this trust agreement.

The terms of this agreement may not be modified by the Grantor in such manner as to increase the obligations or alter the rates of the commissions of the Trustee without its written consent.

18.   DEFINITIONS. Whenever used in this trust agreement, the words "child," "children," or "issue" are intended to include not only persons who are descendants by blood, but also persons and issue of persons who have been adopted according to law prior to their attaining the age of eighteen (18) years.

Masculine, feminine and neuter pronouns shall each include all genders, and the singular shall include the plural and vice versa, where the context or facts so admit.

The captions and paragraph headings of this trust agreement are inserted only as a matter of convenience and for reference and in no way define, limit or describe the scope or intent of this agreement, nor in any way affect this agreement.

19.   EXECUTION. This trust agreement, and any amendments hereto, shall be effective when executed by the Grantor, notwithstanding that the signature of the Trustee is provided for, the Trustee's signature being intended to denote the acceptance of the Trustee to serve in that capacity only.

This trust agreement may be executed in any number of counterparts with the same effect as if all of the parties had signed the same document. All counterparts shall be construed together and shall constitute one agreement.

_____   _____, Grantor
Witness

_____   _____, Trustee
Witness

STATE OF NEW HAMPSHIRE
COUNTY OF _____

The foregoing instrument was acknowledged before me on _____, 2005, by _____.

_____
Notary Public/Justice of the Peace
My Commission Expires:
(Seal)

Page 645: Substitute this form for Form 38 in the text:

FORM 38   Revocable Trust for a Single Person

THE _____ REVOCABLE TRUST OF _____

TRUST AGREEMENT, made on _____, 2009, between _____, residing in _____, New Hampshire (hereinafter called the "Grantor"), and _____, residing in _____, New Hampshire (hereinafter called the "Trustee").

At the time of the signing of this trust, the Grantor's children are _____, _____ and _____.

1.   <u>TRUST PROPERTY</u>. All property transferred and delivered to the Trustee, which the Trustee may, at any time, hold or acquire, including cash, securities, or other property, shall be referred to collectively as the "trust estate" and held and administered and disposed of by the Trustee for the uses and purposes, and upon the terms and conditions, herein set forth.

2.   <u>DISPOSITIVE PROVISIONS: LIFETIME</u>. The Trustee shall hold, manage, invest and reinvest the trust estate, and shall collect the income thereof and dispose of the net income and principal as follows:

A.   Pay such parts of the income, if any, and such parts of the principal of this trust to, or for the benefit of, the Grantor as the Grantor directs from time to time for the Grantor's support in reasonable comfort, education (including college, graduate, and professional education), and maintenance in health (including medical, dental, hospital, nursing and nursing home expenses). Any income accrued or accumulated at the time of the Grantor's death shall be paid and transferred to principal, to be administered according to the terms hereinafter provided.

B.   In addition, during the lifetime of the Grantor, if the Grantor becomes so incapacitated that the Grantor cannot exercise the Grantor's rights under sub-paragraph 2.A. above, and there are sufficient assets in this trust to do so, the Trustee is authorized to pay such parts of the income, if any, and such parts of the principal of this trust to, or for the benefit of, the Grantor and the Grantor's children as it deems advisable for their support in reasonable comfort, education (including college, graduate, and professional education), and maintenance in health (including medical, dental, hospital, nursing and nursing home expenses), taking into consideration the amount of their income from sources other than this trust.

It is the Grantor's intention that the support in reasonable comfort, education (including college, graduate, and professional education), and maintenance in health (including medical, dental, hospital, nursing and nursing home expenses) of the Grantor shall be of primary concern, and the Trustee shall exercise its discretion in using principal for the Grantor, considering all other beneficiaries to be secondary and without liability to any other beneficiary for the use of principal for the Grantor.

153

C. Further, the Trustee is authorized to give, transfer or convey any of the trust estate to persons of the Grantor's natural affection to whom the Grantor would normally consider making such gifts, transfers or conveyances, whether outright or in trust, having in mind the ultimate objective of such gifts, transfers or conveyances is either (i) the qualification for state or federal medical, welfare or other assistance programs for the Grantor's benefit, or (ii) the reduction of the state and federal estate, inheritance, transfer, legacy and succession taxes and any interest and penalties thereon imposed by reason of the Grantor's death.

3. DISPOSITIVE PROVISIONS: AFTER DEATH. Upon the death of the Grantor, the trust estate shall be held and administered and disposed of as follows:

A. The Trustee shall distribute all items of tangible personal property and household effects which are then part of the trust estate, including furniture, clothing, jewelry, silver, books, pictures, china, automobiles and their equipment, other vehicles and their equipment, and other articles of personal and household use or ornament, outright and free of trust, to the Grantor's issue who survive the Grantor, such issue to take per stirpes.

The Grantor expresses the hope that said beneficiaries will dispose of said tangible personal property and household effects according to the Grantor's wishes, however said wishes may be made known to them.

If a division of the property under this distribution is required among the beneficiaries, such division shall be made by the beneficiaries, in appropriate shares, as they may amicably agree.

The Grantor prefers that said beneficiaries shall agree upon the manner in which said property is to be divided, but should they not agree among themselves as to the division thereof within ninety (90) days after the Grantor's death, the Trustee shall have full power and authority to divide said property among said beneficiaries, in appropriate shares, and its determination with respect thereto shall, insofar as permitted by law, be binding and conclusive upon such beneficiaries.

B. After the distributions, if any, in sub-paragraph 3.A. above, all of the remaining trust estate shall be held and administered and disposed of as follows:

1. So long as the youngest living child of the Grantor shall be less than twenty-five (25) years of age, the Trustee may pay over to the children of the Grantor or may use, apply or expend for their direct or indirect benefit, so much of the income and principal of the trust estate, at such times and in such proportions as the Trustee may determine, in its sole, absolute, and uncontrolled discretion, for their support in reasonable comfort, education (including college, graduate, and professional

education), and maintenance in health (including medical, dental, hospital, nursing and nursing home expenses).

Such payments or applications need not be apportioned equally among said children, but may be made according to their needs, as determined by the Trustee, taking into consideration their respective ages, talents, educational needs, health and other available resources.

   a. If any child of the Grantor has predeceased the Grantor leaving issue then living or shall die leaving issue then living during the administration of the trust estate under the provisions of this sub-paragraph, the Trustee may pay over to or may use, apply or expend for the direct or indirect benefit of such issue, so much of the income and principal of the trust estate, at such times and in such proportions as the Trustee may determine, in its sole, absolute, and uncontrolled discretion, for their support in reasonable comfort, education (including college, graduate, and professional education), and maintenance in health (including medical, dental, hospital, nursing and nursing home expenses).

   Such payments or applications need not be apportioned equally among said issue, but may be made according to their needs, as determined by the Trustee, taking into consideration their respective ages, talents, educational needs, health and other available resources.

   b. It is the Grantor's hope and desire that the benefit accorded to such issue, as a group, would approximate the benefit which would have been accorded to the Grantor's deceased child, the parent of such issue.

   The Trustee's determinations hereunder, however, shall be final.

2. At such time when the youngest of the Grantor's living children shall have reached the age of twenty-five (25) years, whether at the time of the death of the Grantor or thereafter, or at such time when all of the Grantor's children shall be deceased before the youngest has reached the age of twenty-five (25) years, whichever event shall first occur, the Trustee shall apportion the remaining principal and undistributed income of the trust estate into equal shares as follows:

   one (1) such share to each of the Grantor's living children, and

   one (1) such share to each family group composed of the living issue of any child of the Grantor who is then deceased.

   Said equal shares shall then be held and administered and disposed of as follows:

   a. In the case of each share apportioned to a living child of the

155

Grantor, the Trustee may, in each and every year beginning with the date of said apportionment, pay over to said child or use, apply or expend for said child's direct or indirect benefit, so much or all of the net income or principal of said share as the Trustee may, in its sole, absolute, and uncontrolled discretion, deem wise and safely consistent with said child's support in reasonable comfort, education (including college, graduate, and professional education), and maintenance in health (including medical, dental, hospital, nursing and nursing home expenses).

i. Whenever, at or after said time of apportionment, said child shall have attained the age of twenty-five (25) years, he shall have the right to request in writing and to receive one-third (1/3) of the balance of his share; and

ii. Whenever, at or after said time of apportionment, said child shall have attained the age of thirty (30) years, he shall have the right to request in writing and to receive an additional one-half (1/2) of the balance of his share; and

iii. Whenever, at or after said time of apportionment, said child shall have attained the age of forty (40) years, he shall have the right to request in writing and to receive the entire balance of his share, at which time his trust shall terminate.

iv. It is the Grantor's belief that, in some circumstances, it may be beneficial for said child to leave the management of his trust share in the hands of the Trustee. Therefore, said child may elect to leave his trust share, or any portion thereof, in the hands of the Trustee, as a separate fund, to be held and administered and disposed of as said child shall direct.

v. The share held by the Trustee for the benefit of a child as described above shall, from the time of the death of said child after the time above set for apportionment into shares, be administered for the benefit of said child's issue in the manner described below.

b. In the case of each share apportioned to the living issue of a deceased child of the Grantor, said share shall be administered for the benefit as a family group of such of the issue of said deceased child as from time to time shall be living.

The Trustee may pay over to the issue, or may use, apply or expend for their direct or indirect benefit, so much of the income and principal of the trust estate, at such times and in such proportions as the Trustee may determine, in its sole, absolute, and uncontrolled discretion, for support in reasonable comfort, education, (including college, graduate, and professional education), and maintenance in health (including medical, dental, hospital, nursing and nursing home expenses).

The Trustee may make such payments, use, application, expenditure or accumulation of the income and principal thereof as it shall think proper for the direct or indirect benefit of the members of said family group without being required to observe any precept or rule of equality of enjoyment as between said members.

Final distribution shall be made of whatever shall remain of said share, per stirpes, among said living issue and free and clear of all trusts when the youngest then living child of the Grantor's deceased child attains the age of thirty (30) years.

c. If at any time before the final distribution of any of the trust shares hereinabove described (after taking into consideration all provisions thereof), there shall be no person in existence who is eligible to have the benefit of the trust of such share, then the share in question shall be reapportioned in equal shares among the other shares of the trust estate apportioned pursuant to sub-paragraph 3.B.2. above, and each equal share shall continue to be held and administered in trust, or distributed free and clear of all trusts, as the case may be, to or for the benefit of persons then and thereafter living, in accordance with the fortunes of the share to which said reapportionment is made.

3. If, at any time before the final distribution of all of the trust shares hereinabove described, there shall be no person in existence who is eligible to have the benefit of any trust shares, the Trustee shall distribute all of the trust estate then remaining, outright and free of trust, to those persons then living who would have taken the Grantor's estate, and in such shares thereof as they would have taken, had the Grantor then died intestate, domiciled in New Hampshire.

C. The provisions contained hereinabove which require the Trustee to apportion the trust estate into shares and parts of shares are for purposes of computation only and shall not be construed to require the Trustee to make physical segregation of one share or a part of a share from the others, although the Trustee shall have full right to make such segregation if it thinks it better to do so.

Notwithstanding said provisions, the Trustee shall have the full right to regard the trust estate as one undivided estate for purposes of management and investment.

D. If the Grantor or the executor of the Grantor's estate or any other individual (including any individual who shall transfer property in trust hereunder or the executor or administrator of the estate of such individual), has allocated any portion or all of any Generation Skipping Transfer ("GST") exemption provided by Section 2631(a) of the Internal Revenue Code to any property to be held in trust hereunder, then notwithstanding anything to the contrary contained in this agreement, the Trustee is authorized to establish such number of separate trusts, with identical terms, to hold the property received in trust hereunder as it, in its sole, absolute, and uncontrolled discretion, shall deem advisable, bearing in mind the allocation of the said GST exemption and the desirability that any trust to which all or any portion of the said GST exemption is allocated shall, if practical, have an inclusion ratio of zero.

Further, the Trustee is authorized to allocate such trusts among the trust shares hereinabove created in order to minimize (or eliminate, if possible) any GST tax.

4.   <u>TRUSTEE'S POWERS</u>. In the administration of the trust estate, the Trustee shall have all of the powers granted to trustees by New Hampshire common law and statutory authority (including, but not limited to, the Uniform Trustees' Powers Act, R.S.A. 564-A, and the Uniform Trust Code, R.S.A. 564-B, as they may be amended from time to time), without restrictions.

In addition to such power, and not in limitation thereof, the Trustee shall have the following powers, all of which shall be exercised in a fiduciary capacity and for the benefit of the beneficiaries:

A.   During the lifetime of the Grantor, the Trustee may retain as an investment, unless and until the Grantor by a writing delivered to the Trustee shall otherwise direct, all of the securities and other property originally assigned, transferred, or delivered to the Trustee hereunder or at any time forming a part of the trust estate, whether or not such securities or other property be of the character authorized by the laws of the State of New Hampshire for the investment of trust funds.

Upon the death or incapacity of the Grantor, the Trustee is authorized to purchase, sell, lease, or alter any investment by buy or sell orders transmitted by it, whether by telephone call, electronic facsimile transmission, computer message or other current non-written method of business communication.

B.   To buy, sell and trade in securities of any nature, [on margin], and for such purpose to maintain and operate [margin] accounts with brokers, and to pledge any securities held or purchased by it with such brokers as security for loans and advances made to the Trustee.

C.   *[For Corporate Trustees]* To retain the property of the trust estate in the same investments as when received by it or to vary and transpose such investments and to invest and reinvest the property of the trust estate in such manner and in such securities or other property (including common trust funds or similar funds for the participation of trusts of which _____ is trustee and including securities of _____ and any successor thereto) as it in its uncontrolled discretion shall deem best without accountability for any loss for so doing and without liability for depreciation occasioned by so doing even though the property so retained or the investments so made may not be of the character permitted for the investment of trust funds under the laws of the State of New Hampshire or any other state or federal law.

D. To take and hold title to real estate, and to convey any interest in real estate and improvements thereon held in trust, and no purchaser or third party shall be bound to inquire whether the Trustee has said power or is properly exercising said power, or see to the application of any trust asset paid to the Trustee for a conveyance thereof.

E. To have all of the necessary banking powers to open and manage financial accounts, including but not limited to, checking accounts, savings accounts, financial accounts and other related financial instruments and to conduct all necessary financial business in reference to the management of the financial assets of the trust.

F. To rent a safe deposit box and to retain such assets in said box as the Trustee, in its sole, absolute, and uncontrolled discretion, determines appropriate.

G. To borrow money, with or without security, and mortgage or pledge trust property for a period within or extending beyond the duration of the trust.

H. To loan funds to the Grantor's estate upon such terms and conditions as to interest rates, maturities, and security as the Trustee shall determine.

I. To make payments, transfers or conveyances, to the extent possible, to the estate of the Grantor (after exhaustion of the assets of the Grantor's estate) to satisfy legacies, bequests or devises, if any, made under the Grantor's will or included in the Grantor's estate for other purposes, if the Grantor's estate shall be insufficient to satisfy such legacies, bequests or devises.

J. To invest in common trust funds.

K. To select property, in its sole, absolute, and uncontrolled discretion, to be allocated to any trust hereunder or to be distributed in satisfaction of any gift provided for herein without respect to the income tax basis of such property, and the Trustee is specifically excused from any duty of impartiality with respect to the income tax basis of such property.

L. If at any time during the Grantor's lifetime, there is delivered to the Trustee other than the Grantor, if any, or, if none, then to the successor Trustee, a written opinion, signed by a licensed physician, stating that the

Grantor has become incompetent or incapacitated, then from and after the delivery of such written opinion the Trustee other than the Grantor, or the successor Trustee, as the case may be, shall have those powers and authorities with respect to the trust estate given to the Trustee in this trust agreement.

M. Regardless of the extent of the authority that the Trustee holds to currently distribute income and/or principal of the trust estate to one or more beneficiaries of the trust, the Trustee shall have full power and authority, to be exercised in its sole, absolute, and uncontrolled discretion, to appoint any or all assets held in this trust estate to any other trust or trusts created under will, deed or otherwise, for the benefit of one or more of the beneficiaries hereunder.

This authority shall be subject to the limitations set forth in R.S.A. 564-B:4-418, as amended from time to time, provided that such appointment clause shall be null and void in the event there is a determination that the application of such clause shall result in the inclusion of any of the trust estate in the Grantor's gross estate under any provision of the Internal Revenue Code, including but not limited to Sections 2041 and 2042, which would not otherwise be includable in the Grantor's gross estate.

Provided further, however, that if this Trust qualifies as a "trust instrument" under the Qualified Dispositions in Trust Act, R.S.A. 564-D, as amended from time to time, then the Trustee may only appoint the assets of the trust estate to a new trust which will continue to qualify as a "trust instrument" under such Act and will provide similar protections to the assets held in this trust estate.

N. If, at any time before the final distribution of the principal of any trust share hereinabove described, the value of the principal of said trust share shall be equal to, or less than, ONE HUNDRED THOUSAND DOLLARS ($100,000), then the Trustee may, in its sole discretion, terminate said trust share and distribute the principal of said trust share, and any accumulated and undistributed income thereof, outright and free of trust, to those persons then entitled to benefit from said trust share, and in the proportions in which they are then entitled to benefit from said trust share, notwithstanding any provisions of this trust to the contrary.

O. To exercise all the powers, authorities and discretions herein conferred, after the termination of the trust hereunder, until the complete distribution of the trust estate.

5.   ADDITIONAL PROPERTY. The Grantor, may, by will, trust or during Grantor's lifetime, from time to time, transfer and deliver to the Trustee cash, securities, and other property acceptable to the Trustee, in addition to the property presently transferred and delivered, and such cash, securities, and other property

shall be held, administered, and disposed of by the Trustee in accordance with the provisions of this agreement without the execution of any further instrument or declaration.

6.   <u>REPORTING BY TRUSTEE</u>.

A.   At any time and from time to time, the Grantor shall have the power, by written instrument signed and acknowledged by the Grantor and delivered to the Trustee, to settle the report of the Trustee with respect to principal or income, or with respect to both principal and income, and to release and discharge the Trustee of and from any and every claim, demand, accountability, and liability of every nature, arising from any matter or thing done or omitted to be done, in connection with this agreement or any trust hereby created, during the period in respect of which the report of the Trustee shall have been so settled.

Every such settlement, release, and discharge shall be conclusive and binding upon, and shall be an absolute protection to the Trustee against all claims of any income beneficiaries, remaindermen, or other persons who might then or thereafter have or claim any interest under this agreement, and no such income beneficiary, remainderman, or other person shall have any right of accounting, reporting, any claim, or any cause of action against the Trustee arising from any matter or thing done or omitted to be done in connection with this agreement or any trust hereby created, during any period in respect of which the report of the Trustee shall have been so settled.

B.   After the death or incapacity of the Grantor, the Trustee may, at the Trustee's sole, absolute, and uncontrolled discretion, and shall, to the extent required by the Uniform Trust Code, R.S.A. 564-B, as it may be amended from time to time, render a Trustee's report as described in the Uniform Trust Code, as it may be amended from time to time, at such intervals as the Trustee may choose or at such times as required by the Uniform Trust Code.

C.   A recipient of such a report (or, if under guardianship or conservatorship, then by the Guardian or Conservator, or, if deceased, then by the Executor or Administrator), may, by a written instrument, assent to the report of the Trustee with respect to principal or to income, or with respect to both principal and income.

The assent of the recipient of such report (or, if under guardianship or conservatorship, then by the Guardian or Conservator, or, if deceased, then by the Executor or Administrator) shall make such report binding and conclusive upon all persons then having or who may thereafter have any interest, vested or contingent, in the income or principal of the trust estate and such assent shall forever release and discharge the Trustee of and from any and every claim, demand, accountability, and liability of

161

every nature, arising from any matter or thing done or omitted to be done, in connection with this agreement or any trust hereby created, during the period in respect of which the report of the Trustee shall have been so settled.

D.   The failure of any person to object in writing to the Trustee to such a report within thirty (30) days after the delivery of the same to such person hereunder shall be final and binding to the same extent as the written assent hereinabove provided.

E.   Any person entitled to such a report, accounting, information, notice and the like (or, if under guardianship or conservatorship, then by the Guardian or Conservator, or, if deceased, then by the Executor or Administrator) may by a written instrument signed and acknowledged by him or her or them, as the case may be, and delivered to the Trustee, waive the right to said Trustee's report or to other information otherwise required to be furnished under the Uniform Trust Code, as it may be amended from time to time.

7.   <u>SUCCESSOR TRUSTEE</u>. The following provisions shall govern the addition, removal and succession of the Trustee:

A.   The Grantor may, during the Grantor's lifetime, add any additional Trustee, or remove any Trustee hereunder and appoint a successor Trustee.

B.   If _____ shall be unable or unwilling to serve in the capacity of Trustee for any reason, then _____ shall serve in his/her stead.

If _____ shall be unable or unwilling to serve in the capacity of Trustee for any reason, then _____ shall serve in his/her stead.

If _____ shall be unable or unwilling to serve in the capacity of Trustee for any reason, then _____ shall serve in his/her stead.

C.   In the event there shall be no successor Trustee who shall be able or willing to serve in the capacity of Trustee, then a majority of the beneficiaries to whom or for whose use the current net income of the trust estate is at the time authorized or required to be paid or applied, either,

1.   acting individually, if then eighteen (18) years of age, or,

2.   by his or her natural parent, or natural guardian, or Court appointed guardian or Court appointed conservator, if then under guardianship or conservatorship,

shall appoint a successor Trustee.

D.   In the event that any beneficiary of the trust, other than the Grantor, shall serve in the capacity of co-Trustee, then the discretionary powers to determine whether income or principal is to be distributed to said beneficiary or to any person to whom said beneficiary owes an obligation of support shall be exercisable only by the remaining Trustee.

It is the Grantor's intention by this sub-paragraph to prohibit said beneficiary from benefiting himself or herself as beneficiary in any way by the exercise of such discretionary powers vested in the Trustee as a group.

E. In the event that any beneficiary of the trust, other than the Grantor, shall serve in the capacity of sole Trustee and the Trustee has discretionary powers to distribute income or principal to himself, herself, or to any person to whom he or she owes an obligation of support, then such distributions of income or principal shall be exercisable by the sole Trustee. The maximum amount that may be withdrawn annually by each such beneficiary under this sub-paragraph, however, shall not exceed the maximum amount over which an individual may have a power of withdrawal without its lapse in such year being deemed to be a release of such power under Section 2514(e) of the Internal Revenue Code.

F. No successor Trustee shall be liable or responsible in any way for any actions or defaults of any predecessor Trustee, nor for any loss or expense from or occasioned by anything done or neglected to be done by any predecessor Trustee. Any successor Trustee shall have, from and after its appointment or succession to office hereunder and without any assignment or other action by any person, all the rights, interests, and powers, including discretionary rights and powers, which are by the provisions of this trust agreement granted to and vested in the Trustee named herein.

8. <u>FIDUCIARIES</u>. No person dealing with the Trustee shall be responsible for the application of any money, securities, or other property paid or delivered, and the receipt of the Trustee shall be a full discharge; and no person dealing with the Trustee, and no issuer, transfer agent, or other agent of any issuer of any securities shall be under any obligation to ascertain or inquire into the power of the Trustee to purchase, sell, exchange, transfer, mortgage, pledge, create a security interest in, lease, distribute, or otherwise dispose of or deal with any money, securities, or other property.

The Trustee shall not at any time be held liable for any action taken or not taken, including any action intended to lessen or eliminate the impact of estate or generation-skipping transfer taxes with respect to any generation or beneficiary, whether or not such action is successful in achieving the results sought and without regard to its effect on other beneficiaries in the same or different generations, or for any loss or depreciation in the value of any property in any trust created herein, whether due to an error of judgment or otherwise, where the Trustee has exercised good faith and ordinary diligence in the exercise of its duties.

The Trustee shall receive reasonable compensation for its services in the administration of the trusts created herein, including reimbursement for amounts reasonably expended for bookkeeping services, investment services and advice, and other professional or paraprofessional services. In addition to the compensation herein provided, the Trustee shall receive reasonable compensation for any legal services provided for the benefit of the trust estate, such as handling any litigation involving the trust, preparing state or federal income tax returns, and transferring any real estate.

9.   PERPETUITIES. All trusts established under this instrument shall be exempt from the application of the rule against perpetuities. This provision is intended to comply with New Hampshire R.S.A. 564:24, and accordingly, the Grantor specifically authorizes the Trustee to sell, mortgage or lease property for any period of time beyond the period that is required for an interest created under this instrument to vest in order to be valid under the rule against perpetuities, as measured by the period defined hereinabove.

The trusts created hereunder shall be perpetual to the fullest extent permitted by the governing law. If any trust created hereunder is deemed to be subject to the law of a jurisdiction (including, but only to the extent applicable to real property) that has a rule against perpetuities or similar rule which limits the period during which property can be held in trust, then such trust (other than a trust created by the exercise of a power of appointment conferred hereunder which exercise commences a new rule against perpetuities period under the law of such jurisdiction) shall terminate in all events upon the expiration of the longest period that property may be held in trust under this trust agreement under the law of such jurisdiction (including any applicable period in gross, such as 21 years, 90 years or 110 years); provided, however, that if the jurisdiction has a rule against perpetuities or similar rule which applies only to certain types of property, such as real property, the provisions of this paragraph shall apply only to such property. If under the law of such jurisdiction the longest period that property may be held in trust may be determined (or alternatively determined) with reference to the death of the last survivor of a group of individuals in being upon the date of this trust agreement, those individuals shall consist of all of the descendants of the Grantor's parents who were in being on the date of this trust agreement. Upon termination of a trust pursuant to the provisions of this paragraph, the trust property shall be transferred, conveyed and paid over to the persons then entitled to receive or have the benefit of the income from the trust in the proportions in which they are entitled thereto, or if their interests are indefinite, then in equal shares.

10.   SPENDTHRIFT PROVISION. Except as herein otherwise provided, the interest of any beneficiary hereunder, either as to income or principal, shall not be anticipated, alienated or in any other manner assigned or pledged or promised by such beneficiary, and shall not be reached by, or be subject to, any legal, equitable or other process, including any bankruptcy or divorce proceeding, or be subject to the interference or control of creditors or others in any way or manner, and all payments to, or the interest of, any beneficiary shall be free from the control or claim of any parent or spouse or former spouse or any other third party. Moreover,

no power of appointment or power of withdrawal shall be subject to involuntary exercise. Provided, however, this spendthrift provision shall not restrict the exercise of a disclaimer or the exercise of a power of appointment or withdrawal right granted by this trust agreement. This provision is intended to be a material provision of this trust and any other trust established hereunder.

11.   TAX PROVISION. The trust estate shall not be charged with the payment of any estate, inheritance, legacy, death taxes or duties of any nature (state or federal), or any interest or penalty thereon, except to the extent that the other assets in the Grantor's estate (excluding any assets which may be exempted from the payment of such taxes by the last will of the Grantor) shall be insufficient to discharge such taxes, interest or penalties or shall be insufficiently liquid to satisfy the same. The Trustee may rely conclusively upon written certification from the executor of the Grantor's estate, or if no probate administration of the Grantor's estate is required under applicable law, upon request of the person or persons nominated as executor under the Grantor's will or upon any other evidence, as to the existence of such insufficiency and the amount thereof; provided, however, that the Trustee shall not pay any additional tax imposed under Section 2032A or 2057 of the Internal Revenue Code or any generation-skipping transfer taxes imposed under Chapter 13 of the Internal Revenue Code imposed by reason of the Grantor's death.

If the Trustee shall be required to pay any such taxes, they shall be charged against the principal of the trust estate as an expense without apportionment.

Provided, that in the event that no probate administration of the Grantor's estate is required under applicable law, the Trustee shall have all the powers and authority given the executor under the Grantor's will in relation to such taxes, including all elections and allocation of the generation-skipping transfer tax exemption under Section 2631 of the Internal Revenue Code.

12.   DEBTS AND EXPENSES. The trust estate shall not be charged with the payment of legal debts of the Grantor's estate, funeral expenses or expenses of administration of the Grantor's estate except to the extent that the other assets in the Grantor's estate shall be insufficient to discharge such debts and expenses, or shall be insufficiently liquid to satisfy the same. The Trustee may rely conclusively upon written certification from the executor of the Grantor's estate, or if no probate administration of the Grantor's estate is required under applicable law, upon request of the person or persons nominated as executor under the Grantor's will, or upon any other evidence, as to the existence of such insufficiency and the amount thereof. If the Trustee shall be required to pay any such debts and expenses, the same shall be treated as debts and expenses of the trust estate (to the extent the assets of the Grantor's estate are insufficient to satisfy the same) or as loans to the Grantor's estate (to the extent the liquid assets of the Grantor's estate are insufficient to satisfy the same) if any such debts and expenses are deducted for federal estate tax purposes in computing the value of the Grantor's taxable estate under Section 2053 of the Internal Revenue Code.

If any such debts and expenses are either not so deducted or deductible under

Section 2053 of the Internal Revenue Code, however, the same shall be charged against the principal of the trust estate as an expense without apportionment.

This provision shall confer no rights upon anyone except the executor of the Grantor's estate.

13.   SURVIVAL REQUIREMENT. No person shall be deemed to have survived the Grantor, or any other person or event under the terms of this trust, unless such person survives the end of the period commencing with the close of the calendar day of the Grantor's death, the death of such other person or on which such event occurs, and ending with the close of the thirtieth (30th) calendar day thereafter.

14.   DISTRIBUTIONS TO MINORS. In any case where property or funds become distributable to a minor, then the Trustee shall have the additional power to distribute the same in any one or more of the following ways: (1) by distribution directly to the minor; (2) by distribution to the legal guardian of the minor; (3) by distribution to a parent, relative or friend of the minor for the minor's support in reasonable comfort, education and maintenance in health; (4) by applying the same directly for the minor's support in reasonable comfort, education and maintenance in health; (5) by depositing the same in a bank account in the name of the minor or by transferring property to or purchasing property in the name of a custodian for his or her benefit under a Uniform Law relating to transfers or gifts to minors; or (6) by holding the same hereunder in trust or in custody for the minor's support in reasonable comfort, education and maintenance in health and by distributing the remainder thereof to the minor upon coming of age or otherwise to the minor's estate in case of the death of the minor. The receipt of the person to whom property or funds are actually distributed in accordance with any of the foregoing provisions shall fully discharge the Trustee from further accountability therefor.

15.   GOVERNING LAW AND SITUS. The Grantor declares that this agreement and the trust created hereby shall be construed and administered under the laws of the State of New Hampshire, that the validity and effect of this agreement and of this trust shall be determined in accordance with the laws of that State.

Further, the trust shall be under the jurisdiction of the courts of the State of New Hampshire and the Trustee shall voluntarily enter a general appearance in any legal action relating to an accounting of the trust or a declaratory judgment interpreting this trust agreement. The Trustee shall not be chargeable in any court other than one of the courts of that State.

16.   AMENDMENT AND REVOCATION. The Grantor reserves the right at any time or from time to time without the consent of any person and without notice to any person other than the Trustee to revoke or modify the trust hereby created, in whole or in part, to change the beneficiaries hereof, or to withdraw the whole or any part of the trust estate by filing notice of such revocation, modification, change, or withdrawal with the Trustee; provided, however, that the

terms of this agreement may not be modified by the Grantor in such manner as to increase the obligations or alter the rates of the commissions of the Trustee without its written consent.

17.   DEFINITIONS. Whenever used in this trust agreement, the words "child," "children," or "issue" are intended to include not only persons who are descendants by blood, but also persons and issue of persons who have been adopted according to law prior to their attaining the age of eighteen (18) years.

References to the "Internal Revenue Code" or "Code" or to provisions thereof are to the Internal Revenue Code of 1986, as amended at the time in question. References to the "Treasury Regulations," "Regulations" and "Regs." are to the Treasury Regulations under the Code. If, by the time in question, a particular provision of the Code has been renumbered, or the Code has been superseded by a subsequent federal tax law, the reference shall be deemed to be to the renumbered provision or the corresponding provision of the subsequent law, unless to do so would clearly be contrary to the Grantor's intent as expressed in this Trust Agreement, and a similar rule shall apply to references to the Regulations.

Masculine, feminine and neuter pronouns shall each include all genders, and the singular shall include the plural and vice versa, where the context or facts so admit.

The captions and paragraph headings of this trust agreement are inserted only as a matter of convenience and for reference and in no way define, limit or describe the scope or intent of this agreement, nor in any way affect this agreement.

18.   EXECUTION. This trust agreement, and any amendments hereto, shall be effective when executed by the Grantor, notwithstanding that the signature of the Trustee is provided for, the Trustee's signature being intended to denote the acceptance of the Trustee to serve in that capacity only.

This trust agreement may be executed in any number of counterparts with the same effect as if all of the parties had signed the same document. All counterparts shall be construed together and shall constitute one agreement.

_____   _____
Witness   _____ , Grantor
_____   _____
Witness   _____ , Trustee

STATE OF NEW HAMPSHIRE
COUNTY OF _____

The foregoing instrument was acknowledged before me on _____, 2009, by _____.

Notary Public/Justice of the Peace
My Commission Expires:
(Seal)

Page 663: Substitute this form for Form 39 in the text:

FORM 39   **Testamentary Trust**
LAST WILL
OF

I, _____, of _____, County of _____, State of New Hampshire, do make this will and hereby revoke all other wills and codicils previously made by me.

1.   <u>DEBTS, EXPENSES AND TAXES</u>. I direct that all my legal debts, funeral expenses and expenses of administration be paid as soon after my death as practical. I further direct that all such debts and expenses, as well as all estate, inheritance, transfer, legacy or succession taxes (state and federal), and any interest or penalties thereon which may be assessed or imposed with respect to my estate, or any part thereof, wheresoever situated, whether or not passing under my will, including the taxable value of all policies of insurance on my life and all transfers, powers, rights or interests includible in my estate for purposes of such taxes and duties, shall be paid out of my residuary estate as an expense of administration and without apportionment, and shall not be prorated or charged against any of the other gifts in this will or against property not passing under this will.

2.   <u>REAL ESTATE</u>. If my spouse, _____, survives me, I give and devise to my said spouse absolutely, all of my right, title and interest, whatever it may be, in the real estate used as our home property or properties at the time of my death. If my said spouse does not survive me, said home property or properties shall be given and devised to my issue who so survive me, such issue to take <u>per stirpes</u>.

3.   <u>TANGIBLE PERSONAL PROPERTY</u>. If my spouse, _____, survives me, I give and bequeath to my said spouse absolutely, all of my tangible personal property and household effects owned by me at the time of my death, including furniture, clothing, jewelry, silver, books, pictures, china, automobiles and their equipment, other vehicles and their equipment, and other articles of personal and household use or ornament. If my said spouse does not survive me, I give and bequeath the same absolutely, to my issue who so survive me, such issue to take <u>per stirpes</u>.

I express the hope that said beneficiaries will dispose of said tangible personal property and household effects according to my wishes, however my wishes may be made known to them, but I expressly declare that I do not intend to create any trust in law or in equity with respect to said tangible personal property.

If a division of the property under this bequest is required among the beneficiaries, such division shall be made by the beneficiaries, in appropriate shares, as they may amicably agree. I prefer that said beneficiaries shall agree upon the manner in which said property is to be divided, but should they not agree

169

among themselves as to the division thereof within ninety (90) days after my death, I give my executor full power and authority to divide said property among said beneficiaries, in appropriate shares, and his determination with respect thereto shall, insofar as permitted by law, be binding and conclusive upon such beneficiaries.

4.   <u>RESIDUARY ESTATE</u>. All the rest, residue and remainder of my estate, of whatever kind or nature, wherever found and however acquired, including any property over which I have a power of appointment, I give, devise and bequeath to my spouse, _____, if she survives me.

If my said spouse does not survive me, then all the rest, residue and remainder of my estate, of whatever kind or nature, wherever found and however acquired, including any property over which I have a power of appointment, I give, devise and bequeath to my trustee, in trust, and my trustee shall apportion said residue into equal shares as follows: one (1) such share to each of my then living children, and one (1) such share to each family group composed of the living issue of any child of mine who is then deceased.

Said equal shares shall then be held and administered and distributed as follows:

A. In the case of each share apportioned to a living child of mine, said share shall be held by my trustee, and my trustee may, in each and every year beginning with the date of said apportionment, pay over to such child so much or all of the net income from the said share for that year as my trustee, in his sole discretion, shall determine, said payments to be made at least annually; and

My trustee shall also have full power and authority, to be exercised in his sole and uncontrolled discretion, to pay over to such child or to use, apply or expend for such child's direct or indirect benefit, so much or all of the principal as he shall deem wise and safely consistent with such child's support in reasonable comfort, education (including college and professional education), and maintenance in health (including medical, dental, hospital, nursing and nursing home expenses).

1. Whenever, at or after said time of apportionment, such child shall have attained the age of _____ (_____) years, he shall have the right to request in writing and to receive distribution of the principal of his share, and any undistributed income, at which time his trust, if so requested and received, shall terminate.

However, it is my belief that, in some circumstances, it may be beneficial for such child to leave his trust share in the hands of the trustee. Therefore, such child may elect to leave his trust share, or any portion thereof, in the hands of the trustee, as a separate fund, to be held and managed and distributed as such child shall direct.

2. If such child shall die while a trust is still being administered for his benefit, the share held by my trustee for the benefit of such child as hereinabove described shall, from the time of the death of such child after the time hereinabove set for apportionment into shares, be administered

for the benefit of such child's issue in the manner hereinbelow described in sub-paragraph 4.B., except that the period of twenty-one (21) years therein specified shall, for the purposes of this sub-paragraph, be taken to run from the date of such child's death.

B. Each share apportioned to the living issue of a deceased child of mine shall be administered for the benefit as a family group of such of the issue of said deceased child as from time to time shall be living; and my trustee may make such payments, use, application, expenditure or accumulation of the income and principal thereof as he shall think proper for the direct or indirect benefit of the members of said family group, without being required to observe any precept or rule of equality of enjoyment as between said members.

Final distribution shall be made of whatever shall remain of said share, per stirpes, among said living issue and free and clear of all trusts, at a time to be chosen by my trustee but not later than twenty-one (21) years after the date hereinabove set for said apportionment.

C. If, at any time before the final distribution of any of the trust shares described above, there shall be no person in existence who is eligible to have the benefit of such trust share, then the share in question shall be reapportioned in equal shares among the other shares pursuant to Paragraph 4 above, and each equal share shall continue to be held in trust or shall be distributed free and clear of all trusts, as the case may be, to or for the benefit of persons then and thereafter living, in accordance with the fortunes of the share to which said reapportionment is made.

D. If at any time before the final distribution of all of the trust shares hereinabove described, there shall be no person in existence who is eligible to have the benefit of any trust shares, the trustee shall divide all of the trust estate then remaining into two (2) equal parts which shall be distributed, outright and free of trust, as follows:

1. One (1) part to those persons then living who would have taken my estate, and in such shares thereof as they would have taken, had I then died intestate, domiciled in New Hampshire; and

2. One (1) part to those persons then living who would have taken my spouse's estate, and in such shares thereof as they would have taken had [he/she] then died intestate, domiciled in New Hampshire.

E. All trusts established under this instrument shall be exempt from the application of the rule against perpetuities. This provision is intended to comply with New Hampshire R.S.A. 564:24, and accordingly, I specifically authorizes my Trustee to sell, mortgage or lease property for any period of time beyond the period that is required for an interest created under this instrument to vest in order to be valid under the rule against perpetuities, as measured by the period defined hereinabove.

The trusts created hereunder shall be perpetual to the fullest extent permitted by the governing law. If any trust created hereunder is deemed to be subject to the law of a jurisdiction (including, but only to the extent applicable to real property)

171

that has a rule against perpetuities or similar rule which limits the period during which property can be held in trust, then such trust (other than a trust created by the exercise of a power of appointment conferred hereunder which exercise commences a new rule against perpetuities period under the law of such jurisdiction) shall terminate in all events upon the expiration of the longest period that property may be held in trust under this trust agreement under the law of such jurisdiction (including any applicable period in gross, such as 21 years, 90 years or 110 years); provided, however, that if the jurisdiction has a rule against perpetuities or similar rule which applies only to certain types of property, such as real property, the provisions of this paragraph shall apply only to such property. If under the law of such jurisdiction the longest period that property may be held in trust may be determined (or alternatively determined) with reference to the death of the last survivor of a group of individuals in being upon the date this trust agreement becomes irrevocable, those individuals shall consist of all of the descendants of my parents who are in being on the date this trust agreement becomes irrevocable. Upon termination of a trust pursuant to the provisions of this paragraph, the trust property shall be transferred, conveyed and paid over to the persons then entitled to receive or have the benefit of the income from the trust in the proportions in which they are entitled thereto, or if their interests are indefinite, then in equal shares.

F. Except as herein otherwise provided, the interest of any beneficiary hereunder, either as to income or principal, shall not be anticipated, alienated or in any other manner assigned or pledged or promised by such beneficiary, and shall not be reached by, or be subject to, any legal, equitable or other process, including any bankruptcy or divorce proceeding, or be subject to the interference or control of creditors or others in any way or manner, and all payments to, or the interest of, any beneficiary shall be free from the control or claim of any parent or spouse or former spouse or any other third party.

5.   ADMINISTRATIVE POWERS. My executor hereinafter named, and any other administrator, executor, or trustee administering my estate shall have the powers, in addition to those granted by law, as are granted to trustees by the Uniform Trustees' Powers Act, R.S.A. 564-A and the Uniform Trust Code, R.S.A. 564-B, as they may be amended from time to time, without restrictions. Where the context of this statute requires, the word "executor" or "administrator" shall be substituted for the word "trustee" and the word "estate" shall be substituted for the word "trust."

6.   SURVIVAL REQUIREMENT. No person shall be deemed to have survived me, or any other person or event under the terms of this will, unless such person survives the end of the period commencing with the close of the calendar day of my death, the death of such other person or on which such event occurs, and ending with the close of the thirtieth (30th) calendar day thereafter.

7.   EXECUTORS. I nominate my spouse, _____, as executrix under this will.

If my said spouse should be unable or unwilling to serve in this capacity for any reason, then I nominate _____ as successor.

It is my desire that the executrix and the designated alternate shall be allowed to serve with the minimum bond required by the Probate Court.

8.   <u>TRUSTEES</u>. I nominate _____ as trustee of the trusts created hereunder.

If _____ should be unable or unwilling to serve in this capacity for any reason, then I nominate _____ as successor.

It is my desire that the Trustee and the designated alternate shall be allowed to serve with the minimum bond required by the Probate Court.

9.   <u>GUARDIANS</u>. If my spouse, _____, survives me, I nominate her to be guardian of the person and property of each of my children who shall be a minor at the time of my death (and I request the Court having jurisdiction thereof to make appointment accordingly).

If my said spouse does not survive me or should be unable or unwilling to act in this capacity for any reason, then I nominate _____ to serve in as successor guardian.

It is my desire that my said spouse and the designated alternate shall be allowed to serve with the minimum bond required by the Probate Court.

10.   <u>EXPRESS INTENT</u>. Except as otherwise expressly provided by this will, I intentionally make no provision for the benefit of any child of mine, nor the issue of any child of mine, whether now alive, now deceased, or hereafter born or deceased.

11.   <u>NON-RECIPROCAL WILLS</u>. Although it is my understanding that my spouse, _____, is or may be executing a last will at or about the time of the execution of this, my last will, it is not my or our intention that such wills be construed or deemed mutual, reciprocal or dependent one upon the other, nor are such wills executed pursuant to a contract.

12.   <u>DEFINITIONS</u>. Whenever used in this will the words "child," "children," or "issue" are intended to include not only persons who are descendants by blood, but also persons, and issue of persons, who have been adopted according to law prior to their attaining the age of eighteen (18) years.

Masculine, feminine, and neuter pronouns shall each include all genders, and the singular shall include the plural, and vice versa, where the context or facts so admit.

The captions and paragraph headings of this will are inserted only as a matter of convenience and for reference, and in no way define, limit or describe the scope or intent of this will, nor in any way affect this will.

IN WITNESS WHEREOF, I hereunto set my hand and, in the presence of two (2) witnesses, declare this to be my will, on _____, 2005. For identification, I have signed each of the _____ (_____) pages of this will.

Signed and declared by the said _____ as and for his will, in the presence of us, who, at his request, in his presence, and in the presence of each other, hereunto subscribe our names as witnesses.

_____ residing at _____

_____ residing at _____

ACKNOWLEDGEMENT AND AFFIDAVIT FOR
SELF-PROVING WILL PURSUANT TO R.S.A. 551:2-a

THE STATE OF NEW HAMPSHIRE

COUNTY OF _____, SS.

The foregoing instrument was acknowledged before me this _____, 2005, by _____, the testator; _____ and _____, the witnesses, who under oath do swear as follows:

1. The testator signed the instrument as his will or expressly directed another to sign for him.

2. This was the testator's free and voluntary act for the purposes expressed in the will.

3. Each witness signed at the request of the testator, in his presence, and in the presence of the other witness.

4. To the best of my knowledge, at the time of the signing the testator was at least 18 years of age, or if under 18 years was a married person, and was of sane mind and under no constraint or undue influence.

_____

Notary Public/Justice of the Peace

My Commission Expires:

(Seal)

Page 670: Substitute this form for Form 40 in the text:

FORM 40   Irrevocable Insurance Trust

THE _____ IRREVOCABLE TRUST OF 2009

THIS AGREEMENT OF TRUST, made on _____, 2009, by and between _____, of _____, County of _____, State of New Hampshire (hereinafter referred to as the "Grantor"), and _____, of _____, County of _____, State of _____ (hereinafter referred to as the "Trustee"), to establish an irrevocable trust to be known as THE _____ IRREVOCABLE TRUST OF 2009.

1.   <u>STATEMENT OF PURPOSE AND RECITATION OF FACTS</u>. This trust has been established for the benefit of the Grantor's spouse and children. Nonetheless, it is not the Grantor's intention that this agreement directly substitute distributions from this trust for payments that the Grantor is obligated to make during lifetime, but, rather, it is the Grantor's intention and direction that the Trustee shall make distributions from this trust from time to time in its sole, absolute, and uncontrolled discretion pursuant to the terms of this trust.

The Grantor does hereby declare that the Grantor has this day irrevocably transferred to the Trustee the property listed in **SCHEDULE A** attached hereto, to have and to hold the same and any cash, securities, or other property which the Trustee may, pursuant to any of the provisions hereof, at any time hereafter, hold or acquire, all of such property being hereinafter referred to collectively as the "trust estate," for the uses and purposes and upon the terms and conditions herein set forth.

At the time of the signing of this trust, the Grantor's spouse is _____, and the Grantor's children are _____.

2.   <u>DISPOSITIVE PROVISIONS: DURING LIFETIME OF THE GRANTOR</u>. During the lifetime of the Grantor, the Trustee shall hold, administer and dispose of the trust estate, as follows:

A.   During the lifetime of the Grantor, the Trustee may pay such parts of the income, if any, and principal of the trust to, or for the benefit of, the Grantor's spouse, so long as the Grantor's spouse shall be living, and the Grantor's children, as from time to time shall be living, as the Trustee may, in its sole, absolute, and uncontrolled discretion, deem appropriate for their support in reasonable comfort, education (including college, graduate, and professional education), and maintenance in health (including medical, dental, hospital, nursing and nursing home expenses).

B.   No payments of income or of principal shall be made to the Grantor during the Grantor's lifetime.

C.   So long as the Grantor's spouse shall be living, and the Grantor's children, or any of them, shall be living, and unless the Grantor or any other transferor so directs to the contrary in writing, the Trustee shall send

175

a written notice to the beneficiaries of a contribution to the trust, that said spouse and each such child (hereinafter sometimes collectively referred to as "beneficiaries" and individually as a "beneficiary") who receives such a written notice shall have the absolute and unrestricted right, as hereinafter provided, to demand and promptly receive from the trust, outright and free from such trust, an amount of property or a sum of cash equal to such beneficiary's pro rata share of any inter vivos gift or transfer, including the initial transfer indicated on **SCHEDULE A** hereof, made to the trust.

The pro rata share of each such beneficiary in any inter vivos gift or transfer to the trust shall be equal to a fraction having as its numerator the amount of the inter vivos gift or transfer and having as its denominator the total number of such beneficiaries then living.

The maximum amount that may be withdrawn annually by each such beneficiary under this sub-paragraph shall not exceed the lesser of:

(1) the maximum amount over which an individual may have a power of withdrawal without its lapse in such year being deemed to be a release of such power under Section 2514(e) of the Internal Revenue Code, and

(2) the maximum amount excludable from a donor's taxable gifts for such year in respect to gifts to any donee under Section 2503(b) of the Code, taking into account for a married donor under Section 2513 of the Code.

Further, a beneficiary shall have no right of withdrawal during any period in which such beneficiary shall be subject to any voluntary or involuntary receivership, insolvency or bankruptcy proceeding under the laws of the United States, or of any other Country, or of any State or political subdivision.

The Trustee shall give each said beneficiary written notice that the trust has received inter vivos gifts or transfers of cash or property in which said beneficiary has a demand right within a reasonable period after such receipt.

The demand right of each such beneficiary shall be noncumulative and such beneficiary must exercise his demand right in writing before the thirtieth (30th) day after receipt by such beneficiary of notice of the inter vivos gift or transfer.

If any such beneficiary is, for any reason, under a legal disability to exercise said beneficiary's demand right, it may be exercised on said beneficiary's behalf by the beneficiary's natural or legal guardian in the same manner as by said beneficiary himself.

3.   DISPOSITIVE PROVISIONS: AFTER DEATH OF GRANTOR. Upon the death of the Grantor, the Trustee shall hold, administer and dispose of the then

remaining trust estate, as follows:

A. **Distribution of Certain Income and Principal During Grantor's Spouse's Lifetime**. After the date of death of the Grantor, if the Grantor dies within three (3) years after the assignment of any life insurance policy to this trust, or if for any other reason the proceeds of any insurance paid to this trust are included in the Grantor's estate under any provision of the Internal Revenue Code, including but not limited to Sections 2035(a) or 2042, and if the Grantor's spouse, _____, survives the Grantor, the proceeds of such insurance shall be held and administered and disposed of by the Trustee as follows:

1. The Trustee shall pay over to the Grantor's spouse all of the net income of said trust estate during said spouse's life, at least annually, but at more frequent intervals if the Grantor's spouse shall, in writing, direct.

    Also, the Trustee may pay over to the Grantor's spouse whatever part or parts of the principal of said trust estate as the Trustee may deem proper or necessary for said spouse's support in reasonable comfort, education (including college, graduate, and professional education), and maintenance in health (including medical, dental, hospital, nursing and nursing home expenses).

2. The Grantor's spouse shall have the absolute right, once during each and every calendar year between December 1 and December 31 inclusive, to withdraw any amount from the principal of said trust estate, in cash or in kind.

    The maximum amount that may be withdrawn annually under this sub-paragraph, however, shall not exceed the maximum amount over which an individual may have a power of withdrawal without its lapse in such year being deemed to be a release of such power under Section 2514(e) of the Internal Revenue Code.

    Such right to withdraw shall be noncumulative.

3. Upon the death of the Grantor's spouse, the Trustee shall pay and transfer all income accrued but undistributed at the date of death of the Grantor's spouse to principal, to be administered according to the terms hereinafter provided.

    The Trustee shall then dispose of the remaining principal as follows:

    a. The Trustee shall first pay to the executor of the Grantor's spouse's estate, out of the principal of said trust estate, the full amount by which estate, inheritance, transfer, legacy or succession taxes (federal and state), and including penalties or interest thereon, imposed by reason of the Grantor's spouse's death, are increased as a result of the inclusion of this trust in the Grantor's spouse's

177

estate for such tax purposes. The final determination of the amount due hereunder shall be based upon the values as finally determined for federal estate tax purposes in the Grantor's spouse's estate.

The Grantor's spouse may waive said spouse's estate's right to payment under this sub-paragraph by making specific reference in said spouse's will to the right to payment hereby given to said spouse's estate.

b. The Trustee shall then pay over the principal, if any, remaining at the Grantor's spouse's death and after the payment required under sub-paragraph 3.A.3.a. has been made, to the trust estate held pursuant to sub-paragraph 3.C. below, and thereafter said additional principal shall be administered as part thereof.

4. If the Grantor's spouse or the Grantor's spouse's executor disclaims said spouse's interest in and power over any property of said trust estate, then the Trustee shall add the disclaimed trust estate to the trust estate held pursuant to sub-paragraph 3.C. below, to be administered thereafter as part thereof.

B. Distribution of Remaining Income and Principal During Grantor's Spouse's Lifetime. After the date of death of the Grantor, the remainder of the trust estate which has not been heretofore previously allocated shall be held and administered and disposed of by the Trustee as follows:

1. If the Grantor's spouse, _____, survives the Grantor, during said spouse's lifetime, the Trustee may pay over to the Grantor's spouse or may use, apply or expend for said spouse's direct or indirect benefit, so much or all of the income of the trust estate and so much or all of the principal of said trust estate as the Trustee may deem proper or necessary for said spouse's support in reasonable comfort, education (including college, graduate, and professional education), and maintenance in health (including medical, dental, hospital, nursing and nursing home expenses); provided, however, that in exercising its sole, absolute, and uncontrolled discretion the Trustee shall take into account other resources of the Grantor's spouse.

2. The Trustee may also pay over to or use, apply or expend for the direct or indirect benefit of the Grantor's children who are from time to time living during said period, or pay to the Grantor's spouse for their benefit, so much or all of the income or principal of the trust hereby created as the Trustee may deem proper or necessary for their support in reasonable comfort, education (including college, graduate, and professional education), and maintenance in health (including medical, dental, hospital, nursing and nursing home expenses).

3. If it becomes necessary for the Trustee to make any payments to or for

the benefit of the Grantor's spouse from the principal of the trust hereinbefore established in sub-paragraph 3.A., or from the principal of this trust, the Trustee is directed, when it is practicable to do so, to make such payments of principal, if any, from the principal of the trust hereinbefore established before making any payment from the principal of this trust.

However, it is the Grantor's intention that the support in reasonable comfort, education (including college, graduate, and professional education), and maintenance in health (including medical, dental, hospital, nursing and nursing home expenses) of the Grantor's spouse shall be of primary concern, and the Trustee shall exercise it sole, absolute, and uncontrolled discretion in using principal for the Grantor's spouse, considering all other beneficiaries to this trust to be secondary and without liability to any other beneficiary for the use of principal for the Grantor's spouse.

4. In addition, after the trust hereinbefore established in sub-paragraph 3.A. has been exhausted, the Grantor's spouse shall have the absolute right once during each and every calendar year, between December 1 and December 31 inclusive, to withdraw any amount from the principal of this trust, in cash or in kind. The maximum amount that may be withdrawn annually under this sub-paragraph, however, shall not exceed the maximum amount over which an individual may have a power of withdrawal without its lapse in such year being deemed to be a release of such power under Section 2514(e) of the Internal Revenue Code. Such right to withdraw shall be noncumulative.

C. Distribution to Children and Issue. Upon the death of the Grantor's spouse, or upon the Grantor's death if the Grantor's spouse does not survive the Grantor, the Trustee shall apportion the trust estate into equal shares as follows:

one (1) such share to each of the Grantor's living children, and

one (1) such share to each family group composed of the living issue of any child of the Grantor who is then deceased.

In the event that the trust estate then consists of proceeds from life insurance on the Grantor's life, then notwithstanding the above equal apportionment, the Trustee shall allocate said life insurance proceeds among said trust shares in the following manner: the Trustee shall calculate a fraction for each share of the trust estate, the numerator of which shall be each beneficiary's (or, in the case of the family group composed of the issue of a deceased child of the Grantor, such beneficiary's parent's) deemed contribution to the payment of the premiums on said insurance policy and the denominator of which shall be

179

the total premiums deemed paid by all of the beneficiaries on said insurance policy.

Each trust share shall then be allocated its fractional portion of said life insurance proceeds.

Said shares, after adjustments, if any, shall then be held and administered and disposed of as follows:

1. In the case of each share apportioned to a living child of the Grantor, the Trustee may, in each and every year beginning with the date of said apportionment, pay over to said child or use, apply or expend for said child's direct or indirect benefit, so much or all of the net income of said share and so much or all of the principal of said share as the Trustee may, in its sole, absolute, and uncontrolled discretion, deem wise and safely consistent with said child's support in reasonable comfort, education (including college, graduate, and professional education), and maintenance in health (including medical, dental, hospital, nursing and nursing home expenses).

    a. Whenever, at or after said time of apportionment, said child shall have attained the age of thirty (30) years, he shall have the right to request in writing and to receive one-third (1/3) of the principal of his share; and

    b. Whenever, at or after said time of apportionment, said child shall have attained the age of thirty-five (35) years, he shall have the right to request in writing and to receive an additional one-half (1/2) of the balance of the principal of his share; and

    c. Whenever, at or after said time of apportionment, said child shall have attained the age of forty (40) years, he shall have the right to request in writing and to receive the entire balance of the principal and undistributed income of his share, at which time his trust shall terminate.

    d. It is the Grantor's belief that, in some circumstances, it may be beneficial for said child to leave the management of his trust share in the hands of the Trustee.

        Therefore, said child may elect to leave his trust share, or any portion thereof, in the hands of the Trustee, as a separate fund, to be held and administered and disposed of as said child shall direct.

    e. The share held by the Trustee for the benefit of a child as described above shall, from the time of the death of said child after the time above set for apportionment into shares, be administered for the benefit of said child's issue in the manner described below.

2. In the case of each share apportioned to the living issue of a deceased child of the Grantor, said share shall be administered for the benefit as a family group of such of the issue of said deceased child as from time to time shall be living.

   The Trustee may pay over to the issue, or may use, apply or expend for their direct or indirect benefit, so much of the income and principal of the trust estate, at such times and in such proportions as the Trustee may determine, in its sole, absolute, and uncontrolled discretion, for support in reasonable comfort, education, (including college, graduate, and professional education), and maintenance in health (including medical, dental, hospital, nursing and nursing home expenses).

   The Trustee may make such payments, use, application, expenditure or accumulation of the income and principal thereof as it shall think proper for the direct or indirect benefit of the members of said family group without being required to observe any precept or rule of equality of enjoyment as between said members.

   Final distribution shall be made of whatever shall remain of said share, per stirpes, among said living issue and free and clear of all trusts when the youngest then living child of the Grantor's deceased child attains the age of thirty (30) years.

3. If at any time before the final distribution of any of the trust shares hereinabove described (after taking into consideration all provisions thereof), there shall be no person in existence who is eligible to have the benefit of the trust of such share, then the share in question shall be reapportioned in equal shares among the other shares of the trust estate apportioned pursuant to sub-paragraph 3.C. above, and each equal share shall continue to be held and administered in trust, or distributed free and clear of all trusts, as the case may be, to or for the benefit of persons then and thereafter living, in accordance with the fortunes of the share to which said reapportionment is made.

4. In the case of any share or part of a share apportioned hereinabove, the Trustee shall not be required to make distribution to any beneficiary sooner than two (2) years after the death of the Grantor.

D. If, at any time before the final distribution of all of the trust shares hereinabove described, there shall be no person in existence who is eligible to have the benefit of said trust shares, the Trustee shall divide all of the trust estate then remaining into two (2) equal parts which shall be distributed, outright and free of trust, as follows:

1. One (1) part to those persons then living who would have taken the Grantor's estate, and in such shares thereof as they would have taken, had the Grantor then died intestate, domiciled in New Hampshire;

and

2. One (1) part to those persons then living who would have taken the Grantor's spouse's estate, and in such shares thereof as they would have taken, had the Grantor's spouse then died intestate, domiciled in New Hampshire.

E. The provisions contained hereinabove which require the Trustee to apportion the trust estate into shares and parts of shares are for purposes of computation only and shall not be construed to require the Trustee to make physical segregation of one share or a part of a share from the others, although the Trustee shall have full right to make such segregation if it thinks it better to do so.

Notwithstanding said provisions, the Trustee shall have the full right to regard the trust estate as one undivided estate for purposes of management and investment; provided, however, that all trust shares and parts of shares shall be treated as substantially separate and independent trusts under Sections 663(c), 2041(b)(2) or 2514(e) of the Internal Revenue Code.

4. <u>TRUSTEE'S DUTIES AND POWERS</u>. The assets of the trust shall be held subject to the following terms and conditions, and the Trustee shall have the following powers, in addition to any other powers granted to the Trustee by New Hampshire common law and statutory authority (including, but not limited to, the Uniform Trustees' Powers Act, R.S.A. 564-A, and the Uniform Trust Code, R.S.A. 564-B, as they may be amended from time to time), without restrictions.

In addition to such powers, and not in limitation thereof, the Trustee shall have the following powers, all of which shall be exercised in a fiduciary capacity and for the benefit of the beneficiaries:

A. As to any insurance policies owned by or payable to the trust, in whole or in part, the Trustee is authorized to sell, assign, surrender or hypothecate the policies, to borrow any sum in accordance with the provisions of the insurance contracts, to receive all payments, dividends, surrender values, and benefits or to receive and exercise all privileges of any kind which may occur on account of the policies, all in accordance with the provisions of the insurance contracts.

In making payment upon the policy, the issuing or obligated insurance company shall not be responsible for the proper application or disposition of any funds paid to the Trustee, but the receipt of the Trustee shall be a complete discharge to the insurance company.

The Trustee shall not use any part of the income of the trust estate in order to pay premiums on any insurance policies on the Grantor's life, or on the Grantor's spouse's life, whether or not the trust owns the insurance policies.

B. The Trustee shall have the power to improve, lease for any term or perpetually, rent, sell, exchange, grant and exercise options to buy, any property at any time, to invest and reinvest in real or personal property of any kind, and to retain as a proper investment any property, whether originally a part of the trust estate or subsequently acquired, and to exercise the powers granted hereinabove without being limited by any statute or judicial decision, whenever enacted or announced, imposing requirements as to assets in which investments may be made or the retention or diversification of investments.

The foregoing powers shall include (without limitation of the above described powers) the power to sell any trust assets to, or purchase assets from, the Grantor, the Grantor's spouse, any descendants of the Grantor or the Grantor's spouse, and/or the estate of any such person, whether or not such person is then acting as a Trustee.

The Trustee shall administer, retain, invest and reinvest the trust estate in any property, real or personal, tangible or intangible, including insurance policies on the Grantor's life, or on the Grantor's spouse's life, security holdings, common trust funds, investments and management and administrative vehicles, whether issued, controlled, managed or administered by any corporate or financial institution serving hereunder as Trustee, or otherwise.

Notwithstanding the preceding provisions hereinabove, or any other provision of this instrument, during the time in which the assets of the trust estate consist solely of principal cash, if any, and insurance policies, the Trustee shall not be required to diversify investments nor make any investment recommendations.

C. Any accumulated income which shall not be paid to the beneficiaries by virtue of a provision in this trust shall be added from time to time by the Trustee to the principal of the trust.

D. The Trustee shall have the power to borrow money from any institution or person, including the Trustee, for the benefit of the trust, and to pledge or mortgage any part or all of the trust estate as security.

E. The Trustee shall have power to arbitrate, defend, enforce, release or settle any claim of or against the trust.

F. The Trustee shall have power to vote, in person or by proxy, upon all securities held as a part of the trust estate, to exercise, buy or sell subscription and conversion rights and participate in reorganizations, re-capitalizations, consolidations, mergers, exchanges, foreclosures, liquidations and creditors' and bondholders' agreements.

G. The Trustee shall have power to allocate receipts, disbursements and losses to principal or to income, in accordance with generally accepted accounting practices.

In addition, the Trustee shall have the power to allocate any annuity payment, or any lump-sum or periodic payment from a pension or profit-sharing plan in which the Grantor was a participant, received by the trust to income and/or principal as the Trustee, in the Trustee's sole, absolute, and uncontrolled discretion, deems advisable, irrespective of the treatment for income tax purposes.

Notwithstanding any trust accounting rule to the contrary, the Trustee shall maintain a reasonable reserve for depreciation with respect to any depreciable asset owned by the trust, and the term "net income", wherever used in this instrument, shall mean net income remaining after any addition to a depreciation reserve.

H. In any case in which the Trustee is required physically to divide property held in the trust estate into parts, shares or trusts, or to distribute the same, the Trustee may, in the Trustee's sole, absolute, and uncontrolled discretion, make the division or distribution in kind (including interests in any insurance policies owned by the trust) or in money or partly in kind and partly in money, and may allocate dissimilar property and undivided interests in property to different parts, shares or trusts, without respect to the income tax basis of the property.

The Trustee is specifically excused from any duty of impartiality with respect to the income tax basis of property.

If necessary to value property to be divided or distributed, it shall be valued at the then-current fair market value.

I. The Trustee may take and hold all securities or other personal property in bearer form, in the name of any Trustee, or in the name of a nominee, with or without disclosing any fiduciary relationship, but the Trustee shall be liable for any wrongful act of the nominee with respect to the assets.

J. The Trustee is authorized to employ and pay reasonable compensation to agents, investment counsel and attorneys, including the Trustee and any person, partner-ship, corporation or other entity with which the Trustee may be associated.

The foregoing authority shall include, without limitation, the power to authorize any Trustee, person or persons to withdraw funds from any bank account maintained by the trust and/or to have access to any safe deposit box maintained by the trust.

K. The Trustee is authorized to execute and deliver all necessary or proper deeds or other instruments.

L. No purchaser from and no lender to the Trustee is under any obligation to ensure that the purchase or loan money is applied for the purposes of the trust estate.

The receipt of the Trustee shall be a complete discharge to that person.

M. The Trustee shall have power to take, hold and convey title to real estate or interests in the name of the Trustee or in the name of the nominee of the Trustee without disclosing the trust, and in accepting title to the real estate neither the Trustee nor the nominee shall be held to have assumed the payment of any encumbrances.

All conveyances executed and delivered by the Trustee or the nominee shall be without covenants of warranty except as against the Trustee's or nominee's own acts.

N. The Trustee shall not be personally liable upon any contract of indebtedness of or claims against the trust estate or upon a mortgage, trust deed, note or other instrument executed under these provisions.

O. The Trustee shall be protected in continuing to make distributions of income or principal until the Trustee shall have actual knowledge of the happening of an event such as attainment of a certain age, death or other occurrence which would affect such distributions.

P. Any Trustee or successor Trustee may accept and rely upon any accounting made by or on behalf of any predecessor Trustee, and any statement or representation made by any fiduciary as to the assets comprising this trust estate or as to any other fact bearing upon the prior administration of the trust.

A Trustee or successor Trustee shall not be liable for having accepted and relied upon the accounting, statement or representation if it is later proved to be incomplete, inaccurate or untrue.

Q. If the Grantor or the executor of the Grantor's estate or any other individual (including any individual who shall transfer property in trust hereunder or the executor or administrator of the estate of such individual), has allocated any portion or all of any Generation Skipping Transfer ("GST") exemption provided by Section 2631(a) of the Internal Revenue Code to any property to be held in trust hereunder, then notwithstanding anything to the contrary contained in this agreement, the Trustee is authorized to establish such number of separate trusts, with identical terms, to hold the property received in trust hereunder as it, in its sole, absolute, and uncontrolled discretion, shall deem advisable, bearing in mind the allocation of the said GST exemption and the desirability that any trust to which all or any portion of the said GST exemption is allocated shall, if practical, have an inclusion ratio of zero.

Further, the Trustee is authorized to allocate such trusts among the trust shares hereinabove created in order to minimize (or eliminate, if possible) any GST tax.

R. If, after the death of the Grantor, THE _____ REVOCABLE TRUST OF _____ or THE _____ REVOCABLE TRUST OF _____ is still in existence and the terms of any trust established under either trust, or any other trust, are substantially similar to this, THE _____ IRREVOCABLE TRUST OF _____, the Trustee is authorized and empowered to consolidate this trust with such similar trust as one trust, unless such consolidation shall be contrary to law or inconsistent with the terms of any instrument supplemental hereto; provided that such consolidation clause shall be null and void in the event there is a determination that the application of such clause shall result in the inclusion of any of the trust estate in the Grantor's gross estate or in the Grantor's spouse's gross estate under any provision of the Internal Revenue Code, including but not limited to Sections 2041 and 2042.

S. The Trustee shall have full power and authority, to be exercised in its sole, absolute, and uncontrolled discretion, to merge any trust created hereunder with any other trust or trusts created under will, deed or otherwise, if the terms of such trust are then substantially similar and held for the primary benefit of the same persons.

T. Regardless of the extent of the authority that the Trustee holds to currently distribute income and/or principal of the trust estate to one or more beneficiaries of the trust, the Trustee shall have full power and authority, to be exercised in its sole, absolute, and uncontrolled discretion, to appoint any or all assets held in this trust estate to any other trust or trusts created under will, deed or otherwise, for the benefit of one or more of the beneficiaries hereunder.

This authority shall be subject to the limitations set forth in R.S.A. 564-B:4-418, as amended from time to time, provided that such appointment clause shall be null and void in the event there is a determination that the application of such clause shall result in the inclusion of any of the trust estate in the Grantor's gross estate under any provision of the Internal Revenue Code, including but not limited to Sections 2041 and 2042, which would not otherwise be includable in the Grantor's gross estate.

Provided further, however, that if this Trust qualifies as a "trust instrument" under the Qualified Dispositions in Trust Act, R.S.A. 564-D, as amended from time to time, then the Trustee may only appoint the assets of the trust estate to a new trust which will continue to qualify as a "trust instrument" under such Act and will provide similar protections to the assets held in this trust estate.

U. After the Grantor's death, the Trustee may borrow or make loans or purchases and sales from and to the Grantor's estate and from and to the Trustee serving under any other trust established by the Grantor, on such terms as the Trustee shall think proper, and all judgments, decisions and actions so taken shall be final and binding upon all persons if made reasonably and in good faith, even though the person serving as executor of the Grantor's estate, or Trustee under such trust, shall be the same as the fiduciary under this trust.

V. In the event that any beneficiary of the trust shall serve in the capacity of co-Trustee, then the discretionary powers to determine whether income or principal is to be distributed to said beneficiary or to any person to whom said beneficiary owes an obligation of support shall be exercisable only by the remaining co-Trustee.

It is the Grantor's intention by this sub-paragraph to prohibit said beneficiary from benefiting himself or herself as beneficiary in any way by the exercise of such discretionary powers vested in the Trustee as a group.

W. In the event that any beneficiary of the trust shall serve in the capacity of sole Trustee and the Trustee has discretionary powers to distribute income or principal to himself, herself, or to any person to whom he or she owes an obligation of support, then such distributions of income or principal shall be exercisable by the sole Trustee.

The maximum amount that may be withdrawn annually by each such beneficiary under this sub-paragraph, however, shall not exceed the maximum amount over which an individual may have a power of withdrawal without its lapse in such year being deemed to be a release of such power under Section 2514(e) of the Internal Revenue Code.

X. If, at any time before the final distribution of the principal of any trust share hereinabove described, the value of the principal of said trust share shall be equal to, or less than, ONE HUNDRED THOUSAND DOL-LARS ($100,000), then the Trustee may, in its sole, absolute, and uncontrolled discretion, terminate said trust share and distribute the principal of said trust share, and any accumulated and undistributed income thereof, outright and free of trust, to those persons then entitled to benefit from said trust share, and in the proportions in which they are then entitled to benefit from said trust share, notwithstanding any provisions of this trust to the contrary.

5. <u>TRUST PROTECTOR</u>.

A. The Grantor appoints _____, of _____, _____, as the Trust Protector.

If _____ shall be unable or unwilling to serve in this capacity for any reason, then _____, of _____, _____, shall serve instead.

If _____ shall be unable or unwilling to serve in this capacity for any reason, then _____, of _____, _____, shall serve instead.

The Trust Protector is authorized, in its sole, absolute, and uncontrolled discretion, to remove any Trustee acting hereunder. Any vacancy resulting from such removal shall be filled pursuant to the provisions hereinbelow.

Any removal of a Trustee shall be evidenced by an acknowledged instrument in writing and shall be delivered to the Trustee so removed and to each remaining Trustee (if any).

B. If all Trust Protectors cease to act as to any one or more trusts hereunder, a successor Trust Protector may be appointed by the "Appointment Committee" (as defined hereunder); provided, however that notwithstanding anything contained herein to the contrary, there may not be appointed as successor Trust Protector, either

1. the Grantor, or

2. the Grantor's spouse, or

3. any beneficiary of a trust hereunder, or

4. any spouse of a beneficiary, or

5. any person who is a related or subordinate party within the meaning of section 672(c) of the Code with respect to any beneficiary of this trust.

6. The Appointment Committee shall be as follows:

a. the Grantor's then living and competent adult children, over the age of twenty-five (25) years, by majority vote, or, if no child of the Grantor is then living, adult, competent and over the age of twenty-five (25) years,

b. such of the Grantor's descendants as are then living, adult and competent, over the age of thirty (30) years, by majority vote, or, if there is no such then adult and competent descendant over the age of thirty (30) years,

c. the Trust Protector, if any.

C. The Grantor is not imposing any fiduciary responsibility on the Trust Protector to monitor the actions of the Trustee.

Except for any matter involving the Trust Protector's own individual willful misconduct or negligence proved by clear and convincing evidence, no Trust Protector shall incur any liability by reason of any error of judgment, mistake of law, or action of any kind taken or omitted to be taken hereunder if in good faith reasonably believed by such Trust Protector to be in accordance with the provisions and intent hereof.

The Trust Protector shall not be liable for the failure to remove any Trustee even if such Trustee may be guilty of a gross violation of his or her fiduciary duties hereunder.

D.   Any appointment of a successor Trust Protector pursuant to the provisions hereunder shall be evidenced by an acknowledged instrument in writing and shall be effective upon acceptance thereof by the Trust Protector so appointed.

Any successor Trust Protector shall have all the powers of the initial Trust Protector.

Different trusts hereunder may, but need not, have different Trust Protectors.

More than one person may act collectively as a Trust Protector for any given trust hereunder, in which case decisions of the Trust Protector shall be made by majority vote if more than two (2) persons are so acting collectively.

Any Trust Protector may resign from office with respect to any one or more trusts hereunder at any time by delivery of a written, acknowledged instrument of resignation to the persons who are authorized to appoint a successor Trust Protector hereunder, or, if none, to the Trustees then in office.

The Trust Protector shall act without compensation hereunder but shall be reimbursed for any expenses in carrying out his or her duties hereunder.

6.   <u>TRUST ESTATE</u>.

A.   The Trustee acknowledges receipt of the property listed in **SCHEDULE A** attached hereto and will hold, manage, invest and reinvest the trust estate upon the terms herein set forth.

The Trustee may accept and administer hereunder whatever property, including cash, securities, life insurance policies, or other property, may by virtue of any gift, Will, Codicil or any other instrument be irrevocably given, devised, bequeathed or appointed to the Trustee hereunder by the Grantor or by any other person.

B.   The Trustee shall possess and own all incidents of ownership, rights, powers, interests, privileges, and benefits of every kind that may accrue on account of all property, including insurance policies, composing part of the trust estate, and the Grantor shall have no interest or right of any

189

kind in or to any of the said trust property.

7.   <u>REPORTING BY TRUSTEE.</u>

A.   The Trustee may, at the Trustee's sole, absolute, and uncontrolled discretion, and shall, to the extent required by the Uniform Trust Code, R.S.A. 564-B, as it may be amended from time to time, render a Trustee's report as described in the Uniform Trust Code, as it may be amended from time to time, at such intervals as the Trustee may choose or at such times as required by the Uniform Trust Code.

B.   A recipient of such a report (or, if under guardianship or conservatorship, then by the Guardian or Conservator, or, if deceased, then by the Executor or Administrator), may, by a written instrument, assent to the report of the Trustee with respect to principal or to income, or with respect to both principal and income.

The assent of the recipient of such report (or, if under guardianship or conservatorship, then by the Guardian or Conservator, or, if deceased, then by the Executor or Administrator) shall make such report binding and conclusive upon all persons then having or who may thereafter have any interest, vested or contingent, in the income or principal of the trust estate and such assent shall forever release and discharge the Trustee of and from any and every claim, demand, accountability, and liability of every nature, arising from any matter or thing done or omitted to be done, in connection with this agreement or any trust hereby created, during the period in respect of which the report of the Trustee shall have been so settled.

C.   The failure of any person to object in writing to the Trustee to such a report within thirty (30) days after the delivery of the same to such person hereunder shall be final and binding to the same extent as the written assent hereinabove provided.

D.   Any person entitled to such a report, accounting, information, notice and the like (or, if under guardianship or conservatorship, then by the Guardian or Conservator, or, if deceased, then by the Executor or Administrator) may by a written instrument signed and acknowledged by him or her or them, as the case may be, and delivered to the Trustee, waive the right to said Trustee's report or to other information otherwise required to be furnished under the Uniform Trust Code, as it may be amended from time to time.

8.   <u>SUCCESSOR TRUSTEE.</u>

A.   If _____ shall be unable or unwilling to serve in the capacity of Trustee for any reason, then _____, of _____, shall serve as successor Trustee.

B.   If all Trustees shall be unable or unwilling to serve in the capacity of

Trustee for any reason, then a majority of the beneficiaries to whom or for whose use the current net income of the trust estate is at the time authorized or required to be paid or applied, either,

   (a) acting individually, if then eighteen (18) years of age, or,

   (b) by his or her natural parent, or natural guardian, or Court appointed guardian or Court appointed conservator, if then under guardianship or conservatorship,

shall appoint a successor Trustee.

C. Each Trustee hereunder (whether originally designated herein or appointed as successor) shall have the right to resign at any time by giving thirty (30) written notice to that effect to the current income beneficiary (or beneficiaries) of the trust.

D. In the event that a corporation or financial institution shall be appointed as successor Trustee hereunder, such successor Trustee shall be a trust company or bank qualified to act as such, possessing trust powers.

E. No successor Trustee shall be liable or responsible in any way for any actions or defaults of any predecessor Trustee, nor for any loss or expense from or occasioned by anything done or neglected to be done by any predecessor Trustee. Any successor Trustee shall have, from and after its appointment or succession to office hereunder and without any assignment or other action by any person, all the rights, interests, and powers, including discretionary rights and powers, which are by the provisions of this trust agreement granted to and vested in the Trustee named herein.

F. At no time shall the Grantor serve as Trustee hereunder.

9. FIDUCIARIES.

A. No person dealing with the Trustee shall be responsible for the application of any money, securities, or other property paid or delivered, and the receipt of the Trustee shall be a full discharge; and no person dealing with the Trustee, and no issuer, transfer agent, or other agent of any issuer of any securities shall be under any obligation to ascertain or inquire into the power of the Trustee to purchase, sell, exchange, transfer, mortgage, pledge, create a security interest in, lease, distribute, or otherwise dispose of or deal with any money, securities, or other property.

B. The Trustee hereby accepts the trust created by this trust agreement and it agrees to carry out the provisions hereof on its part according to the best of its ability; provided, however, that, in addition to the provisions of this trust agreement, no Trustee shall be held liable for any action taken or not taken, including any action intended to lessen or eliminate the impact of estate or generation-skipping transfer taxes with respect to any generation or beneficiary, whether or not such action is successful in achieving the results sought and without regard to its effect on other beneficiaries in the same or different generations, or for any loss or depreciation in the value of any property in any trust created herein, whether due to an error of judgment or otherwise, where the Trustee has exercised good faith and ordinary diligence in the exercise of its duties.

C.   The Trustee shall receive reasonable compensation for its services in the administration of the trusts created herein, including reimbursement for amounts reasonably expended for bookkeeping services, investment services and advice, and other professional or para-professional services. In addition to the compensation herein provided, the Trustee shall receive reasonable compensation for any legal services provided for the benefit of the trust estate, such as handling any litigation involving the trust, preparing state or federal income tax returns, and transferring any real estate.

D.   The Trustee shall be permitted to serve without bond or surety on its bond, except as required by law, and any successor Trustee shall be permitted to serve without bond or surety on its bond.

E.   A certificate signed by any Trustee hereunder and acknowledged before a Notary Public shall be conclusive evidence upon all persons and for all purposes of the facts stated in said certificate with regard to the terms of this trust, the text thereof, and who is from time to time Trustee here-under.

F.   Any individual acting as a Trustee hereunder or any firm or corporation of which it is a member or employee may act as attorney for, deal and contract with, and be employed by the Trustee hereunder, and any individual acting as a Trustee hereunder may act as attorney, director, officer, agent or employee of any corporation in which the Grantor's estate or the trust are interested, directly or indirectly, as a stockholder or otherwise, all in the same manner and with the same freedom as though not a Trustee or the employee of a Trustee hereunder and without accountability for any compensation received in connection with such action.

10.   PERPETUITIES. All trusts established under this instrument shall be exempt from the application of the rule against perpetuities. This provision is intended to comply with New Hampshire R.S.A. 564:24, and accordingly, the Grantor specifically authorizes the Trustee to sell, mortgage or lease property for any period of time beyond the period that is required for an interest created under this instrument to vest in order to be valid under the rule against perpetuities, as measured by the period defined hereinabove.

The trusts created hereunder shall be perpetual to the fullest extent permitted by the governing law. If any trust created hereunder is deemed to be subject to the law of a jurisdiction (including, but only to the extent applicable to real property) that has a rule against perpetuities or similar rule which limits the period during which property can be held in trust, then such trust (other than a trust created by the exercise of a power of appointment conferred hereunder which exercise commences a new rule against perpetuities period under the law of such jurisdiction) shall terminate in all events upon the expiration of the longest period that property may be held in trust under this trust agreement under the law of such jurisdiction (including any applicable period in gross, such as 21 years, 90 years or 110 years); provided, however, that if the jurisdiction has a rule against perpetuities or similar rule which applies only to certain types of property, such as real property, the provisions of this paragraph shall apply only to such property. If under the law of such jurisdiction the longest period that property may be held in trust may be determined (or alternatively determined) with reference to the death of the last survivor of a group of individuals in being upon the date of this trust agreement, those individuals shall consist of all of the descendants of the Grantor's parents who were in being on the date of this trust agreement. Upon termination of a trust pursuant to the provisions of this paragraph, the trust property shall be transferred, conveyed and paid over to the persons then entitled to receive or have the benefit of the income from the trust in the proportions in which they are entitled thereto, or if their interests are indefinite, then in equal shares.

11.   SPENDTHRIFT PROVISION. Except as herein otherwise provided, the interest of any beneficiary hereunder, either as to income or principal, shall not be anticipated, alienated or in any other manner assigned or pledged or promised by such beneficiary, and shall not be reached by, or be subject to, any legal, equitable or other process, including any bankruptcy or divorce proceeding, or be subject to the interference or control of creditors or others in any way or manner, and all payments to, or the interest of, any beneficiary shall be free from the control or claim of any parent or spouse or former spouse or any other third party. Moreover, no power of appointment or power of withdrawal shall be subject to involuntary exercise. Provided, however, this spendthrift provision shall not restrict the exercise of a disclaimer or the exercise of a power of appointment or withdrawal right granted by this trust agreement. This provision is intended to be a material provision of this trust and any other trust established hereunder.

12.   TAX APPORTIONMENT. The assets held in this trust shall not be liable for any tax, including without limitation, legacy, estate and/or inheritance taxes, paid by or due and payable by the Grantor's estate, irrespective of whether these taxes, if any, are attributable to assets held by this trust. The Trustee of this trust has no authority to, and is not authorized to, pay these taxes, if any, from any trust assets, whether principal or income.

13.   SURVIVAL REQUIREMENT. No person shall be deemed to have survived any person or event under the terms of this trust, unless such person survives the end of the period commencing with the close of the calendar day of the death of such person or on which such event occurs, and ending with the close of the thirtieth (30th) calendar day thereafter.

14.   <u>DISTRIBUTIONS TO MINORS</u>. In any case where property or funds become distributable to a minor, then the Trustee shall have the additional power to distribute the same in any one or more of the following ways: (1) by distribution directly to the minor; (2) by distribution to the legal guardian of the minor; (3) by distribution to a parent, relative or friend of the minor for the minor's support in reasonable comfort, education and maintenance in health; (4) by applying the same directly for the minor's support in reasonable comfort, education and maintenance in health; (5) by depositing the same in a bank account in the name of the minor or by transferring property to or purchasing property in the name of a custodian for his or her benefit under a Uniform Law relating to transfers or gifts to minors; or (6) by holding the same hereunder in trust or in custody for the minor's support in reasonable comfort, education and maintenance in health and by distributing the remainder thereof to the minor upon coming of age or otherwise to the minor's estate in case of the death of the minor. The receipt of the person to whom property or funds are actually distributed in accordance with any of the foregoing provisions shall fully discharge the Trustee from further accountability therefor.

15.   <u>GOVERNING LAW AND SITUS</u>. The Grantor declares that this agreement and the trust created hereby shall be construed under and regulated by the laws of the State of New Hampshire and that the validity and effect of this agreement and of this trust shall be determined in accordance with the laws of that State.

Further, the trust shall be under the jurisdiction of the courts of the State of New Hampshire and the Trustee shall voluntarily enter a general appearance in any legal action relating to an accounting of the trust or a declaratory judgment interpreting this trust agreement. The Trustee shall not be chargeable in any court other than one of the courts of that State.

[OPTIONAL] However, the Trustee, at any time and from time to time, in its discretion, may, (1) remove all or part of the trust estate and hold and administer the same in any other jurisdiction where the Trustee shall be then located, (2) change the situs of administration of any trust from one jurisdiction to another jurisdiction; and (3) elect that the law of such other jurisdiction shall thereafter govern the trust to such extent as may be necessary and appropriate, and to amend the administrative provisions of the trust as the Trustee deems appropriate to ensure compliance and compatibility with such law, whereupon the courts of such other jurisdiction shall have the power to effectuate the purposes of this trust agreement to such extent. The determination of the Trustee as to any such removal of assets or change of situs or governing law shall be conclusive and binding on all persons interested in such trust.

16.   <u>IRREVOCABILITY</u>.

A. This trust is irrevocable and the Grantor severs permanently any control over the assets of the trust.

The significance of the irrevocability of this trust has been fully explained to the Grantor by the Grantor's legal counsel.

The Grantor hereby expressly acknowledges that the Grantor shall have no right or power, whether alone or in conjunction with others, in whatever capacity, to alter, amend, revoke or terminate the trust, or any of the terms of the trust, in whole or in part, or to designate the persons who shall possess or enjoy the trust estate or the income therefrom.

By this trust instrument, the Grantor intends to and does hereby relinquish absolutely and forever all possession or enjoyment of, or right to the income from, the trust estate, whether directly, indirectly or constructively, and every interest of any nature, present or future, in the trust estate.

B. Notwithstanding anything contained in this agreement expressly or impliedly to the contrary, no power enumerated herein or accorded to the Trustee generally pursuant to law shall be construed,

(1) to enable the Grantor or any "non-adverse party" (as defined in IRC Section 672(b)), or both of them, to borrow all or any part of the trust estate or income therefrom, directly or indirectly, without adequate interest or adequate security or to permit the Grantor to revest in the Grantor title to any or all of the trust estate, nor

(2) without the approval or consent of an "adverse party" (as defined in IRC Section 672(a)), to enable the Grantor or such non-adverse party, or both of them, to purchase, exchange or otherwise deal with or dispose of any or all of the trust estate or income therefrom for less than an adequate consideration in money or money's worth or to enable any or all of the income from the trust to be distributed to, or be held or accumulated for future distribution to the Grantor (by discharging a support obligation or otherwise), nor

(3) to enable the Grantor to remove a successor Trustee or co-Trustee, nor

(4) to permit any person other than the Trustee to have or exercise the power to vote or direct the voting of stock or other securities of the trust, to control the investment of the trust estate either by directing or vetoing investments or reinvestments, or to reacquire the trust estate by substituting other property of an equivalent value.

C. The Trustee, in its sole, absolute, and uncontrolled discretion, may from time to time amend this trust agreement to address changes in federal or state tax law.

In the event of repeal of the federal estate or generation-skipping transfer tax provisions (as currently set forth in Chapters 11 and 13 of the Internal

195

Revenue Code), the Trustee, in the Trustee's sole, absolute, and uncontrolled discretion, may terminate the trust by distribution, outright and free of trust, to those persons then entitled to benefit from this trust, and in the proportions in which they are then entitled to benefit from this trust at the time of said repeal, notwithstanding any provisions of this trust to the contrary.

In exercising such power, the Trustee shall, in addition to the factors set forth herein, consider the following:

The enactment of any federal income, capital gains or other tax which would impact adversely on, or offset the tax benefits of, any proposed trust termination;

The benefits afforded to the beneficiaries by the continuation of the trust, such as protection against the claims of judgment creditors and the insulation from the reach of government agencies;

The likelihood of re-enactment of a federal estate, gift or generation-skipping transfer or comparable tax which would subject the trust principal to imposition of such tax or taxes in the hands of, or upon lifetime or testamentary transfers by, the beneficiaries to whom the trust principal would have been distributed upon termination.

17.   DEFINITIONS. Whenever used in this trust agreement, the words "child", "children", or "issue" are intended to include not only persons who are descendants by blood, but also persons and issue of persons who have been adopted according to law prior to their attaining the age of eighteen (18) years.

References to the "Internal Revenue Code" or "Code" or to provisions thereof are to the Internal Revenue Code of 1986, as amended at the time in question. References to the "Treasury Regulations," "Regulations" and "Regs." are to the Treasury Regulations under the Code. If, by the time in question, a particular provision of the Code has been renumbered, or the Code has been superseded by a subsequent federal tax law, the reference shall be deemed to be to the renumbered provision or the corresponding provision of the subsequent law, unless to do so would clearly be contrary to the Grantor's intent as expressed in this Trust Agreement, and a similar rule shall apply to references to the Regulations.

Masculine, feminine and neuter pronouns shall each include all genders, and the singular shall include the plural, and vice versa, where the context or facts so admit.

The captions and paragraph headings of this trust agreement are inserted only as a matter of convenience and for reference and in no way define, limit or describe the scope or intent of this agreement, nor in any way affect this agreement.

18.   EXECUTION. This trust agreement shall be effective when executed by the Grantor, notwithstanding that the signature of the Trustee is provided for, the

Trustee's signature being intended to denote the acceptance of the Trustee to serve in that capacity only.

This trust agreement may be executed in any number of counterparts with the same effect as if all of the parties had signed the same document. All counterparts shall be construed together and shall constitute one agreement.

IN WITNESS WHEREOF, the said Grantor and the Trustee have set their hands and seals on _____, 2009.

In The Presence Of:

_____

_____   _____
Witness   Grantor

_____   _____
Witness   Trustee

STATE OF NEW HAMPSHIRE
COUNTY OF _____

The foregoing instrument was acknowledged before me on _____, 2009, by _____.

_____
Notary Public/Justice of the Peace
My Commission Expires:
(Seal)

STATE OF NEW HAMPSHIRE
COUNTY OF _____

The foregoing instrument was acknowledged before me on _____, 2009, by _____.

_____
Notary Public/Justice of the Peace
My Commission Expires:
(Seal)

SCHEDULE A

CASH:
ACCEPTED: _____, 2009

_____
_____, Trustee

Page 692: Substitute this form for Form 41 in the text:

FORM 41   Irrevocable Joint and Survivor Insurance Trust

THE _____ FAMILY

IRREVOCABLE TRUST OF 2009

THIS AGREEMENT OF TRUST, made on _____, 2009, by and between _____, of _____, County of _____, State of New Hampshire, and _____, of _____, County of _____, State of New Hampshire (hereinafter individually referred to as the "Grantor" and collectively referred to as the "Grantors"), and _____, of _____, County of _____, State of New Hampshire (hereinafter referred to as the "Trustee"), to establish an irrevocable trust to be known as **THE _____ FAMILY IRREVOCABLE TRUST OF _____.**

1.   <u>STATEMENT OF PURPOSE AND RECITATION OF FACTS</u>. This trust has been established for the benefit of the Grantors' issue. Nonetheless, it is not the Grantors' intention that this agreement directly substitute distributions from this trust for payments that the Grantors are obligated to make during the Grantors' lifetimes, but, rather, it is the Grantors' intention and direction that the Trustee shall make distributions from this trust from time to time in its sole, absolute, and uncontrolled discretion pursuant to the terms of this trust.

The Grantors do hereby declare that the Grantors have this day irrevocably transferred to the Trustee the property listed in **SCHEDULE A** attached hereto, to have and to hold the same and any cash, securities, or other property which the Trustee may, pursuant to any of the provisions hereof, at any time hereafter, hold or acquire, all of such property being hereinafter referred to collectively as the "trust estate", for the uses and purposes and upon the terms and conditions herein set forth.

At the time of the signing of this trust, the Grantors' children are _____.

2.   <u>DISPOSITIVE PROVISIONS: DURING LIFETIMES OF THE GRANTORS</u>.

A.   Except as otherwise hereinafter provided, the Trustee shall apportion the trust estate into equal shares as follows:

one (1) such equal share to each of the Grantors' living children, and

one (1) such equal share, allocated <u>per stirpes</u>, to the living issue of any child of the Grantors who is deceased.

1.   With respect to any <u>inter vivos</u> gift or other transfer to the Trustee at any time hereafter, the donor or transferor may by written designation direct the Trustee to apportion, equally or unequally, said gift or transfer among one or more of said shares or parts of shares.

In the event that the donor or transferor does not make such a written designation, then the Trustee shall apportion said gift or transfer equally among said shares.

2. Unless the Grantor or any other transferor so directs to the contrary in writing, the Trustee shall give each beneficiary written notice that the trust has received <u>inter</u> <u>vivos</u> gifts or transfers of cash or property in which said beneficiary has a Demand Right, as hereinafter provided, made to the trust within a reasonable period after receipt of such gift or transfer.

Upon receipt of written notice from the Trustee, each beneficiary shall have the absolute and unrestricted right, as hereinafter provided, to demand and promptly receive from said beneficiary's trust, outright and free from trust, an amount of property or a sum of cash equal to the amount apportioned to said beneficiary's share in accordance with sub-paragraph 2.A. above of any <u>inter</u> <u>vivos</u> gift or transfer, including the initial transfer indicated on **SCHEDULE A** hereof (the "Demand Right").

Provided, however, that the maximum amount that can be withdrawn annually by each such beneficiary under this sub-paragraph shall not exceed the maximum amount excludable from a donor's taxable gifts for such year in respect to gifts to any donee under Section 2503(b) of the Internal Revenue Code, taking into account for a married donor under Section 2513 of the Code.

Notwithstanding the foregoing, a beneficiary shall have no right of withdrawal during any period in which said beneficiary shall be subject to any voluntary or involuntary receivership, insolvency or bankruptcy proceeding under the laws of the United States, or of any other country, or of any state or political sub-division.

The Demand Right of each said beneficiary shall be non-cumulative and said beneficiary must exercise his demand right in writing before the thirtieth (30th) day after receipt by said beneficiary of notice of the <u>inter</u> <u>vivos</u> gift or transfer.

If any such beneficiary is, for any reason, under a legal disability to exercise his Demand Right, it may be exercised on his behalf by the natural or legal guardian of said beneficiary in the same manner as by said beneficiary himself.

3. Said shares shall then be held and administered and disposed of as provided for below.

B. During the lifetimes of the Grantors, the shares and parts of shares apportioned above shall be held and administered and disposed of as follows:

1. In the case of each share apportioned to a living child of the Grantors,

the Trustee may make such payments, use, application, expenditure or accumulation of the income and principal thereof as it shall think proper for the direct or indirect benefit of said child for support in reasonable comfort, education (including college, graduate, and professional education), and maintenance in health (including medical, dental, hospital, nursing and nursing home expenses).

2. In the case of each part of a share allocated per stirpes to the living issue of a deceased child of the Grantors (hereinafter each individually referred to as a "beneficiary"), the Trustee may make such payments, use, application, expenditure or accumulation of the income and principal thereof as it shall think proper for the direct or indirect benefit of said beneficiary for support in reasonable comfort, education (including college, graduate, and professional education) and maintenance in health (including medical, dental, hospital, nursing and nursing home expenses).

C. No payments of income or of principal shall be made to the Grantors during the Grantors' lifetimes.

D. The provisions contained above which require the Trustee to apportion the trust estate into shares and parts of shares are for purposes of computation only and shall not be construed to require the Trustee to make physical segregation of one share or a part of a share from the others, although the Trustee shall have full right to make such segregation if it thinks it better to do so.

Notwithstanding said provisions, the Trustee shall have the full right to regard the trust estate as one undivided estate for purposes of management and investment; provided, however, that all trust shares and parts of shares shall be treated as substantially separate and independent trusts under Sections 663(c), 2041(b)(2) and 2514(e) of the Internal Revenue Code.

3. DISPOSITIVE PROVISIONS: AFTER DEATH OF THE SURVIVING GRANTOR. Upon the death of the surviving Grantor, the trust shares, and parts of shares, above apportioned shall be held and administered and disposed of, as follows:

A. In the event the trust estate consists of proceeds from life insurance on the Grantors' lives, then notwithstanding the above equal apportionment, the Trustee shall allocate said life insurance proceeds among said trust shares in the following manner:

The Trustee shall calculate a fraction for each share of the trust estate, the numerator of which shall be each beneficiary's (or, in the case of the family group composed of the issue of a deceased child of the Grantors, such beneficiary's parent's) deemed contribution to the payment of premiums on said insurance policy, and the denominator of which shall be the total premiums deemed paid by all of the beneficiaries on said insurance policy;

Each trust share shall then be allocated its fractional portion of said life insurance proceeds.

B. In the case of each share, if any, administered for the benefit of a living child of the Grantors, during the lifetime of the child, the Trustee may, in its sole, absolute, and uncontrolled discretion, accumulate the income of each trust share, or, pay over to such child or use, apply or expend for such child's direct or indirect benefit, so much or all of the net income of his trust share, and so much or all of the principal of his trust share, as the Trustee may deem proper or necessary for his support in reasonable comfort, education (including college, graduate, and professional education), and maintenance in health (including medical, dental, hospital, nursing and nursing home expenses), taking into consideration the amount of such child's assets and income from sources other than this trust; provided, however, that the Trustee shall not be required to make any distributions sooner than two (2) years after the date of the death of the surviving Grantor.

1. Whenever said child shall have attained the age of twenty-five (25) years, he shall have the right to request in writing and to receive one third (1/3) of the principal of his share; and

Whenever said child shall have attained the age of thirty (30) years, he shall have the right to request in writing and to receive an additional one-half (1/2) of the principal of his share; and

Whenever said child shall have attained the age of thirty-five (35) years, he shall have the right to request in writing and to receive the entire balance of the principal and undistributed income of his share, at which time said child's trust shall terminate.

2. It is the Grantors' belief that, in some circumstances, it may be beneficial for said child to leave the management of his trust share in the hands of the Trustee. Therefore, said child may elect to leave his trust share, or any portion thereof, in the hands of the Trustee, as a separate fund, to be held and administered and disposed of as said child shall direct.

C. In the case of each part of a share allocated per stirpes to the living issue of a deceased child of the Grantors, the Trustee may make such payments, use, application, expenditure or accumulation of the income and principal thereof as it shall think proper for the direct or indirect benefit of said issue for support in reasonable comfort, education (including college, graduate, and professional education) and maintenance in health (including medical, dental, hospital, nursing and nursing home expenses).

201

Final distribution shall be made of whatever shall remain of said share, free and clear of all trusts when the youngest then living child of the Grantors' deceased child attains the age of thirty (30) years; provided, however, that the Trustee shall not be required to make any distributions sooner than two (2) years after the date of the death of the surviving Grantor.

4.   <u>DISPOSITIVE PROVISIONS: DEATH OF A BENEFICIARY</u>. Regardless of whether or not either Grantor is living, if any beneficiary dies prior to full distribution of said beneficiary's trust share, the following shall apply:

A.   To the extent any portion of said beneficiary's share would otherwise be subject to and require payment of (1) the Generation Skipping Transfer Tax imposed under Chapter 13 of the Internal Revenue Code if distributed to said beneficiary's issue or held in trust for the benefit of said beneficiary's issue under the terms of this trust, or (2) the Estate Tax under Chapter 11 of the Internal Revenue Code as a result of said beneficiary's death after lapse of his right of withdrawal pursuant to sub-paragraph 2.B.3. above, said beneficiary shall have a general power of appointment over such interest in the principal and accumulated income remaining in his trust share, free of all trusts and exercisable by himself alone, by his will, duly proved and allowed, either in favor of his estate or of others, or in favor of his estate and of others, as he shall choose; provided, however, that said general power of appointment shall be exercisable by said beneficiary by reference in his will to said general power of appointment hereby created.

B.   To the extent any portion of said beneficiary's trust share would not otherwise be subject to (1) Generation Skipping Transfer Tax or (2) Estate Tax, said beneficiary shall have a limited power of appointment over such interest in the principal and accumulated income remaining in his trust share, free of all trusts and exercisable by himself alone, by his will, duly proved and allowed, in favor of his issue and the issue of the Grantors, as he shall choose; provided, however, that said limited power of appointment shall be exercisable by said beneficiary by reference in his will to said limited power of appointment hereby created; provided, further, that in no event shall said limited power of appointment be exercisable in favor of said beneficiary, his estate, his creditors, or the creditors of his estate.

C.   Any principal remaining in said beneficiary's trust share on the death of said beneficiary and which has not been fully appointed by his will in accordance with the powers above vested in him, shall be reapportioned among the issue of the Grantor in accordance with the provisions of sub-paragraph 2.A. above and administered pursuant to the applicable provisions of Paragraph 2. or Paragraph 3., as the case may be.

D.   If at any time before the final distribution of all of the trust shares, and parts of shares described above there shall be no person in existence who is eligible to have the benefit of said trust shares, and parts of shares, the Trustee shall divide all of the trust estate then remaining into two (2) equal parts, which shall be distributed, outright and free of trust, as follows:

1. One (1) part to those persons then living who would have taken _____'s estate, and in such shares thereof as they would have taken, had he then died intestate, domiciled in New Hampshire; and

2. One (1) part to those persons then living who would have taken _____'s estate, and in such shares thereof as they would have taken, had she then died intestate, domiciled in New Hampshire.

5. <u>TRUSTEE'S DUTIES AND POWERS</u>. The assets of the trust shall be held subject to the following terms and conditions, and the Trustee shall have the following powers, in addition to any other powers granted to the Trustee by New Hampshire common law and statutory authority (including, but not limited to, the Uniform Trustees' Powers Act, R.S.A. 564-A, and the Uniform Trust Code, R.S.A. 564-B, as they may be amended from time to time), without restrictions.

In addition to such powers, and not in limitation thereof, the Trustee shall have the following powers, all of which shall be exercised in a fiduciary capacity and for the benefit of the beneficiaries:

A. As to any insurance policies owned by or payable to the trust, in whole or in part, the Trustee is authorized to sell, assign, surrender or hypothecate the policies, to borrow any sum in accordance with the provisions of the insurance contracts, to receive all payments, dividends, surrender values, and benefits or to receive and exercise all privileges of any kind which may occur on account of the policies, all in accordance with the provisions of the insurance contracts.

In making payment upon the policy, the issuing or obligated insurance company shall not be responsible for the proper application or disposition of any funds paid to the Trustee, but the receipt of the Trustee shall be a complete discharge to the insurance company.

The Trustee shall not use any part of the income of the trust estate in order to pay premiums on any insurance policies on the Grantors' lives, whether or not the trust owns the insurance policies.

B. The Trustee shall have the power to improve, lease for any term or perpetually, rent, sell, exchange, grant and exercise options to buy, any property at any time, to invest and reinvest in real or personal property of any kind, and to retain as a proper investment any property, whether originally a part of the trust estate or subsequently acquired, and to exercise the powers granted herein without being limited by any statute or judicial decision, whenever enacted or announced, imposing require-

203

ments as to assets in which investments may be made or the retention or diversification of investments.

The foregoing powers shall include (without limitation of the above described powers) the power to sell any trust assets to, or purchase assets from, the Grantors, any descendants of the Grantors, and/or the estate of any such person, whether or not such person is then acting as a Trustee.

The Trustee shall administer, retain, invest and reinvest the trust estate in any property, real or personal, tangible or intangible, including insurance policies on the Grantors' lives, security holdings, common trust funds, investments and management and administrative vehicles, whether issued, controlled, managed or administered by any corporate or financial institution serving hereunder as Trustee, or otherwise.

Notwithstanding the preceding provisions, or any other provision of this instrument, during the time in which the assets of the trust estate consist solely of principal cash, if any, and insurance policies, the Trustee shall not be required to diversify investments nor make any investment recommendations.

C. Any accumulated income which shall not be paid to the beneficiaries by virtue of a provision in this trust shall be added from time to time by the Trustee to the principal of the trust.

D. The Trustee shall have the power to borrow money from any institution or person, including the Trustee, for the benefit of the trust, and to pledge or mortgage any part or all of the trust estate as security.

E. The Trustee shall have power to arbitrate, defend, enforce, release or settle any claim of or against the trust.

F. The Trustee shall have power to vote, in person or by proxy, upon all securities held as a part of the trust estate, to exercise, buy or sell subscription and conversion rights and participate in reorganizations, recapitalizations, consolidations, mergers, exchanges, foreclosures, liquidations and creditors' and bondholders' agreements.

G. The Trustee shall have power to allocate receipts, disbursements and losses to principal or to income, in accordance with generally accepted accounting practices.

In addition, the Trustee shall have the power to allocate any annuity payment, or any lump-sum or periodic payment from a pension or profit-sharing plan in which either Grantor was a participant, received by the trust to income and/or principal as the Trustee, in the Trustee's sole, absolute, and uncontrolled discretion, deems advisable, irrespective of the treatment of the payment for income tax purposes.

Notwithstanding any trust accounting rule to the contrary, the Trustee shall maintain a reasonable reserve for depreciation with respect to any depreciable asset owned by the trust, and the term "net income", wherever used in this instrument, shall mean net income remaining after any addition to a depreciation reserve.

H. In any case in which the Trustee is required physically to divide property held in the trust estate into parts, shares or trusts, or to distribute the same, the Trustee may, in the Trustee's sole, absolute, and uncontrolled discretion, make the division or distribution in kind (including interests in any insurance policies owned by the trust) or in money or partly in kind and partly in money, and may allocate dissimilar property and undivided interests in property to different parts, shares or trusts, without respect to the income tax basis of the property.

The Trustee is specifically excused from any duty of impartiality with respect to the income tax basis of property.

If necessary to value property to be divided or distributed, it shall be valued at the then-current fair market value.

I. The Trustee may take and hold all securities or other personal property in bearer form, in the name of any Trustee, or in the name of a nominee, with or without disclosing any fiduciary relationship, but the Trustee shall be liable for any wrongful act of the nominee with respect to the assets.

J. The Trustee is authorized to employ and pay reasonable compensation to agents, investment counsel and attorneys, including the Trustee and any person, partnership, corporation or other entity with which the Trustee may be associated.

The foregoing authority shall include, without limitation, the power to authorize any Trustee, person or persons to withdraw funds from any bank account maintained by the trust and/or to have access to any safe deposit box maintained by the trust.

K. The Trustee is authorized to execute and deliver all necessary or proper deeds or other instruments.

L. No purchaser from and no lender to the Trustee is under any obligation to ensure that the purchase or loan money is applied for the purposes of the trust estate.

The receipt of the Trustee shall be a complete discharge to that person.

M. The Trustee shall have power to take, hold and convey title to real estate or interests in the name of the Trustee or in the name of the nominee of the Trustee without disclosing the trust, and in accepting title to the real estate neither the Trustee nor the nominee shall be held to have assumed the payment of any encumbrances.

205

All conveyances executed and delivered by the Trustee or the nominee shall be without covenants of warranty except as against the Trustee's or nominee's own acts.

N. The Trustee shall not be personally liable upon any contract of indebtedness of or claims against the trust estate or upon a mortgage, trust deed, note or other instrument executed under these provisions.

O. The Trustee shall be protected in continuing to make distributions of income or principal until the Trustee shall have actual knowledge of the happening of an event such as attainment of a certain age, death or other occurrence which would affect such distributions.

P. Any Trustee or successor Trustee may accept and rely upon any accounting made by or on behalf of any predecessor Trustee, and any statement or representation made by any fiduciary as to the assets comprising this trust estate or as to any other fact bearing upon the prior administration of the trust.

A Trustee or successor Trustee shall not be liable for having accepted and relied upon the accounting, statement or representation if it is later proved to be incomplete, inaccurate or untrue.

Q. If the Grantors or the executors of the Grantors' estates or any other individual (including any individual who shall transfer property in trust hereunder or the executor or administrator of the estate of such individual), has allocated any portion or all of any Generation Skipping Transfer ("GST") exemption provided by Section 2631(a) of the Internal Revenue Code to any property to be held in trust hereunder, then notwithstanding anything to the contrary contained in this agreement, the Trustee is authorized to establish such number of separate trusts, with identical terms, to hold the property received in trust hereunder as it, in its sole, absolute, and uncontrolled discretion, shall deem advisable, bearing in mind the allocation of the said GST exemption and the desirability that any trust to which all or any portion of the said GST exemption is allocated shall, if practical, have an inclusion ratio of zero.

Further, the Trustee is authorized to allocate such trusts among the trust shares above created in order to minimize (or eliminate, if possible) any GST tax.

R. If, after the death of the surviving Grantor, **THE** _____ **REVOCABLE TRUST OF** _____ or **THE** _____ **REVOCABLE TRUST OF** _____ is still in existence and the terms of any trust established under either trust, or any other trust, are substantially similar to this, **THE** _____ **FAMILY IRREVOCABLE TRUST OF** _____, the Trustee is authorized and empowered to consolidate this trust with such similar trust as one trust, unless such consolidation shall be contrary to law or inconsistent with the terms of any instrument supplemental hereto; provided that such consolidation clause shall be null and void in the event there is a determination that the application of such clause shall result in the inclusion of any of the trust estate in either Grantor's gross estate under any provision of the Internal Revenue Code, including but not limited to Sections 2041 and 2042.

S. The Trustee shall have full power and authority, to be exercised in its sole, absolute, and uncontrolled discretion, to merge any trust created hereunder with any other trust or trusts created under will, deed or otherwise, if the terms of such trust are then substantially similar and held for the primary benefit of the same persons.

T. Regardless of the extent of the authority that the Trustee holds to currently distribute income and/or principal of the trust estate to one or more beneficiaries of the trust, the Trustee shall have full power and authority, to be exercised in its sole, absolute, and uncontrolled discretion, to appoint any or all assets held in this trust estate to any other trust or trusts created under will, deed or otherwise, for the benefit of one or more of the beneficiaries hereunder.

This authority shall be subject to the limitations set forth in R.S.A. 564-B:4-418, as amended from time to time, provided that such appointment clause shall be null and void in the event there is a determination that the application of such clause shall result in the inclusion of any of the trust estate in the Grantor's gross estate under any provision of the Internal Revenue Code, including but not limited to Sections 2041 and 2042, which would not otherwise be includable in the Grantor's gross estate.

Provided further, however, that if this Trust qualifies as a "trust instrument" under the Qualified Dispositions in Trust Act, R.S.A. 564-D, as amended from time to time, then the Trustee may only appoint the assets of the trust estate to a new trust which will continue to qualify as a "trust instrument" under such Act and will provide similar protections to the assets held in this trust estate.

U. After the surviving Grantor's death, the Trustee may borrow or make loans or purchases and sales from and to the surviving Grantor's estate and from and to the Trustee serving under any other trust established by the Grantors, on such terms as the Trustee shall think proper, and all judgments, decisions and actions so taken shall be final and binding upon all persons if made reasonably and in good faith, even though the person serving as executor of the surviving Grantor's estate, or Trustee under such trust, shall be the same as the fiduciary under this trust.

V. In the event that any beneficiary of the trust shall serve in the capacity of co-Trustee then the discretionary powers to determine whether income or principal is to be distributed to said beneficiary or to any person to whom said beneficiary owes an obligation of support shall be exercisable only by the remaining Trustee.

It is the Grantors' intention by this sub-paragraph to prohibit said beneficiary from benefiting himself or herself as beneficiary in any way by the exercise of such discretionary powers vested in the Trustee as a group.

W. If, at any time before the final distribution of the principal of any trust share above described, the value of the principal of said trust share shall be equal to, or less than, ONE HUNDRED THOUSAND DOLLARS ($100,000), then the Trustee may, in its sole, absolute, and uncontrolled discretion, terminate said trust share and distribute the principal of said trust share, and any accumulated and undistributed income thereof, outright and free of trust, to those persons then entitled to benefit from said trust share, and in the proportions in which they are then entitled to benefit from said trust share, notwithstanding any provisions of this trust to the contrary.

6. <u>TRUST PROTECTOR</u>.

A. The Grantors appoint _____, of _____, _____, as the Trust Protector.

If _____ shall be unable or unwilling to serve in this capacity for any reason, then _____, of _____, _____, shall serve instead.

If _____ shall be unable or unwilling to serve in this capacity for any reason, then _____, of _____, _____, shall serve instead.

The Trust Protector is authorized, in its sole, absolute, and uncontrolled discretion, to remove any Trustee acting hereunder. Any vacancy resulting from such removal shall be filled pursuant to the provisions below.

Any removal of a Trustee shall be evidenced by an acknowledged instrument in writing and shall be delivered to the Trustee so removed and to each remaining Trustee (if any).

B. If all Trust Protectors cease to act as to any one or more trusts hereunder, a successor Trust Protector may be appointed by the "Appointment Committee" (as defined hereunder); provided, however that notwithstanding anything contained herein to the contrary, there may not be appointed as successor Trust Protector, either

1. the Grantors, or

2. any beneficiary of a trust hereunder, or

3. any spouse of a beneficiary, or

4. any person who is a related or subordinate party within the meaning of section 672(c) of the Code with respect to any beneficiary of this trust.

5. The Appointment Committee shall be as follows:

   a. the Grantors' then living and competent adult children, over the age of twenty-five (25) years, by majority vote, or, if no child of the Grantors are then living, adult, competent and over the age of twenty-five (25) years,

   b. such of the Grantors' descendants as are then living, adult and competent, over the age of thirty (30) years, by majority vote, or, if there is no such then adult and competent descendant over the age of thirty (30) years,

   c. the Trust Protector, if any.

C. The Grantors are not imposing any fiduciary responsibility on the Trust Protector to monitor the actions of the Trustee.

Except for any matter involving the Trust Protector's own individual willful misconduct or negligence proved by clear and convincing evidence, no Trust Protector shall incur any liability by reason of any error of judgment, mistake of law, or action of any kind taken or omitted to be taken hereunder if in good faith reasonably believed by such Trust Protector to be in accordance with the provisions and intent hereof.

The Trust Protector shall not be liable for the failure to remove any Trustee even if such Trustee may be guilty of a gross violation of his or her fiduciary duties hereunder.

D. Any appointment of a successor Trust Protector pursuant to the provisions hereunder shall be evidenced by an acknowledged instrument in writing and shall be effective upon acceptance thereof by the Trust Protector so appointed.

Any successor Trust Protector shall have all the powers of the initial Trust Protector.

Different trusts hereunder may, but need not, have different Trust Protectors.

More than one person may act collectively as a Trust Protector for any given trust hereunder, in which case decisions of the Trust Protector shall be made by majority vote if more than two (2) persons are so acting collectively.

Any Trust Protector may resign from office with respect to any one or more trusts hereunder at any time by delivery of a written, acknowledged instrument of resignation to the persons who are authorized to appoint a successor Trust Protector hereunder, or, if none, to the Trustees then in office.

The Trust Protector shall act without compensation hereunder but shall be reimbursed for any expenses in carrying out his or her duties hereunder.

7.   <u>TRUST ESTATE.</u>

A.   The Trustee acknowledges receipt of the property listed in **SCHEDULE A** attached hereto and will hold, manage, invest and reinvest the trust estate upon the terms herein set forth.

The Trustee may accept and administer hereunder whatever property, including cash, securities, life insurance policies, or other property, may by virtue of any gift, Will, Codicil or any other instrument be irrevocably given, devised, bequeathed or appointed to the Trustee hereunder by the Grantors or by any other person.

B.   The Trustee shall possess and own all incidents of ownership, rights, powers, interests, privileges, and benefits of every kind that may accrue on account of all property, including insurance policies, composing part of the trust estate, and the Grantors shall have no interest or right of any kind in or to any of the said trust property.

8.   <u>REPORTING BY TRUSTEE.</u>

A.   The Trustee may, at the Trustee's sole, absolute, and uncontrolled discretion, and shall, to the extent required by the Uniform Trust Code, R.S.A. 564-B, as it may be amended from time to time, render a Trustee's report as described in the Uniform Trust Code, as it may be amended from time to time, at such intervals as the Trustee may choose or at such times as required by the Uniform Trust Code.

B.   A recipient of such a report (or, if under guardianship or conservatorship, then by the Guardian or Conservator, or, if deceased, then by the Executor or Administrator), may, by a written instrument, assent to the report of the Trustee with respect to principal or to income, or with respect to both principal and income.

The assent of the recipient of such report (or, if under guardianship or conservatorship, then by the Guardian or Conservator, or, if deceased, then by the Executor or Administrator) shall make such report binding and conclusive upon all persons then having or who may thereafter have any interest, vested or contingent, in the income or principal of the trust estate and such assent shall forever release and discharge the Trustee of and from any and every claim, demand, accountability, and liability of every nature, arising from any matter or thing done or omitted to be done, in connection with this agreement or any trust hereby created, during the period in respect of which the report of the Trustee shall have been so settled.

C. The failure of any person to object in writing to the Trustee to such a report within thirty (30) days after the delivery of the same to such person hereunder shall be final and binding to the same extent as the written assent above provided.

D. Any person entitled to such a report, accounting, information, notice and the like (or, if under guardianship or conservatorship, then by the Guardian or Conservator, or, if deceased, then by the Executor or Administrator) may by a written instrument signed and acknowledged by him or her or them, as the case may be, and delivered to the Trustee, waive the right to said Trustee's report or to other information otherwise required to be furnished under the Uniform Trust Code, as it may be amended from time to time.

9.   SUCCESSOR TRUSTEE.

A. If _____ shall be unable or unwilling to serve in the capacity of Trustee for any reason, then _____ shall serve as successor Trustee.

B. If all Trustees shall be unable or unwilling to serve in the capacity of Trustee for any reason, then a majority of the beneficiaries to whom or for whose use the current net income of the trust estate is at the time authorized or required to be paid or applied, either,

(1) acting individually, if then eighteen (18) years of age, or,

(2) by his or her natural parent, or natural guardian, or Court appointed guardian or Court appointed conservator, if then under guardianship or conservatorship,

shall appoint a successor Trustee.

C. Each Trustee hereunder (whether originally designated herein or appointed as successor) shall have the right to resign at any time by giving thirty (30) days written notice to that effect to the current income beneficiary (or beneficiaries) of the trust.

D. In the event that a corporation or financial institution shall be appointed as successor Trustee hereunder, such successor Trustee shall be a trust company or bank qualified to act as such, possessing trust powers.

E. In the event that a corporation or financial institution shall be serving as Trustee hereunder, a majority of the beneficiaries to whom or for whose use the current net income of the trust estate is at the time authorized or required to be paid or applied and who shall be acting individually if at least eighteen (18) years of age, or, by his or her natural parent, or natural guardian, or Court appointed guardian or Court appointed conservator, if then under guardianship or conservatorship, may by a written instrument signed and acknowledged by them and delivered to such corporation or financial institution remove said Trustee and appoint as its successor, any corporation or financial institution having a trust department capable of rendering financial advice concerning the investments of the trust estate.

F. No successor Trustee shall be liable or responsible in any way for any actions or defaults of any predecessor Trustee, nor for any loss or expense from or occasioned by anything done or neglected to be done by any predecessor Trustee. Any successor Trustee shall have, from and after its appointment or succession to office hereunder and without any assignment or other action by any person, all the rights, interests, and powers, including discretionary rights and powers, which are by the provisions of this trust agreement granted to and vested in the Trustee named herein.

G. At no time shall the Grantors serve as Trustee hereunder.

10. <u>FIDUCIARIES</u>.

A. No person dealing with the Trustee shall be responsible for the application of any money, securities, or other property paid or delivered, and the receipt of the Trustee shall be a full discharge; and no person dealing with the Trustee, and no issuer, transfer agent, or other agent of any issuer of any securities shall be under any obligation to ascertain or inquire into the power of the Trustee to purchase, sell, exchange, transfer, mortgage, pledge, create a security interest in, lease, distribute, or otherwise dispose of or deal with any money, securities, or other property.

B. The Trustee hereby accepts the trust created by this trust agreement and it agrees to carry out the provisions hereof on its part according to the best of its ability; provided, however, that, in addition to the provisions of this trust agreement, no Trustee shall be held liable for any action taken or not taken, including any action intended to lessen or eliminate the impact of estate or generation-skipping transfer taxes with respect to any generation or beneficiary, whether or not such action is successful in achieving the results sought and without regard to its effect on other beneficiaries in the same or different generations, or for any loss or depreciation in the value of any property in any trust created herein, whether due to an error of judgment or otherwise, where the Trustee has exercised good faith and ordinary diligence in the exercise of its duties.

C. The Trustee shall receive reasonable compensation for its services in the administration of the trusts created herein, including reimbursement for amounts reasonably expended for bookkeeping services, investment services and advice, and other professional or para-professional services. In addition to the compensation herein provided, the Trustee shall receive reasonable compensation for any legal services provided for the benefit of the trust estate, such as handling any litigation involving the trust, preparing state or federal income tax returns and transferring any real estate.

D.   The Trustee shall be permitted to serve without bond or surety on its bond, except as required by law, and any successor Trustee shall be permitted to serve without bond or surety on its bond.

E.   A certificate signed by any Trustee hereunder and acknowledged before a Notary Public shall be conclusive evidence upon all persons and for all purposes of the facts stated in said certificate with regard to the terms of this trust, the text thereof, and who is from time to time Trustee hereunder.

F.   Any individual acting as a Trustee hereunder or any firm or corporation of which it is a member or employee may act as attorney for, deal and contract with, and be employed by the Trustee hereunder, and any individual acting as a Trustee hereunder may act as attorney, director, officer, agent or employee of any corporation in which the Grantors' estates or the trust are interested, directly or indirectly, as a stockholder or otherwise, all in the same manner and with the same freedom as though not a Trustee or the employee of a Trustee hereunder and without accountability for any compensation received in connection with such action.

11.   PERPETUITIES. All trusts established under this instrument shall be exempt from the application of the rule against perpetuities. This provision is intended to comply with New Hampshire R.S.A. 564:24, and accordingly, the Grantor specifically authorizes the Trustee to sell, mortgage or lease property for any period of time beyond the period that is required for an interest created under this instrument to vest in order to be valid under the rule against perpetuities, as measured by the period defined above.

The trusts created hereunder shall be perpetual to the fullest extent permitted by the governing law. If any trust created hereunder is deemed to be subject to the law of a jurisdiction (including, but only to the extent applicable to real property) that has a rule against perpetuities or similar rule which limits the period during which property can be held in trust, then such trust (other than a trust created by the exercise of a power of appointment conferred hereunder which exercise commences a new rule against perpetuities period under the law of such jurisdiction) shall terminate in all events upon the expiration of the longest period that property may be held in trust under this trust agreement under the law of such jurisdiction (including any applicable period in gross, such as 21 years, 90 years or 110 years); provided, however, that if the jurisdiction has a rule against perpetuities or similar rule which applies only to certain types of property, such as real property, the provisions of this paragraph shall apply only to such property. If under the law of such jurisdiction the longest period that property may be held in trust may be determined (or alternatively determined) with reference to the death of the last survivor of a group of individuals in being upon the date of this trust agreement, those individuals shall consist of all of the descendants of the Grantor's parents who were in being on the date of this trust agreement. Upon termination of a trust pursuant to the provisions of this paragraph, the trust property shall be transferred, conveyed and paid over to the persons then entitled to receive or have the benefit of the income from the trust in the proportions in which they are entitled thereto, or if their interests are indefinite, then in equal shares.

12.   SPENDTHRIFT PROVISION. Except as herein otherwise provided, the interest of any beneficiary hereunder, either as to income or principal, shall not be anticipated, alienated or in any other manner assigned or pledged or promised by such beneficiary, and shall not be reached by, or be subject to, any legal, equitable or other process, including any bankruptcy or divorce proceeding, or be subject to the interference or control of creditors or others in any way or manner, and all payments to, or the interest of, any beneficiary shall be free from the control or claim of any parent or spouse or former spouse or any other third party. Moreover, no power of appointment or power of withdrawal shall be subject to involuntary exercise. Provided, however, this spendthrift provision shall not restrict the exercise of a disclaimer or the exercise of a power of appointment or withdrawal right granted by this trust agreement. This provision is intended to be a material provision of this trust and any other trust established hereunder.

13.   TAX APPORTIONMENT. The assets held in this trust shall not be liable for any tax, payable by either Grantors' estate, including without limitation, legacy, estate and/or inheritance taxes, paid by or due and payable by the Grantors' estates, irrespective of whether these taxes, if any, are attributable to assets held by this trust. The Trustee of this trust has no authority to, and is not authorized to, pay these taxes, if any, from any trust assets, whether principal or income.

14.   SURVIVAL REQUIREMENT. No person shall be deemed to have survived any other person or event under the terms of this trust, unless such person survives the end of the period commencing with the close of the calendar day of the death of such person or on which such event occurs and ending with the close of the thirtieth (30th) calendar day thereafter.

15.   DISTRIBUTIONS TO MINORS. In any case where property or funds become distributable to a minor, then the Trustee shall have the additional power to distribute the same in any one or more of the following ways: (1) by distribution directly to the minor; (2) by distribution to the legal guardian of the minor; (3) by distribution to a parent, relative or friend of the minor for the minor's support in reasonable comfort, education and maintenance in health; (4) by applying the same directly for the minor's support in reasonable comfort, education and maintenance in health; (5) by depositing the same in a bank account in the name of the minor or by transferring property to or purchasing property in the name of a custodian for his or her benefit under a Uniform Law relating to transfers or gifts to minors; or (6) by holding the same hereunder in trust or in custody for the minor's support in reasonable comfort, education and maintenance

in health and by distributing the remainder thereof to the minor upon coming of age or otherwise to the minor's estate in case of the death of the minor.

The receipt of the person to whom property or funds are actually distributed in accordance with any of the foregoing provisions shall fully discharge the Trustee from further accountability therefor.

16. <u>GOVERNING LAW AND SITUS</u>. The Grantors declare that this agreement and the trust created hereby shall be construed under and regulated by the laws of the State of New Hampshire and that the validity and effect of this agreement and of this trust shall be determined in accordance with the laws of that State.

Further, the trust shall be under the jurisdiction of the courts of the State of New Hampshire and the Trustee shall voluntarily enter a general appearance in any legal action relating to an accounting of the trust or a declaratory judgment interpreting this trust agreement. The Trustee shall not be chargeable in any court other than one of the courts of that State.

[OPTIONAL] However, the Trustee, at any time and from time to time, in its discretion, may, (1) remove all or part of the trust estate and hold and administer the same in any other jurisdiction where the Trustee shall be then located, (2) change the situs of administration of any trust from one jurisdiction to another jurisdiction; and (3) elect that the law of such other jurisdiction shall thereafter govern the trust to such extent as may be necessary and appropriate, and to amend the administrative provisions of the trust as the Trustee deems appropriate to ensure compliance and compatibility with such law, whereupon the courts of such other jurisdiction shall have the power to effectuate the purposes of this trust agreement to such extent. The determination of the Trustee as to any such removal of assets or change of situs or governing law shall be conclusive and binding on all persons interested in such trust.

17. <u>IRREVOCABILITY</u>.

A. This trust is irrevocable and the Grantors sever permanently any control over the assets of the trust.

The significance of the irrevocability of this trust has been fully explained to the Grantors by the Grantors' legal counsel.

The Grantors hereby expressly acknowledge that the Grantors shall have no right or power, whether alone or in conjunction with others, in whatever capacity, to alter, amend, revoke or terminate the trust, or any of the terms of the trust, in whole or in part, or to designate the persons who shall possess or enjoy the trust estate or the income therefrom.

By this trust instrument, the Grantors intend to and do hereby relinquish absolutely and forever all possession or enjoyment of, or right to the income from, the trust estate, whether directly, indirectly or constructively, and every interest of any nature, present or future, in the trust estate.

B. Notwithstanding anything contained in this agreement expressly or impliedly to the contrary, no power enumerated herein or accorded to the Trustee generally pursuant to law shall be construed,

(1) to enable the Grantors or any "non-adverse party" (as defined in Section 672(b) of the Internal Revenue Code), or both of them, to borrow all or any part of the trust estate or income therefrom, directly or indirectly, without adequate interest or adequate security or to permit the Grantors to revest in themselves title to any or all of the trust estate, nor

(2) without the approval or consent of an "adverse party" (as defined in Section 672(a) of the Internal Revenue Code), to enable the Grantors or such non-adverse party, or both of them, to purchase, exchange or otherwise deal with or dispose of any or all of the trust estate or income therefrom for less than an adequate consideration in money or money's worth or to enable any or all of the income from the trust to be distributed to, or be held or accumulated for future distribution to the Grantors (by discharging a support obligation or otherwise), nor

(3) to enable the Grantors to remove a successor Trustee or co-Trustee, nor

(4) to permit any person other than the Trustee to have or exercise the power to vote or direct the voting of stock or other securities of the trust, to control the investment of the trust estate either by directing or vetoing investments or reinvestments, or to reacquire the trust estate by substituting other property of an equivalent value.

C. The Trustee, in its sole, absolute, and uncontrolled discretion, may from time to time amend this trust agreement to address changes in federal or state tax law.

In the event of repeal of the federal estate or generation-skipping transfer tax provisions (as currently set forth in Chapters 11 and 13 of the Internal Revenue Code), the Trustee, in the Trustee's sole, absolute, and uncontrolled discretion, may terminate the trust by distribution, outright and free of trust, to those persons then entitled to benefit from this trust, and in the proportions in which they are then entitled to benefit from this trust at the time of said repeal, notwithstanding any provisions of this trust to the contrary.

In exercising such power, the Trustee shall, in addition to the factors set forth herein, consider the following:

The enactment of any federal income, capital gains or other tax which would impact adversely on, or offset the tax benefits of, any proposed trust termination;

The benefits afforded to the beneficiaries by the continuation of the trust, such as the age and maturity of the beneficiaries, protection against the claims of judgment creditors and the insulation from the reach of government agencies;

The likelihood of re-enactment of a federal estate, gift or generation-skipping transfer or comparable tax which would subject the trust principal to imposition of such tax or taxes in the hands of, or upon lifetime or testamentary transfers by, the beneficiaries to whom the trust principal would have been distributed upon termination.

18.   DEFINITIONS. Whenever used in this trust agreement, the words "child", "children" or "issue" are intended to include not only persons who are descendants by blood, but also persons, and issue of persons, who have been adopted according to law prior to their attaining the age of eighteen (18) years.

References to the "Internal Revenue Code" or "Code" or to provisions thereof are to the Internal Revenue Code of 1986, as amended at the time in question. References to the "Treasury Regulations," "Regulations" and "Regs." are to the Treasury Regulations under the Code. If, by the time in question, a particular provision of the Code has been renumbered, or the Code has been superseded by a subsequent federal tax law, the reference shall be deemed to be to the renumbered provision or the corresponding provision of the subsequent law, unless to do so would clearly be contrary to the Grantor's intent as expressed in this Trust Agreement, and a similar rule shall apply to references to the Regulations.

Masculine, feminine and neuter pronouns shall each include all genders, and the singular shall include the plural and vice versa, where the context or facts so admit.

The captions and paragraph headings of this trust agreement are inserted only as a matter of convenience and for reference and in no way define, limit or describe the scope or intent of this agreement, nor in any way affect this agreement.

19.   EXECUTION. This trust agreement shall be effective when executed by the Grantors, notwithstanding that the signature of the Trustee is provided for, the Trustee's signature being intended to denote the acceptance of the Trustee to serve in that capacity only.

This trust agreement may be executed in any number of counterparts with the same effect as if all of the parties had signed the same document. All counterparts shall be construed together and shall constitute one agreement.

IN WITNESS WHEREOF, the Grantors and the Trustee have set their hands and seals on _____, 2009.

In the Presence Of:

_____   _____
Witness   , Grantor

_____ _____
Witness   , Grantor

_____ _____
Witness   , Trustee

STATE OF NEW HAMPSHIRE
COUNTY OF _____

The foregoing instrument was acknowledged before me on _____,
2009 by _____.

_____
Notary Public/Justice of the Peace
My Commission Expires:
(Seal)

STATE OF NEW HAMPSHIRE
COUNTY OF _____

The foregoing instrument was acknowledged before me on _____,
2009 by _____.

_____
Notary Public/Justice of the Peace
My Commission Expires:
(Seal)

STATE OF NEW HAMPSHIRE
COUNTY OF _____

The foregoing instrument was acknowledged before me on _____,
2009 by _____.

_____
Notary Public/Justice of the Peace
My Commission Expires:
(Seal)

SCHEDULE A

CASH: Ten Dollars ($10.00)

ACCEPTED: _____, 2009.

_____

_____ , Trustee

Page 712: Substitute this form for Form 42 in the text:

FORM 42 Irrevocable Trust for Grandchildren

THE _____ FAMILY GRANDCHILDREN'S IRREVOCABLE TRUST OF 2005

THIS AGREEMENT OF TRUST, made on _____, 2005, by and between _____, of _____, County of _____, State of _____, and _____, of _____, County of _____, State of New Hampshire (hereinafter individually referred to as the "Grantor" and collectively referred to as the "Grantors"), and _____, of _____, County of _____, State of _____ (hereinafter referred to as the "Trustee"), to establish an irrevocable trust to be known as "The _____ Family Grandchildren's Irrevocable Trust of 2005".

1. STATEMENT OF PURPOSE AND RECITATION OF FACTS. This trust has been established for the benefit of the Grantors' grandchild. Nonetheless, it is not the Grantors' intention that this agreement directly substitute distributions from this trust for payments anyone is obligated to make to the Grantors' said grandchild, but, rather, it is the Grantors' intention and direction that the Trustee shall make distributions from this trust from time to time in its sole discretion pursuant to the terms of this trust.

The Grantors do hereby declare that they have this day irrevocably transferred to the Trustee the property listed in **SCHEDULE A** attached hereto, to have and to hold the same and any cash, securities, or other property which the Trustee may, pursuant to any of the provisions hereof, at any time hereafter, hold or acquire, all of such property being hereinafter referred to collectively as the "trust estate", for the uses and purposes and upon the terms and conditions herein set forth.

2. DISPOSITIVE PROVISIONS.

A. The Trustee shall hold, manage, invest and reinvest the trust estate, and shall collect the income thereof and dispose of the net income and principal primarily for the benefit of the Grantors' grandchild, _____, _____ and _____, as follows:

During the lifetime of said grandchild, the Trustee may pay over to said grandchild or may use, apply or expend for said grandchild's direct or indirect benefit, so much or all of the net income and so much or all of the principal of the trust estate as the Trustee may deem proper or necessary for support in reasonable comfort, education (including college and professional education), and maintenance in health (including medical, dental, hospital, nursing and nursing home expenses).

Said grandchild shall have the following rights with regard to withdrawal of fractions of the principal of said trust estate:

1. Whenever said grandchild shall have attained the age of thirty (30) years, said grandchild shall have the right to request in writing and to

219

receive one-third (1/3) of the principal of said trust estate;

Whenever said grandchild shall have attained the age of thirty-five (35) years, said grandchild shall have the right to request in writing and to receive one-half (1/2) of the balance of the principal of said trust estate;

Whenever said grandchild shall have attained the age of forty (40) years, said grandchild shall have the right to request in writing and to receive the entire balance of the principal and undistributed income of said trust estate, at which time this trust shall terminate.

2. It is the Grantors' belief that, in some circumstances, it may be beneficial for said grandchild to leave the management of said trust estate in the hands of the Trustee.

Therefore, said grandchild may elect to leave said trust estate, or any portion thereof, in the hands of the Trustee, as a separate fund, to be held and administered and disposed of as said grandchild shall direct.

3. Upon the death of said grandchild, if said grandchild dies prior to full distribution of the trust estate, if said grandchild is then under the age of eighteen (18) years, then the remaining principal and undistributed income of said trust estate shall be paid over to said grandchild's estate, to be disposed of pursuant to the provisions thereof.

If said grandchild shall have attained the age of eighteen (18) years at the time of death, then said grandchild shall have a general power of appointment over the remaining principal and undistributed income of said trust estate, free of all trusts and exercisable by said grandchild alone, by last will, duly proved and allowed, either in favor of said grandchild's estate or of others, or in favor of said grandchild's estate and of others, as said grandchild shall choose; provided, however, that said general power of appointment shall be exercisable by said grandchild by reference in said grandchild's last will to said general power of appointment hereby created.

In the event said grandchild fails to validly exercise said general power of appointment, in whole or in part, then, upon the death of said grandchild, the Trustee shall apportion said trust estate not so apportioned to the living issue of said deceased grandchild, per stirpes.

B. The shares hereinabove apportioned to said grandchild's living issue shall be held and administered and disposed of as follows:

1. In the case of each share apportioned, per stirpes, to the living issue of said deceased grandchild (hereinafter each individually called "issue"), the Trustee may, in each and every year beginning with the date of said

apportionment, pay over to said issue or use, apply, or expend for said issue's direct or indirect benefit, so much or all of the net income and so much or all of the principal of said share as the Trustee may deem proper or necessary for support in reasonable comfort, education (including college and professional education), and maintenance in health (including medical, dental, hospital, nursing and nursing home expenses).

Final distribution shall be made of whatever shall remain of said share to said living issue and free and clear of all trusts, at a time determined by the Trustee, but in no event later than twenty-one (21) years after the death of the Grantors' said grandchild.

2. If at any time before the final distribution of any per stirpes share hereinabove described there shall be no person in existence who is eligible to have the benefit of the trust of such share, then the share in question shall be reapportioned, per stirpes, among the other shares apportioned to the living issue of said deceased grandchild, and each such reapportioned share shall continue to be held and administered in trust, in the manner provided for hereinabove, for the benefit of persons then living, in accordance with the fortunes of the share to which reapportionment is made.

C. If at any time before the final distribution of all of the trust shares hereinabove described, there shall be no person in existence who is eligible to have the benefit of said trust estate, then the Trustee shall distribute the remaining principal and undistributed income of said trust estate, outright and free of trust, to the Grantors' own child, _____ and _____, if then living, or, if not, then to said child's remaining living issue, per stirpes.

If said _____ and _____ is not then living, and, further, has no remaining living issue, then the Trustee shall divide said trust estate then remaining into two (2) equal parts which shall be distributed, outright and free of trust, as follows:

1. One (1) part to those persons then living who would have taken's estate, and in such shares thereof as they would have taken, had he then died intestate, domiciled in New Hampshire; and

2. One (1) part to those persons then living who would have taken's estate, and in such shares thereof as they would have taken, had she then died intestate, domiciled in New Hampshire.

D. So long as the Grantors' said children, or any of them, shall be living, and unless the Grantor or any other transferor so directs to the contrary in writing the Trustee shall send a written notice to the beneficiaries of a contribution to the trust, that each child who receives a written notice shall have the absolute and unrestricted right, as hereinafter provided, to demand and promptly receive from the trust, outright and free from such trust, an amount of property or a sum of cash equal to such beneficiary's pro rata share of any inter vivos gift or transfer, including the initial transfer indicated on **SCHEDULE A** hereof, made to the trust.

The pro rata share of each such beneficiary in any inter vivos gift or transfer to the trust shall be equal to a fraction having as its numerator the amount of the inter vivos gift or transfer and having as its denominator the total number of such beneficiaries then living.

The maximum amount that may be withdrawn annually by each such beneficiary under this sub-paragraph shall not exceed the lesser of:

1. the maximum amount over which an individual may have a power of withdrawal without its lapse in such year being deemed to be a release of such power under Section 2514(e) of the Code of 1986, as amended, and any corresponding Sections of any future Code (the "Code"), and

2. the maximum amount excludable from a donor's taxable gifts for such year in respect to gifts to any donee under Section 2503(b) of the Code, taking into account for a married donor under Section 2513 of the Code.

Notwithstanding the foregoing, a Grantor or any other transferor may by written designation direct the Trustee to apportion, equally or unequally, the said gift or transfer among one or more of said beneficiaries, rather than the gift or transfer being apportioned on a pro rata basis.

In the event that a Grantor or any other transferor does not make such a written designation, then the Trustee shall apportion to each beneficiary his pro rata share of said gift or transfer.

Further, a beneficiary shall have no right of withdrawal during any period in which such beneficiary shall be subject to any voluntary or involuntary receivership, insolvency or bankruptcy proceeding under the laws of the United States, or of any other Country, or of any State or political subdivision.

The Trustee shall give each said beneficiary written notice that the trust has received inter vivos gifts or transfers of cash or property in which said beneficiary has a demand right within a reasonable period after such receipt.

The demand right of each such beneficiary shall be noncumulative and such beneficiary must exercise his demand right in writing before the thirtieth (30th) day after receipt by such beneficiary of notice of the inter vivos gift or transfer.

If any such beneficiary is, for any reason, under a legal disability to exercise said beneficiary's demand right, it may be exercised on said beneficiary's behalf by said beneficiary's natural or legal guardian in the same manner as by such beneficiary himself.

E. The provisions contained hereinabove which require the Trustee to apportion the trust estate into shares are for purposes of computation only and shall not be construed to require the Trustee to make physical segregation of one share or a part of a share from the others, although the Trustee shall have full right to make such segregation if it thinks it better to do so.

Notwithstanding said provisions, the Trustee shall have the full right to regard the trust estate as one undivided estate for purposes of management and investment; provided, however, that all trust shares and parts of shares shall be treated as substantially separate and independent trusts under Sections 663(c), 2041(b)(2) or 2514(e) of the Code of 1986, or any provision successor thereto.

F. If, at any time before the final distribution of the principal of the trust estate hereinabove described, the value of the principal of said trust estate shall be equal to, or less than, ONE HUNDRED THOUSAND DOLLARS ($100,000), then the Trustee may, in its sole discretion, terminate this trust and distribute the principal of this trust, and any accumulated and undistributed income thereof, outright and free of trust, to those persons then entitled to benefit from this trust, and in the proportions in which they are then entitled to benefit from this trust, notwithstanding any provisions of this trust to the contrary.

3.   TRUSTEE'S DUTIES AND POWERS. The assets of the trust shall be held subject to the following terms and conditions, and the Trustee shall have the following powers, in addition to any other powers granted to the Trustee under the Uniform Trustees' Powers Act, R.S.A. 564-A and the Uniform Trust Code, R.S.A. 564-B, as they may be amended from time to time, without restrictions, and shall have all of the powers contained in that act without restrictions.

In addition to such powers, and not in limitation thereof, the Trustee shall have the following powers, all of which shall be exercised in a fiduciary capacity and for the benefit of the beneficiaries:

A. As to any insurance policies owned by or payable to the trust, in whole or in part, the Trustee is authorized to sell, assign, surrender or hypothecate the policies, to borrow any sum in accordance with the provisions of the insurance contracts, to receive all payments, dividends, surrender values, benefits or privileges of any kind which may occur on account of the policies, all in accordance with the provisions of the insurance contracts.

In making payment upon the policy, the issuing or obligated insurance company shall not be responsible for the proper application or disposition of any funds paid to the Trustee, but the receipt of the Trustee shall be a complete discharge to the insurance company.

The Trustee shall not use any part of the income of the trust estate in order to pay premiums on any insurance policies on the Grantors' lives, whether or not the trust owns the insurance policies.

B. The Trustee shall have the power to improve, lease for any term or perpetually, rent, sell, exchange, grant and exercise options to buy, any property at any time, to invest and reinvest in real or personal property (including both tangible and intangible securities) of any kind, and to retain as a proper investment any property, whether originally a part of the trust estate or subsequently acquired, and to exercise the powers granted herein without being limited by any statute or judicial decision, whenever enacted or announced, imposing requirements as to assets in which investments may be made or the retention or diversification of investments.

Notwithstanding the preceding provisions hereinabove, or any other provision of this instrument, during the time in which the assets of the trust estate consist solely of principal cash, if any, and insurance policies, the Trustee shall not be required to diversify investments nor make any investment recommendations.

C. Any accumulated income which shall not be paid to the beneficiaries by virtue of a provision in this trust shall be added from time to time by the Trustee to the principal of the trust.

D. The Trustee shall have the power to borrow money from any institution or person, including the Trustee, for the benefit of the trust, and to pledge or mortgage any part or all of the trust estate as security.

E. The Trustee shall have power to arbitrate, defend, enforce, release or settle any claim of, or against, the trust.

F. The Trustee shall have power to vote, in person or by proxy, upon all securities held as a part of the trust estate, to exercise, buy or sell subscription and conversion rights and participate in reorganizations, recapitalizations, consolidations, mergers, exchanges, foreclosures, liquidations and creditors' and bondholders' agreements.

G. The Trustee shall have power to allocate receipts, disbursements and losses to principal or to income, in accordance with generally accepted accounting practices.

In addition, the Trustee shall have the power to allocate any annuity payment, or any lump-sum or periodic payment from a pension or profit-sharing plan in which either Grantor was a participant, received by the trust to income and/or principal as the Trustee, in the Trustee's sole discretion, deems advisable, irrespective of the treatment of the payment for income tax purposes.

Notwithstanding any trust accounting rule to the contrary, the Trustee shall maintain a reasonable reserve for depreciation with respect to any depreciable asset owned by the trust, and the term "net income", wherever used in this instrument, shall mean net income remaining after any addition to a depreciation reserve.

H. In any case in which the Trustee is required physically to divide property held in the trust estate into parts, shares or trusts, or to distribute the same, the Trustee may, in the Trustee's discretion, make the division or distribution in kind (including interests in any insurance policies owned by the trust) or in money or partly in kind and partly in money, and may allocate dissimilar property and undivided interests in property to different parts, shares or trusts, without respect to the income tax basis of the property.

The Trustee is specifically excused from any duty of impartiality with respect to the income tax basis of property.

If necessary to value property to be divided or distributed, it shall be valued at the then-current fair market value.

I. The Trustee may take and hold all securities or other personal property in bearer form, in the name of any Trustee, or in the name of a nominee, with or without disclosing any fiduciary relationship, but the Trustee shall be liable for any wrongful act of the nominee with respect to the assets.

J. The Trustee is authorized to employ and pay reasonable compensation to agents, investment counsel and attorneys, including the Trustee and any person, partnership, corporation or other entity with which the Trustee may be associated.

The foregoing authority shall include, without limitation, the power to authorize any Trustee, person or persons to withdraw funds from any bank account maintained by the trust and/or to have access to any safe deposit box maintained by the trust.

K. The Trustee is authorized to execute and deliver all necessary or proper deeds or other instruments.

L. No purchaser from, nor lender to, the Trustee is under any obligation to ensure that the purchase or loan money is applied for the purposes of the trust estate.

The receipt of the Trustee shall be a complete discharge to that person.

M. The Trustee shall have power to take, hold and convey title to real estate or interests in the name of the Trustee or in the name of the nominee of the Trustee without disclosing the trust, and in accepting title to the real estate neither the Trustee nor the nominee shall be held to have assumed the payment of any encumbrances.

All conveyances executed and delivered by the Trustee or the nominee shall be without covenants of warranty except as against the Trustee's or nominee's own acts.

N. The Trustee shall not be personally liable upon any contract of indebtedness of or claims against the trust estate or upon a mortgage, trust deed, note or other instrument executed under these provisions.

O. The Trustee shall be protected in continuing to make distributions of income or principal until the Trustee shall have actual knowledge of the happening of an event such as attainment of a certain age, death or other occurrence which would affect such distributions.

P. Any Trustee or successor Trustee may accept and rely upon any accounting made by or on behalf of any predecessor Trustee, and any statement or representation made by any fiduciary as to the assets comprising this trust estate or as to any other fact bearing upon the prior administration of the trust.

A Trustee or successor Trustee shall not be liable for having accepted and relied upon the accounting, statement or representation if it is later proved to be incomplete, inaccurate or untrue.

Q. If the Grantors or the executors of the Grantors' estates or any other individual (including any individual who shall transfer property in trust hereunder or the executor or administrator of the estate of such individual), has allocated any portion or all of any Generation Skipping Transfer ("GST") exemption provided by Section 2631(a) of the Code of 1986, as amended, (and any corresponding sections of any future Code) to any property to be held in trust hereunder, then notwithstanding anything to the contrary contained in this agreement, the Trustee is authorized to establish such number of separate trusts, with identical terms, to hold the property received in trust hereunder as it, in its sole discretion, shall deem advisable, bearing in mind the allocation of the said GST exemption and the desirability that any trust to which all or any portion of the said GST exemption is allocated shall, if practical, have an inclusion ratio of zero.

Further, the Trustee is authorized to allocate such trusts among the trust shares hereinabove created in order to minimize (or eliminate, if possible) any GST tax.

R. If any other trust is in existence and the terms of such other trust are substantially similar to this trust, the Trustee is authorized and empowered to consolidate this trust with such other trust as one trust, unless such consolidation shall be contrary to law or inconsistent with the terms of any instrument supplemental hereto, and provided that such consolidation clause shall be null and void in the event there is a determination that the application of such clause shall result in the inclusion of any of the trust estate in either Grantor's gross estate under any provision of the Code of 1986, as amended, including but not limited to Sections 2041 and 2042 (and any corresponding sections of any future Code).

S.   The Trustee shall have full power and authority, to be exercised in its sole and uncontrolled discretion, to merge any trust created hereunder with any other trust or trusts created under will, deed or otherwise, if the terms of such trust are then substantially similar and held for the primary benefit of the same persons.

T.   In the event that any beneficiary of the trust shall serve in the capacity of co-Trustee then the discretionary powers to determine whether income or principal is to be distributed to said beneficiary or to any person to whom said beneficiary owes an obligation of support shall be exercisable only by the remaining Trustee.

It is the Grantors' intention by this sub-paragraph to prohibit said beneficiary from benefiting himself or herself as beneficiary in any way by the exercise of such discretionary powers vested in the Trustee as a group.

U.   In the event that any beneficiary of the trust shall serve in the capacity of sole Trustee and the Trustee has discretionary powers to distribute income or principal to himself, herself, or to any person to whom he or she owes an obligation of support, then such distributions of income or principal shall be exercisable by the sole Trustee.

The maximum amount that may be withdrawn annually by each such beneficiary under this sub-paragraph, however, shall not exceed the maximum amount over which an individual may have a power of withdrawal without its lapse in such year being deemed to be a release of such power under Section 2514(e) of the Code of 1986, as amended and any corresponding Sections of any future Code.

V.   If the Trustee has discretionary powers to distribute income or principal to any person to whom he or she owes an obligation of support, then said Trustee shall be prohibited from using assets of this trust to make such distributions.

4.   **TRUST ESTATE**.

A.   The Trustee acknowledges receipt of the property listed in **SCHEDULE A** attached hereto and will hold, manage, invest and reinvest the trust estate upon the terms herein set forth.

227

The Trustee may accept and administer hereunder whatever property, including cash, securities, life insurance policies, or other property, may by virtue of any gift, Will, Codicil or any other instrument be irrevocably given, devised, bequeathed or appointed to the Trustee hereunder by the Grantors or by any other person.

B. The Trustee shall possess and own all incidents of ownership, rights, powers, interests, privileges, and benefits of every kind that may accrue on account of all property, including insurance policies, composing part of the trust estate, and the Grantors shall have no interest or right of any kind in or to any of the said trust property.

5. SUCCESSOR TRUSTEE.

A. If _____ shall be unable or unwilling to serve in the capacity of Trustee for any reason, then _____, shall serve as successor Trustee.

If _____ shall be unable or unwilling to serve in the capacity of Trustee for any reason, then _____ shall serve as successor Trustee.

B. If all Trustees shall be unable or unwilling to serve in the capacity of Trustee for any reason, then a majority of the beneficiaries to whom or for whose use the current net income of the trust estate is at the time authorized or required to be paid or applied, either,

1. acting individually, if then eighteen (18) years of age, or,

2. by his or her natural parent, or natural guardian, or Court appointed guardian or Court appointed conservator, if then under guardianship or conservatorship, shall appoint a successor Trustee.

C. No successor Trustee shall be liable or responsible in any way for any actions or defaults of any predecessor Trustee, nor for any loss or expense from or occasioned by anything done or neglected to be done by any predecessor Trustee. Any successor Trustee shall have, from and after its appointment or succession to office hereunder and without any assignment or other action by any person, all the rights, interests, and powers, including discretionary rights and powers, which are by the provisions of this trust agreement granted to and vested in the Trustee named herein.

D. At no time shall either Grantor serve as Trustee.

6. TRUSTEE'S COMPENSATION. The Trustee hereunder may and is hereby authorized to pay itself fair and just compensation for services rendered as Trustee, in the administration of the trusts created herein out of the trust estate for its services hereunder.

The Trustee shall be reimbursed out of the trust estate for any advances made by it and for all reasonable expenses incurred in the management and protection of the trust estate.

7.   TRUSTEE'S LIABILITY. The Trustee hereby accepts the trust created by this trust agreement and it agrees to carry out the provisions hereof on its part according to the best of its ability; provided, however, that, in addition to the provisions of this trust agreement, no Trustee shall be held liable for any action taken or not taken, including any action intended to lessen or eliminate the impact of estate or generation-skipping transfer taxes with respect to any generation or beneficiary, whether or not such action is successful in achieving the results sought and without regard to its effect on other beneficiaries in the same or different generations, or for any loss or depreciation in the value of any property in any trust created herein, whether due to an error of judgment or otherwise, where the Trustee has exercised good faith and ordinary diligence in the exercise of its duties.

8.   TRUSTEE BOND. The Trustee shall be permitted to serve without bond or surety on its bond, except as required by law, and any successor Trustee shall be permitted to serve without bond or surety on its bond.

9.   TRUSTEE CERTIFICATE CONCLUSIVE. A certificate signed by any Trustee hereunder and acknowledged before a Notary Public shall be conclusive evidence upon all persons and for all purposes of the facts stated in said certificate with regard to the terms of this trust, the text thereof, and who is from time to time Trustee hereunder.

10.   TRANSACTIONS WITH INTERESTED TRUSTEE. Any individual acting as a Trustee hereunder or any firm or corporation of which it is a member or employee may act as attorney for, deal and contract with, and be employed by the Trustee hereunder, and any individual acting as a Trustee hereunder may act as attorney, director, officer, agent or employee of any corporation in which the trust is interested, directly or indirectly, as a stockholder or otherwise, all in the same manner and with the same freedom as though not a Trustee or the employee of a Trustee hereunder and without accountability for any compensation received in connection with such action.

11.   ACCOUNTING BY TRUSTEE.

A.   The Trustee shall render accounts of the administration of the trust annually. The assent by a majority of the beneficiaries to whom or to whose use the current net income of the trust is at the time authorized or required to be paid or applied and who at the time shall be at least eighteen (18) years of age (or if under guardianship or conservatorship, then by the Guardian or Conservator or if deceased, then by the Executor or Administrator) shall make such account, in the absence of fraud or manifest error, binding and conclusive upon all persons then having or who may thereafter have any interest, vested or contingent, in the income or principal of the trust estate.

B.   Said majority of the beneficiaries may by a written instrument signed and

229

acknowledged by him or her or them, as the case may be, and delivered to the Trustee, settle the account of the Trustee with respect to principal or to income, or with respect to both principal and income, and release and discharge the Trustee of and from any and every claim, demand, accountability, and liability of every nature, arising from any matter or thing done or omitted to be done, in connection with this agreement or any trust hereby created, during the period in respect of which the account of the Trustee shall have been so settled.

C. The failure of any person to object in writing to the Trustee to such an account within thirty (30) days after the delivery of the same to such person hereunder shall be final and binding to the same extent as the written approval hereinabove provided.

12.   SPENDTHRIFT PROVISION. Except as herein otherwise provided, the interest of any beneficiary hereunder, either as to income or principal, shall not be anticipated, alienated or in any other manner assigned or pledged or promised by such beneficiary, and shall not be reached by, or be subject to, any legal, equitable or other process, including any bankruptcy or divorce proceeding, or be subject to the interference or control of creditors or others in any way or manner, and all payments to, or the interest of, any beneficiary shall be free from the control or claim of any parent or spouse or former spouse or any other third party. Moreover, no power of appointment or power of withdrawal shall be subject to involuntary exercise. Provided, however, this spendthrift provision shall not restrict the exercise of a disclaimer or the exercise of a power of appointment or withdrawal right granted by this trust agreement.

13.   SURVIVAL REQUIREMENT. No person shall be deemed to have survived any person or event under the terms of this trust, unless such person survives the end of the period commencing with the close of the calendar day of death of such person or on which such event occurs and ending with the close of the thirtieth (30th) calendar day thereafter.

14.   TAX APPORTIONMENT. The assets held in this trust shall not be liable for any tax, including without limitation, legacy, estate and/or inheritance taxes, paid by or due and payable by the Grantors' estates, irrespective of whether these taxes, if any, are attributable to assets held by this trust.

The Trustee of this trust has no authority to, and is not authorized to, pay these taxes, if any, from any trust assets, whether principal or income.

15.   DISTRIBUTIONS TO MINORS. In any case where property or funds become distributable to a minor, then the Trustee shall have the additional power to distribute the same in any one or more of the following ways: (1) by distribution directly to the minor; (2) by distribution to the legal guardian of the minor; (3) by applying the same directly for the minor's support in reasonable comfort, education and maintenance in health; (4) by depositing the same in a bank account in the name of the minor or by transferring property to or purchasing property in the name of a custodian for his or her benefit under a Uniform Law

relating to transfers or gifts to minors; or (5) by holding the same hereunder in trust or in custody for the minor's support in reasonable comfort, education and maintenance in health and by distributing the remainder thereof to the minor upon coming of age or otherwise to the minor's estate in case of the death of the minor.

The receipt of the person to whom property or funds are actually distributed in accordance with any of the foregoing provisions shall fully discharge the Trustee from further accountability therefor.

16.   <u>IRREVOCABILITY</u>.

A.   This trust is irrevocable and the Grantors sever permanently any control over the assets of the trust.

The significance of the irrevocability of this trust has been fully explained to the Grantors by their legal counsel.

The Grantors hereby expressly acknowledge that they shall have no right or power, whether alone or in conjunction with others, in whatever capacity, to alter, amend, revoke or terminate the trust, or any of the terms of the trust, in whole or in part, or to designate the persons who shall possess or enjoy the trust estate, or the income therefrom.

By this trust instrument, the Grantors intend to and do hereby relinquish absolutely and forever all possession or enjoyment of, or right to the income from, the trust estate, whether directly, indirectly or constructively, and every interest of any nature, present or future, in the trust estate.

B.   Notwithstanding anything contained in this agreement expressly or impliedly to the contrary, no power enumerated herein or accorded to the Trustee generally pursuant to law shall be construed,

1.   to enable the Grantors or any "non-adverse party" (as defined in Section 672(b) of the Code of 1986, or any provision successor thereto), or both of them, to borrow all or any part of the trust estate or income therefrom, directly or indirectly, without adequate interest or adequate security or to permit the Grantors to revest in themselves title to any or all of the trust estate, nor

2.   without the approval or consent of an "adverse party" (as defined in Section 672(a) of the Code of 1986, or any provision successor thereto), to enable the Grantors or such non-adverse party, or both of them, to purchase, exchange or otherwise deal with or dispose of any or all of the trust estate or income therefrom for less than an adequate consideration in money or money's worth or to enable any or all of the income from the trust to be distributed to, or be held or accumulated for future distribution to the Grantors (by discharging a support obligation or otherwise), nor

231

3. to enable the Grantors to remove a successor Trustee or co-Trustee, nor

4. to permit any person other than the Trustee to have or exercise the power to vote or direct the voting of stock or other securities of the trust, to control the investment of the trust estate either by directing or vetoing investments or reinvestments, or to reacquire the trust estate by substituting other property of an equivalent value.

C. The Trustee, in its sole discretion, may from time to time amend this trust agreement to address changes in federal or state tax law.

In the event of repeal of the federal estate or generation-skipping transfer tax provisions (as currently set forth in Chapters 11 and 13 of the Code of 1986, and any provisions successor thereto), the Trustee, in the Trustee's sole discretion, may terminate the trust by distribution, outright and free of trust, to those persons then entitled to benefit from this trust, and in the proportions in which they are then entitled to benefit from this trust at the time of said repeal, notwithstanding any provisions of this trust to the contrary.

In exercising such power, the Trustee shall, in addition to the factors set forth herein, consider the following:

The enactment of any federal income, capital gains or other tax which would impact adversely on, or offset the tax benefits of, any proposed trust termination;

The benefits afforded to the beneficiaries by the continuation of the trust, such as protection against the claims of judgment creditors and the insulation from the reach of government agencies;

The likelihood of re-enactment of a federal estate, gift or generation-skipping transfer or comparable tax which would subject the trust principal to imposition of such tax or taxes in the hands of, or upon lifetime or testamentary transfers by, the beneficiaries to whom the trust principal would have been distributed upon termination.

17.   PERPETUITIES. All trusts established under this instrument shall be exempt from the application of the rule against perpetuities. This provision is intended to comply with New Hampshire R.S.A. 564:24, and accordingly, the Grantor specifically authorizes the Trustee to sell, mortgage or lease property for any period of time beyond the period that is required for an interest created under this instrument to vest in order to be valid under the rule against perpetuities, as measured by the period defined hereinabove.

The trusts created hereunder shall be perpetual to the fullest extent permitted by the governing law. If any trust created hereunder is deemed to be subject to the law of a jurisdiction (including, but only to the extent applicable to real property) that has a rule against perpetuities or similar rule which limits the period during which property can be held in trust, then such trust (other than a trust created by the exercise of a power of appointment conferred hereunder which exercise commences a new rule against perpetuities period under the law of such jurisdiction) shall terminate in all events upon the expiration of the longest period that property may be held in trust under this trust agreement under the law of such jurisdiction (including any applicable period in gross, such as 21 years, 90 years or 110 years); provided, however, that if the jurisdiction has a rule against perpetuities or similar rule which applies only to certain types of property, such as real property, the provisions of this paragraph shall apply only to such property. If under the law of such jurisdiction the longest period that property may be held in trust may be determined (or alternatively determined) with reference to the death of the last survivor of a group of individuals in being upon the date of this trust agreement, those individuals shall consist of all of the descendants of the Grantor's parents who were in being on the date of this trust agreement. Upon termination of a trust pursuant to the provisions of this paragraph, the trust property shall be transferred, conveyed and paid over to the persons then entitled to receive or have the benefit of the income from the trust in the proportions in which they are entitled thereto, or if their interests are indefinite, then in equal shares.

18. SITUS. The Grantors declare that this agreement and the trust created hereby shall be construed under and regulated by the laws of the State of New Hampshire and that the validity and effect of this agreement and of this trust shall be determined in accordance with the laws of that State, and that the Trustee shall not be chargeable in any court other than one of the courts of that State.

Further, the trust shall be under the jurisdiction of the courts of the State of New Hampshire and the Trustee shall voluntarily enter a general appearance in any legal action relating to an accounting of the trust or a declaratory judgment interpreting this trust agreement.

19. DEFINITIONS. Whenever used in this trust agreement, the words "child", "children", or "issue" are intended to include not only persons who are descendants by blood, but also persons and issue of persons who have been adopted according to law prior to their attaining the age of eighteen (18) years.

References to the "Internal Revenue Code" or "Code" or to provisions thereof are to the Internal Revenue Code of 1986, as amended at the time in question. References to the "Treasury Regulations," "Regulations" and "Regs." are to the Treasury Regulations under the Code. If, by the time in question, a particular provision of the Code has been renumbered, or the Code has been superseded by a subsequent federal tax law, the reference shall be deemed to be to the renumbered provision or the corresponding provision of the subsequent law, unless to do so would clearly be contrary to the Grantor's intent as expressed in this Trust Agreement, and a similar rule shall apply to references to the Regulations.

Masculine, feminine and neuter pronouns shall each include all genders, and the singular shall include the plural and vice versa, where the context or facts so admit.

The captions and paragraph headings of this trust agreement are inserted only as a matter of convenience and for reference and in no way define, limit or describe the scope or intent of this agreement, nor in any way affect this agreement.

Masculine, feminine and neuter pronouns shall each include all genders, and the singular shall include the plural, and vice versa, where the context or facts so admit.

The captions and paragraph headings of this trust agreement are inserted only as a matter of convenience and for reference and in no way define, limit or describe the scope or intent of this agreement, nor in any way affect this agreement.

20.   <u>EXECUTION</u>. This trust agreement shall be effective when executed by the Grantors, notwithstanding that the signature of the Trustee is provided for, the Trustee's signature being intended to denote the acceptance of the Trustee to serve in that capacity only.

This trust agreement may be executed in any number of counterparts with the same effect as if all of the parties had signed the same document. All counterparts shall be construed together and shall constitute one agreement.

IN WITNESS WHEREOF, the said Grantors and the Trustee have set their hands and seals on _____, 2005.

In the Presence Of:

_____   _____
Witness   , Grantor

_____   _____
Witness   , Grantor

_____   _____
Witness   , Trustee

STATE OF NEW HAMPSHIRE
COUNTY OF _____

The foregoing instrument was acknowledged before me on _____, 2005 by _____.

_____
Notary Public/Justice of the Peace
My Commission Expires:
(Seal)

STATE OF NEW HAMPSHIRE
COUNTY OF _____

The foregoing instrument was acknowledged before me on _____,
2005 by _____.

_____

_____
Notary Public/Justice of the Peace
My Commission Expires:
(Seal)

SCHEDULE A

CASH: Ten Dollars ($10.00)

Page 739: Substitute this form for Form 47 in the text:

FORM 47   Special Needs Trust [Dual-Grantor]

THE _____FAMILY REVOCABLE TRUST OF 2009

TRUST AGREEMENT, made on _____, 2009, between _____, residing in _____, New Hampshire, and _____, residing in _____, New Hampshire (hereinafter individually called the "Grantor" and collectively called the "Grantors"), and _____, residing in _____, New Hampshire, and _____, residing in _____, New Hampshire (hereinafter individually and collectively called the "Trustee").

At the time of the signing of this trust, the Grantor's spouse is _____, and the Grantor's children are _____.

1.   TRUST PROPERTY. All property transferred and delivered to the Trustee, which the Trustee may, at any time, hold or acquire, including cash, securities, or other property, shall be referred to collectively as the "trust estate" and held and administered and disposed of by the Trustee for the uses and purposes, and upon the terms and conditions, herein set forth.

2.   DISPOSITIVE PROVISIONS: LIFETIMES. The Trustee shall hold, manage, invest and reinvest the trust estate, and shall collect the income thereof and dispose of the net income and principal as follows:

A.   Pay such parts of the income, if any, and such parts of the principal of this trust to, or for the benefit of, the Grantors as the Grantors direct from time to time for the Grantors' support in reasonable comfort, education (including college, graduate, and professional education), and maintenance in health (including medical, dental, hospital, nursing and nursing home expenses). Any income accrued or accumulated at the time of the surviving Grantor's death shall be paid and transferred to principal, to be administered according to the terms hereinafter provided.

B.   In addition, during the lifetimes of the Grantors, if either Grantor becomes so incapacitated that he or she cannot exercise his or her rights under sub-paragraph 2.A. above, and there are sufficient assets in this trust to do so, the Trustee is authorized to pay such parts of the income, if any, and such parts of the principal of this trust to, or for the benefit of, the Grantors as it deems advisable for their support in reasonable comfort, education (including college, graduate, and professional education), and maintenance in health (including medical, dental, hospital, nursing and nursing home expenses), taking into consideration the amount of their income from sources other than this trust.

Further, the Trustee is authorized to give, transfer or convey any of the trust estate to persons of the Grantors' natural affection to whom the Grantors would normally consider making such gifts, transfers or conveyances, whether outright or in trust, having in mind the ultimate objective of such gifts, transfers or conveyances is either (i) the qualification for state or federal medical, welfare or other assistance programs for their benefit, or (ii) the reduction of the state and federal estate, inheritance, transfer, legacy and succession taxes and any interest and penalties thereon imposed by reason of their deaths.

In the case of _____, however, the Trustee shall make no such gift, transfer or conveyance which conflicts with the provisions of sub-paragraph 3.B.1. or the intent of the Grantors as stated in sub-paragraph 3.B.1.a.

3.   DISPOSITIVE PROVISIONS: AFTER DEATHS. Upon the death of the surviving Grantor, the trust estate shall be held and administered and disposed of as follows:

A.   The Trustee shall distribute all of the tangible personal property and household effects which are then part of the trust estate, including furniture, clothing, jewelry, silver, books, pictures, china, automobiles and their equipment, other vehicles and their equipment, and other articles of personal and household use or ornament, outright and free of trust, to the Grantors' issue who are then living, such issue to take per stirpes.

In the case of _____, however, the Trustee shall make no such gift, transfer or conveyance which conflicts with the provisions of sub-paragraph 3.B.1. or the intent of the Grantors as stated in sub-paragraph 3.B.1.a.

The Grantors express the hope that said beneficiaries will dispose of said tangible personal property and household effects according to the Grantors' wishes, however said wishes may be made known to them.

If a division of the property under this distribution is required among the beneficiaries, such division shall be made by the beneficiaries, in appropriate shares, as they may amicably agree.

The Grantors prefer that said beneficiaries shall agree upon the manner in which said property is to be divided, but should they not agree among themselves as to the division thereof within ninety (90) days after the surviving Grantor's death, the Trustee shall have full power and authority to divide said property among said beneficiaries, in appropriate shares, and its determination with respect thereto shall, insofar as permitted by law, be binding and conclusive upon such beneficiaries.

B.   After the distributions, if any, in sub-paragraph 3.A. above, the Trustee shall apportion the trust estate then remaining into equal shares as follows:

one (1) such share to each of the Grantors' living children, and

one (1) such share to each family group composed of the living issue of

237

any child of the Grantors who is then deceased.

Said equal shares shall then be held and administered and disposed of as follows:

1. In the case of the share apportioned to _____ (hereinafter referred to as the "beneficiary"), if he shall survive the surviving Grantor, during his lifetime, the Trustee may, in each and every year beginning with the date of said apportionment, pay over to said beneficiary so much or all of the net income from the said share for that year as the Trustee, in its sole, absolute, and uncontrolled discretion, may determine; and

The Trustee shall also have full power and authority to be exercised in its sole, absolute, and uncontrolled discretion, to pay over to said beneficiary or to use, apply, or expend for said beneficiary's direct or indirect benefit, so much or all of the principal it may deem wise.

Said beneficiary shall have no right whatsoever to demand or require payment of any amount of principal or income.

   a. The intent of the Grantors is for the Trustee to use the income and principal to promote the happiness, welfare and development of said beneficiary without in any way reducing the services or the financial assistance in basic maintenance, support, medical, psychological or dental care said beneficiary receives without charge from any local, state or federal government or agency or department thereof or any private agency or any private contractor and without using any portion of the income and principal to reimburse any local, state or federal government or agency or department thereof or any private agency or any private contractor for basic maintenance, support, medical, psychological and dental care received by said beneficiary.

   The Trustee may pay to or apply for the benefit of said beneficiary such sums out of the income or principal of said trust share as the Trustee, in the Trustee's sole, absolute, and uncontrolled discretion, considers necessary or appropriate for said beneficiary's special needs.

   As used herein, "special needs" refers to the requisites for maintaining said beneficiary's good health, safety and welfare when, in the discretion of the Trustee, such requisites are not being provided by any public agency, office or department of any state, or of the United States.

   "Special needs" shall include, but not be limited to, medical and dental expenses, clothing and equipment, programs of training, education and treatment, residential care, transportation and essential dietary needs, spending money (e. g., money to purchase appropriate gifts for relatives and friends), small visual and/or audio equipment for entertainment purposes (e. g., radio, record player, television set), vacations, movies and trips; provided, however, that the Trustee is under no obligation to expend principal or income for such needs, but if the Trustee, in its sole, absolute, and uncontrolled discretion, decides to do so, in no case shall the Trustee pay or reimburse any amounts to the federal or state governments, or any subdivision thereof.

The intent of the Grantors is that the income and principal is not to be considered income to, nor an asset of, said beneficiary for any purposes including but not limited to determination of income or assets as stated in any rules or regulations set forth by any local, state or federal government or agency or department thereof or any private agency or any private contractor. The Trustee shall honor these intentions.

b. In order to determine the happiness, welfare and development of said beneficiary, a family member, if any, serving as Trustee hereunder shall, to the extent possible:

    i. Visit said beneficiary at least quarterly;

    ii. Evaluate the physical and mental condition of the beneficiary including, as appropriate, examinations and services by independent physicians, dentists and psychiatrists or other appropriate professional personnel;

    iii. Evaluate education and training programs available to said beneficiary;

    iv. Evaluate work and earning opportunities available to said beneficiary;

    v. Evaluate recreation, leisure and social needs of said beneficiary;

    vi. Determine appropriateness of existing residential and program services available to said beneficiary; and

    vii. Determine legal rights of said beneficiary and public assistance available to said beneficiary.

In addition to the above, it is the Grantors' intent that because said beneficiary is disabled and unable to maintain and support himself independently, the Trustee may, in its sole, absolute, and uncontrolled discretion, seek support and maintenance for said beneficiary from all available public resources, including but not limited to, Social Security Administration benefits, Veterans Administration benefits, Supplemental Security Income (SSI), U.S. Civil Service Commission benefits, State medical benefits, Medicaid and federal Social Security Disability Insurance (SSDI); and the Trustee may, in its sole, absolute, and uncontrolled discretion, initiate administrative and/or judicial proceedings for the purpose of determining eligibility, and all costs related thereto, including reasonable attorneys' fees, shall be a proper charge to the trust share.

c. No interest in the income or principal of the trust share shall be liable for any present or future debt of said beneficiary to any state or to any other creditor and neither said beneficiary nor her guardian shall have the power to anticipate, alienate or encumber any interest in the trust's principal or income.

d. The Trustee shall regard the trust share as existing primarily for the benefit of said beneficiary and secondarily for the benefit of the takers of the remainder.

Accordingly, the Trustee shall exercise its discretion as to disbursements and investments with this standard in mind.

e. In the event of a lawful determination by a court or agency or contractor or competent authority, that the trust share, or any portion or share thereof, is liable for basic maintenance, support, medical, psychological or dental care for said beneficiary, which would otherwise be provided by local, state or federal government or agency or department thereof or private agency or private contractor, or a determination that any principal or income of the trust share not actually paid out to said beneficiary is to be counted as a resource or income in determining eligibility for local, state or federal government or private aid, then all right and interest of said beneficiary in and to the trust share shall thereupon terminate as though said beneficiary had died, and the Trustee shall distribute the then remaining principal and undistributed income of the trust share, as if _____ had then died.

In that regard, the Grantors request, but do not direct, that such recipients conserve, manage and distribute the proceeds of the terminated trust share for the benefit of said beneficiary, during his lifetime, in accordance with the provisions set forth in this trust for his benefit.

f. Upon the death of _____ after the time hereinabove set for apportionment into shares, any and all rights of said beneficiary under this trust shall terminate and the principal and undistributed income of the trust share, if any, apportioned to said beneficiary shall be administered for the benefit of said beneficiary's issue from time to time living in the manner described below.

If said deceased beneficiary has no such living issue, then said share shall be reapportioned in equal shares among the remaining shares of the trust estate apportioned pursuant to sub-paragraph 3.B. above, and each such reapportioned share shall continue to be held and administered in trust, or distributed free and clear of all trusts, as the case may be, to or for the benefit of persons then and thereafter living, in accordance with the fortunes of the share to which reapportionment is made.

2. In the case of each share apportioned to the Grantors' children _____, _____, and _____, the Trustee may, in each and every year beginning with the date of said apportionment, pay over to said child or use, apply or expend for said child's direct or indirect benefit, so much or all of the net income of said share and so much or all of the principal of said share as the Trustee may, in its sole, absolute, and uncontrolled discretion, deem wise and safely consistent with said child's support in reasonable comfort, education (including college, graduate, and professional education), and maintenance in health (including medical, dental, hospital, nursing and nursing home expenses).

    a. Whenever, at or after said time of apportionment, said child shall have attained the age of thirty (30) years, he shall have the right to request in writing and to receive one-third (1/3) of the balance of his share; and

    b. Whenever, at or after said time of apportionment, said child shall have attained the age of thirty-five (35) years, he shall have the right to request in writing and to receive an additional one-half (1/2) of the balance of his share; and

    c. Whenever, at or after said time of apportionment, said child shall have attained the age of forty (40) years, he shall have the right to receive the entire balance of his share, at which time his trust shall terminate.

    d. It is the Grantors' belief that, in some circumstances, it may be beneficial for said child to leave the management of his trust share in the hands of the Trustee.

        Therefore, said child may elect to leave his trust share, or any portion thereof, in the hands of the Trustee, as a separate fund, to be held and administered and disposed of as said child shall direct.

    e. The share held by the Trustee for the benefit of a child as described above shall, from the time of the death of the child after the time

241

above set for apportionment into shares, be administered for the benefit of the child's issue in the manner described below.

3. In the case of each share apportioned to the living issue of a deceased child of the Grantors, said share shall be administered for the benefit as a family group of such of the issue of said deceased child as from time to time shall be living.

The Trustee may pay over to the issue, or may use, apply or expend for their direct or indirect benefit, so much of the income and principal of the trust estate, at such times and in such proportions as the Trustee may determine, in its sole, absolute, and uncontrolled discretion, for support in reasonable comfort, education, (including college, graduate, and professional education), and maintenance in health (including medical, dental, hospital, nursing and nursing home expenses).

The Trustee may make such payments, use, application, expenditure or accumulation of the income and principal thereof as it shall think proper for the direct or indirect benefit of the members of said family group without being required to observe any precept or rule of equality of enjoyment as between said members.

Final distribution shall be made of whatever shall remain of said share, per stirpes, among said living issue and free and clear of all trusts when the youngest then living child of the Grantor's deceased child attains the age of thirty (30) years.

4. If at any time before the final distribution of any of the trust shares hereinabove described (after taking into consideration all provisions thereof), there shall be no person in existence who is eligible to have the benefit of the trust of such share, then the share in question shall be reapportioned in equal shares among the other shares of the trust estate apportioned pursuant to sub-paragraph 3.B. above, and each equal share shall continue to be held and administered in trust, or distributed free and clear of all trusts, as the case may be, to or for the benefit of persons then and thereafter living, in accordance with the fortunes of the share to which said reapportionment is made.

C. If, at any time before the final distribution of all of the trust shares hereinabove described, there shall be no person in existence who is eligible to have the benefit of any trust shares, the Trustee shall divide all of the trust estate then remaining into two (2) equal parts which shall be distributed, outright and free of trust, as follows:

1. One (1) part to those persons then living who would have taken _____'s estate, and in such shares thereof as they would have taken, had he then died intestate, domiciled in New Hampshire; and

2. One (1) part to those persons then living who would have taken

_____'s estate, and in such shares thereof as they would have taken, had she then died intestate, domiciled in New Hampshire.

D. The provisions contained hereinabove which require the Trustee to apportion the trust estate into shares and parts of shares are for purposes of computation only and shall not be construed to require the Trustee to make physical segregation of one share or a part of a share from the others, although the Trustee shall have full right to make such segregation if it thinks it better to do so.

Notwithstanding said provisions, the Trustee shall have the full right to regard the trust estate as one undivided estate for purposes of management and investment.

E. If the Grantors or the executors of the Grantors' estates or any other individual (including any individual who shall transfer property in trust hereunder or the executor or administrator of the estate of such individual), has allocated any portion or all of any Generation Skipping Transfer ("GST") exemption provided by Section 2631(a) of the Internal Revenue Code to any property to be held in trust hereunder, then notwithstanding anything to the contrary contained in this agreement, the Trustee is authorized to establish such number of separate trusts, with identical terms, to hold the property received in trust hereunder as it, in its sole, absolute, and uncontrolled discretion, shall deem advisable, bearing in mind the allocation of the said GST exemption and the desirability that any trust to which all or any portion of the said GST exemption is allocated shall, if practical, have an inclusion ratio of zero.

Further, the Trustee is authorized to allocate such trusts among the trust shares hereinabove created in order to minimize (or eliminate, if possible) any GST tax.

4.   TRUSTEE'S POWERS. In the administration of the trust estate, the Trustee shall have all of the powers granted to trustees by New Hampshire common law and statutory authority (including, but not limited to, the Uniform Trustees' Powers Act, R.S.A. 564-A, and the Uniform Trust Code, R.S.A. 564-B, as they may be amended from time to time), without restrictions.

In addition to such power, and not in limitation thereof, the Trustee shall have the following powers, all of which shall be exercised in a fiduciary capacity and for the benefit of the beneficiaries:

A. During the lifetime of the Grantor, the Trustee may retain as an investment, unless and until the Grantor by a writing delivered to the Trustee shall otherwise direct, all of the securities and other property originally assigned, transferred, or delivered to the Trustee hereunder or at any time forming a part of the trust estate, whether or not such securities or other property be of the character authorized by the laws of the State of New Hampshire for the investment of trust funds.

Upon the death or incapacity of the Grantor, the Trustee is authorized to purchase, sell, lease, or alter any investment by buy or sell orders transmitted by it, whether by telephone call, electronic facsimile transmission, computer message or other current non-written method of business communication.

B. To buy, sell and trade in securities of any nature, on margin, and for such purpose to maintain and operate margin accounts with brokers, and to pledge any securities held or purchased by it with such brokers as security for loans and advances made to the Trustee.

C. *[For Corporate Trustees]* To retain the property of the trust estate in the same investments as when received by it or to vary and transpose such investments and to invest and reinvest the property of the trust estate in such manner and in such securities or other property (including common trust funds or similar funds for the participation of trusts of which any corporation or financial institution serving as Trustee hereunder is trustee and including securities of said corporation or financial institution and any affiliate, subsidiary and successor thereto) as it in its uncontrolled discretion shall deem best without accountability for any loss for so doing and without liability for depreciation occasioned by so doing even though the property so retained or the investments so made may not be of the character permitted for the investment of trust funds under the laws of the State of New Hampshire or any other state or federal law.

D. To take and hold title to real estate, and to convey any interest in real estate and improvements thereon held in trust, and no purchaser or third party shall be bound to inquire whether the Trustee has said power or is properly exercising said power, or see to the application of any trust asset paid to the Trustee for a conveyance thereof.

E. To invest in and hold property which is used as the principal residence, furniture, automobile, and other such items meeting the special needs of _____ despite the fact that such property is non-income-producing.

F. To have all of the necessary banking powers to open and manage financial accounts, including but not limited to, checking accounts, savings accounts, financial accounts and other related financial instruments and to conduct all necessary financial business in reference to the management of the financial assets of the trust.

G. To rent a safe deposit box and to retain such assets in said box as the Trustee, in its sole, absolute, and uncontrolled discretion, determines appropriate.

H. To borrow money, with or without security, and mortgage or pledge trust property for a period within or extending beyond the duration of the trust.

I. To loan funds to the Grantor's estate upon such terms and conditions as to interest rates, maturities, and security as the Trustee shall determine.

J. To make payments, transfers or conveyances, to the extent possible, to the estate of the Grantor (after exhaustion of the assets of the Grantor's estate) to satisfy legacies, bequests or devises, if any, made under the Grantor's will or included in the Grantor's estate for other purposes, if the Grantor's estate shall be insufficient to satisfy such legacies, bequests or devises.

K. To invest in common trust funds.

L. To select property, in its sole, absolute, and uncontrolled discretion, to be allocated to any trust hereunder or to be distributed in satisfaction of any gift provided for herein without respect to the income tax basis of such property, and the Trustee is specifically excused from any duty of impartiality with respect to the income tax basis of such property.

M. If at any time during the Grantor's lifetime, there is delivered to the Trustee other than the Grantor, if any, or, if none, then to the successor Trustee, a written opinion, signed by a licensed physician, stating that the Grantor has become incompetent or incapacitated, then from and after the delivery of such written opinion the Trustee other than the Grantor, or the successor Trustee, as the case may be, shall have those powers and authorities with respect to the trust estate given to the Trustee in this trust agreement.

N. Regardless of the extent of the authority that the Trustee holds to currently distribute income and/or principal of the trust estate to one or more beneficiaries of the trust, the Trustee shall have full power and authority, to be exercised in its sole, absolute, and uncontrolled discretion, to appoint any or all assets held in this trust estate to any other trust or trusts created under will, deed or otherwise, for the benefit of one or more of the beneficiaries hereunder.

This authority shall be subject to the limitations set forth in R.S.A. 564-B:4-418, as amended from time to time, provided that such appointment clause shall be null and void in the event there is a determination that the application of such clause shall result in the inclusion of any of the trust estate in the Grantor's gross estate under any provision of the Internal Revenue Code, including but not limited to Sections 2041 and 2042, which would not otherwise be includable in the Grantor's gross estate.

Provided further, however, that if this Trust qualifies as a "trust instrument" under the Qualified Dispositions in Trust Act, R.S.A. 564-D, as amended from time to time, then the Trustee may only appoint the assets of the trust estate to a new trust which will continue to qualify as a "trust instrument" under such Act and will provide similar protections to the assets held in this trust estate.

O. If, at any time before the final distribution of the principal of any trust share hereinabove described, the value of the principal of said trust share shall be equal to, or less than, ONE HUNDRED THOUSAND DOLLARS ($100,000), then the Trustee may, in its sole discretion, terminate said trust share and distribute the principal of said trust share, and any accumulated and undistributed income thereof, outright and free of trust, to those persons then entitled to benefit from said trust share, and in the proportions in which they are then entitled to benefit from said trust share, notwithstanding any provisions of this trust to the contrary.

P. To exercise all the powers, authorities and discretions herein conferred, after the termination of the trust hereunder, until the complete distribution of the trust estate.

5.   ADDITIONAL PROPERTY. The Grantors may, by will, trust or during their lifetimes, from time to time, transfer and deliver to the Trustee cash, securities, and other property acceptable to the Trustee, in addition to the property presently transferred and delivered, and such cash, securities, and other property shall be held and administered and disposed of by the Trustee in accordance with the provisions of this agreement without the execution of any further instrument or declaration.

6.   REPORTING BY TRUSTEE.

A. At any time and from time to time, the Grantors, acting jointly if both are competent or the sole competent Grantor acting alone, shall have the power, by written instrument signed and acknowledged by the said Grantor(s) and delivered to the Trustee, to settle the report of the Trustee with respect to principal or income, or with respect to both principal and income, and to release and discharge the Trustee of and from any and every claim, demand, accountability, and liability of every nature, arising from any matter or thing done or omitted to be done, in connection with this agreement or any trust hereby created, during the period in respect of which the report of the Trustee shall have been so settled.

Every such settlement, release, and discharge shall be conclusive and binding upon, and shall be an absolute protection to the Trustee against all claims of any income beneficiaries, remaindermen, or other persons who might then or thereafter have or claim any interest under this agreement, and no such income beneficiary, remainderman, or other person shall have any right of accounting, reporting, any claim, or any cause of action against the Trustee arising from any matter or thing done or omitted to be done in connection with this agreement or any trust hereby created, during any period in respect of which the report of the Trustee shall have been so settled.

B. After the death or incapacity of the surviving Grantor, the Trustee may, at the Trustee's sole, absolute, and uncontrolled discretion, and shall, to the extent required by the Uniform Trust Code, R.S.A. 564-B, as it may be amended from time to time, render a Trustee's report as described in the Uniform Trust Code, as it may be amended from time to time, at such intervals as the Trustee may choose or at such times as required by the Uniform Trust Code.

C. A recipient of such a report (or, if under guardianship or conservatorship, then by the Guardian or Conservator, or, if deceased, then by the Executor or Administrator), may, by a written instrument, assent to the report of the Trustee with respect to principal or to income, or with respect to both principal and income.

The assent of the recipient of such report (or, if under guardianship or conservatorship, then by the Guardian or Conservator, or, if deceased, then by the Executor or Administrator) shall make such report binding and conclusive upon all persons then having or who may thereafter have any interest, vested or contingent, in the income or principal of the trust estate and such assent shall forever release and discharge the Trustee of and from any and every claim, demand, accountability, and liability of every nature, arising from any matter or thing done or omitted to be done, in connection with this agreement or any trust hereby created, during the period in respect of which the report of the Trustee shall have been so settled.

D. The failure of any person to object in writing to the Trustee to such a report within thirty (30) days after the delivery of the same to such person hereunder shall be final and binding to the same extent as the written assent hereinabove provided.

E. Any person entitled to such a report, accounting, information, notice and the like (or, if under guardianship or conservatorship, then by the Guardian or Conservator, or, if deceased, then by the Executor or Administrator) may by a written instrument signed and acknowledged by him or her or them, as the case may be, and delivered to the Trustee, waive the right to said Trustee's report or to other information otherwise required to be furnished under the Uniform Trust Code, as it may be amended from time to time.

7.   <u>SUCCESSOR TRUSTEE</u>. The following provisions shall govern the addition, removal and succession of the Trustee:

A. The Grantors may, during their lifetimes, add any additional Trustee, or remove any Trustee hereunder and appoint a successor Trustee.

B. If either _____ or _____ shall be unable or unwilling to

serve in the capacity of Trustee for any reason, then no successor shall serve in his or her stead, as the case may be, and the remaining Trustee shall continue to serve hereunder.

1. If both _____ and _____ shall be unable or unwilling to serve in the capacity of Trustee for any reason, then _____, of _____, New Hampshire, shall serve in their stead.

2. If _____ shall be unable or unwilling to serve in the capacity of Trustee for any reason, then _____, of _____, New Hampshire, shall serve in _____ stead.

C. In the event there shall be no successor Trustee who shall be able or willing to serve in the capacity of Trustee, then a majority of the beneficiaries to whom or for whose use the current net income of the trust estate is at the time authorized or required to be paid or applied, either,

1. acting individually, if then eighteen (18) years of age, or,

2. by his or her Guardian or Conservator, if then under guardianship or conservatorship,

shall appoint a successor Trustee.

D. In the event that any beneficiary of the trust, other than the Grantors, shall serve in the capacity of co-Trustee, then the discretionary powers to determine whether income or principal is to be distributed to said beneficiary or to any person to whom said beneficiary owes an obligation of support shall be exercisable only by the remaining Trustee.

It is the Grantors' intention by this sub-paragraph to prohibit said beneficiary from benefiting himself or herself as beneficiary in any way by the exercise of such discretionary powers vested in the Trustee as a group.

E. In the event that any beneficiary of the trust, other than the Grantors, shall serve in the capacity of sole Trustee and the Trustee has discretionary powers to distribute income or principal to himself, herself, or to any person to whom he or she owes an obligation of support, then such distributions of income or principal shall be exercisable by the sole Trustee. The maximum amount that may be withdrawn annually by each such beneficiary under this sub-paragraph, however, shall not exceed the maximum amount over which an individual may have a power of withdrawal without its lapse in such year being deemed to be a release of such power under Section 2514(e) of the Internal Revenue Code.

F. No successor Trustee shall be liable or responsible in any way for any actions or defaults of any predecessor Trustee, nor for any loss or expense from or occasioned by anything done or neglected to be done by any predecessor Trustee. Any successor Trustee shall have, from and after its appointment or succession to office hereunder and without any assignment or other action by any person, all the rights, interests, and powers, including discretionary rights and powers, which are by the provisions of this trust agreement granted to and vested in the Trustee named herein.

8.   <u>FIDUCIARIES</u>. No person dealing with the Trustee shall be responsible for the application of any money, securities, or other property paid or delivered, and the receipt of the Trustee shall be a full discharge; and no person dealing with the Trustee, and no issuer, transfer agent, or other agent of any issuer of any securities shall be under any obligation to ascertain or inquire into the power of the Trustee to purchase, sell, exchange, transfer, mortgage, pledge, create a security interest in, lease, distribute, or otherwise dispose of or deal with any money, securities, or other property.

The Trustee shall not at any time be held liable for any action taken or not taken, including any action intended to lessen or eliminate the impact of estate or generation-skipping transfer taxes with respect to any generation or beneficiary, whether or not such action is successful in achieving the results sought and without regard to its effect on other beneficiaries in the same or different generations, or for any loss or depreciation in the value of any property in any trust created herein, whether due to an error of judgment or otherwise, where the Trustee has exercised good faith and ordinary diligence in the exercise of its duties.

The Trustee shall receive reasonable compensation for its services in the administration of the trusts created herein, including reimbursement for amounts reasonably expended for bookkeeping services, investment services and advice, and other professional or para-professional services. In addition to the compensation herein provided, the Trustee shall receive reasonable compensation for any legal services provided for the benefit of the trust estate, such as handling any litigation involving the trust, preparing state or federal income tax returns, and transferring any real estate.

9.   <u>PERPETUITIES</u>. All trusts established under this instrument shall be exempt from the application of the rule against perpetuities. This provision is intended to comply with New Hampshire R.S.A. 564:24, and accordingly, the Grantor specifically authorizes the Trustee to sell, mortgage or lease property for any period of time beyond the period that is required for an interest created under this instrument to vest in order to be valid under the rule against perpetuities, as measured by the period defined hereinabove.

The trusts created hereunder shall be perpetual to the fullest extent permitted by the governing law. If any trust created hereunder is deemed to be subject to the law of a jurisdiction (including, but only to the extent applicable to real property) that has a rule against perpetuities or similar rule which limits the period during which property can be held in trust, then such trust (other than a trust created by the exercise of a power of appointment conferred hereunder which exercise commences a new rule against perpetuities period under the law of such jurisdiction) shall terminate in all events upon the expiration of the longest period that property may be held in trust under this trust agreement under the law of such jurisdiction (including any applicable period in gross, such as 21 years, 90 years or 110 years); provided, however, that if the jurisdiction has a rule against perpetuities or similar rule which applies only to certain types of property, such as real property, the provisions of this paragraph shall apply only to such property. If under the law of such jurisdiction the longest period that property may be held in trust may be determined (or alternatively determined) with reference to the death of the last survivor of a group of individuals in being upon the date of this trust agreement, those individuals shall consist of all of the descendants of the Grantor's parents who were in being on the date of this trust agreement. Upon termination of a trust pursuant to the provisions of this paragraph, the trust property shall be transferred, conveyed and paid over to the persons then entitled to receive or have the benefit of the income from the trust in the proportions in which they are entitled thereto, or if their interests are indefinite, then in equal shares.

10.   <u>SPENDTHRIFT PROVISION</u>. Except as herein otherwise provided, the interest of any beneficiary hereunder, either as to income or principal, shall not be anticipated, alienated or in any other manner assigned or pledged or promised by such beneficiary, and shall not be reached by, or be subject to, any legal, equitable or other process, including any bankruptcy or divorce proceeding, or be subject to the interference or control of creditors or others in any way or manner, and all payments to, or the interest of, any beneficiary shall be free from the control or claim of any parent or spouse or former spouse or any other third party. Moreover, no power of appointment or power of withdrawal shall be subject to involuntary exercise. Provided, however, this spendthrift provision shall not restrict the exercise of a disclaimer or the exercise of a power of appointment or withdrawal right granted by this trust agreement. This provision is intended to be a material provision of this trust and any other trust established hereunder.

Furthermore, the Grantors intend that because part of this trust is to be conserved and maintained for the special needs of _____, no part of the corpus thereof, neither principal nor undistributed income, shall be subject to the claims of voluntary or involuntary creditors for the provision of care and services, including residential care, by any public entity, office, department or agency or any state, or of the United States.

11.   <u>TAX PROVISION</u>. The trust estate shall not be charged with the payment of any estate, inheritance, legacy, death taxes or duties of any nature (state or federal), or any interest or penalty thereon, except to the extent that the other assets in the Grantors' estates (excluding any assets which may be exempted from the payment of such taxes by the last wills of the Grantors) shall be insufficient to discharge such taxes, interest or penalties or shall be insufficiently liquid to satisfy the same. The Trustee may rely conclusively upon written certification from the executors of the Grantors' estates, or if no probate administration of the Grantors' estates is required under applicable law, upon request of the person or persons nominated as executor under the Grantors' wills

or upon any other evidence, as to the existence of such insufficiency and the amount thereof; provided, however, that the Trustee shall not pay any additional tax imposed under Section 2032A of the Internal Revenue Code or any generation-skipping transfer taxes imposed under Chapter 13 of the Internal Revenue Code imposed by reason of the Grantors' deaths. If the Trustee shall be required to pay any such taxes, they shall be charged against the principal of the trust estate as an expense without apportionment.

Provided, that in the event that no probate administration of the Grantors' estates is required under applicable law, the Trustee shall have all the powers and authority given the executors under the Grantors' wills in relation to such taxes, including all elections and allocation of the generation-skipping transfer tax exemption under Section 2631 of the Internal Revenue Code.

12.   <u>DEBTS AND EXPENSES</u>. The trust estate shall not be charged with the payment of legal debts of the Grantors' estates, funeral expenses or expenses of administration of the Grantors' estates except to the extent that the other assets in the Grantors' estates shall be insufficient to discharge such debts and expenses, or shall be insufficiently liquid to satisfy the same. The Trustee may rely conclusively upon written certification from the executors of the Grantors' estates, or if no probate administration of the Grantors' estates is required under applicable law, upon request of the person or persons nominated as executor under the Grantors' wills, or upon any other evidence, as to the existence of such insufficiency and the amount thereof. If the Trustee shall be required to pay any such debts and expenses, the same shall be treated as debts and expenses of the trust estate (to the extent the assets of the Grantors' estates are insufficient to satisfy the same) or as loans to the Grantors' estates (to the extent the liquid assets of the Grantors' estates are insufficient to satisfy the same) if any such debts and expenses are deducted for federal estate tax purposes in computing the value of the Grantors' taxable estates under Section 2053 of the Internal Revenue Code. If any such debts and expenses are either not so deducted or deductible under Section 2053 of the Internal Revenue Code, however, the same shall be charged against the principal of the trust estate as an expense without apportionment.

This provision shall confer no rights upon anyone except the executor of the Grantors' estates.

13.   <u>SURVIVAL REQUIREMENT</u>. No person shall be deemed to have survived the surviving Grantor, or any other person or event under the terms of this trust, unless such person survives the end of the period commencing with the close of the calendar day of the surviving Grantor's death, the death of such other person or on which such event occurs, and ending with the close of the thirtieth (30th) calendar day thereafter.

14.   <u>DISTRIBUTIONS TO MINORS</u>. In any case where property or funds become distributable to a minor, then the Trustee shall have the additional power to distribute the same in any one or more of the following ways: (1) by distribution directly to the minor; (2) by distribution to the legal guardian of the minor; (3) by distribution to a parent, relative or friend of the minor for the

minor's support in reasonable comfort, education and maintenance in health; (4) by applying the same directly for the minor's support in reasonable comfort, education and maintenance in health; (5) by depositing the same in a bank account in the name of the minor or by transferring property to or purchasing property in the name of a custodian for his or her benefit under a Uniform Law relating to transfers or gifts to minors; or (6) by holding the same hereunder in trust or in custody for the minor's support in reasonable comfort, education and maintenance in health and by distributing the remainder thereof to the minor upon coming of age or otherwise to the minor's estate in case of the death of the minor. The receipt of the person to whom property or funds are actually distributed in accordance with any of the foregoing provisions shall fully discharge the Trustee from further accountability therefor.

15.   GOVERNING LAW AND SITUS. The Grantors declare that this agreement and the trust created hereby shall be construed and administered under the laws of the State of New Hampshire, that the validity and effect of this agreement and of this trust shall be determined in accordance with the laws of that State.

Further, the trust shall be under the jurisdiction of the courts of the State of New Hampshire and the Trustee shall voluntarily enter a general appearance in any legal action relating to an accounting of the trust or a declaratory judgment interpreting this trust agreement. The Trustee shall not be chargeable in any court other than one of the courts of that State.

[OPTIONAL] However, the Trustee, at any time and from time to time, in its discretion, may, (1) remove all or part of the trust estate and hold and administer the same in any other jurisdiction where the Trustee shall be then located, (2) change the situs of administration of any trust from one jurisdiction to another jurisdiction; and (3) elect that the law of such other jurisdiction shall thereafter govern the trust to such extent as may be necessary and appropriate, and to amend the administrative provisions of the trust as the Trustee deems appropriate to ensure compliance and compatibility with such law, whereupon the courts of such other jurisdiction shall have the power to effectuate the purposes of this trust agreement to such extent. The determination of the Trustee as to any such removal of assets or change of situs or governing law shall be conclusive and binding on all persons interested in such trust.

16.   AMENDMENT AND REVOCATION. The Grantors reserve the right together at any time or from time to time without the consent of any person and without notice to any person other than the Trustee to revoke or modify the trust hereby created, in whole or in part, to change the beneficiaries hereof, or to withdraw the whole or any part of the trust estate by filing notice of such revocation, modification, change, or withdrawal with the Trustee; provided, however, that the terms of this agreement may not be modified by the Grantors in such manner as to increase the obligations or alter the rates of the commissions of the Trustee without its written consent; provided, further, that following the death

of the first Grantor, the surviving Grantor shall alone have all the rights and powers listed above in this paragraph.

The Trustee, may, in its sole, absolute, and uncontrolled discretion, at any time and from time to time, amend said trust agreement in any manner consistent with maintaining _____'s eligibility for services and financial assistance which _____ receives without charge from any local, state or federal government or agency or department thereof or any private agency or any private contractor, taking into consideration changes in their programs, policies, regulations and laws.

17. DEFINITIONS. Whenever used in this trust agreement, the words "child," "children," or "issue" are intended to include not only persons who are descendants by blood, but also persons and issue of persons who have been adopted according to law prior to their attaining the age of eighteen (18) years.

References to the "Internal Revenue Code" or "Code" or to provisions thereof are to the Internal Revenue Code of 1986, as amended at the time in question. References to the "Treasury Regulations," "Regulations" and "Regs." are to the Treasury Regulations under the Code. If, by the time in question, a particular provision of the Code has been renumbered, or the Code has been superseded by a subsequent federal tax law, the reference shall be deemed to be to the renumbered provision or the corresponding provision of the subsequent law, unless to do so would clearly be contrary to the Grantor's intent as expressed in this Trust Agreement, and a similar rule shall apply to references to the Regulations.

Masculine, feminine and neuter pronouns shall each include all genders, and the singular shall include the plural and vice versa, where the context or facts so admit.

The captions and paragraph headings of this trust agreement are inserted only as a matter of convenience and for reference and in no way define, limit or describe the scope or intent of this agreement, nor in any way affect this agreement.

18. EXECUTION. This trust agreement, and any amendments hereto, shall be effective when executed by the Grantors, notwithstanding that the signature of the Trustee is provided for, the Trustee's signature being intended to denote the acceptance of the Trustee to serve in that capacity only.

This trust agreement may be executed in any number of counterparts with the same effect as if all of the parties had signed the same document. All counterparts shall be construed together and shall constitute one agreement.

Witness	, Grantor
Witness	, Grantor
Witness	, Trustee

_____   _____
Witness   , Trustee

STATE OF NEW HAMPSHIRE
COUNTY OF _____

The foregoing instrument was acknowledged before me on _____,
2009 by _____.

_____
Notary Public/Justice of the Peace
My Commission Expires:
(Seal)

STATE OF NEW HAMPSHIRE
COUNTY OF _____

The foregoing instrument was acknowledged before me on _____,
2009 by _____.

_____
Notary Public/Justice of the Peace
My Commission Expires:
(Seal)

Page 760: Add this new form after Form 48 in the text:

FORM 48-A   Exemption from the Rule Against Perpetuities

<u>PERPETUITIES</u>. All trusts established under this instrument shall be exempt from the application of the rule against perpetuities. This provision is intended to comply with New Hampshire R.S.A. 564:24, and accordingly, the Grantor specifically authorizes the Trustee to sell, mortgage or lease property for any period of time beyond the period that is required for an interest created under this instrument to vest in order to be valid under the rule against perpetuities, as measured by the period defined hereinabove.

The trusts created hereunder shall be perpetual to the fullest extent permitted by the governing law. If any trust created hereunder is deemed to be subject to the law of a jurisdiction (including, but only to the extent applicable to real property) that has a rule against perpetuities or similar rule which limits the period during which property can be held in trust, then such trust (other than a trust created by the exercise of a power of appointment conferred hereunder which exercise commences a new rule against perpetuities period under the law of such jurisdiction) shall terminate in all events upon the expiration of the longest period that property may be held in trust under this trust agreement under the law of such jurisdiction (including any applicable period in gross, such as 21 years, 90 years or 110 years); provided, however, that if the jurisdiction has a rule against perpetuities or similar rule which applies only to certain types of property, such as real property, the provisions of this paragraph shall apply only to such property. If under the law of such jurisdiction the longest period that property may be held in trust may be determined (or alternatively determined) with reference to the death of the last survivor of a group of individuals in being upon the date of this trust agreement, those individuals shall consist of all of the descendants of the Grantor's parents who were in being on the date of this trust agreement. Upon termination of a trust pursuant to the provisions of this paragraph, the trust property shall be transferred, conveyed and paid over to the persons then entitled to receive or have the benefit of the income from the trust in the proportions in which they are entitled thereto, or if their interests are indefinite, then in equal shares.

255

Page 771: Delete Form 58 [New Hampshire Living Will] from the text:

Page 773: Substitute this form for Form 59 in the text:

FORM 59   New Hampshire Advance Directive [Combined Durable Power of Attorney for Health Care, Living Will, and Designation of Personal Representative and Authorization to Release Health Information (HIPAA)]

INFORMATION CONCERNING THE DURABLE POWER OF

ATTORNEY FOR HEALTH CARE

THIS IS AN IMPORTANT LEGAL DOCUMENT. BEFORE SIGNING IT, YOU SHOULD

KNOW THESE IMPORTANT FACTS:

Except if you say otherwise in the directive, this directive gives the person you name as your health care agent the power to make any and all health care decisions for you when you lack the capacity to make health care decisions for yourself (in other words, you no longer have the ability to understand and appreciate generally the nature and consequences of a health care decision, including the significant benefits and harms of and reasonable alternatives to any proposed health care). "Health care" means any treatment, service or procedure to maintain, diagnose or treat your physical or mental condition. Your health care agent, therefor, will have the power to make a wide range of health care decisions for you. Your health care agent may consent (in other words, give permission), refuse to consent, or withdraw consent to medical treatment, and may make decisions about withdrawing or withholding life-sustaining treatment. Your health care agent cannot consent to or direct any of the following: commitment to a state institution, sterilization, or termination of treatment if you are pregnant and if the withdrawal of that treatment is deemed likely to terminate the pregnancy, unless the treatment will be physically harmful to you or prolong severe pain which cannot be alleviated by medication.

You may state in this directive any treatment you do not want, or any treatment you want to be sure you receive. Your health care agent's power will begin when your doctor certifies that you lack the capacity to make health care decisions (in other words, that you are not able to make health care decisions). If for moral or religious reasons you do not want to be treated by a doctor or to be examined by a doctor to certify that you lack capacity, you must say so in the directive and you must name someone who can certify your lack of capacity. That person cannot be your health care agent or alternate health care agent or any person who is not eligible to be your health care agent. You may attach additional pages to the document if you need more space to complete your statement.

If you want to give your health care agent power to withhold or withdraw medically administered nutrition and hydration, you must say so in your directive. Otherwise, your health care agent will not be able to direct that. Under no conditions will your health care agent be able to direct the withholding of food and drink that you are able to eat and drink normally.

Your agent shall be directed by your written instructions in this document when making decisions on your behalf, and as further guided by your medical condition or prognosis. Unless you state otherwise in the directive, your agent will have the same power to make decisions about your health care as you would have made, if those decisions by your health care agent are made consistent with state law.

It is important that you discuss this directive with your doctor or other health care providers before you sign it, to make sure that you understand the nature and range of decisions which could be made for you by your health care agent. If you do not have a health care provider, you should talk with someone else who is knowledgeable about these issues and can answer your questions. Check with your community hospital or hospice for trained staff. You do not need a lawyer's assistance to complete this directive, but if there is anything in this directive that you do not understand, you should ask a lawyer to explain it to you.

The person you choose as your health care agent should be someone you know and trust, and he or she must be at least 18 years old. If you choose your health or residential care provider (such as your doctor, advanced registered nurse practitioner, or an employee of a hospital, nursing home, home health agency, or residential care home, other than a relative), that person will have to choose between acting as your health care agent or as your health or residential care provider, because the law does not allow a person to do both at the same time. You should consider choosing an alternate health care agent, in case your health care agent is unwilling, unable, unavailable or not eligible to act as your health care agent. Any alternate health care agent you choose will then have the same authority to make health care decisions for you.

You should tell the person you choose that you want him or her to be your health care agent. You should talk about this directive with your health care agent and your doctor or advanced registered nurse practitioner and give each one a signed copy. You should write on the directive itself the people and institutions who will have signed copies. Your health care agent will not be liable for health care decisions made in good faith on your behalf.

EVEN AFTER YOU HAVE SIGNED THIS DIRECTIVE, YOU HAVE THE RIGHT TO MAKE HEALTH CARE DECISIONS FOR YOURSELF AS LONG AS YOU ARE ABLE TO DO SO, AND TREATMENT CANNOT BE GIVEN TO YOU OR STOPPED OVER YOUR CLEAR OBJECTION. You have the right to revoke the power given to your health care agent by telling him or her, or by telling your health care provider, orally or in writing, that you no longer want that person to be your health care agent.

YOU HAVE THE RIGHT TO EXCLUDE OR STRIKE REFERENCES TO ARNP'S IN YOUR ADVANCE DIRECTIVE AND IF YOU DO SO, YOUR ADVANCE DIRECTIVE SHALL STILL BE VALID AND ENFORCEABLE.

Once this directive is executed it cannot be changed or modified. If you want to make changes, you must make an entirely new directive.

THIS POWER OF ATTORNEY WILL NOT BE VALID UNLESS IT IS SIGNED IN THE PRESENCE OF A NOTARY PUBLIC OR JUSTICE OF THE PEACE OR TWO (2) OR MORE QUALIFIED WITNESSES, WHO MUST BOTH BE PRESENT WHEN YOU SIGN AND WHO WILL ACKNOWLEDGE YOUR SIGNATURE ON THE DOCUMENT. THE FOLLOWING PERSONS MAY NOT ACT AS WITNESSES:

- The person you have designated as your health care agent;
- Your spouse or heir at law;
- Your attending physician or ARNP, or person acting under the direction or control of the attending physician or ARNP;

ONLY ONE OF THE TWO WITNESSES MAY BE YOUR HEALTH OR RESIDENTIAL CARE PROVIDER OR ONE OF YOUR PROVIDER'S EMPLOYEES.

NEW HAMPSHIRE ADVANCE DIRECTIVE
I. DURABLE POWER OF ATTORNEY FOR HEALTH CARE

I, _____ , of _____ , hereby appoint my _____ ,
     (name)   (city, state)   (relationship)
_____ , of _____ ,
  (name)   (city, state)

as my agent to make any and all health care decisions for me, except to the extent I state otherwise in this directive or as prohibited by law. This durable power of attorney for health care shall take effect in the event I lack the capacity to make my own health care decisions.

In the event the person I appoint above is unable, unwilling or unavailable, or ineligible to act as my health care agent, I hereby appoint my _____ ,
                                            (relationship)
_____ , of _____ , as alternate agent.
  (name)   (city, state)

STATEMENT OF DESIRES, SPECIAL PROVISIONS,
AND LIMITATIONS REGARDING HEALTH CARE DECISIONS.

For your convenience in expressing your wishes, some general statements concerning the withholding or removal of life-sustaining treatment are set forth below. (Life-sustaining treatment is defined as procedures without which a person would die, such as but not limited to the following: mechanical respiration, kidney dialysis or the use of other external mechanical and technological devices, drugs to maintain blood pressure, blood transfusions, and antibiotics.) There is also a section which allows you to set forth specific directions for these or other matters. If you wish, you may indicate your agreement or disagreement with any of the following statements and give your agent power to act in those specific circumstances.

A. LIFE-SUSTAINING TREATMENT.

1. If I am near death and lack the capacity to make health care decisions, I

authorize my agent to direct that: *(Initial beside your choice of (a) or (b).)*

_____ (a) life-sustaining treatment not be started, or if started, be discontinued.

-or-

_____ (b) life-sustaining treatment continue to be given to me.

2. Whether near death or not, if I become permanently unconscious I authorize my agent to direct that: *(Initial beside your choice of (a) or (b).)*

_____ (a) life-sustaining treatment not be started, or if started, be discontinued.

-or-

_____ (b) life-sustaining treatment continue to be given to me.

B. MEDICALLY ADMINISTERED NUTRITION AND HYDRATION.

1. I realize that situations could arise in which the only way to allow me to die would be to not start or to discontinue medically administered nutrition and hydration. In carrying out any instructions I have given in this document, I authorize my agent to direct that: *(Initial beside your choice of (a) or (b).)*

_____ (a) medically administered nutrition and hydration not be started or, if started, be discontinued.

-or-

_____ (b) even if all other forms of life-sustaining treatment have been withdrawn, medically administered nutrition and hydration continue to be given to me.

(If you fail to complete item B, your agent will not have the power to direct the withholding or withdrawal of medically administered nutrition and hydration.)

C. TREATMENT AGAINST OBJECTION.

1. There may be situations, such as in advanced cases of dementia, in which you may want your agent's decisions to be honored, even if you vocalize an objection to those decisions. In this context, please consider the following statement: *Even if I am incapacitated and I object to treatment, treatment may be given to me against my objection. (Initial beside your choice of (a) or (b).)*

_____ (a) Yes, even if I am incapacitated and I object to treatment, treatment **may** be given to me against my objection.

259

-or-

_____ (b) No, even if I am incapacitated and I object to treatment, treatment **may not** be given to me against my objection.

D. ADDITIONAL INSTRUCTIONS.

Here you may include any specific desires or limitations you deem appropriate, such as when or what life-sustaining treatment you would want used or withheld, or instructions about refusing any specific types of treatment that are inconsistent with your religious beliefs or are unacceptable to you for any other reason. You may leave this question blank if you desire.

_____

_____

_____

I hereby acknowledge that I have been provided with a disclosure statement explaining the effect of this directive. I have read and understand the information contained in the disclosure statement.

The original of this directive will be kept at McLane, Graf, Raulerson and Middleton, Professional Association, 900 Elm Street, P.O. Box 326, Manchester, New Hampshire 03105, and the following persons and institutions will have signed copies:

_____

_____

Signed on _____, 2009 _____

                              Print Name: _____, Principal

We declare that the principal appears to be of sound mind and free from duress at the time the durable power of attorney for health care is signed and that the principal affirms that he or she is aware of the nature of the directive and is signing it freely and voluntarily.

Witness: _____   Address: _____

_____   _____(city, state)_____

Witness: _____   Address: _____

_____   _____(city, state)_____

STATE OF NEW HAMPSHIRE
COUNTY OF _____

The foregoing durable power of attorney for health care was acknowledged before me this on _____, 2009, by _____ (the "Principal").

Notary Public/Justice of the Peace
My Commission Expires:
(Seal)

II. LIVING WILL

I specifically intend for Part I, the Durable Power of Attorney for Health Care, to take precedence over this Living Will. It is my intention that my doctors, ARNP and other health care providers recognize that my Health Care Agent's decisions with respect to my health care shall be controlling.

I, _____ , of _____ , of being of sound mind, willfully and
   (name)   (city, state)
voluntarily make known my desire that my dying shall not be artificially prolonged under the circumstances set forth below, do hereby declare:

If at any time I should have an incurable injury, disease, or illness and I am certified to be near death or in a permanently unconscious condition by two (2) physicians or a physician and an ARNP, and two (2) physicians or a physician and an ARNP have determined that my death is imminent whether or not life-sustaining treatment is utilized and where the application of life-sustaining treatment would serve only to artificially prolong the dying process, or that I will remain in a permanently unconscious condition, I direct that such procedures be withheld or withdrawn, and that I be permitted to die naturally with only the administration of medication, the natural ingestion of food or fluids by eating and drinking, or the performance of any medical procedure deemed necessary to provide me with comfort care. I realize that situations could arise in which the only way to allow me to die would be to discontinue medically administered nutrition and hydration.

In carrying out any instruction I have given under this section, I authorize that:
(Initial beside your choice of (a) or (b).)

_____ (a) medically administered nutrition and hydration not be started or, if started, be discontinued,

-or-

_____ (b) even if all other forms of life-sustaining treatment have been withdrawn, medically administered nutrition and hydration continue to be given to me.

In the absence of my ability to give directions regarding the use of such life-sustaining treatment, it is my intention that this declaration shall be honored by my family and health care providers as the final expression of my right to refuse medical or surgical treatment and accept the consequences of such refusal. I understand the full import of this declaration, and I am emotionally and mentally competent to make this declaration.

Signed on _____, 2009.

Print Name: _____, Principal

We declare that the principal appears to be of sound mind and free from duress at the time the living will is signed and that the principal affirms that he or she is aware of the nature of the directive and is signing it freely and voluntarily.

Witness: _____   Address: _____

_____   _____(city, state)_____

Witness: _____   Address: _____

_____   _____(city, state)_____

STATE OF NEW HAMPSHIRE

COUNTY OF _____

The foregoing living will was acknowledged before me on _____, 2009, by _____ (the "Principal").

_____

Notary Public/Justice of the Peace

My Commission Expires:

(Seal)

DESIGNATION OF PERSONAL REPRESENTATIVE AND AUTHORIZATION TO RELEASE HEALTH INFORMATION

I, _____ , of _____ , hereby appoint my _____ ,
   (name)   (city, state)   (relationship)
_____ , of _____, as my personal representative, under the
   (name)   (city, state)
Health Insurance Portability and Accountability Act of 1996, as it may be amended, and the regulations thereunder (hereinafter "HIPAA").

In the event the person I appoint above is unable, unwilling or unavailable, or ineligible to act as my personal representative, I hereby appoint my _____ , _____ , of _____, as alternate personal repre-
(relationship)   (name)   (city, state)
sentative.

Upon request of my personal representatives, I hereby direct any covered entity and/or business associate of a covered entity to disclose my individually identifiable health information to such requesting personal representative. I hereby acknowledge that such individually identifiable health information may be subject to re-disclosure by my requesting personal representative and no longer protected under HIPAA.

Covered entities and their business associates may rely upon the representation of my requesting personal representative as to all matters pertaining to the disclosure of my individually identifiable health information, and no covered entity or business associate who acts in reliance upon the representation of my requesting personal representative pursuant to the authority granted hereunder to my personal representatives shall incur any liability to me or my estate as a result of complying with the request of my personal representative unless prior notice was provided to such covered entity or business associate that the authority granted to my personal representative hereunder was revoked as provided below.

The authority granted herein to my personal representatives shall continue in effect until (i) I revoke this designation and authorization in writing and notice to that effect is provided to such covered entity and/or such business associate, or (ii) I die and a fiduciary (e.g., executor or administrator) of my estate is appointed by a court of competent jurisdiction and notice of such appointment is provided to such covered entity and/or such business associate, whichever occurs first. If a fiduciary of my estate is so appointed, such fiduciary or co-fiduciaries, as the case may be, shall thereafter be my personal representative under HIPAA.

As used herein the terms "personal representative", "individually identifiable health information", "covered entities" and "business associates" shall all have the same meanings as set forth in HIPAA.

IN WITNESS WHEREOF, I have set my hand on _____ , 2009.
Witness: _____
                                                              Print name: _____

STATE OF _____
COUNTY OF _____

The foregoing instrument was acknowledged before me on _____, 2009, by _____

_____
Notary Public/Justice of the Peace
My Commission Expires:
(Seal)

Page 778: Substitute this form for Form 60 in the text:

FORM 60   Statutory Power of Attorney (R.S.A. 564-E:301)

NEW HAMPSHIRE

STATUTORY POWER OF ATTORNEY

INFORMATION CONCERNING THE POWER OF ATTORNEY

THIS IS AN IMPORTANT LEGAL DOCUMENT. BEFORE SIGNING THIS DOCUMENT YOU SHOULD KNOW THESE IMPORTANT FACTS:

Notice to the Principal: As the "Principal," you are using this Power of Attorney to grant power to another person (called the "Agent") to make decisions, including, but not limited to, decisions concerning your money, property, or both, and to use your money, property, or both on your behalf. If this Power of Attorney does not limit the powers that you give to your Agent, your Agent will have broad and sweeping powers to sell or otherwise dispose of your property, and to spend your money without advance notice to you or approval by you. Unless you have expressly provided otherwise in this Power of Attorney, your Agent will have these powers before you become incapacitated, and unless you have expressly provided otherwise in this Power of Attorney, your Agent will continue to have these powers after you become incapacitated. You have the right to retain this Power of Attorney and to release it later or to request that another person retain this Power of Attorney on your behalf and release it only if one or more conditions specified in advance by you are satisfied. You have the right to revoke or take back this Power of Attorney at any time, so long as you are of sound mind. If there is anything about this Power of Attorney that you do not understand, you should seek professional advice.

Principal's Signature: _____

Date: _____

1. DESIGNATION OF AGENT

I, (Name of Principal), of (Address of Principal), name the following person as my agent:

    Name of Agent: _____

    Agent's Address: _____

2. DESIGNATION OF SUCCESSOR AGENT(S) (OPTIONAL)

If my agent is unable or unwilling to act for me, I name the following person as my successor agent:

    Name of Successor Agent: _____

    Successor Agent's Address: _____

If my successor agent is unable or unwilling to act for me, I name the following person as my second successor agent:

    Name of Second Successor Agent: _____

Second Successor Agent's Address: _____

3. REVOCATION OF EXISTING POWERS OF ATTORNEY

(Initial the following statement if it is your choice.)

_____ This Power of Attorney revokes all existing powers of attorney previously executed by me.

4. GRANT OF GENERAL AUTHORITY

(Initial beside your choice of A or B, but not both.)

_____ A. I grant my agent general authority to act for me in all matters, including, without limitation, all of the subjects enumerated in B below.

_____ B. I grant my agent general authority over the following subjects as defined in the following sections of the Uniform Power of Attorney Act:

(Initial each subject you want to include in the agent's general authority.)

_____ Real Property as defined in RSA 564-E:204

_____ Tangible Personal Property as defined in RSA 564-E:205

_____ Stocks and Bonds as defined in RSA 564-E:206

_____ Commodities and Options as defined in RSA 564-E:207

_____ Banks and Other Financial Institutions as defined in RSA 564-E:208

_____ Operation of Entity or Business as defined in RSA 564-E:209

_____ Insurance and Annuities as defined in RSA 564-E:210

_____ Estates, Trusts and Other Beneficial Interests as defined in RSA 564-E:211

_____ Claims and Litigation as defined in RSA 564-E:212

_____ Personal and Family Maintenance as defined in RSA 564-E:213

_____ Benefits from Governmental Programs or Civil or Military Service as defined in RSA 564-E:214

_____ Retirement Plans as defined in RSA 564-E:215

_____ Taxes as defined in RSA 564-E:216

_____ Digital Assets

5. GRANT OF SPECIFIC AUTHORITY (OPTIONAL)

(Initial each subject you want to include in the agent's authority. CAUTION: As to some of the following subjects, granting your agent authority will give your agent the authority to take actions that could significantly reduce your property or change how your property is distributed at your death.)

_____ My agent MAY NOT do any of the following specific acts for me UNLESS I have INITIALED the specific authority listed below:

6. LIMITATION ON AGENT'S AUTHORITY (OTHER THAN GIFTING)

_____ Create, amend, revoke, or terminate an inter vivos trust

_____ Make a gift, subject to the limitations of RSA 564-E:217 of the Uniform Power of Attorney Act

(If you have granted your agent the authority to make a gift, then as to each of the following statements, initial beside it if it is your choice.)

_____ My agent may make a gift, even if it will leave me without sufficient assets or income to provide for my care without relying on Medicaid, other public assistance or charity.

_____ My agent may make a gift to himself or herself and to any individual to whom my agent owes a legal obligation of support.

_____ Create or change rights of survivorship

_____ Create or change a beneficiary designation

_____ Delegate authority granted under this Power of Attorney to another person

_____ Waive my right to be a beneficiary of a joint and survivor annuity, including a survivor benefit under a retirement plan

_____ Exercise the fiduciary power(s) that I have the authority to delegate as specified in the "Special Instructions" in Paragraph 7 of this Power of Attorney

_____ Exercise authority over the content of electronic communication sent or received by me

_____ Exercise authority with respect to intellectual property, including, without limitation, copyrights, contracts for payment of royalties, and trademarks

(If an agent (including successor agent) named in this Power of Attorney is someone other than an ancestor of yours, your spouse, or a descendant of yours, you must initial the following statement if it is your choice that such agent have the following authority. An agent who is an ancestor of yours, your spouse, or a descendant of yours already has the following authority under New Hampshire law.)

_____ My agent may exercise authority under this Power of Attorney to create in my agent, or in an individual to whom my agent owes a legal obligation of support, an interest in my property by any manner (other than a gift), including, without limitation, by right of survivorship, beneficiary designation, or disclaimer.

7. SPECIAL INSTRUCTIONS (OPTIONAL)

(Here you may include special instructions. You may leave this Paragraph blank. You may attach additional pages as necessary.)

8. EFFECTIVE DATE AND AUTHORITY OF AGENT

This Power of Attorney is effective immediately unless I have stated otherwise in the Special Instructions in Paragraph 7 of this Power of Attorney. An agent (including successor agent) named in this Power of Attorney will have no authority to act as my agent until he or she has signed and affixed to this Power of Attorney an acknowledgment that is substantially the same as the Acknowledgment at the end of this Power of Attorney.

9. GOVERNING LAW

This Power of Attorney shall be governed by the laws of the State of New Hampshire.

10. RELIANCE ON THIS POWER OF ATTORNEY

Any person, including my agent, may rely upon this Power of Attorney if it is acknowledged before a notary public or other individual authorized to take acknowledgements (or a copy of the acknowledged Power of Attorney), unless that person knows it is void, invalid, or terminated.

SIGNATURE AND ACKNOWLEDGMENT

(You must date and sign this Power of Attorney. If you are physically unable to sign, it may be signed by someone else writing your name, in your presence and at your express direction. This Power of Attorney must be acknowledged before a notary public or other individual authorized by law to take acknowledgments.)

Principal's Signature: _____

Principal's Printed Name: _____

Principal's Address: _____

Date: _____

STATE OF NEW HAMPSHIRE

COUNTY OF _____

The foregoing Power of Attorney was acknowledged before me on _____, by _____, known to me or satisfactorily proven to be the person named herein

Signature of Notarial Officer: _____

Title (and Rank): _____

My commission expires: _____

AGENT ACKNOWLEDGMENT

Notice to Agent: You will have no authority to act as agent under this Power of Attorney until you sign and affix this acknowledgment to the Power of Attorney.

I, _____, have read the attached power of attorney and am the person identified as the agent for the principal. I hereby acknowledge that when I act as agent I am given power under the power of attorney to make decisions about money, property, or both belonging to the principal, and to spend the principal's money, property, or both on the principal's behalf, in accordance with the terms of the power of attorney. When acting as agent, I have duties (called "fiduciary duties") to act in the principal's best interest, to act in good faith, and to act only within the scope of authority granted in the power of attorney, as well as other duties imposed by law to the extent not provided otherwise in the power of attorney. As an agent, I am not entitled to use the money or property for my own benefit or to make gifts to myself or others unless the power of attorney specifically gives me the authority to do so. As an agent, my authority under the power of attorney will end when the principal dies and I will not have authority to manage or dispose of any property or administer the estate of the principal. If I violate a fiduciary duty under the power of attorney, I may be liable for damages and may be subject to criminal prosecution. If there is anything about this power of attorney, or my duties under it, that I do not understand, I understand that I should seek professional advice.

Agent's Signature: _____

Date: _____

Page 780: Substitute this form for Form 61 in the text:

FORM 61   Durable Power of Attorney for Financial Affairs with Notice to Principal and Statement by Agent Forms and Directive Letter to Law Firm

DURABLE GENERAL POWER OF ATTORNEY

_____

_____

_____, 2009

_____, Esq.

_____

_____

Re: Escrow Letter for my Durable General Powers of Attorney

Dear Attorney_____:

Enclosed are my signed Durable General Powers of Attorney. It is my request that you hold these documents in escrow and that you release them to my named agents either (i) when I request in writing in the future, or (ii) when you determine that I have become subsequently disabled or incompetent. You may consult with and obtain the advice of my physician regarding my competency.

If you determine that I become disabled or incompetent, you may release the Durable General Power of Attorney to the first available and willing of my named agents as follows:

(1) First, you shall release the Durable General Power of Attorney naming my _____, _____, and my _____, _____, to them.

(2) Second, if my said _____ and my said _____ are unable or unwilling to serve in the capacity of attorney-in-fact, you shall then release the Durable General Power of Attorney naming my _____, _____, and my _____, _____, to them.

I understand that my agent shall be required to sign a "Statement by Agent" or any other legally mandated document prior to the release of any Durable General Power of Attorney.

If you should be unable for any reason to make any decisions regarding the release of said Durable General Powers of Attorney, I authorize a partner of the law firm of _____, or any successor law firm, to release said Durable General Powers of Attorney upon the same terms and conditions.

269

Very truly yours,

_____

DURABLE GENERAL POWER OF ATTORNEY

KNOW ALL BY THESE PRESENTS, that I, _____, of _____, New Hampshire, do hereby appoint _____ of _____, New Hampshire, as my agent and attorney-in-fact to act on my behalf with regard to the following:

1.   To receive dividends, interest and income arising from my assets; to endorse checks drawn to my order; to withdraw funds standing in my name from time to time on deposit in any bank or trust company; to purchase, sell or exchange any bonds or shares of stock now held by me or which I may hereafter acquire; to vote in person or by proxy all such stock or other securities; to delegate investment decisions to an investment manager or agent; and to execute such instruments of transfer and assignment as may be necessary or desirable in connection therewith;

2.   To act in all respects regarding any insurance policies which I own or in which I have or may have a beneficial interest, including but not limited to the following acts: transfer of ownership, change of beneficiary, cancellation of policy, purchase of insurance or additional insurance and exercise of any options available with respect to said policies;

OR

To pay any premium owed on any insurance policy which I own or to purchase additional insurance on my behalf and exercise any options available with respect to such additional insurance policies. Specifically, subject to the provisions of Paragraph 13. below, my attorney-in-fact shall not have the power to transfer ownership, change the beneficiary, or cancel an existing insurance policy which I own or in which I have or may have a beneficial interest;

3.   To borrow such sums of money as may be necessary or desirable and to execute notes from time to time in my name, giving such security as my attorney-in-fact may determine;

4.   To sell and dispose of any real or personal property which I own or in which I have any interest to such person or persons, for such amount, and on such terms as my attorney-in-fact may determine; in my name to execute and deliver instruments of transfer and assignment to convey my interest in said property;

5.   To purchase or acquire any real or personal property which my attorney-in-fact may determine to be in my interest and for such amount and on such terms as my attorney-in-fact may determine; in my name, to execute and deliver any consideration, documents or instruments of transfer which may be required to purchase or acquire said property;

6.   To have full access to any safe deposit box rented in my name, to remove the contents, and surrender the box;

7. To give, transfer or convey any of my assets to charities and persons of natural affection to whom I would normally consider making such gifts, transfers or conveyances, (including gifts to the attorney-in-fact) having in mind the ultimate objective of such gifts, transfers or conveyances being the qualification for state or federal medical, welfare or other assistance programs for my benefit or for the reduction of state and federal estate and inheritance taxes on my estate or my spouse's estate;

[OPTIONAL] provided, however, that my attorney-in-fact, individually, shall not be able to make gifts, transfers or conveyances to himself, his estate, his creditors or the creditors of his estate, in excess of the maximum amount over which an individual may have a power of withdrawal without its lapse in such year being deemed to be a release of such power under Section 2514(e) of the Internal Revenue Code of 1986, as amended and any corresponding Sections of any future Internal Revenue Code;

OR

To give, transfer or convey any of my assets to charities, to my attorney-in-fact, and persons of natural affection to whom I would normally consider making such gifts, transfers or conveyances, having in mind the ultimate objective of such gifts, transfers or conveyances being the qualification for state or federal medical, welfare or other assistance programs for my benefit or for the reduction of state and federal estate and inheritance taxes on my estate, whether or not such gift, transfer or conveyance may leave me without sufficient assets or income to provide for my care without relying on Medicaid, other public assistance or charity;

8. To disclaim any assets to which I may be entitled;

9. To exercise and to otherwise deal in any way with any power of appointment, general, special, limited or otherwise, of which I may be a donee;

[OPTIONAL] provided, however, that my attorney-in-fact, individually, shall not be able to make gifts, transfers or conveyances to himself, his estate, his creditors or the creditors of his estate, in excess of the maximum amount over which an individual may have a power of withdrawal without its lapse in such year being deemed to be a release of such power under Section 2514(e) of the Internal Revenue Code of 1986, as amended and any corresponding Sections of any future Internal Revenue Code;

10. To establish a new domicile;

11. To make out and execute all returns which may be required for the purpose of determining income or other taxes imposed by the United States government or by any state government as well as execute an IRS Form 2848 "Power of Attorney and Declaration of Representative" appointing the attorney-in-fact or anyone else to serve;

12. To commence and prosecute, or to defend, all actions or proceedings involving any matter in which I have or may have any interest or concern, and to

compromise, settle and adjust all claims and demands whatsoever due and hereafter to become due or belonging to me;

13.   To transfer all or any part of my assets, real or personal, tangible or intangible, to any trust which is in existence or which I may now or in the future create;

14.   To apply to the Social Security Administration to become representative payee of my Social Security benefit payments, and to then act as my representative payee in accordance with applicable law;

15.   To make any and all applications to other state or federal medical, welfare or other assistance programs for benefits to which I may be entitled;

16.   To continue or participate in the operation of any business or other enterprise;

17.   To employ as investment counsel, custodians, brokers, accountants, appraisers, attorneys-at-law, or other agents or such persons, firms or organizations (including any of my said attorneys and any firm of which any of my said attorneys may be a member or employee) as deemed necessary or desirable, and to pay such persons, firms, or organizations such compensation as is deemed reasonable; and to determine whether or not to act upon the advice of any such agent without liability for acting or failing to act thereon;

18.   To establish one or more "individual retirement accounts" or other retirement plans or arrangements in my name. In connection with any pension, profit sharing or stock bonus plan, individual retirement arrangement, Roth IRA, § 401(k), § 403(b) annuity or account, § 457 plan, or any other retirement plan, arrangement or annuity in which I am a participant or of which I am a beneficiary (whether established by my agent or otherwise) (each of which is hereinafter referred to as "such Plan"), my agent shall have the following powers, in addition to all other applicable powers granted by this instrument:

A. To make contributions (including "rollover" contributions) or cause contributions to be made to such Plan with my funds or otherwise on my behalf.

B. To receive and endorse checks or other distributions to me from such Plan, or to arrange for the direct deposit of the same in any account in my name or in the name of any trust which is in existence or which I may now or in the future create.

C. To elect a form of payment of benefits from such Plan, to withdraw benefits from such Plan, to make contributions to such Plan and to make, exercise, waive or consent to any and all elections and/or options that I may have regarding contributions to, investments or administration of, distribution from, or form of benefits under, such Plan.

D. To designate one or more beneficiaries or contingent beneficiaries for any benefits payable under such Plan on account of my death, and to change any such prior designation of beneficiary made by me or by my agent, subject to the following limitation: My agent shall have no power to designate my agent directly or indirectly as a beneficiary or contingent beneficiary to receive a greater share or proportion of any such benefits than my agent would have otherwise received, unless such change is consented to by all other beneficiaries who would have received the benefits but for the proposed change. The preceding limitation shall not apply to any designation of my agent as beneficiary in a fiduciary capacity, with no beneficial interest.

19.   To act as my personal representative solely for the purpose of obtaining and receiving any and all Protected Health Information related to my health care and related to payments in regard to such health care, in accordance with the Health Care Insurance Portability and Accountability Act of 1996 (Pub. L. 104-191), 45 CFR Sections 160 and 164 ("HIPAA").

20.   To have full power to act in the management and disposition of all of my estate, affairs, and property of every kind and wherever situate, in such manner and with such authority as I myself might exercise if personally present, and to do all acts which my attorney-in-fact deems necessary in carrying out the foregoing.

My agent, in addition to the above powers and authority, shall have all of the powers granted to trustees by New Hampshire common law and statutory authority (including, but not limited to, the Uniform Trustees' Powers Act, R.S.A. 564-A, and the Uniform Trust Code, R.S.A. 564-B, as they may be amended from time to time), without restrictions. Where the context of this statute requires, the word "attorney-in-fact" or "agent" shall be substituted for the word "trustee" and the words "property", "assets" or "matters" shall be substituted for the word "trust estate".

This power of attorney is executed pursuant to New Hampshire Revised Statutes Annotated 506:6 and shall not be affected by my subsequent disability or incompetence or the passage of time. If there shall be any uncertainty whether I am dead or alive, all acts done by my attorney-in-fact shall have the same effect and inure to the benefit of and bind me and my distributees, devisees, legatees, and personal representatives as if I were alive, competent and not disabled.

IN WITNESS WHEREOF, I have set my hand on _____, 2009.

_____   _____
Witness

_____   _____
Witness

STATE OF NEW HAMPSHIRE
COUNTY OF _____

The foregoing instrument was acknowledged before me on _____, 2009, by _____.

273

Notary Public/Justice of the Peace
My Commission Expires:
(Seal)

INFORMATION CONCERNING THE DURABLE GENERAL POWER OF ATTORNEY

THIS IS AN IMPORTANT LEGAL DOCUMENT.
BEFORE SIGNING THIS DOCUMENT YOU SHOULD KNOW THESE IMPORTANT FACTS:

Notice to Principal

As the "principal," you are using this Durable General Power of Attorney to grant power to another person (called the "Agent" or "Attorney-in-Fact") to make decisions, including, but not limited to, decisions concerning your money, property, or both, and to use your money, property or both on your behalf. If this written Durable General Power of Attorney does not limit the powers that you give to your Agent, upon its release, your Agent will have broad and sweeping powers to sell or otherwise dispose of your property and to spend your money without advance notice to you or approval by you.

You have designated your attorney as the person to retain this Power in escrow and not to release this Power until you instruct your attorney to so release it to your Agent pursuant to written instructions or upon the condition that your attorney determines that you have become subsequently disabled or incompetent.

You have the right to revoke or take back this Durable General Power of Attorney at any time, so long as you are of sound mind.

If there is anything about this Durable General Power of Attorney that you do not understand, you should seek professional advice.

RECEIVED:

_____, 2009 _____

_____, Principal

STATE OF NEW HAMPSHIRE
COUNTY OF _____

The foregoing instrument was received and acknowledged before me on _____, 2009, by _____.

Notary Public/Justice of the Peace
My Commission Expires:
(Seal)

INFORMATION CONCERNING THE DURABLE GENERAL POWER OF ATTORNEY

THIS IS AN IMPORTANT LEGAL DOCUMENT. BEFORE SIGNING THIS DOCUMENT YOU SHOULD KNOW THESE IMPORTANT FACTS:

Statement by Agent

I, _____, have read the attached Durable General Power of Attorney and am the person identified as the Agent for the Principal. I hereby acknowledge that when I act as Agent or "Attorney-in-Fact," I am given power under this Durable General Power of Attorney to make decisions about money, property, or both belonging to the Principal, and to spend the Principal's money, property, or both on the Principal's behalf, in accordance with the terms of this Durable General Power of Attorney.

This Durable General Power of Attorney is valid only if the Principal is of sound mind when the Principal signs it. When acting in the capacity of Agent, I am under a duty (called a "fiduciary duty") to observe the standards observed by a prudent person, which means the use of those powers that is reasonable in view of the interests of the Principal and in view of the way in which a person of ordinary judgment would act in carrying out the person's own affairs. If the exercise of my acts is called into question, the burden will be upon me to prove that I acted under the standards of fiduciary duty.

As the Agent, I am not entitled to use the money or property for my own benefit or to make gifts to myself or others unless the Durable General Power of Attorney specifically gives me the authority to do so.

As the Agent, my authority under this Durable General Power of Attorney will end when the Principal dies and I will not have authority to manage or dispose of any property or administer the estate unless I am authorized to do so by a New Hampshire Probate Court. If I violate my fiduciary responsibility duty under this Durable General Power of Attorney, I may be liable for damages and may be subject to criminal prosecution. If there is anything about this Durable General Power of Attorney, or my duties under it, that I do not understand, I understand that I should seek professional advice.

_____, 2009

_____, Agent

STATE OF NEW HAMPSHIRE
COUNTY OF _____

The foregoing instrument was received and acknowledged before me on
_____, 2009, by _____.

Notary Public/Justice of the Peace
My Commission Expires:
(Seal)

Page 788: Substitute this form for Form 62 in the text:

FORM 62   Letter of Instruction to Agent or Attorney-in-Fact

**Important Information for the
Agent/Attorney-In-Fact
Under a Power of Attorney**

To the Agent/Attorney-in-Fact:

As you know, a POWER OF ATTORNEY is a document in which an individual, called the Principal, appoints another individual, called the Agent or the Attorney-in-Fact, as his or her legal representative. The Agent/Attorney-in-Fact is authorized to transact business on behalf of the Principal. A list of the authorities conferred is contained in the Power itself, and, as you can see, they are very broad. The purpose of a Power of Attorney is to enable an individual to appoint another individual as his or her legal representative without the need for the appointment of a guardian through probate court procedure. Normally, it is not intended that the Power of Attorney be used by the Agent unless there is an incompetency on the part of the Principal, or unless the Principal is otherwise physically restricted from handling his or her own affairs.

It is important for you to keep in mind that a Power of Attorney creates a fiduciary relationship between the Agent and the Principal. This means that you have the legal responsibility and duty to use the Principal's assets solely for the benefit of the Principal. Even though the Power of Attorney may give you the ability to make gifts of the Principal's property in order to effectuate estate or Medicaid planning, you must have the Principal's welfare foremost in mind when disposing of any assets. A breach of the fiduciary duty imposed under a Power of Attorney or abuse of that fiduciary duty can result in severe criminal and civil sanctions.

Is also very important for you to segregate the assets of the Principal from your own. These assets should always be held in the name of the Principal, not in your name, and they should never be co-mingled with your or any one else's assets. You should also keep separate, accurate records of the Principal's assets showing receipts and disbursements. You should prepare an annual statement of how the Principal's assets have been invested and spent. A copy should be given to the Principal and other family members if appropriate.

Under the law, any person interested in the assets of the Principal may at any time petition the Probate Court or the Superior Court to ask for an accounting for your actions under the Power of Attorney. See the Revised Statutes of New Hampshire, Chapter 564-E. This procedure is relatively simple to initiate and, if initiated, will result in an open hearing in the Probate or Superior Court upon your actions under the Power of Attorney. It has been our experience, that the Probate and Superior Courts scrutinize very carefully an agent's actions under a Power of Attorney. They particularly frown upon any evidence that the Agent is using the Power of Attorney for his or her own benefit. Also, it is important, in case such a hearing is held, to make sure that all of your actions under the Power of Attorney have a "paper trail." Therefore, we advise you to not engage in any cash transactions, but all receipts should be carefully itemized on deposit slips and all disbursements should be made by check. Cash transactions should not be used at all.

You should seek the advice of your attorney if you have any questions regarding your duties under this Power of Attorney.

Received by:

_____   _____
Witness

Page 798: Substitute this form for Form 64 found in the text:

FORM 64   Alternate Antenuptial Agreement

ANTENUPTIAL AGREEMENT

This Antenuptial Agreement (the "Agreement") is made this _____ day of _____, _____, by and between _____, of ____, and ____, of ____, .

1.   **Representations**.   and   represent and acknowledge the following to be true and correct as of the Date of this Agreement:

     1.1   and   intend to be married in the reasonably foreseeable future.

     1.2   is the owner of tangible personal property which is listed on Exhibit A attached hereto, all of which has been fully disclosed to and discussed with   .

     1.3   has an ownership interest in the following real estate: _____ _____ , _____ .

     1.4   has reasonable prospects of earning income from his participation in the management of the his business entities and employment, all of which have been disclosed to and discussed with   .

     1.5   has reviewed Exhibit A and acknowledges that   's disclosure of his personal property, real property and entities is satisfactory to her; she hereby waives further disclosure by   of the same.

     1.6   is the owner of real property, personal property and other interests which are listed on Exhibit B attached hereto, all of which have been disclosed to and discussed with

     1.7   has reasonable prospects of earning income from her real property, personal property and other interests all of which have been fully disclosed to and discussed with

     1.8   has reviewed Exhibit B and acknowledges that   's disclosure of her real and personal property and other interests is satisfactory to him; he hereby waives further disclosure by   of the same.

     1.9   's separate property shall be defined as:

        a.   All of his personal property, real property and entities identified under Exhibit A attached hereto and the proceeds thereof;

     b.   Any interest in any personal property, real property and entities which may hereafter acquire through the investment of his separate property as defined by this Agreement, or through the investment of any funds which   has borrowed individually and, if secured, has secured by collateral assignment or other security interest in his separate property and which is paid for from   's separate property or income received by   from his separate property;

     c.   Any gifts or inheritance, regardless of kind or type, specifically given to or left to   ;

     d.   Any dividends, interest, capital gains, return of principal, compensation or other income, (including, without limitation, all salary and bonuses) derived from the above separate property ;

     e.   Any and all retirement benefits, IRA accounts, profit sharing plans, stock options and/or Keogh plans received because of his present or future contribution or by benefit of his present or future employment; and

     f.   Any property he may individually acquire during the parties' marriage that is specifically designated as separate property in a writing signed by him and   .

     1.10   desires that except as provided in this Agreement, his separate property and any increase or appreciation in its value in the future, whether caused by his efforts or otherwise, be free from any claim that   might otherwise acquire by an action for divorce, legal separation, separate maintenance or through any temporary or permanent order of any court. (Hereinafter all of the aforementioned property is sometimes referred to as his "Separate Property").

     1.11   's separate property shall be defined as:

     a.   All of her personal property, real property and business interests identified on Exhibit B attached hereto and the proceeds thereof;

     b.   Any interest in any personal and real property and business interests which may hereafter acquire through the investment of her separate property as defined by this Agreement, or through the investment of her separate property as defined by this Agreement, or through the investment of any funds which   has borrowed individually and, if secured, has secured by collateral assignment or the security interest in her separate property and which is paid for from   's separate property or income received by   from her separate property;

     c.   Any gifts or inheritance, regardless of kind or type, specifically given to or left to   ;

    d. Any dividends, interest, capital gains, return of principal compensation or other income, (including, without limitation, all salary and bonuses) derived from the above separate property;

    e. Any and all retirement benefits, IRA accounts, profit sharing plans, stock options and/or Keogh plans received because of her present or future contribution or by benefit of her present of future employment; and

    f. Any property she may individually acquire during the parties' marriage that is specifically designated as separate property in a writing signed by her and

  1.12 desires that except as provided for in this Agreement, her separate property or any increase or appreciation in its value in the future whether caused by her efforts or otherwise be free from any claim that   might otherwise acquire by action for divorce, legal separation, separate maintenance or through any temporary or permanent order of the court (hereinafter all of the aforementioned property is sometimes referred to as her "Separate Property").

  1.13 The parties shall have marital property which shall be equally divided between the parties upon the parties' separation, upon the dissolution of the parties' marriage, or upon the death of either party. Marital Property shall be defined as:

    a. All property, real estate, bank accounts, stock and business interests which the parties hold under joint names even if acquired by either party's separate funds;

    b. Any interest in any personal property, real property and business interests which may be acquired through the investment of Marital Property as defined by this Agreement, through the investment of any funds jointly borrowed by the parties, and if secured, has been secured by collateral assignment or other security interest in their marital property;

    c. Any gifts or inheritances, regardless of kind or type, specifically given to or left to both   and   ; and

    d. Any dividends, interests, capital gains, return of principal, compensation or other income (without limitation, also salaries and bonuses) derived from the above marital property or otherwise earned by them jointly.

  1.14 has agreed to accept the provisions of this Agreement in lieu of all of her property rights in the Separate Property of   , except as otherwise provided in this Agreement, to which she might be entitled either as his wife during his lifetime, as his separate spouse or divorced former spouse, or as his widow, heir-at-law, next of kin, or distributee upon his death.

  1.15 has agreed to accept the provisions of this Agreement in lieu of all of his property rights in the separate property of   , except as otherwise provided in this

Agreement, to which he might be entitled either as her husband during his lifetime, as her separate spouse or divorced former spouse, or as her widower, heir-at-law, next of kin, or distributee upon her death.

1.16 _____ has agreed that, effective upon the lawful marriage of the parties, he shall pay to _____.

1.17 Both _____ and _____ have expressed their intent and desire to enter into this Agreement notwithstanding their understanding and acknowledgment that either or both of their financial health and other circumstances may change substantially in the future, including disability, incapacity, substantial handicap, the birth of children, and the loss or lack of earning capacity.

NOW THEREFORE, in consideration of the mutual promises, covenants and conditions herein set forth, the parties hereto agree as follows:

2. **Separate Property**. Any real or personal property or interests in any entity which are owned or acquired by either party before their marriage, or which are owned or acquired by either party after their marriage, as their separate property except as otherwise provided in this Agreement:

2.1 Shall be the separate property of the party owning or acquiring it with the absolute right of such party to manage, dispose of or otherwise deal with it;

2.2 Shall be subject to no claim nor any demand on or against it by the other party; and

2.3 That after the parties' marriage, both parties shall execute any documents necessary to waive his/her interest in the other parties' separate property.

3. **Release of Certain Marital Rights by** _____:

3.1 Agrees that he shall not during the lifetime of _____, or after her death, should her death occur before his, take, claim, demand or receive community property or any dower, homestead, forced share against her present or any future will or other right or interest in any of her Separate Property except as set forth in Sections 1.14, 6 and 9 of this Agreement;

3.2 Expressly releases all property rights in _____'s separate property except as set forth in Sections 1.14, 6 and 9 of this Agreement to which he might be entitled during her lifetime under the laws of the State of New Hampshire, or of any other state, jurisdiction or country, with the intent that the property rights to the separate property of each of the parties described in this Agreement remains separate and distinct during their lifetimes as if the contemplated marriage had not taken place; and

3.3   Expressly releases all property rights to any inheritance to which   may be entitled and in any direct or indirect equity ownership that   may acquire in any business as if the contemplated marriage had not taken place.

4.   **Release of Certain Marital Rights by**   :

4.1   Agrees that she shall not during the lifetime of   , or after his death, should his death occur before hers, take, claim, demand or receive community property or any dower, homestead, forced share against his present or any future will or other right or interest in any of his separate property except as set forth in Sections 1.14, 6 and 8 of this Agreement;

4.2   Expressly releases all property rights in   's separate property except as set forth in Sections 1.14, 6 and 8 of this Agreement to which she might be entitled during his lifetime under the laws of the State of New Hampshire, or of any other state, jurisdiction or country, with the intent that the property rights to the Separate Property of each of the parties described in this Agreement remains separate and distinct during their lifetimes as if the contemplated marriage had not taken place; and

4.3   Expressly releases all property rights to any inheritance to which   may be entitled and in any direct or indirect equity ownership that   may acquire in any business including, without limitation, the Business Entities, as if the contemplated marriage had not taken place.

4.4   In the event of the death of   ,   shall have the right to remain in the parties' marital residence located in   ,   , for a period not to exceed ten (10) years from the date of death of   ; provided, however, that   and   were lawfully married and residing together with no legal separation or divorce proceedings pending in any court of competent jurisdiction. Further provided, that   shall be responsible or the upkeep, maintenance and expenses of the property during her residency.

5.   **Dissolution of the Marriage**.   and   , each representing that he or she has the current capacity and ability to independently support himself or herself, agree that if, after their marriage, either of the parties for alleged cause or otherwise files a proceeding for annulment, separation, separate maintenance or other form of dissolution of their marriage arrangement or violates the bonds of matrimony as provided by the statutes of the State of New Hampshire or any state, jurisdiction or country in which they may be domiciled, then, except as otherwise provided by this Agreement, neither of them shall demand, take, receive, make claim to or be entitled to any real or personal property or stock or business interests which have been designated or described as the present or future Separate Property of the other party by virtue of the contemplated termination or the termination of the marriage between them.

         agrees that, in the event of a dissolution of the marriage, he will pay over to the following amounts:

5.1   For each year, to a maximum of fifteen (15) years, the parties were lawfully married and residing together and no legal separation or divorce proceedings were pending in any court of competent jurisdiction,   shall pay over to   the sum of   ($). The maximum amount   will pay to   pursuant to this provision is   ($). Payment pursuant to this provision shall be made within one hundred twenty (120) days from expiration of the period for filing an appeal from the final order of the Court setting forth the terms for dissolution of the parties' marriage.

5.2   In the event the parties were lawfully married and residing together with no legal separation or divorce proceedings pending in any court of competent jurisdiction for a period exceeding fifteen (15) years, then the provisions herein provided shall govern any additional asset distribution from   to   as a result of the dissolution of the parties marriage.

6.   **Marital Property of the Parties**. The parties agree that nothing set forth in this Agreement shall be deemed a waiver of any rights that either of them may acquire in Marital Property by virtue of their marriage. Each party hereto understands and agrees that this Agreement is meant to affect only their Separate Property as defined and described herein and not their Marital Property. If either party files an action for legal separation or separate maintenance or the termination of the marriage, then, in that event, the Marital Property shall be equally divided between the parties.

7.   **Joint Releases**.   and   represent that they have adequate independent means of support. In the event either of them after consummation of the marriage, find, for cause or otherwise, that they are unable or unwilling to continue the marriage arrangement, or if either of the parties hereto violates the bonds of matrimony as provided by the statutes of the State of New Hampshire or of any jurisdiction in which they may be domiciled, or if either party files an action for legal separation, separate maintenance or termination of the marriage, then, and in that event,   and   agree that neither of them shall be entitled to any alimony, support, costs, attorney's fees or to any other money by virtue of the termination of the marriage between them except as otherwise provided in this Agreement. The parties agree that nothing set forth herein shall be deemed to be a waiver of either party's right to claim or right to receive child support for the support of any children born of their marriage or legally adopted during their marriage. These provisions may be cited by either party hereto in any court of competent jurisdiction as a waiver and release of any money payment as aforesaid by one to the other.

8.   **Release of Homestead Rights of the Parties**. The parties agree that:

8.1   The settlement made hereinabove is intended to be made in lieu of   's homestead right, distributive share, or either of them, in   's estate and in compliance with the provisions of New Hampshire Revised Statutes Annotated, Chapter 560:15, or as may be subsequently amended.

8.2   The settlement made hereinabove is intended to be made in lieu of   's homestead right, distributive share, or either of them, in   's estate and in compliance with the provisions of New Hampshire Revised Statutes Annotated, Chapter 560:16, or as may be subsequently amended.

9.   **Transfer Between the Parties**. Subject to the provisions of this Agreement, either party hereto shall have the right to transfer or convey to the other party, any property or interest which may be lawfully conveyed or transferred during his or her lifetime, or by will or otherwise upon death, and neither party intends by this Agreement to limit or restrict in any way the right and power to receive any such transfer or conveyance from the other party made in addition to any provisions set forth herein.

10.   **Confidentiality of Disclosures in this Agreement**. Each party has been advised by the other party that the disclosures of the property set forth in this Agreement are confidential and not available to the public and contain confidential information. Each party agrees that disclosure of said confidential information will be damaging to the other party. Accordingly as a material inducement to enter into this Agreement, each party hereto agrees that he or she will not disclose to third parties the information disclosed by the other party in this Agreement without written consent of the other party and each party agrees that this confidentiality covenant and agreement will survive the termination of their marriage or the death of either of them; provided however, that it will not be a breach thereof for either party hereto to disclose such information to his or her attorney or to any court of competent jurisdiction in which an action relating to their marriage is pending; provided further, however, that the party filing this Agreement, in, or disclosing this Agreement to, such a court, seeks a protective order under which this Agreement will not be available for inspection by the public or the media. Each party hereto agrees that there is no adequate remedy at law for violation of this confidentiality covenant and therefore agrees to waive any defense based thereon and agrees that equitable relief, including specific performance of said covenant by injunction, would be an appropriate remedy for the breach or threatened breach of this confidentiality agreement and covenant.

11.   **Further Assurances**. Each party shall, on the request of the other party, execute, acknowledge and deliver any additional instruments or documents that may be reasonably required to carry out the intention of this Agreement, including such instruments as may be required by the laws of any state, jurisdiction, or country now in effect or hereafter enacted, which may affect the property rights of the parties as between themselves or with others.

12.   **Full Disclosure**. Each of the parties represents that they have made a full disclosure to the other party of all material property presently owned or otherwise held by them and of all present earnings of each such party.

13.   **Entire Agreement**. This Agreement contains the entire understanding of the parties and may be rescinded, terminated, modified or amended at any time before or after the solemnization of the marriage only by a subsequent written agreement between   and   . The Parties each acknowledge that the other is relying upon the accuracy of the information being provided herein and in Exhibits A and B in entering into this Agreement.

14.   **Effective Date**. This Agreement shall take effect only on the solemnization of the marriage now contemplated by   and   ; provided that the confidentiality covenant and

agreement set in forth in Section 11 shall be effective upon the execution of this Agreement by the parties and shall remain in effect between them even if their marriage is never solemnized.

15.   **Severability**. In the event that any condition of this Agreement shall be held invalid or unenforceable by any Court of competent jurisdiction or rendered invalid or unenforceable by any governmental legislative or other action, such holding or action shall not invalidate or render unenforceable any other provision of this Agreement, and the offending provisions shall be severed from this Agreement and shall be null, void and of no further force and effect.

16.   **Consideration**. The consideration for this Agreement consists of mutual promises of the parties,   and   , as set forth in this Agreement and the obligations required of and   in Sections 1.11, 1.13, 6, 8 and 9 of this Agreement.

17.   **Binding Effect**. This Agreement shall inure to the benefit of the parties hereto and there respective legal representatives, guardians, successors and assigns.

18.   **Governing Law**. The interpretation, construction and effect of this Agreement shall be made in accordance with the laws of the State of New Hampshire in effect at the time of its execution. In the event of the dissolution of the marriage, legal separation or death of either party, the laws of the State of   's and   's then residence will apply in determining their respective rights as to matters not covered by this Agreement.

19.   **Counsel**. The parties hereby acknowledge as indicated on page 10 of this Agreement that each of them has had the opportunity to be represented by counsel of his or her choice in the negotiation and preparation of this Agreement, that each party has had the opportunity to be represented by additional counsel of his or her choice, that each party has read the foregoing Agreement, that each party has had the opportunity to be fully advised by counsel of his or her choice of their property rights and the legal significance of the foregoing Agreement, that each party has a full and complete understanding of the foregoing Agreement and that each of them is freely and voluntarily executing this Agreement. It is further understood between the parties that   was willing to postpone the date of the marriage should   desire more time to deliberate, review and negotiate the terms and provisions of this Agreement.   shall not seek to set aside the terms of this Agreement and any subsequent proceeding by claiming that there was not adequate time for her to freely negotiate the terms of this Agreement or by claiming that she has entered into it under any pressures, duress or coercion. It is further understood between the parties that   was willing to postpone the date of the marriage should   desire more time to deliberate, review and negotiate the terms and provisions of this Agreement.   shall not seek to set aside the terms of this Agreement and any subsequent proceeding by claiming that there was not adequate time for him to freely negotiate the terms of this Agreement or by claiming that he has entered into it under any pressures, duress or coercion.

IN WITNESS WHEREOF, the parties have hereto signed, sealed and acknowledged this Agreement on the date first above written.

_____

STATE OF NEW HAMPSHIRE
COUNTY OF _____

    Personally appeared before me,   , a person known to me, and made oath that the foregoing instrument is his free voluntary act and deed.

_____
                            Notary Public/Justice of the Peace

STATE OF NEW HAMPSHIRE
COUNTY OF _____

    Personally appeared before me,   , a person known to me, and made oath that the foregoing instrument is her free voluntary act and deed.

_____
                            Notary Public/Justice of the Peace

ACKNOWLEDGMENT OF

I hereby certify that I have had the opportunity to consult with counsel of my choice and to be fully advised of my property rights and of the legal significance of the foregoing Agreement, and that I hereby acknowledge a full and complete understanding of the legal consequences of the terms and provisions of the foregoing Agreement and that I am freely and voluntarily executing this Agreement.

_____

ACKNOWLEDGMENT OF

I hereby certify that I have had the opportunity to consult with counsel of my choice and to be fully advised of my property rights and of the legal significance of the foregoing Agreement, and that I hereby acknowledge a full and complete understanding of the legal consequences of the terms and provisions of the foregoing Agreement and that I am freely and voluntarily executing this Agreement.

_____

EXHIBIT A

PROPERTY OF

Asset	Value

EXHIBIT B

PROPERTY OF
_____

_____ County of _____ State of New
Asset _____ of _____ Value

Page 819: Substitute this form for Form 67 in the text:

FORM 67   International Will

LAST WILL
OF

_____

I, _____, of _____, County of _____, State of New Hampshire, do make this will as an international will pursuant to R.S.A. 551-A, and hereby revoke all other wills and codicils previously made by me.

1.   <u>DEBTS, EXPENSES AND TAXES</u>. I direct that all my legal debts, funeral expenses and expenses of administration be paid as soon after my death as practical. I further direct that all such debts and expenses, as well as all estate, inheritance, transfer, legacy or succession taxes (state and federal), and any interest or penalties thereon which may be assessed or imposed with respect to my estate, or any part thereof, wheresoever situated, whether or not passing under my will, including the taxable value of all policies of insurance on my life and all transfers, powers, rights or interests includible in my estate for purposes of such taxes and duties, shall be paid out of my residuary estate as an expense of administration and without apportionment, and shall not be prorated or charged against any of the other gifts in this will or against property not passing under this will.

2.   <u>REAL ESTATE</u>. I give and devise to _____ absolutely, all of my right, title and interest, whatever it may be, in the real estate used as our home property or properties at the time of my death.

3.   <u>TANGIBLE PERSONAL PROPERTY</u>. I give and bequeath to absolutely, all of my tangible personal property and household effects owned by me at the time of my death, including furniture, clothing, jewelry, silver, books, pictures, china, automobiles and their equipment, other vehicles and their equipment, and other articles of personal and household use or ornament.

I express the hope that said beneficiaries will dispose of said tangible personal property and household effects according to my wishes, however my wishes may be made known to them, but I expressly declare that I do not intend to create any trust in law or in equity with respect to said tangible personal property.

If a division of the property under this bequest is required among the beneficiaries, such division shall be made by the beneficiaries, in appropriate shares, as they may amicably agree. I prefer that said beneficiaries shall agree upon the manner in which said property is to be divided, but should they not agree among themselves as to the division thereof within ninety (90) days after my death, I give my executor full power and authority to divide said property among said beneficiaries, in appropriate shares, and his determination with respect thereto shall, insofar as permitted by law, be binding and conclusive upon such beneficiaries.

4.   <u>RESIDUARY ESTATE</u>. All the rest, residue and remainder of my estate,

of whatever kind or nature, wherever found and however acquired, including any property over which I have a power of appointment, I give, devise and bequeath to _____ if _____ he/she survives me.

If _____ shall not survive me, then I give, devise and bequeath my residuary estate to my issue who so survive me, such issue to take per stirpes.

5.   ADMINISTRATIVE POWERS. My executor hereinafter named, and any other administrator, executor, or trustee administering my estate shall have the powers, in addition to those granted by law, as are granted to trustees by the Uniform Trustees' Powers Act, R.S.A. 564-A and the Uniform Trust Code, R.S.A. 564-B, as they may be amended from time to time, without restrictions. Where the context of this statute requires, the word "executor" or "administrator" shall be substituted for the word "trustee" and the word "estate" shall be substituted for the word "trust."

6.   SURVIVAL REQUIREMENT. No person shall be deemed to have survived me, or any other person or event under the terms of this will, unless such person survives the end of the period commencing with the close of the calendar day of my death, the death of such other person or on which such event occurs, and ending with the close of the thirtieth (30th) calendar day thereafter.

7.   EXECUTORS. I nominate my _____, _____, as executor under this will.

If my said _____ should be unable or unwilling to serve in this capacity for any reason, then I nominate my _____, _____, of _____, _____ as successor.

It is my desire that the executor and the designated alternate shall be allowed to serve with the minimum bond required by the Probate Court.

8.   GUARDIANS. If my former spouse, _____, of _____, _____, survives me, I nominate my said former spouse to be the guardian of the person and property of each of the children of our marriage who shall be a minor at the time of my death (and I request the Court having jurisdiction thereof to make appointment accordingly).

If my said former spouse does not survive me or should be unable or unwilling to act in this capacity for any reason, then I nominate my _____, _____, of _____, _____, to serve in the stead of my former spouse.

It is my desire that my said former spouse and the designated alternates shall be allowed to serve with the minimum bond required by the Probate Court.

9.   EXPRESS INTENT. Except as otherwise expressly provided by this will, I intentionally make no provision for the benefit of any child of mine, nor the issue of any child of mine, whether now alive, now deceased, or hereafter born or deceased.

10.   DEFINITIONS. Whenever used in this will the words "child," "children," or "issue" are intended to include not only persons who are

descendants by blood, but also persons, and issue of persons, who have been adopted according to law prior to their attaining the age of eighteen (18) years.

Masculine, feminine and neuter pronouns shall each include all genders, and the singular shall include the plural, and vice versa, where the context or facts so admit.

The captions and paragraph headings of this will are inserted only as a matter of convenience and for reference, and in no way define, limit or describe the scope or intent of this will, nor in any way affect this will.

IN WITNESS WHEREOF, I hereunto set my hand and, in the presence of two (2) witnesses, declare this to be my will, on _____, 2005. For identification, I have signed each of the _____ (_____) pages of this will.

_____

_____

Signed and declared by the said _____ as and for his will, in the presence of us, who at his request, in his presence, and in the presence of each other, hereunto subscribe our names as witnesses and authorized person.

_____ residing at _____

_____ residing at _____

_____ residing at _____
Authorized Person

ACKNOWLEDGEMENT AND AFFIDAVIT FOR
SELF-PROVING WILL PURSUANT TO R.S.A. 551:2-a

THE STATE OF NEW HAMPSHIRE
COUNTY OF _____, SS.

The foregoing instrument was acknowledged before me on _____, 2005, by _____, the testator; _____ and _____, the witnesses, and _____, the authorized person, who under oath do swear as follows:

1. The testator signed the instrument as his will or expressly directed another to sign for him.

2. This was the testator's free and voluntary act for the purposes expressed in the will.

3. Each witness signed at the request of the testator, in his presence, in the presence of the other witness, and in the presence of the authorized person.

4. To the best of my knowledge, at the time of the signing the testator was at least 18 years of age, or if under 18 years was a married person, and was of sane mind and under no constraint or undue influence.

Notary Public/Justice of the Peace
My Commission Expires:
(Seal)

CERTIFICATE

I, _____, of _____
　　　　(name)　　　　　　　　　　(address)

in my capacity as _____, a person authorized in connection with international wills, certify that on _____, 2005, at _____, New Hampshire, the testator, _____, of _____, _____, New Hampshire, born on _____, in _____, _____, in my presence and that of the witnesses:

(a) _____
　　　　　　(name, address, date and place of birth)

(b) _____
　　　　　　(name, address, date and place of birth)

has declared that the attached document is his last will and that he knows the content thereof.

I furthermore certify that:

(a) In my presence and in that of the witnesses the testator has signed the will or has acknowledged his signature previously affixed;

(b) the witnesses and I have signed the will;

(c) each page of the will has been signed by the testator and numbered;

(d) I have satisfied myself as to the identity of the testator and of the witnesses as designed above;

(e) the witnesses met the conditions requisite to act as such according to the law under which I am acting;

(f) for safekeeping purposes, the testator directs that the original of this will shall be kept at the offices of McLane, Graf, Raulerson & Middleton, P.A., at 900 Elm Street, Manchester, New Hampshire.

PLACE OF EXECUTION: Manchester, New Hampshire

DATE: _____, 2005

SIGNATURE and, if　　_____
necessary, SEAL:　　　　Authorized Person

Page 829: Substitute this form for Form 69 in the text:

FORM 69   Revocable Qualified Terminable Interest Property (QTIP) Trust with Qualified Subchapter S Corporation (QSST) Provisions

THE _____ REVOCABLE TRUST OF 2009

TRUST AGREEMENT, made on _____, 2009, between _____, residing in _____, _____, (hereinafter called the "Grantor"), and _____, residing in _____, _____ (hereinafter called the "Trustee").

At the time of the signing of this trust, the Grantor's spouse is _____, and the Grantor's children are _____.

1.   TRUST PROPERTY. All property transferred and delivered to the Trustee, which the Trustee may, at any time, hold or acquire, including cash, securities, or other property, shall be referred to collectively as the "trust estate" and held and administered and disposed of by the Trustee for the uses and purposes, and upon the terms and conditions, herein set forth.

2.   DISPOSITIVE PROVISIONS: LIFETIME. The Trustee shall hold, manage, invest and reinvest the trust estate, and shall collect the income thereof and dispose of the net income and principal as follows:

A. Pay such parts of the income, if any, and such parts of the principal of this trust to, or for the benefit of, the Grantor as the Grantor directs from time to time for the Grantor's support in reasonable comfort, education (including college, graduate, and professional education), and maintenance in health (including medical, dental, hospital, nursing and nursing home expenses). Any income accrued or accumulated at the time of the Grantor's death shall be paid and transferred to principal, to be administered according to the terms hereinafter provided.

B. In addition, during the lifetime of the Grantor, if the Grantor becomes so incapacitated that the Grantor cannot exercise the Grantor's rights under sub-paragraph 2.A. above, and there are sufficient assets in this trust to do so, the Trustee is authorized to pay such parts of the income, if any, and such parts of the principal of this trust to, or for the benefit of, the Grantor, the Grantor's spouse and the Grantor's children as it deems advisable for their support in reasonable comfort, education (including college, graduate, and professional education), and maintenance in health (including medical, dental, hospital, nursing and nursing home expenses), taking into consideration the amount of their income from sources other than this trust.

It is the Grantor's intention that the support in reasonable comfort, education (including college, graduate, and professional education), and maintenance in health (including medical, dental, hospital, nursing and nursing home expenses) of the Grantor and the Grantor's spouse shall be of primary concern, and the Trustee shall exercise its discretion in using principal for the Grantor and the Grantor's spouse, considering all other beneficiaries to be secondary and without liability to any other beneficiary for the use of principal for the Grantor and the Grantor's spouse.

C.   Further, the Trustee is authorized to give, transfer or convey any of the trust estate to persons of the Grantor's natural affection to whom the Grantor would normally consider making such gifts, transfers or conveyances, whether outright or in trust, having in mind the ultimate objective of such gifts, transfers or conveyances is either (i) the qualification for state or federal medical, welfare or other assistance programs for the Grantor's or the Grantor's spouse's benefit, or (ii) the reduction of the state and federal estate, inheritance, transfer, legacy and succession taxes and any interest and penalties thereon imposed by reason of the Grantor's death or the Grantor's spouse's death.

3.   <u>DISPOSITIVE PROVISIONS: AFTER DEATH</u>. Upon the death of the Grantor, the Trustee shall thereafter apply and distribute the trust estate as follows:

A.   If the Grantor's spouse, _____, survives the Grantor, the Trustee shall distribute to the Grantor's said spouse, outright and free of trust, all items of tangible personal property and household effects which are then part of the trust estate, including furniture, clothing, jewelry, silver, books, pictures, china, automobiles and their equipment, other vehicles and their equipment, and other articles of personal and household use or ornament.

If the Grantor's said spouse shall not survive the Grantor, said tangible personal property and household effects shall be distributed, outright and free of trust, to the Grantor's issue who so survive the Grantor, such issue to take <u>per</u> <u>stirpes</u>.

The Grantor expresses the hope that said beneficiaries will dispose of said tangible personal property and household effects according to the Grantor's wishes, however said wishes may be made known to them.

If there is found with this trust agreement a written memorandum regarding certain items of tangible personal property and if said items of tangible personal property are then part of the trust estate, the Grantor expresses the hope that the Trustee will distribute the items of tangible personal property contained on said memorandum as therein provided.

If a division of the property under this distribution is required among the beneficiaries, such division shall be made by the beneficiaries, in appropriate shares, as they may amicably agree.

The Grantor prefers that said beneficiaries shall agree upon the manner in which said property is to be divided, but should they not agree among themselves as to the division thereof within ninety (90) days after the

295

Grantor's death, the Trustee shall have full power and authority to divide said property among said beneficiaries, in appropriate shares, and its determination with respect thereto shall, insofar as permitted by law, be binding and conclusive upon such beneficiaries.

B. If the Grantor's spouse, _____, survives the Grantor, the Trustee shall divide the remaining trust estate into two parts, one to be known as the "Marital QTIP Trust," and the other as the "Family Trust."

    1. The Marital QTIP Trust shall consist of an amount equal to the maximum allowable federal estate tax marital deduction as calculated by law in effect at the time of the Grantor's death, diminished by the value for federal estate tax purposes of all items in the Grantor's gross estate which qualify for said deduction and which pass or have passed to the Grantor's spouse under the Grantor's will, by survivorship in joint tenancy or tenancy by the entirety property, by life insurance settlement, by operation of law or otherwise.

        Provided, however, that if the amount of the maximum allowable federal estate tax marital deduction in the Grantor's estate is greater than the amount needed to reduce the federal estate tax to zero, after considering the available unified tax credit (the applicable credit amount or applicable exclusion amount) and state death tax credit or deduction allowable in determining such tax (provided that the state death tax credit or deduction shall be taken into account only to the extent that doing so would not result in an increase in state death taxes which would otherwise be payable), then the amount set aside in the Marital QTIP Trust shall be equal only to that portion of such marital deduction that is needed to reduce the federal estate tax on the Grantor's estate to zero.

    2. For the purpose of determining the amount to be transferred into the Marital QTIP Trust, values shall be those which are finally determined for federal estate tax purposes. Elections made by the Grantor's executor with respect to taking certain deductions for income tax purposes rather than for estate tax purposes shall determine the aforesaid values and the amount to constitute the Marital QTIP Trust. The words "which pass" or "has passed" shall have the same meaning as under the Internal Revenue Code for marital deduction purposes and no assets shall be transferred to the Marital QTIP Trust that do not qualify for the marital deduction.

    3. In making allocation or distribution to the Marital QTIP Trust the Trustee is authorized to satisfy the Marital QTIP Trust in cash or in kind, or in combination of both, provided that all assets placed in the Marital QTIP Trust shall be valued for the purpose of being placed in the Marital QTIP Trust at their fair market value as determined as of

the dates of respective distributions to the Marital QTIP Trust, which dates shall be the dates on which the Trustee makes specific allocation on its books of account (if such assets are in negotiable form), or when delivery is made in proper form for transfer, or a deed is executed (if real estate), and the aggregate fair market value thereof shall be no less than the amount required to completely fund the Marital QTIP Trust. The Trustee is further authorized to estimate the size of the Marital QTIP Trust and to fund the trust, subject, however, to any adjustments which may be required upon final determination of the federal estate tax on the Grantor's estate.

4. No debts, funeral expenses, expenses of administration of the Grantor's estate, inheritance, estate, transfer, legacy or succession taxes (state and federal), and any interest or penalties thereon shall be apportioned against or paid from the Marital QTIP Trust. Provided, however, with regard to expenses of administration of the Grantor's estate which are not deducted for federal estate tax purposes, to the extent the assets of both the Grantor's estate and the Family Trust hereinafter created are insufficient for this purpose, then said expenses shall be apportioned against or paid from the Marital QTIP Trust.

5. If the Grantor's spouse or the Grantor's spouse's executor disclaims said spouse's interest in and power over any property of the Marital QTIP Trust, then the Trustee shall pay the disclaimed trust assets over to the Family Trust and thereafter said assets shall be administered as part thereof.

6. If the Grantor or the executor of the Grantor's estate or any other individual (including any individual who shall transfer property in trust hereunder or the executor or administrator of the estate of such individual), deems it necessary to allocate any portion of the trust estate to a separate trust share which will allow such assets to qualify for a state marital deduction pursuant to any applicable provision of state law, then notwithstanding anything to the contrary contained in this agreement, the Trustee is authorized to establish a separate Marital QTIP Trust, the terms of which will qualify for the state marital deduction, to hold the property received in trust hereunder as it, in its sole, absolute, and uncontrolled discretion, shall deem advisable; provided, however, that the amount set aside in the state Marital QTIP Trust shall be equal only to that portion of such marital deduction that is needed to reduce the state estate tax on the Grantor's estate to zero.

C. Marital QTIP Trust. The Marital QTIP Trust shall be held and administered and disposed of as follows:

1. The Trustee shall pay over to the Grantor's spouse all of the net income

of this Marital QTIP Trust, including all of the income of any retirement plan payable to this Marital QTIP Trust, during Grantor's spouse's life, at least annually, but at more frequent intervals if the Grantor's spouse shall, in writing, direct.

The Grantor's spouse may at any time by written notice, require the Trustee either to make any nonproductive property of this Trust productive or to convert such nonproductive property to productive property within a reasonable time.

Also, the Trustee may pay over to the Grantor's spouse whatever part or parts of the principal as the Trustee may deem proper or necessary for Grantor's spouse's support in reasonable comfort, education (including college, graduate, and professional education), and maintenance in health (including medical, dental, hospital, nursing and nursing home expenses).

2. The Trustee shall make no distribution of income or principal of the Marital QTIP Trust to any person other than the Grantor's spouse during said spouse's lifetime.

3. The Grantor's spouse shall have the absolute right once during each and every calendar year, between December 1 and December 31 inclusive, to withdraw any amount from the principal of the Marital QTIP Trust, in cash or in kind. The maximum amount that may be withdrawn annually by said spouse from the principal of the Marital QTIP Trust, however, shall not exceed the maximum amount over which an individual may have a power of withdrawal without its lapse in such year being deemed to be a release of such power under Section 2514(e) of the Code. Such right to withdraw shall be non-cumulative.

4. Upon the death of the Grantor's spouse, the Trustee shall pay and transfer all income accrued but undistributed at the date of death of the Grantor's spouse to principal, to be administered according to the terms hereinafter provided.

The Trustee shall then dispose of the then remaining principal as follows:

a. The Trustee shall first pay, out of the principal of the trust estate, the full amount by which estate, inheritance, transfer, legacy or succession taxes (federal and state), and including penalties or interest thereon, imposed by reason of the Grantor's spouse's death, are increased as a result of the inclusion of this Marital QTIP Trust in the Grantor's spouse's estate for such tax purposes.

The final determination of the amount due hereunder shall be based upon the values as finally determined for federal estate tax purposes in the Grantor's spouse's estate.

The Grantor's spouse may waive the rights said spouse's estate to payment under this sub-paragraph by making specific reference in said spouse's will to the right to payment hereby given to said spouse's estate.

b. The Trustee shall then pay over the principal, if any, remaining at the Grantor's spouse's death and after the payment required under sub-paragraph 3.C.4.a. has been made, to the Family Trust and thereafter said additional principal shall be apportioned, allocated and administered as part thereof, pursuant to the provisions hereinbelow.

D. Family Trust—Family Corporation Share. If any portion of the Family Trust shall consist of stock in a corporation for which an S Corporation election under Section 1362 of the Code, is then in effect (hereinafter, the "S Corporation Stock"), the Trustee may allocate said S Corporation Stock to this, the Family Corporation Share of the Family Trust.

Said Family Corporation Share of the Family Trust shall be held and administered and disposed of by the Trustee as follows:

1. If the Grantor's spouse, _____, survives the Grantor, then, during said spouse's lifetime, the Trustee shall pay over to said spouse, at least as often as annually, all of the income of said Family Corporation Share and so much or all of the principal of said share as the Trustee may deem proper or necessary for said spouse's support in reasonable comfort, education (including college, graduate, and professional education), and maintenance in health (including medical, dental, hospital, nursing and nursing home expenses).

The Trustee shall make no distribution of income or principal of said Family Corporation Share to any person other than the Grantor's spouse during said spouse's lifetime.

2. Upon the death of the Grantor's spouse, or upon the Grantor's death if the Grantor's spouse does not survive the Grantor, the Trustee shall apportion the remaining principal of the Family Corporation Share of the Family Trust into equal shares as follows:

one (1) such share to each of the Grantor's living children, and

one (1) such share, allocated, per stirpes, to the living issue of any child of the Grantor who is then deceased.

Said equal shares shall then be held and administered and disposed of as follows:

a. In the case of each share apportioned to a living child of the Grantor, the Trustee shall, in each and every year beginning with the date of said apportionment, pay over to said child, at least as often as annually, all of the income of said child's share.

The Trustee shall also have full power and authority to be exercised in its sole, absolute, and uncontrolled discretion, to pay over to said child or to use, apply, or expend for said child's direct or indirect benefit, so much or all of the principal as it may deem wise and safely consistent with said child's support in reasonable comfort, education (including college, graduate, and professional education), and maintenance in health (including medical, dental, hospital, nursing and nursing home expenses).

The Trustee shall make no distribution of income or principal of said child's trust share to any person other than said child during his lifetime.

    i.   Whenever, at or after said time of apportionment, said child shall have attained the age of twenty-five (25) years, he shall have the right to request in writing and to receive one-third (1/3) of the balance of his share; and

    ii. Whenever, at or after said time of apportionment, said child shall have attained the age of thirty (30) years, he shall have the right to request in writing and to receive an additional one-half (1/2) of the balance of his share; and

    iii. Whenever, at or after said time of apportionment, said child shall have attained the age of thirty-five (35) years, he shall have the right to request in writing and to receive the entire balance of his share, at which time his trust shall terminate.

    iv. The share held by the Trustee for the benefit of a child as described above shall, from the time of the death of said child after the time above set for apportionment into shares, be administered for the benefit of said child's issue, per stirpes, in the manner described below.

b. In the case of each part of a share allocated, per stirpes, to the living issue of a deceased child of the Grantor (hereinafter each individually called "issue"), the Trustee shall, in each and every year beginning with the date of said allocation, pay over to said issue, at least as often as annually, all of the income of said issue's trust part.

The Trustee shall also have full power and authority to be exercised in its sole, absolute, and uncontrolled discretion, to pay over to said issue or to use, apply, or expend for said issue's direct or indirect benefit, so much or all of the principal as it may deem wise and safely consistent with said issue's support in reasonable comfort, education (including college, graduate, and professional education), and maintenance in health (including medical, dental, hospital, nursing and nursing home expenses).

The Trustee shall make no distribution of income or principal of said issue's trust part to any person other than said issue during his lifetime.

i.   Final distribution shall be made of whatever shall remain of said part of a share to said living issue and free and clear of all trusts when said issue attains the age of thirty (30) years.

ii.   If said issue shall die before final distribution of said issue's per stirpes part of a share then the part of a share in question shall be reallocated as follows:

    (a) per stirpes, among said issue's issue, if any, and if none then

    (b) per stirpes, among the other parts of shares allocated to the living issue of the same deceased child of the Grantor,

        and each such reallocated part of a share shall continue to be held and administered in trust, or distributed free and clear of all trust, as the case may be, in the manner provided for in sub-paragraph 3.D.2.b., for the benefit of persons then living, in accordance with the fortunes of the part of a share to which said reallocation is made.

c.   If at any time before the final distribution of any of the trust shares hereinabove described, there shall be no person in existence who is eligible to have the benefit of the trust of such share, then the share in question shall be reapportioned in equal shares among the other shares of said Family Corporation Share apportioned pursuant to sub-paragraph 3.D.2. above, and each equal share shall continue to be held and administered in trust, or distributed, free and clear of all trusts, as the case may be, to or for the benefit of persons then living, in accordance with the fortunes of the share to which said reapportionment is made.

3. The Trustee shall request the current income beneficiary of each separate trust created under sub-paragraph 3.D.2., or the legal representative of such current income beneficiary, to file a timely election under Section 1361(d)(2) of the Internal Revenue Code, with respect to each S Corporation Stock held in such trust.

E. Family Trust—Discretionary Share. All the remainder of the Family Trust not allocated to the Family Corporation Share as hereinabove provided in sub-paragraph 3.D. shall be allocated to this, the Discretionary Share of the Family Trust.

Said Discretionary Share of the Family Trust shall be held and administered and disposed of by the Trustee as follows:

1. If the Grantor's spouse, _____, survives the Grantor, then, during said spouse's lifetime, the Trustee may pay over to said spouse or may use, apply or expend for said spouse's direct or indirect benefit, so much or all of the income of the Discretionary Share hereby created and so much or all of the principal of said trust as the Trustee may deem proper or necessary for said spouse's support in reasonable comfort, education (including college, graduate, and professional education), and maintenance in health (including medical, dental, hospital, nursing and nursing home expenses).

    The Trustee may also pay over to or use, apply or expend for the direct or indirect benefit of the Grantor's children who are from time to time living during said period, or pay to the Grantor's spouse for their benefit, so much or all of the income or principal of the Discretionary Share hereby created as the Trustee may deem proper or necessary for their support in reasonable comfort, education (including college, graduate, and professional education), and maintenance in health (including medical, dental, hospital, nursing and nursing home expenses).

    a. If it becomes necessary for the Trustee to make any payments to or for the benefit of the Grantor's spouse from the principal of the Marital QTIP Trust hereinbefore established, or from the principal of the Discretionary Share of the Family Trust, the Trustee is directed, when it is practicable to do so, to make such payments of principal, if any, from the principal of the Marital QTIP Trust before making any payment from the principal of the Discretionary Share of the Family Trust.

        However, it is the Grantor's intention that the support in reasonable comfort, education (including college, graduate, and professional education), and maintenance in health (including medical, dental, hospital, nursing and nursing home expenses) of the Grantor's spouse shall be of primary concern, and the Trustee shall exercise its discretion in using principal for the Grantor's spouse, considering all other beneficiaries to this trust to be secondary and without liability to any other beneficiary for the use of principal for the Grantor's spouse.

    b. In addition, after the Marital QTIP Trust has been exhausted, the Grantor's spouse shall have the absolute right once during each and every calendar year, between December 1 and December 31 inclusive, to withdraw any amount from the principal of the

Discretionary Share of the Family Trust, in cash or in kind. The maximum amount that may be withdrawn annually by said spouse from the Discretionary Share of the Family Trust, however, shall not exceed the maximum amount over which an individual may have a power of withdrawal without its lapse in such year being deemed to be a release of such power under Section 2514(e) of the Internal Revenue Code. Such right to withdraw shall be non-cumulative.

c. The Grantor's spouse shall have a limited power of appointment over said spouse's entire interest in the principal and accumulated income of the Discretionary Share of the Family Trust, in favor of the Grantor's issue, in such shares, proportion, manner and amount, whether outright, in trust, or otherwise, as the Grantor's spouse, by her last will, duly proved and allowed, may appoint; provided, however, that this limited power of appointment is specifically referred to by the terms of said will; and provided, further, that in no event shall said limited power of appointment be exercisable in favor of the Grantor's said spouse, said spouse's estate, said spouse's creditors, or the creditors of said spouse's estate.

Such property remaining in the Discretionary Share of the Family Trust on the death of the Grantor's spouse which has not been appointed by said spouse's last will, in accordance with the power hereinabove vested in Grantor's spouse, shall be administered in accordance with the provisions hereinbelow.

2. Upon the death of the Grantor's spouse, or upon the Grantor's death if the Grantor's spouse does not survive the Grantor, the Trustee shall apportion the unappointed balance of the principal and accumulated income of the Discretionary Share of the Family Trust, or the remaining principal and accumulated income of said Discretionary Share, as the case may be, into equal shares as follows:

one (1) such share to each of the Grantor's living children, and

one (1) such share to each family group composed of the living issue of any child of the Grantor who is then deceased.

Said equal shares shall then be held and administered and disposed of as follows:

a. In the case of each share apportioned to a living child of the Grantor, the Trustee may, in each and every year beginning with the date of said apportionment, pay over to said child or use, apply or expend for said child's direct or indirect benefit, so much or all of the net income of said share and so much or all of the principal of said share as the Trustee may, in its sole, absolute, and uncontrolled discretion, deem wise and safely consistent with said child's support in reasonable comfort, education (including college, graduate, and professional education), and maintenance in health (including medical, dental, hospital, nursing and nursing home expenses).

i. Whenever, at or after said time of apportionment, said child shall have attained the age of twenty-five (25) years, he shall have the right to request in writing and to receive one-third (1/3) of the balance of his share; and

ii. Whenever, at or after said time of apportionment, said child shall have attained the age of thirty (30) years, he shall have the right to request in writing and to receive an additional one-half (1/2) of the balance of his share; and

iii. Whenever, at or after said time of apportionment, said child shall have attained the age of thirty-five (35) years, he shall have the right to request in writing and to receive the entire balance of his share, at which time his trust shall terminate.

iv. It is the Grantor's belief that, in some circumstances, it may be beneficial for such child to leave the management of his trust share in the hands of the Trustee. Therefore, such child may elect to leave his trust share, or any portion thereof, in the hands of the Trustee, as a separate fund, to be held and administered and disposed of as such child shall direct.

v. The share held by the Trustee for the benefit of a child as described above shall, from the time of the death of the child after the time above set for apportionment into shares, be administered for the benefit of said child's issue, <u>per stirpes</u>, in the manner described below.

b. In the case of each share apportioned to the living issue of a deceased child of the Grantors, said share shall be administered for the benefit as a family group of such of the issue of said deceased child as from time to time shall be living.

The Trustee may pay over to the issue, or may use, apply or expend for their direct or indirect benefit, so much of the income and principal of the trust estate, at such times and in such proportions as the Trustee may determine, in its sole, absolute, and uncontrolled discretion, for support in reasonable comfort, education, (including college, graduate, and professional education), and maintenance in health (including medical, dental, hospital, nursing and nursing home expenses).

The Trustee may make such payments, use, application, expenditure or accumulation of the income and principal thereof as it shall think proper for the direct or indirect benefit of the members of said family group without being required to observe any precept or rule of equality of enjoyment as between said members.

Final distribution shall be made of whatever shall remain of said share, per stirpes, among said living issue and free and clear of all trusts when the youngest then living child of the Grantor's deceased child attains the age of thirty (30) years.

   c. If at any time before the final distribution of any of the trust shares hereinabove described, there shall be no person in existence who is eligible to have the benefit of the trust of such share, then the share in question shall be reapportioned in equal shares among the other shares of said Discretionary Share apportioned pursuant to sub-paragraph 3.E.2. above, and each equal share shall continue to be held and administered in trust, or distributed free and clear of all trusts, as the case may be, to or for the benefit of persons then and thereafter living, in accordance with the fortunes of the share to which said reapportionment is made.

F. If, at any time before the final distribution of all of the trust shares of either the Family Corporation Share of the Family Trust or the Discretionary Share of the Family Trust hereinabove described, there shall be no person in existence who is eligible to have the benefit of any trust shares, the Trustee shall divide all of the trust estate then remaining into two (2) equal parts which shall be distributed, outright and free of trust, as follows:

   1. One (1) part to those persons then living who would have taken the Grantor's estate, and in such shares thereof as they would have taken, had the Grantor then died intestate, domiciled in New Hampshire; and

   2. One (1) part to those persons then living who would have taken the Grantor's spouse's estate, and in such shares thereof as they would have taken, had the Grantor's spouse then died intestate, domiciled in New Hampshire.

G. If the Grantor's residential real estate is held in the trust estate and used by the Grantor's said spouse as a residence, then, during said spouse's lifetime, said spouse shall be permitted exclusive use and occupancy of said residential real estate.

Also, the Grantor's said spouse may, during said spouse's lifetime, in writing, delivered to the Trustee, request the Trustee to sell said residential real estate and to provide a substitute residence, of approximately equal or lesser value to the residence then occupied by the Grantor's said spouse.

Upon receipt of such written request, the Trustee shall then have full power and authority to make reasonable efforts to obtain such substitute residence and to sell the residential real estate then occupied by the Grantor's said spouse.

The costs of selling said residential real estate, of obtaining such substitute residence and of moving the Grantor's said spouse and said spouse's belongings out of said spouse's then occupied residence and into said substitute residence may, in the Trustee's sole, absolute, and uncontrolled discretion, be borne by the trust share to which such real estate has been allocated, to the extent there shall be sufficiently liquid assets to satisfy same.

The Trustee shall have full power and authority to execute any and all documents necessary to carry out the foregoing purpose.

The Trustee shall not be responsible, directly or indirectly, for the success, failure or ultimate satisfaction of the Grantor's said spouse in connection therewith.

The costs and expenses of maintenance and repairs to keep such residential real estate in the same condition it is in at the commencement of said use (reasonable wear and tear excepted), real estate taxes and other normal costs of maintenance and upkeep of said residential real estate, including fire and casualty insurance, may, in the Trustee's sole, absolute, and uncontrolled discretion, be borne by the trust share to which such real estate has been allocated, to the extent there shall be sufficiently liquid assets to satisfy same.

H. Notwithstanding any provision hereinabove to the contrary, the Trustee shall not make any distribution of income or principal from the Marital QTIP Trust, or of income or principal from the Family Corporation Share or the Discretionary Share of the Family Trust, to the Grantor's spouse, _____, if the Grantor's said spouse waives testate distribution of the Grantor's will and claims said spouse's statutory share of the Grantor's estate under R.S.A. 560:10, or any provisions successor thereto.

In such event, the trust estate benefiting the Grantor's spouse shall be administered as if the Grantor's spouse were not then living.

I. The provisions contained hereinabove which require the Trustee to apportion and allocate the trust estate into shares and parts of shares are for purposes of computation only and shall not be construed to require the Trustee to make physical segregation of one share or a part of a share from the others, although the Trustee shall have full right to make such segregation if it thinks it better to do so.

Notwithstanding said provisions, the Trustee shall have the full right to regard the trust estate as one undivided estate for purposes of management and investment; provided, however, that all trust shares created under the Family Corporation Share of the Family Trust shall be treated as substantially separate and independent trusts under Section 663(c) of the Internal Revenue Code.

J. If the Grantor or the executor of the Grantor's estate or any other individual (including any individual who shall transfer property in trust hereunder or the executor or administrator of the estate of such individual), has allocated any portion or all of any Generation Skipping Transfer ("GST") exemption provided by Section 2631(a) of the Internal Revenue Code to any property to be held in trust hereunder, then notwithstanding anything to the contrary contained in this agreement, the Trustee is authorized to establish such number of separate trusts, with identical terms, to hold the property received in trust hereunder as it, in its sole, absolute, and uncontrolled discretion, shall deem advisable, bearing in mind the allocation of the said GST exemption and the desirability that any trust to which all or any portion of the said GST exemption is allocated shall, if practical, have an inclusion ratio of zero.

Further, the Trustee is authorized to allocate such trusts among the trust shares hereinabove created in order to minimize (or eliminate, if possible) any GST tax.

4.   TRUSTEE'S POWERS. In the administration of the trust estate, the Trustee shall have all of the powers granted to trustees by New Hampshire common law and statutory authority (including, but not limited to, the Uniform Trustees' Powers Act, R.S.A. 564-A, and the Uniform Trust Code, R.S.A. 564-B, as they may be amended from time to time), without restrictions.

In addition to such power, and not in limitation thereof, the Trustee shall have the following powers, all of which shall be exercised in a fiduciary capacity and for the benefit of the beneficiaries:

A. During the lifetime of the Grantor, the Trustee may retain as an investment, unless and until the Grantor by a writing delivered to the Trustee shall otherwise direct, all of the securities and other property originally assigned, transferred, or delivered to the Trustee hereunder or at any time forming a part of the trust estate, whether or not such securities or other property be of the character authorized by the laws of the State of New Hampshire for the investment of trust funds.

Upon the death or incapacity of the Grantor, the Trustee is authorized to purchase, sell, lease, or alter any investment by buy or sell orders transmitted by it, whether by telephone call, electronic facsimile transmission, computer message or other current non-written method of business communication.

B.   To buy, sell and trade in securities of any nature, on margin, and for such purpose to maintain and operate margin accounts with brokers, and to pledge any securities held or purchased by it with such brokers as security for loans and advances made to the Trustee.

C.   *[For Corporate Trustees]* To retain the property of the trust estate in the same investments as when received by it or to vary and transpose such investments and to invest and reinvest the property of the trust estate in such manner and in such securities or other property (including common trust funds or similar funds for the participation of trusts of which any corporation or financial institution serving as Trustee hereunder is trustee and including securities of said corporation or financial institution and any affiliate, subsidiary and successor thereto) as it in its uncontrolled discretion shall deem best without accountability for any loss for so doing and without liability for depreciation occasioned by so doing even though the property so retained or the investments so made may not be of the character permitted for the investment of trust funds under the laws of the State of New Hampshire or any other state or federal law.

D.   To take and hold title to real estate, and to convey any interest in real estate and improvements thereon held in trust, and no purchaser or third party shall be bound to inquire whether the Trustee has said power or is properly exercising said power, or see to the application of any trust asset paid to the Trustee for a conveyance thereof.

E.   To have all of the necessary banking powers to open and manage financial accounts, including but not limited to, checking accounts, savings accounts, financial accounts and other related financial instruments and to conduct all necessary financial business in reference to the management of the financial assets of the trust.

F.   To rent a safe deposit box and to retain such assets in said box as the Trustee, in its sole, absolute, and uncontrolled discretion, determines appropriate.

G.   To borrow money, with or without security, and mortgage or pledge trust property for a period within or extending beyond the duration of the trust.

H.   To loan funds to the Grantor's estate upon such terms and conditions as to interest rates, maturities, and security as the Trustee shall determine.

I.   To make payments, transfers or conveyances, to the extent possible, to the estate of the Grantor (after exhaustion of the assets of the Grantor's estate) to satisfy legacies, bequests or devises, if any, made under the Grantor's will or included in the Grantor's estate for other purposes, if the Grantor's estate shall be insufficient to satisfy such legacies, bequests or devises.

J. To invest in common trust funds.

K. To select property, in its sole, absolute, and uncontrolled discretion, to be allocated to any trust hereunder or to be distributed in satisfaction of any gift provided for herein without respect to the income tax basis of such property, and the Trustee is specifically excused from any duty of impartiality with respect to the income tax basis of such property.

In the event that residential real estate is held in the trust estate, the Trustee may allocate said residential real estate to any trust created hereunder, to be held and administered and disposed of pursuant to the provisions thereof.

L. To allocate S Corporation stock to either the Family Trust Family Corporation Share or the Family Trust Discretionary Share and to make an election to treat the Family Trust Discretionary Share as an Electing Small Business Trust under Section 1361(c)(2)(v) of the Internal Revenue Code if any S Corporation stock is allocated to the Family Trust Discretionary Share.

M. To elect to recognize gain or loss upon the distribution of assets in kind under Section 643(e)(3) of the Internal Revenue Code.

N. If at any time during the Grantor's lifetime, there is delivered to the Trustee other than the Grantor, if any, or, if none, then to the successor Trustee, a written opinion, signed by a licensed physician, stating that the Grantor has become incompetent or incapacitated, then from and after the delivery of such written opinion the Trustee other than the Grantor, or the successor Trustee, as the case may be, shall have those powers and authorities with respect to the trust estate given to the Trustee in this trust agreement.

O. If, after the death of the Grantor and the Grantor's spouse, _____, as it may be amended from time to time, is still in existence and the terms of any trust established by said trust are substantially similar to the terms of any trust established by this, _____, the Trustee is authorized and empowered to consolidate such trust with such similar trust established by _____ and to administer them as one trust, unless such consolidation shall be contrary to law or inconsistent with the terms of any instrument supplemental hereto.

P. Regardless of the extent of the authority that the Trustee holds to currently distribute income and/or principal of the trust estate to one or more beneficiaries of the trust, the Trustee shall have full power and authority, to be exercised in its sole, absolute, and uncontrolled discretion, to appoint any or all assets held in this trust estate to any other trust or trusts created under will, deed or otherwise, for the benefit of one or more of the beneficiaries hereunder.

This authority shall be subject to the limitations set forth in R.S.A. 564-B:4-418, as amended from time to time, provided that such appointment clause shall be null and void in the event there is a determination that the application of such clause shall result in the inclusion of any of the trust estate in the Grantor's gross estate under any provision of the Internal Revenue Code, including but not limited to Sections 2041 and 2042, which would not otherwise be includable in the Grantor's gross estate.

Q. If, at any time before the final distribution of the principal of any trust share hereinabove described, the value of the principal of said trust share shall be equal to, or less than, ONE HUNDRED THOUSAND DOLLARS ($100,000), then the Trustee may, in its sole discretion, terminate said trust share and distribute the principal of said trust share, and any accumulated and undistributed income thereof, outright and free of trust, to those persons then entitled to benefit from said trust share, and in the proportions in which they are then entitled to benefit from said trust share, notwithstanding any provisions of this trust to the contrary.

R. To exercise all the powers, authorities and discretions herein conferred, after the termination of the trust hereunder, until the complete distribution of the trust estate.

5.   CLOSELY-HELD BUSINESS. The Grantor owns at present stock and other securities which represents a significant interest in _____.

The Grantor anticipates that at the time of the Grantor's death the Grantor will own stock in a corporation, or in a successor thereto, or that the Grantor will own a significant interest in another business enterprise (whether operated in the form of a corporation, a limited liability company, a partnership or a sole proprietorship), hereinafter referred to as the "business", and consequently the Grantor expects that some such business enterprise will be in the Grantor's estate or in this trust at the time of the Grantor's death and if in the Grantor's estate, then subsequently in this trust.

Since the Grantor desires that the Trustee may continue to hold and operate each such business as part of the trust herein created, the Grantor hereby vests said Trustee, including any successors, with the following powers and authority, as supplemental to the ones contained hereinabove, the applicability of which to the business the Grantor confirms, without limitation by reason of specification, and in addition to powers conferred by law, all of which may be exercised with respect to every such business, whether a corporation, a limited liability company, a partnership or a sole proprietorship:

A. To retain and continue to operate the business for such period as the Trustee may deem advisable.

B. To control, direct and manage the business; in this connection, the Trustee in its sole, absolute, and uncontrolled discretion, shall determine the manner and extent of its active participation in the operation, and the Trustee may delegate all or any part of its power to supervise and operate, to such person or persons as it may select, including any associate, partner, officer or employee of the business.

C. To hire and discharge officers and employees, fix their compensation and define their duties; and similarly to employ, compensate and discharge agents, attorneys, consultants, accountants and such other representatives as the Trustee may deem appropriate, including the right to employ any beneficiary (or individual Trustee) in any of the foregoing capacities.

D. To invest other trust funds in such business, to pledge other assets of the trust as security for loans made to such business; and to loan funds from the trust to such business, and to borrow from any bank or other lending institution, including any named corporate fiduciary, on such terms as are currently competitive.

E. To organize a corporation, a partnership, a limited liability company or other business under the laws of this or any other state or country and to transfer thereto all or any part of the business or other property held in the estate or trust, and to receive in exchange therefor such stocks, partnership interests, membership interests, bonds and other securities as the Trustee may deem advisable.

F. To take any action required to convert any corporation into a partnership, a limited liability company or sole proprietorship.

G. To treat the business as an entity separate from the trust; in its accountings to the court and to any beneficiaries, the Trustee shall only be required to report the earnings and condition of the business in accordance with standard corporate accounting practice.

H. To retain in the business such amount of the net earnings for working capital and other purposes of the business as the Trustee may deem advisable in conformity with sound business practice.

I. To purchase, process and sell merchandise of every kind and description, and to purchase and sell machinery and equipment, furniture and fixtures and supplies of all kinds.

J. To sell or liquidate all or any part of any business at such time and price and upon such terms and conditions (including credit) as the Trustee may determine, whether or not said business shall, in the Trustee's sole and uncontrolled determination, be a productive investment of the trust estate; the Trustee is specifically authorized and empowered to make such sale to any partner, officer or employee of the business (or to any individual Trustee) or to any beneficiary hereunder.

311

K. To exercise any of the rights and powers herein conferred in conjunction with another or others.

L. To diminish, enlarge or change the scope or nature of any business.

M. To elect, continue, revoke or terminate an existing S Corporation election under Section 1362 of the Internal Revenue Code.

N. To cause the redemption of shares of stock in _____, or in any successor corporation, to obtain funds for payment of estate, inheritance, legacy and succession taxes (including any interest collected thereon) payable from the Grantor's estate, and to the extent permitted, for funeral expenses and expenses of administration, in such manner as to take full advantage of Sections 302 and 303 of the Internal Revenue Code.

The Grantor is aware that certain risks are inherent in the operation of any business and expects that decisions will be required of a "businessman's risk" nature as contrasted with the "prudent man rule." Therefore, the Grantor directs that the Trustee shall not be liable for any loss arising out of the retention and operation of any business unless such loss shall result from the Trustee's bad faith or willful misconduct. In determining any question of liability for loss, it should be considered that the Trustee is engaging in a speculative enterprise at the Grantor's express request.

If any business operated by the Trustee pursuant to the authorization contained in the trust shall be unincorporated, then the Grantor directs that all liabilities arising therefrom shall be satisfied first from the business itself and second out of the trust. It is the Grantor's intention that in no event shall any such liability be enforced against the Trustee personally. If the Trustee shall be held personally liable, it shall be entitled to indemnity first from the business and second from the trust.

It is recognized that any business interest which may be included in any trust may require additional efforts and expertise on the part of the fiduciary. Accordingly, additional fees may be required. Such fees may be taken as a director's fee, which will be remitted to the fiduciary, and/or as a management consultant charge by the fiduciary.

Notwithstanding the foregoing, the Trustee shall have no power or authority with respect to shares of any Sub-Chapter S Corporation allocated to any trust share which power or authority would cause said trust share not to qualify as either a Qualified Sub-Chapter S Trust or an Electing Small Business Trust, as the case may be, under the Code.

6. <u>ADDITIONAL PROPERTY</u>. The Grantor, or the Grantor's spouse may, by will, trust or during their lifetimes, from time to time, transfer and deliver to the Trustee cash, securities, and other property acceptable to the Trustee, in addition to the property presently transferred and delivered, and such cash, securities, and other property shall be held, administered, and disposed of by the Trustee in accordance with the provisions of this agreement without the execution

of any further instrument or declaration.

7.   REPORTING BY TRUSTEE.

A.   At any time and from time to time, the Grantor shall have the power, by written instrument signed and acknowledged by the Grantor and delivered to the Trustee, to settle the report of the Trustee with respect to principal or income, or with respect to both principal and income, and to release and discharge the Trustee of and from any and every claim, demand, accountability, and liability of every nature, arising from any matter or thing done or omitted to be done, in connection with this agreement or any trust hereby created, during the period in respect of which the report of the Trustee shall have been so settled.

Every such settlement, release, and discharge shall be conclusive and binding upon, and shall be an absolute protection to the Trustee against all claims of any income beneficiaries, remaindermen, or other persons who might then or thereafter have or claim any interest under this agreement, and no such income beneficiary, remainderman, or other person shall have any right of accounting, reporting, any claim, or any cause of action against the Trustee arising from any matter or thing done or omitted to be done in connection with this agreement or any trust hereby created, during any period in respect of which the report of the Trustee shall have been so settled.

B.   After the death or incapacity of the Grantor, the Trustee may, at the Trustee's sole, absolute, and uncontrolled discretion, and shall, to the extent required by the Uniform Trust Code, R.S.A. 564-B, as it may be amended from time to time, render a Trustee's report as described in the Uniform Trust Code, as it may be amended from time to time, at such intervals as the Trustee may choose or at such times as required by the Uniform Trust Code.

C.   A recipient of such a report (or, if under guardianship or conservatorship, then by the Guardian or Conservator, or, if deceased, then by the Executor or Administrator), may, by a written instrument, assent to the report of the Trustee with respect to principal or to income, or with respect to both principal and income.

The assent of the recipient of such report (or, if under guardianship or conservatorship, then by the Guardian or Conservator, or, if deceased, then by the Executor or Administrator) shall make such report binding and conclusive upon all persons then having or who may thereafter have any interest, vested or contingent, in the income or principal of the trust estate and such assent shall forever release and discharge the Trustee of and from any and every claim, demand, accountability, and liability of every nature, arising from any matter or thing done or omitted to be done, in connection with this agreement or any trust hereby created, during the

313

period in respect of which the report of the Trustee shall have been so settled.

D.   The failure of any person to object in writing to the Trustee to such a report within thirty (30) days after the delivery of the same to such person hereunder shall be final and binding to the same extent as the written assent hereinabove provided.

E.   Any person entitled to such a report, accounting, information, notice and the like (or, if under guardianship or conservatorship, then by the Guardian or Conservator, or, if deceased, then by the Executor or Administrator) may by a written instrument signed and acknowledged by him or her or them, as the case may be, and delivered to the Trustee, waive the right to said Trustee's report or to other information otherwise required to be furnished under the Uniform Trust Code, as it may be amended from time to time.

8.   SUCCESSOR TRUSTEE. The following provisions shall govern the addition, removal and succession of the Trustee:

A.   The Grantor may, during Grantor's lifetime, add any additional Trustee, or remove any Trustee hereunder and appoint a successor Trustee.

B.   If _____ shall be unable or unwilling to serve in the capacity of Trustee for any reason, then _____, of _____, _____, shall serve as successor Trustee.

1.   If _____ shall be unable or unwilling to serve in the capacity of Trustee for any reason, then _____, of _____, _____, shall serve as successor Trustee.

2.   If _____ shall be unable or unwilling to serve in the capacity of Trustee for any reason, then _____, of _____, _____, shall serve as successor Trustee.

C.   In the event there shall be no successor Trustee who shall be able or willing to serve in the capacity of Trustee, then a majority of the beneficiaries to whom or for whose use the current net income of the trust estate is at the time authorized or required to be paid or applied, either,

1.   acting individually, if then eighteen (18) years of age, or,

2.   by his or her natural parent, or natural guardian, or Court appointed guardian or Court appointed conservator, if then under guardianship or conservatorship,

shall appoint a successor Trustee.

D.   In the event that any beneficiary of the trust, other than the Grantor, shall serve in the capacity of co-Trustee, then the discretionary powers to determine whether income or principal is to be distributed to said beneficiary or to any person to whom said beneficiary owes an obligation of support shall be exercisable only by the remaining Trustee.

It is the Grantor's intention by this sub-paragraph to prohibit said beneficiary from benefiting himself or herself as beneficiary in any way by the exercise of such discretionary powers vested in the Trustee as a group.

E. In the event that any beneficiary of the trust, other than the Grantor or the Grantor's spouse, shall serve in the capacity of sole Trustee and the Trustee has discretionary powers to distribute income or principal to himself, herself, or to any person to whom he or she owes an obligation of support, then such distributions of income or principal shall be exercisable by the sole Trustee. The maximum amount that may be withdrawn annually by each such beneficiary under this sub-paragraph, however, shall not exceed the maximum amount over which an individual may have a power of withdrawal without its lapse in such year being deemed to be a release of such power under Section 2514(e) of the Internal Revenue Code.

F. In the event that an attorney, an accountant, a certified financial planner or a corporation or financial institution shall be serving as Trustee hereunder, a majority of the beneficiaries to whom or for whose use the current net income of the trust estate is at the time authorized or required to be paid or applied and who shall at the time be at least eighteen (18) years of age may by a written instrument signed and acknowledged by them and delivered to such attorney, accountant, certified financial planner or corporation or financial institution remove said Trustee and, subject to the successor trustee appointments herein, appoint as its successor Trustee, any attorney, accountant, certified financial planner or corporation or financial institution having a trust department capable of rendering financial advice concerning the investments of the trust estate.

G. No change of name of any corporation shall affect its appointment and capacity as Trustee hereunder. Any corporation into which it may merge or with which it may be consolidated, or any corporation resulting from any merger or consolidation to which it may be a party, shall be the successor of the Trustee hereunder without the execution or filing of any additional instrument or the performance of any further act.

H. Each Trustee hereunder (whether originally designated herein or appointed as successor) shall have the right to resign at any time by giving thirty (30) days written notice to that effect to the current income beneficiary (or beneficiaries) of the trust.

Thereafter, such beneficiary (or a majority of such beneficiaries) who shall at the time be at least eighteen (18) years of age shall have the right within such thirty (30) day period to appoint a successor Trustee, subject to the provisions hereinabove, and shall notify the resigning Trustee of such appointment.

In the event that a corporation or financial institution shall be appointed as successor Trustee hereunder, such successor Trustee shall be a trust company or bank qualified to act as such, possessing trust powers.

In the event the current income beneficiary (or beneficiaries) shall fail to designate a successor Trustee within the time specified, the then-acting Trustee shall appoint a successor Trustee as herein provided.

I. No successor Trustee shall be liable or responsible in any way for any actions or defaults of any predecessor Trustee, nor for any loss or expense from or occasioned by anything done or neglected to be done by any predecessor Trustee. Any successor Trustee shall have, from and after its appointment or succession to office hereunder and without any assignment or other action by any person, all the rights, interests, and powers, including discretionary rights and powers, which are by the provisions of this trust agreement granted to and vested in the Trustee named herein.

9.   FIDUCIARIES. No person dealing with the Trustee shall be responsible for the application of any money, securities, or other property paid or delivered, and the receipt of the Trustee shall be a full discharge; and no person dealing with the Trustee, and no issuer, transfer agent, or other agent of any issuer of any securities shall be under any obligation to ascertain or inquire into the power of the Trustee to purchase, sell, exchange, transfer, mortgage, pledge, create a security interest in, lease, distribute, or otherwise dispose of or deal with any money, securities, or other property.

The Trustee shall not at any time be held liable for any action taken or not taken, including any action intended to lessen or eliminate the impact of estate or generation-skipping transfer taxes with respect to any generation or beneficiary, whether or not such action is successful in achieving the results sought and without regard to its effect on other beneficiaries in the same or different generations, or for any loss or depreciation in the value of any property in any trust created herein, whether due to an error of judgment or otherwise, where the Trustee has exercised good faith and ordinary diligence in the exercise of its duties.

The Trustee shall receive reasonable compensation for its services in the administration of the trusts created herein, including reimbursement for amounts reasonably expended for bookkeeping services, investment services and advice, and other professional or para-professional services. In addition to the compensation herein provided, the Trustee shall receive reasonable compensation for any legal services provided for the benefit of the trust estate, such as handling any litigation involving the trust, preparing state or federal income tax returns, and transferring any real estate.

10.   PERPETUITIES. All trusts established under this instrument shall be exempt from the application of the rule against perpetuities. This provision is

intended to comply with New Hampshire R.S.A. 564:24, and accordingly, the Grantor specifically authorizes the Trustee to sell, mortgage or lease property for any period of time beyond the period that is required for an interest created under this instrument to vest in order to be valid under the rule against perpetuities, as measured by the period defined hereinabove.

The trusts created hereunder shall be perpetual to the fullest extent permitted by the governing law. If any trust created hereunder is deemed to be subject to the law of a jurisdiction (including, but only to the extent applicable to real property) that has a rule against perpetuities or similar rule which limits the period during which property can be held in trust, then such trust (other than a trust created by the exercise of a power of appointment conferred hereunder which exercise commences a new rule against perpetuities period under the law of such jurisdiction) shall terminate in all events upon the expiration of the longest period that property may be held in trust under this trust agreement under the law of such jurisdiction (including any applicable period in gross, such as 21 years, 90 years or 110 years); provided, however, that if the jurisdiction has a rule against perpetuities or similar rule which applies only to certain types of property, such as real property, the provisions of this paragraph shall apply only to such property. If under the law of such jurisdiction the longest period that property may be held in trust may be determined (or alternatively determined) with reference to the death of the last survivor of a group of individuals in being upon the date of this trust agreement, those individuals shall consist of all of the descendants of the Grantor's parents who were in being on the date of this trust agreement. Upon termination of a trust pursuant to the provisions of this paragraph, the trust property shall be transferred, conveyed and paid over to the persons then entitled to receive or have the benefit of the income from the trust in the proportions in which they are entitled thereto, or if their interests are indefinite, then in equal shares.

11. SPENDTHRIFT PROVISION. Except as herein otherwise provided, the interest of any beneficiary hereunder, either as to income or principal, shall not be anticipated, alienated or in any other manner assigned or pledged or promised by such beneficiary, and shall not be reached by, or be subject to, any legal, equitable or other process, including any bankruptcy or divorce proceeding, or be subject to the interference or control of creditors or others in any way or manner, and all payments to, or the interest of, any beneficiary shall be free from the control or claim of any parent or spouse or former spouse or any other third party. Moreover, no power of appointment or power of withdrawal shall be subject to involuntary exercise. Provided, however, this spendthrift provision shall not restrict the exercise of a disclaimer or the exercise of a power of appointment or withdrawal right granted by this trust agreement. This provision is intended to be a material provision of this trust and any other trust established hereunder.

12. TAX PROVISION. The trust estate shall not be charged with the payment of any estate, inheritance, legacy, death taxes or duties of any nature (state or federal), or any interest or penalty thereon, except to the extent that the

other assets in the Grantor's estate (excluding any assets which may be exempted from the payment of such taxes by the last will of the Grantor) shall be insufficient to discharge such taxes, interest or penalties or shall be insufficiently liquid to satisfy the same. The Trustee may rely conclusively upon written certification from the executor of the Grantor's estate, or if no probate administration of the Grantor's estate is required under applicable law, upon request of the person or persons nominated as executor under the Grantor's will or upon any other evidence, as to the existence of such insufficiency and the amount thereof; provided, however, that the Trustee shall not pay any additional tax imposed under Section 2032A or 2057 of the Internal Revenue Code or any generation-skipping transfer taxes imposed under Chapter 13 of the Internal Revenue Code imposed by reason of the Grantor's death.

If the Trustee shall be required to pay any such taxes, they shall be charged first against the Discretionary Share of the Family Trust as an expense without apportionment, and, if such trust share shall be insufficient, then against the Family Corporation Share of the Family Trust, as an expense without apportionment.

Provided, that in the event that no probate administration of the Grantor's estate is required under applicable law, the Trustee shall have all the powers and authority given the executor under the Grantor's will in relation to such taxes, including all elections and allocation of the generation-skipping transfer tax exemption under Section 2631 of the Internal Revenue Code.

13.   <u>DEBTS AND EXPENSES</u>. The trust estate shall not be charged with the payment of legal debts of the Grantor's estate, funeral expenses or expenses of administration of the Grantor's estate except to the extent that the other assets in the Grantor's estate shall be insufficient to discharge such debts and expenses, or shall be insufficiently liquid to satisfy the same. The Trustee may rely conclusively upon written certification from the executor of the Grantor's estate, or if no probate administration of the Grantor's estate is required under applicable law, upon request of the person or persons nominated as executor under the Grantor's will, or upon any other evidence, as to the existence of such insufficiency and the amount thereof. If the Trustee shall be required to pay any such debts and expenses, the same shall be treated as debts and expenses of the trust estate (to the extent the assets of the Grantor's estate are insufficient to satisfy the same) or as loans to the Grantor's estate (to the extent the liquid assets of the Grantor's estate are insufficient to satisfy the same) if any such debts and expenses are deducted for federal estate tax purposes in computing the value of the Grantor's taxable estate under Section 2053 of the Internal Revenue Code.

If any such debts and expenses are either not so deducted or deductible under Section 2053 of the Internal Revenue Code, however, the same shall be charged first against the Discretionary Share of the Family Trust as an expense without apportionment, and, if such trust share shall be insufficient, then against the Family Corporation Share of the Family Trust, as an expense without apportionment.

This provision shall confer no rights upon anyone except the executor of the Grantor's estate.

14.   SURVIVAL REQUIREMENT. No person shall be deemed to have survived the Grantor, or any other person or event under the terms of this trust, unless such person survives the end of the period commencing with the close of the calendar day of the Grantor's death, the death of such other person or on which such event occurs, and ending with the close of the thirtieth (30th) calendar day thereafter.

15.   DISTRIBUTIONS TO MINORS. In any case where property or funds become distributable to a minor, then the Trustee shall have the additional power to distribute the same in any one or more of the following ways: (1) by distribution directly to the minor; (2) by distribution to the legal guardian of the minor; (3) by distribution to a parent, relative or friend of the minor for the minor's support in reasonable comfort, education and maintenance in health; (4) by applying the same directly for the minor's support in reasonable comfort, education and maintenance in health; (5) by depositing the same in a bank account in the name of the minor or by transferring property to or purchasing property in the name of a custodian for his or her benefit under a Uniform Law relating to transfers or gifts to minors; or (6) by holding the same hereunder in trust or in custody for the minor's support in reasonable comfort, education and maintenance in health and by distributing the remainder thereof to the minor upon coming of age or otherwise to the minor's estate in case of the death of the minor. The receipt of the person to whom property or funds are actually distributed in accordance with any of the foregoing provisions shall fully discharge the Trustee from further accountability therefor.

16.   GOVERNING LAW AND SITUS. The Grantor declares that this agreement and the trust created hereby shall be construed and administered under the laws of the State of New Hampshire, that the validity and effect of this agreement and of this trust shall be determined in accordance with the laws of that State.

Further, the trust shall be under the jurisdiction of the courts of the State of New Hampshire and the Trustee shall voluntarily enter a general appearance in any legal action relating to an accounting of the trust or a declaratory judgment interpreting this trust agreement. The Trustee shall not be chargeable in any court other than one of the courts of that State.

[OPTIONAL] However, the Trustee, at any time and from time to time, in its discretion, may, (1) remove all or part of the trust estate and hold and administer the same in any other jurisdiction where the Trustee shall be then located, (2) change the situs of administration of any trust from one jurisdiction to another jurisdiction; and (3) elect that the law of such other jurisdiction shall thereafter govern the trust to such extent as may be necessary and appropriate, and to amend the administrative provisions of the trust as the Trustee deems appropriate to ensure compliance and compatibility with such law, whereupon the courts of such other jurisdiction shall

have the power to effectuate the purposes of this trust agreement to such extent. The determination of the Trustee as to any such removal of assets or change of situs or governing law shall be conclusive and binding on all persons interested in such trust.

17.   AMENDMENT AND REVOCATION. The Grantor reserves the right at any time or from time to time without the consent of any person and without notice to any person other than the Trustee to revoke or modify the trust hereby created, in whole or in part, to change the beneficiaries hereof, or to withdraw the whole or any part of the trust estate by filing notice of such revocation, modification, change, or withdrawal with the Trustee; provided, however, that the terms of this agreement may not be modified by the Grantor in such manner as to increase the obligations or alter the rates of the commissions of the Trustee without its written consent.

18.   DEFINITIONS. Whenever used in this trust agreement, the words "child," "children," or "issue" are intended to include not only persons who are descendants by blood, but also persons and issue of persons who have been adopted according to law prior to their attaining the age of eighteen (18) years.

References to the "Internal Revenue Code" or "Code" or to provisions thereof are to the Internal Revenue Code of 1986, as amended at the time in question. References to the "Treasury Regulations," "Regulations" and "Regs." are to the Treasury Regulations under the Code. If, by the time in question, a particular provision of the Code has been renumbered, or the Code has been superseded by a subsequent federal tax law, the reference shall be deemed to be to the renumbered provision or the corresponding provision of the subsequent law, unless to do so would clearly be contrary to the Grantor's intent as expressed in this Trust Agreement, and a similar rule shall apply to references to the Regulations.

Masculine, feminine and neuter pronouns shall each include all genders, and the singular shall include the plural and vice versa, where the context or facts so admit.

The captions and paragraph headings of this trust agreement are inserted only as a matter of convenience and for reference and in no way define, limit or describe the scope or intent of this agreement, nor in any way affect this agreement.

Whenever used in this trust agreement, the word "income" shall refer to the amount of income calculated in accordance with Section 643(b) of the Internal Revenue Code of 1986 and Treasury Regulation Section 1.643(b)(1), or any provisions successor thereto, plus all capital gains realized by any S Corporation the stock of which is held in the trust hereunder, which is taxable to the income beneficiary of such trust. All other capital gains shall be allocated to principal.

19.   EXECUTION. This trust agreement, and any amendments hereto, shall be effective when executed by the Grantor, notwithstanding that the signature of the Trustee is provided for, the Trustee's signature being intended to denote the

acceptance of the Trustee to serve in that capacity only.

This trust agreement may be executed in any number of counterparts with the same effect as if all of the parties had signed the same document. All counterparts shall be construed together and shall constitute one agreement.

_____   _____,
Witness   Grantor

_____   _____,
Witness   Trustee

STATE OF NEW HAMPSHIRE
COUNTY OF _____

The foregoing instrument was acknowledged before me on _____, 2009, by _____

Notary Public/Justice of the Peace
My Commission Expires:
(Seal)

Page 859: Substitute this form for Form 70 in the text:

FORM 70   Revocable Qualified Terminable Interest Property (QTIP) Trust with Qualified Domestic Trust (QDOT) Provisions

THE _____ REVOCABLE TRUST OF 2009

TRUST AGREEMENT, made on _____, 2009, between _____, residing in _____, New Hampshire (hereinafter called the "Grantor"), and _____, residing in _____, New Hampshire (hereinafter called the "Trustee").

At the time of the signing of this trust, the Grantor's spouse is _____, and the Grantor's children are _____.

1.   <u>TRUST PROPERTY</u>. All property transferred and delivered to the Trustee, which the Trustee may, at any time, hold or acquire, including cash, securities, or other property, shall be referred to collectively as the "trust estate" and held and administered and disposed of by the Trustee for the uses and purposes, and upon the terms and conditions, herein set forth.

2.   <u>DISPOSITIVE PROVISIONS: LIFETIME</u>. The Trustee shall hold, manage, invest and reinvest the trust estate, and shall collect the income thereof and dispose of the net income and principal as follows:

A.   Pay such parts of the income, if any, and such parts of the principal of this trust to, or for the benefit of, the Grantor as the Grantor directs from time to time for the Grantor's support in reasonable comfort, education (including college, graduate, and professional education), and maintenance in health (including medical, dental, hospital, nursing and nursing home expenses). Any income accrued or accumulated at the time of the Grantor's death shall be paid and transferred to principal, to be administered according to the terms hereinafter provided.

B.   In addition, during the lifetime of the Grantor, if the Grantor becomes so incapacitated that the Grantor cannot exercise the Grantor's rights under sub-paragraph 2.A. above, and there are sufficient assets in this trust to do so, the Trustee is authorized to pay such parts of the income, if any, and such parts of the principal of this trust to, or for the benefit of, the Grantor, the Grantor's spouse and the Grantor's children as it deems advisable for their support in reasonable comfort, education (including college, graduate, and professional education), and maintenance in health (including medical, dental, hospital, nursing and nursing home expenses), taking into consideration the amount of their income from sources other than this trust.

It is the Grantor's intention that the support in reasonable comfort, education (including college, graduate, and professional education), and maintenance in health (including medical, dental, hospital, nursing and nursing home expenses) of the Grantor and the Grantor's spouse shall be of primary concern, and the Trustee shall exercise its discretion in using principal for the Grantor and the Grantor's spouse, considering all other beneficiaries to be secondary and without liability to any other beneficiary for the use of principal for the Grantor and the Grantor's spouse.

C. Further, the Trustee is authorized to give, transfer or convey any of the trust estate to persons of the Grantor's natural affection to whom the Grantor would normally consider making such gifts, transfers or conveyances, whether outright or in trust, having in mind the ultimate objective of such gifts, transfers or conveyances is either (i) the qualification for state or federal medical, welfare or other assistance programs for the Grantor's or the Grantor's spouse's benefit, or (ii) the reduction of the state and federal estate, inheritance, transfer, legacy and succession taxes and any interest and penalties thereon imposed by reason of the Grantor's death or the Grantor's spouse's death.

3.   <u>DISPOSITIVE PROVISIONS: AFTER DEATH</u>. Upon the death of the Grantor, the Trustee shall thereafter apply and distribute the trust estate as follows:

A. If the Grantor's spouse, _____, survives the Grantor, the Trustee shall distribute to the Grantor's said spouse, outright and free of trust, all items of tangible personal property and household effects which are then part of the trust estate, including furniture, clothing, jewelry, silver, books, pictures, china, automobiles and their equipment, other vehicles and their equipment, and other articles of personal and household use or ornament.

If the Grantor's said spouse shall not survive the Grantor, said tangible personal property and household effects shall be distributed, outright and free of trust, to the Grantor's issue who so survive the Grantor, such issue to take <u>per stirpes</u>.

The Grantor expresses the hope that said beneficiaries will dispose of said tangible personal property and household effects according to the Grantor's wishes, however said wishes may be made known to them.

If a division of the property under this distribution is required among the beneficiaries, such division shall be made by the beneficiaries, in appropriate shares, as they may amicably agree.

The Grantor prefers that said beneficiaries shall agree upon the manner in which said property is to be divided, but should they not agree among themselves as to the division thereof within ninety (90) days after the Grantor's death, the Trustee shall have full power and authority to divide said property among said beneficiaries, in appropriate shares, and its determination with respect thereto shall, insofar as permitted by law, be binding and conclusive upon such beneficiaries.

B. After the distributions, if any, in sub-paragraph 3.A. above, if the

Grantor's spouse, _____, survives the Grantor, the Trustee shall divide the remaining trust estate into two parts, one to be known as the "Marital Share" and the other as the "Family Trust."

1. The Marital Share shall consist of an amount equal to the maximum allowable federal estate tax marital deduction as calculated by law in effect at the time of the Grantor's death, diminished by, either,

    a. if the Grantor's spouse is then a citizen of the United States, or becomes a citizen of the United States so as to qualify for the estate tax marital deduction in accordance with Section 2056(d)(4) of the Internal Revenue Code the value for federal estate tax purposes of all items in the Grantor's gross estate which qualify for said deduction and which pass or have passed to the Grantor's spouse under the Grantor's will, by survivorship in joint tenancy or tenancy by the entirety property, by life insurance settlement, by operation of law or otherwise, or,

    b. if the Grantor's spouse is not then a citizen of the United States, the value for federal estate tax purposes of all items in the Grantor's gross estate which qualify for said deduction and which pass or have passed to any other qualified domestic trust not incorporated in this trust agreement.

    Provided, however, that if the amount of the maximum allowable federal estate tax marital deduction in the Grantor's estate is greater than the amount needed to reduce the federal estate tax to zero, after considering the available unified tax credit (the applicable credit amount or applicable exclusion amount) and state death tax credit or deduction allowable in determining such tax (provided that the state death tax credit or deduction shall be taken into account only to the extent that doing so would not result in an increase in state death taxes which would otherwise be payable), then the amount set aside in the Marital Share shall be equal only to that portion of such marital deduction that is needed to reduce the federal estate tax on the Grantor's estate to zero.

2. For the purpose of determining the amount to be transferred into the Marital Share, values shall be those which are finally determined for federal estate tax purposes.

    Elections made by the Grantor's executor with respect to taking certain deductions for income tax purposes rather than for estate tax purposes shall determine the aforesaid values and the amount to constitute the Marital Share.

    The words "which pass" or "has passed" shall have the same meaning as under the Internal Revenue Code for marital deduction purposes and no assets shall be transferred to the Marital Share that do not qualify for the marital deduction.

3. In making allocation or distribution to the Marital Share the Trustee is authorized to satisfy the Marital Share in cash or in kind, or in combination of both, provided that all assets placed in the Marital Share shall be valued for the purpose of being placed in the Marital Share at their fair market value as determined as of the dates of respective distributions to the Marital Share, which dates shall be the dates on which the Trustee makes specific allocation on its books of account (if such assets are in negotiable form), or when delivery is made in proper form for transfer, or a deed is executed, if real estate, and the aggregate fair market value thereof shall be no less than the amount required to completely fund the Marital Share.

   The Trustee is further authorized to estimate the size of the Marital Share and to fund the trust, subject, however, to any adjustments which may be required upon final determination of the federal estate tax on the Grantor's estate.

4. No debts, funeral expenses, expenses of administration of the Grantor's estate, inheritance, estate, transfer, legacy or succession taxes (state and federal), and any interest or penalties thereon shall be apportioned against or paid from the Marital Share.

   Provided, however, with regard to expenses of administration of the Grantor's estate which are not deducted for federal estate tax purposes, to the extent the assets of both the Grantor's estate and the Family Trust are insufficient for this purpose, then said expenses shall be apportioned against or paid from the Marital Share.

5. In the event that any provision of this trust agreement shall be finally determined, by a court of competent jurisdiction or by any agency, agent or officer of the Internal Revenue Service or any other branch of the United States Government, to invalidate or render ineffective a federal estate tax marital deduction for the gift and bequest to the Qualified Domestic Trust created hereinbelow, said provision shall thereupon be deemed to be and shall be null and void and of no effect in its application to said Qualified Domestic Trust; accordingly, the Trustee is hereby directed to take whatever action is necessary in setting up and administering the Qualified Domestic Trust as may be necessary to assure its qualification for said federal estate tax marital deduction, and the provisions of the trust will be construed in accordance with whatever requirements the Secretary of the Treasury may by regulations prescribe to ensure the collection of any estate tax imposed on the trust.

6. If the Grantor's spouse or the Grantor's spouse's executor disclaims

325

said spouse's interest in and power over any property of the Marital Share, then the Trustee shall pay the disclaimed trust assets over to the Family Trust and thereafter said assets shall be administered as part thereof.

7. If the Grantor or the executor of the Grantor's estate or any other individual (including any individual who shall transfer property in trust hereunder or the executor or administrator of the estate of such individual), deems it necessary to allocate any portion of the trust estate to a separate trust share which will allow such assets to qualify for a state marital deduction pursuant to any applicable provision of state law, then notwithstanding anything to the contrary contained in this agreement, the Trustee is authorized to establish a separate Marital Share, the terms of which will qualify for the state marital deduction, to hold the property received in trust hereunder as it, in its sole, absolute, and uncontrolled discretion, shall deem advisable; provided, however, that the amount set aside in the state Marital Share shall be equal only to that portion of such marital deduction that is needed to reduce the state estate tax on the Grantor's estate to zero.

C. <u>Marital Share-Marital QTIP Trust</u>. If the Grantor's spouse, _____, survives the Grantor and is a citizen of the United States upon the Grantor's death, or becomes a citizen of the United States so as to qualify this trust for the estate tax marital deduction in accordance with Section 2056(d)(4) of the Internal Revenue Code the Marital Share shall be designated as the "Marital QTIP Trust" and held and administered and disposed of as follows:

1. The Trustee shall pay over to the Grantor's spouse all of the net income of this Marital QTIP Trust, including all of the income of any retirement plan payable to this Marital QTIP Trust, during said spouse's life, at least annually, but at more frequent intervals if the Grantor's spouse shall, in writing, direct.

   The Grantor's spouse may at any time by written notice, require the Trustee either to make any nonproductive property of this Trust productive or to convert such nonproductive property to productive property within a reasonable time.

   Also, the Trustee may pay over to the Grantor's spouse whatever part or parts of the principal as the Trustee may deem proper or necessary for said spouse's support in reasonable comfort, education (including college, graduate, and professional education), and maintenance in health (including medical, dental, hospital, nursing and nursing home expenses).

   The Trustee shall make no distribution of income or principal of the Marital QTIP Trust to any person other than the Grantor's spouse during said spouse's lifetime.

2. Upon the death of the Grantor's spouse, the Trustee shall pay and transfer all income accrued but undistributed at the date of death of the Grantor's spouse to principal, to be administered according to the terms hereinafter provided.

The Trustee shall then dispose of the then remaining principal as follows:

a. The Trustee shall first pay, out of the principal of the trust estate, the full amount by which estate, inheritance, transfer, legacy or succession taxes (federal and state), and including penalties or interest thereon, imposed by reason of the Grantor's spouse's death, are increased as a result of the inclusion of this Marital QTIP Trust in the Grantor's spouse's estate for such tax purposes.

The final determination of the amount due hereunder shall be based upon the values as finally determined for federal estate tax purposes in the Grantor's spouse's estate.

The Grantor's spouse may waive said spouse's estate's right to payment under this sub-paragraph by making specific reference in said spouse's will to the right to payment hereby given to said spouse's estate.

b. The Trustee shall then pay over the principal, if any, remaining at the Grantor's spouse's death and after the payment required under sub-paragraph 3.C.2.a. has been made, to the Family Trust and thereafter said additional principal shall be apportioned and administered as part thereof, pursuant to the provisions herein-below.

D. Marital Share-Qualified Domestic Trust. If the Grantor's spouse, _____, survives the Grantor and is not a citizen of the United States upon the Grantor's death and does not become a citizen of the United States so as to qualify this trust for the estate tax marital deduction in accordance with Section 2056(d)(4) of the Internal Revenue Code the Marital Share shall be designated as the "Qualified Domestic Trust" and held and administered and disposed of as follows:

1. The Trustee shall pay over to the Grantor's spouse during said spouse's life, all of the net income of this Qualified Domestic Trust, including all of the income of any retirement plan payable to this Qualified Domestic Trust, said payments to be made at least annually, but at more frequent intervals if the Grantor's spouse shall, in writing, direct.

Also, the Trustee may pay over to the Grantor's spouse whatever part or parts of the principal as the Trustee may deem proper or necessary for said spouse's support in reasonable comfort, education (including college, graduate, and professional education), and maintenance in health (including medical, dental, hospital, nursing and nursing home expenses), subject to the provisions of sub-paragraph 3.D.3. below, or on account of said spouse's hardship.

The Trustee shall take into account the other resources of the Grantor's spouse in exercising its discretion.

2. Upon the death of the Grantor's spouse, the Trustee shall pay and transfer all income accrued but undistributed at the date of death of the Grantor's spouse to principal, to be administered according to the terms hereinafter provided.

3. Upon any taxable distribution of the principal of the Qualified Domestic Trust during the lifetime of the Grantor's spouse, and upon the death of the Grantor's spouse, the Trustee shall set aside sufficient funds to satisfy the estate tax liability imposed as a result of such distribution or death, as provided for in sub-paragraph 12.B. below.

4. The Trustee shall then pay over the principal, if any, remaining at the Grantor's spouse's death and after the payments required under sub-paragraphs 3.D.2. and 3.D.3. have been made, to the Family Trust and thereafter said additional principal shall be apportioned and administered pursuant to the provisions thereof.

E. <u>Family Trust</u>. The Family Trust shall consist of all of the remainder of the trust estate which has not been heretofore previously allocated and shall be held and administered and disposed of by the Trustee as follows:

1. If the Grantor's spouse, _____, survives the Grantor, then, during said spouse's lifetime, the Trustee may pay over to the Grantor's spouse or may use, apply or expend for said spouse's direct or indirect benefit, so much or all of the income of the trust hereby created and so much or all of the principal of said trust as the Trustee may deem proper or necessary for said spouse's support in reasonable comfort, education (including college, graduate, and professional education), and maintenance in health (including medical, dental, hospital, nursing and nursing home expenses); provided, however, that in exercising its discretion the Trustee shall take into account other resources of the Grantor's spouse.

a. The Trustee may also pay over to or use, apply or expend for the direct or indirect benefit of the Grantor's children who are from time to time living during said period, or pay to the Grantor's spouse for their benefit, so much or all of the income or principal of the trust hereby created as the Trustee may deem proper or necessary for their support in reasonable comfort, education (including college, graduate, and professional education), and maintenance in health (including medical, dental, hospital, nursing and nursing home expenses).

b. If it becomes necessary for the Trustee to make any payments to or for the benefit of the Grantor's spouse from the principal of the Marital QTIP Trust hereinbefore established, or from the principal of the Family Trust, the Trustee is directed, when it is practicable to do so, to make such payments of principal, if any, from the principal of the Marital QTIP Trust before making any payment from the principal of the Family Trust.

If it becomes necessary for the Trustee to make any payments to or for the benefit of the Grantor's spouse from the principal of the Qualified Domestic Trust hereinbefore established, or from the principal of the Family Trust, the Trustee is directed, when it is practicable to do so to make such payments of principal, if any, from the principal of the Family Trust before making any payment from the principal of the Qualified Domestic Trust. The Trustee shall set aside sufficient funds to satisfy the estate tax liability imposed as a result of any distribution from the Qualified Domestic Trust provided for in sub-paragraph 12.B. below.

However, it is the Grantor's intention that the support in reasonable comfort, education (including college, graduate, and professional education), and maintenance in health (including medical, dental, hospital, nursing and nursing home expenses) of the Grantor's spouse shall be of primary concern, and the Trustee shall exercise its discretion in using principal for the Grantor's spouse, considering all other beneficiaries to this trust to be secondary and without liability to any other beneficiary for the use of principal for the Grantor's spouse.

2. Upon the death of the Grantor's spouse or upon the Grantor's death if the Grantor's spouse does not survive him, the Trustee shall apportion the trust estate into equal shares as follows:

one (1) such share to each of the Grantor's living children, and

one (1) such share to each family group composed of the living issue of any child of the Grantor who is then deceased.

Said equal shares shall then be held and administered and disposed of as follows:

a. In the case of each share apportioned to a living child of the Grantor, the Trustee may, in each and every year beginning with the date of said apportionment, pay over to said child or use, apply or expend for said child's direct or indirect benefit, so much or all of the net income of said share and so much or all of the principal

329

of said share as the Trustee may, in its sole, absolute, and uncontrolled discretion, deem wise and safely consistent with said child's support in reasonable comfort, education (including college, graduate, and professional education), and maintenance in health (including medical, dental, hospital, nursing and nursing home expenses).

i.   Whenever, at or after said time of apportionment, said child shall have attained the age of thirty (30) years, he shall have the right to request in writing and to receive one-third (1/3) of the balance of his share; and

ii. Whenever, at or after said time of apportionment, said child shall have attained the age of thirty-five (35) years, he shall have the right to request in writing and to receive an additional one-half (1/2) of the balance of his share; and

iii. Whenever, at or after said time of apportionment, said child shall have attained the age of forty (40) years, he shall have the right to request in writing and to receive the entire balance of his share, at which time his trust shall terminate.

iv. It is the Grantor's belief that, in some circumstances, it may be beneficial for said child to leave the management of his trust share in the hands of the Trustee.

Therefore, said child may elect to leave his trust share, or any portion thereof, in the hands of the Trustee, as a separate fund, to be held and administered and disposed of as said child shall direct.

v.   The share held by the Trustee for the benefit of a child as described above shall, from the time of the death of said child after the time above set for apportionment into shares, be administered for the benefit of said child's issue in the manner described below.

b. In the case of each share apportioned to the living issue of a deceased child of the Grantors, said share shall be administered for the benefit as a family group of such of the issue of said deceased child as from time to time shall be living.

The Trustee may pay over to the issue, or may use, apply or expend for their direct or indirect benefit, so much of the income and principal of the trust estate, at such times and in such proportions as the Trustee may determine, in its sole, absolute, and uncontrolled discretion, for support in reasonable comfort, education, (including college, graduate, and professional education), and maintenance in health (including medical, dental, hospital, nursing and nursing home expenses).

The Trustee may make such payments, use, application, expenditure or accumulation of the income and principal thereof as it shall think proper for the direct or indirect benefit of the members of said family group without being required to observe any precept or rule of equality of enjoyment as between said members.

Final distribution shall be made of whatever shall remain of said share, per stirpes, among said living issue and free and clear of all trusts when the youngest then living child of the Grantor's deceased child reaches the age of thirty (30) years.

   c. If at any time before the final distribution of any of the trust shares hereinabove described (after taking into consideration all provisions thereof), there shall be no person in existence who is eligible to have the benefit of the trust of such share, then the share in question shall be reapportioned in equal shares among the other shares of the trust estate apportioned pursuant to sub-paragraph 3.E.2. above, and each equal share shall continue to be held and administered in trust, or distributed free and clear of all trusts, as the case may be, to or for the benefit of persons then and thereafter living, in accordance with the fortunes of the share to which said reapportionment is made.

F. If, at any time before the final distribution of all of the trust shares hereinabove described, there shall be no person in existence who is eligible to have the benefit of any trust shares, the Trustee shall divide all of the trust estate then remaining into two (2) equal parts which shall be distributed, outright and free of trust, as follows:

   1. One (1) part to those persons then living who would have taken the Grantor's estate, and in such shares thereof as they would have taken, had the Grantor then died intestate, domiciled in New Hampshire; and

   2. One (1) part to those persons then living who would have taken the Grantor's spouse's estate, and in such shares thereof as they would have taken, had he/she then died intestate, domiciled in New Hampshire.

G. If the Grantor's residential real estate is held in the trust estate and used by the Grantor's said spouse as a residence, then, during said spouse's lifetime, said spouse shall be permitted exclusive use and occupancy of said residential real estate.

Also, the Grantor's said spouse may, during said spouse's lifetime, in writing, delivered to the Trustee, request the Trustee to sell said residential real estate and to provide a substitute residence, of approximately equal or lesser value to the residence then occupied by the Grantor's said spouse.

Upon receipt of such written request, the Trustee shall then have full power and authority to make reasonable efforts to obtain such substitute residence and to sell the residential real estate then occupied by the Grantor's said spouse.

The costs of selling said residential real estate, of obtaining such substitute residence and of moving the Grantor's said spouse and said spouse's belongings out of said spouse's then occupied residence and into said substitute residence may, in the Trustee's sole, absolute, and uncontrolled discretion, be borne by the Family Trust, to the extent there shall be sufficiently liquid assets to satisfy same.

The Trustee shall have full power and authority to execute any and all documents necessary to carry out the foregoing purpose.

The Trustee shall not be responsible, directly or indirectly, for the success, failure or ultimate satisfaction of the Grantor's said spouse in connection therewith.

The costs and expenses of maintenance and repairs to keep such residential real estate in the same condition it is in at the commencement of said use (reasonable wear and tear excepted), real estate taxes and other normal costs of maintenance and upkeep of said residential real estate, including fire and casualty insurance, may, in the Trustee's sole, absolute, and uncontrolled discretion, be borne by the Family Trust, to the extent there shall be sufficiently liquid assets to satisfy same.

H. Notwithstanding any provision hereinabove to the contrary, the Trustee shall not make any distribution of income or principal from the Marital QTIP Trust or the Qualified Domestic Trust or the Family Trust, to the Grantor's spouse, _____, if the Grantor's said spouse waives testate distribution of the Grantor's will and claims a statutory share of the Grantor's estate under R.S.A. 560:10, or any provisions successor thereto.

In such event, the trust estate benefiting the Grantor's spouse shall be administered as if the Grantor's spouse were not then living.

I. The provisions contained hereinabove which require the Trustee to apportion the trust estate into shares and parts of shares are for purposes of computation only and shall not be construed to require the Trustee to make physical segregation of one share or a part of a share from the others, although the Trustee shall have full right to make such segregation if it thinks it better to do so.

Notwithstanding said provisions, the Trustee shall have the full right to regard the trust estate as one undivided estate for purposes of management and investment.

J.   If the Grantor or the executor of the Grantor's estate or any other individual (including any individual who shall transfer property in trust hereunder or the executor or administrator of the estate of such individual), has allocated any portion or all of any Generation Skipping Transfer ("GST") exemption provided by Section 2631(a) of the Internal Revenue Code to any property to be held in trust hereunder, then notwithstanding anything to the contrary contained in this agreement, the Trustee is authorized to establish such number of separate trusts, with identical terms, to hold the property received in trust hereunder as it, in its sole, absolute, and uncontrolled discretion, shall deem advisable, bearing in mind the allocation of the said GST exemption and the desirability that any trust to which all or any portion of the said GST exemption is allocated shall, if practical, have an inclusion ratio of zero.

Further, the Trustee is authorized to allocate such trusts among the trust shares hereinabove created in order to minimize (or eliminate, if possible) any GST tax.

4.   <u>TRUSTEE'S POWERS</u>. In the administration of the trust estate, the Trustee shall have all of the powers granted to trustees by New Hampshire common law and statutory authority (including, but not limited to, the Uniform Trustees' Powers Act, R.S.A. 564-A, and the Uniform Trust Code, R.S.A. 564-B, as they may be amended from time to time), without restrictions.

In addition to such power, and not in limitation thereof, the Trustee shall have the following powers, all of which shall be exercised in a fiduciary capacity and for the benefit of the beneficiaries:

A.   During the lifetime of the Grantor, the Trustee may retain as an investment, unless and until the Grantor by a writing delivered to the Trustee shall otherwise direct, all of the securities and other property originally assigned, transferred, or delivered to the Trustee hereunder or at any time forming a part of the trust estate, whether or not such securities or other property be of the character authorized by the laws of the State of New Hampshire for the investment of trust funds.

Upon the death or incapacity of the Grantor, the Trustee is authorized to purchase, sell, lease, or alter any investment by buy or sell orders transmitted by it, whether by telephone call, electronic facsimile transmission, computer message or other current non-written method of business communication.

B.   To buy, sell and trade in securities of any nature, on margin, and for such purpose to maintain and operate margin accounts with brokers, and to pledge any securities held or purchased by it with such brokers as security for loans and advances made to the Trustee.

C. *[For Corporate Trustees]* To retain the property of the trust estate in the same investments as when received by it or to vary and transpose such investments and to invest and reinvest the property of the trust estate in such manner and in such securities or other property (including common trust funds or similar funds for the participation of trusts of which any corporation or financial institution serving as Trustee hereunder is trustee and including securities of said corporation or financial institution and any affiliate, subsidiary and successor thereto) as it in its uncontrolled discretion shall deem best without accountability for any loss for so doing and without liability for depreciation occasioned by so doing even though the property so retained or the investments so made may not be of the character permitted for the investment of trust funds under the laws of the State of New Hampshire or any other state or federal law.

D. To take and hold title to real estate, and to convey any interest in real estate and improvements thereon held in trust, and no purchaser or third party shall be bound to inquire whether the Trustee has said power or is properly exercising said power, or see to the application of any trust asset paid to the Trustee for a conveyance thereof.

E. To have all of the necessary banking powers to open and manage financial accounts, including but not limited to, checking accounts, savings accounts, financial accounts and other related financial instruments and to conduct all necessary financial business in reference to the management of the financial assets of the trust.

F. To rent a safe deposit box and to retain such assets in said box as the Trustee, in its sole, absolute, and uncontrolled discretion, determines appropriate.

G. To borrow money, with or without security, and mortgage or pledge trust property for a period within or extending beyond the duration of the trust.

H. To loan funds to the Grantor's estate upon such terms and conditions as to interest rates, maturities, and security as the Trustee shall determine.

I. To make payments, transfers or conveyances, to the extent possible, to the estate of the Grantor (after exhaustion of the assets of the Grantor's estate) to satisfy legacies, bequests or devises, if any, made under the Grantor's will or included in the Grantor's estate for other purposes, if the Grantor's estate shall be insufficient to satisfy such legacies, bequests or devises.

J. To invest in common trust funds.

K. To select property, in its sole, absolute, and uncontrolled discretion, to be allocated to any trust hereunder or to be distributed in satisfaction of any gift provided for herein without respect to the income tax basis of such property, and the Trustee is specifically excused from any duty of impartiality with respect to the income tax basis of such property.

In the event that residential real estate is held in the trust estate, the Trustee may allocate said residential real estate to any trust created hereunder, to be held and administered and disposed of pursuant to the provisions thereof.

L.   If at any time during the Grantor's lifetime, there is delivered to the Trustee other than the Grantor, if any, or, if none, then to the successor Trustee, a written opinion, signed by a licensed physician, stating that the Grantor has become incompetent or incapacitated, then from and after the delivery of such written opinion the Trustee other than the Grantor, or the successor Trustee, as the case may be, shall have those powers and authorities with respect to the trust estate given to the Trustee in this trust agreement.

M. If, after the death of the Grantor and the Grantor's spouse, _____, as it may be amended from time to time, is still in existence and the terms of any trust established by said trust are substantially similar to the terms of any trust established by this, _____, the Trustee is authorized and empowered to consolidate such trust with such similar trust established by _____ and to administer them as one trust, unless such consolidation shall be contrary to law or inconsistent with the terms of any instrument supplemental hereto.

N. Regardless of the extent of the authority that the Trustee holds to currently distribute income and/or principal of the trust estate to one or more beneficiaries of the trust, the Trustee shall have full power and authority, to be exercised in its sole, absolute, and uncontrolled discretion, to appoint any or all assets held in this trust estate to any other trust or trusts created under will, deed or otherwise, for the benefit of one or more of the beneficiaries hereunder.

This authority shall be subject to the limitations set forth in R.S.A. 564-B:4-418, as amended from time to time, provided that such appointment clause shall be null and void in the event there is a determination that the application of such clause shall result in the inclusion of any of the trust estate in the Grantor's gross estate under any provision of the Internal Revenue Code, including but not limited to Sections 2041 and 2042, which would not otherwise be includable in the Grantor's gross estate.

O. If, at any time before the final distribution of the principal of any trust share hereinabove described, the value of the principal of said trust share shall be equal to, or less than, ONE HUNDRED THOUSAND DOL-LARS ($100,000), then the Trustee may, in its sole discretion, terminate said trust share and distribute the principal of said trust share, and any accumulated and undistributed income thereof, outright and free of trust, to those persons then entitled to benefit from said trust share, and in the proportions in which they are then entitled to benefit from said trust share, notwithstanding any provisions of this trust to the contrary.

P.   To exercise all the powers, authorities and discretions herein conferred, after the termination of the trust hereunder, until the complete distribution of the trust estate.

5.   ADDITIONAL PROPERTY. The Grantor, or the Grantor's spouse may, by will, trust or during their lifetimes, from time to time, transfer and deliver to the Trustee cash, securities, and other property acceptable to the Trustee, in addition to the property presently transferred and delivered, and such cash, securities, and other property shall be held, administered, and disposed of by the Trustee in accordance with the provisions of this agreement without the execution of any further instrument or declaration.

All tangible personal property and household effects and intangible personal property (including written evidence of intangible personal property, stock certificates, bonds, notes and similar property) which are then part of the trust estate must be physically located in the United States at all times during the administration of the Qualified Domestic Trust of the Marital Share. In addition, securities held in a brokerage account must be held in an account established with a domestic corporation.

After the death of the Grantor, the Grantor's spouse may, within the period allowed by law, transfer or irrevocably assign to the Qualified Domestic Trust of the Marital Share any property which passed from the Grantor to the Grantor's spouse, in accordance with Section 2056(d)(2)(B) of the Internal Revenue Code.

6.   REPORTING BY TRUSTEE.

A.   At any time and from time to time, the Grantor shall have the power, by written instrument signed and acknowledged by the Grantor and delivered to the Trustee, to settle the report of the Trustee with respect to principal or income, or with respect to both principal and income, and to release and discharge the Trustee of and from any and every claim, demand, accountability, and liability of every nature, arising from any matter or thing done or omitted to be done, in connection with this agreement or any trust hereby created, during the period in respect of which the report of the Trustee shall have been so settled.

Every such settlement, release, and discharge shall be conclusive and binding upon, and shall be an absolute protection to the Trustee against all claims of any income beneficiaries, remaindermen, or other persons who might then or thereafter have or claim any interest under this agreement, and no such income beneficiary, remainderman, or other person shall have any right of accounting, reporting, any claim, or any cause of action against the Trustee arising from any matter or thing done or omitted to be done in connection with this agreement or any trust hereby created, during any period in respect of which the report of the Trustee shall have been so settled.

B. After the death or incapacity of the Grantor, the Trustee may, at the Trustee's sole, absolute, and uncontrolled discretion, and shall, to the extent required by the Uniform Trust Code, R.S.A. 564-B, as it may be amended from time to time, render a Trustee's report as described in the Uniform Trust Code, as it may be amended from time to time, at such intervals as the Trustee may choose or at such times as required by the Uniform Trust Code.

C. A recipient of such a report (or, if under guardianship or conservatorship, then by the Guardian or Conservator, or, if deceased, then by the Executor or Administrator), may, by a written instrument, assent to the report of the Trustee with respect to principal or to income, or with respect to both principal and income.

The assent of the recipient of such report (or, if under guardianship or conservatorship, then by the Guardian or Conservator, or, if deceased, then by the Executor or Administrator) shall make such report binding and conclusive upon all persons then having or who may thereafter have any interest, vested or contingent, in the income or principal of the trust estate and such assent shall forever release and discharge the Trustee of and from any and every claim, demand, accountability, and liability of every nature, arising from any matter or thing done or omitted to be done, in connection with this agreement or any trust hereby created, during the period in respect of which the report of the Trustee shall have been so settled.

D. The failure of any person to object in writing to the Trustee to such a report within thirty (30) days after the delivery of the same to such person hereunder shall be final and binding to the same extent as the written assent hereinabove provided.

E. Any person entitled to such a report, accounting, information, notice and the like (or, if under guardianship or conservatorship, then by the Guardian or Conservator, or, if deceased, then by the Executor or Administrator) may by a written instrument signed and acknowledged by him or her or them, as the case may be, and delivered to the Trustee, waive the right to said Trustee's report or to other information otherwise required to be furnished under the Uniform Trust Code, as it may be amended from time to time.

7. SUCCESSOR TRUSTEE. The following provisions shall govern the

addition, removal and succession of the Trustee:

A. The Grantor may, during the Grantor's lifetime, add any additional Trustee, or remove any Trustee hereunder and appoint a successor Trustee.

B. <u>If the Grantor's Spouse is not a United States Citizen</u>. The following provisions shall govern the addition, removal and succession of the Trustee, if the Grantor's spouse is not a citizen of the United States and does not become a citizen of the United States so as to qualify this trust for the estate tax marital deduction in accordance with Section 2056(d)(4) of the Internal Revenue Code.

1. If _____ shall unable or unwilling to serve in the capacity of Trustee for any reason, then the Grantor's spouse, _____, and the Grantor's _____, _____, of _____, _____, shall serve as successor Trustee.

2. If the Grantor's said spouse shall be unable or unwilling to serve in the capacity of Trustee for any reason, then no successor shall serve and the remaining Trustee shall serve as sole Trustee.

3. If _____ shall be unable or unwilling to serve in the capacity of Trustee of said Trust for any reason, then the Grantor's _____, _____, of _____, _____, shall serve as successor.

4. In the event there shall be no successor Trustee who shall be able or willing to serve in the capacity of Trustee, then a majority of the beneficiaries to whom or for whose use the current net income of the trust estate is at the time authorized or required to be paid or applied, either,

   a. acting individually, if then eighteen (18) years of age, or,

   b. by his or her natural parent, or natural guardian, or Court appointed guardian or Court appointed conservator, if then under guardianship or conservatorship,

   shall appoint a successor Trustee, subject to the provisions hereinbelow.

5. At all times after the death of the Grantor, at least one (1) successor Trustee shall be an individual citizen of the United States or domestic corporation.

6. If, upon or at any time after the death of the Grantor, no successor Trustee shall be an individual citizen of the United States or a domestic corporation, then a successor Trustee shall be immediately appointed by the Trustee then serving, which successor Trustee shall be an individual citizen of the United States or a domestic corporation.

The Trustee shall have the sole authority to appoint a United States bank as Trustee if such Trustee is required as set forth hereinbelow.

7. The Trustee shall comply with the requirements for security arrangements for qualified domestic trusts as set forth in Treas. Reg. § 20.2056A-2(d)(1)(i) or (ii), summarized as follows:

     a. Trust in Excess of TWO MILLION DOLLARS ($2,000,000). If the fair market value of the assets passing to the Qualified Domestic Trust (determined without reduction for any indebtedness thereon) exceeds TWO MILLION DOLLARS ($2,000,000) on the relevant valuation date, then the Trustee must at all times during the term of the trust either satisfy the U.S. Bank as Trustee requirement (*see* Treas. Reg. § 20.2056A-2(d)(1)(i)(A), or furnish a bond that satisfies the requirements of Treas. Reg. § 20.2056A-2(d)(1)(i)(B), or furnish an irrevocable letter of credit that satisfies the requirements of Treas. Reg. § 20.2056A-2(d)(1)(i)(C), (hereinafter referred to as the U.S. Bank, Bond, or Letter of Credit Requirement); The Trustee may alternate between any of the security arrangements described in the preceding sentence provided that, at all times during the term of the trust, one of the arrangements is operative;

        If the Trustee elects to furnish a bond or letter of credit as security, then in the event the Internal Revenue Service draws on the instrument in accordance with its terms, neither the U.S. Trustee nor any other person will seek a return of any part of the remittance until after April 15th of the calendar year following the year in which the bond or letter of credit is drawn upon;

     b. Trust of TWO MILLION DOLLARS ($2,000,000) or Less. If the fair market value of the assets passing to the Qualified Domestic Trust (determined without reduction for any indebtedness) is TWO MILLION DOLLARS ($2,000,000) or less on the relevant valuation date, then the Trustee must comply with either the U.S. Bank, Bond, or Letter of Credit Requirement only if more than thirty-five percent (35%) of the fair market value of the trust assets, determined annually on the last day of the taxable year of the trust, consists of real property located outside the United States. For purposes of determining whether more than thirty-five percent (35%) of the trust assets consist of foreign real property, Treas. Reg. § 20.2056A-2(d)(1)(ii)(B) applies;

     c. Determination of Value. For purposes of determining whether the fair market value of the Qualified Domestic Trust assets exceeds TWO MILLION DOLLARS ($2,000,000), the Trustee is authorized to make the election under Treas. Reg. § 20.2056A-

2(d)(1)(iv)(A) with respect to real property used as the Grantor's spouse's personal residence;

d.   Amount of Bond or Letter of Credit. For purposes of determining the amount of the bond or letter of credit, the Trustee is authorized to make the election under Treas. Reg. § 20.2056A-2(d)(1)(iv)(B) with respect to real property used as the Grantor's spouse's personal residence;

e.   Annual Statements. The Trustee is directed to file any annual statements required under Treas. Reg. § 20.2056A-2(d)(3);

f.   General Conduct. Notwithstanding anything contained herein to the contrary, the Trustee is hereby authorized to enter into alternative plans or arrangements with the Internal Revenue Service pursuant to Treas. Reg. § 20.2056A-2(d)(4) to assure collection of the deferred estate tax, in lieu of the provisions contained herein.

8.   No distributions other than a distribution of income may be made to the Grantor's spouse under the provisions of the Qualified Domestic Trust of the Marital Share unless the Trustee serving hereunder who shall be an individual citizen of the United States or a domestic corporation has the right to withhold from such distribution the tax imposed by Section 2056A of the Internal Revenue Code, or any provision successor thereto.

9.   In the event that any beneficiary of the trust, other than the Grantor, shall serve in the capacity of co-Trustee, then the discretionary powers to determine whether income or principal is to be distributed to said beneficiary or to any person to whom said beneficiary owes an obligation of support shall be exercisable only by the remaining Trustee.

It is the Grantor's intention by this sub-paragraph to prohibit said beneficiary from benefiting himself or herself as beneficiary in any way by the exercise of such discretionary powers vested in the Trustee as a group.

10.   In the event that any beneficiary of the trust, other than the Grantor or the Grantor's spouse, shall serve in the capacity of sole Trustee and the Trustee has discretionary powers to distribute income or principal to himself, herself, or to any person to whom he or she owes an obligation of support, then such distributions of income or principal shall be exercisable by the sole Trustee. The maximum amount that may be withdrawn annually by each such beneficiary under this sub-paragraph, however, shall not exceed the maximum amount over which an individual may have a power of withdrawal without its lapse

in such year being deemed to be a release of such power under Section 2514(e) of the Internal Revenue Code.

11. In the event that an attorney, an accountant, a certified financial planner or a corporation or financial institution shall be serving as Trustee hereunder, a majority of the beneficiaries to whom or for whose use the current net income of the trust estate is at the time authorized or required to be paid or applied and who shall at the time be at least eighteen (18) years of age may by a written instrument signed and acknowledged by them and delivered to such attorney, accountant, certified financial planner or corporation or financial institution remove said Trustee and, subject to the successor trustee appointments herein, appoint as its successor Trustee, any attorney, accountant, certified financial planner or corporation or financial institution having a trust department capable of rendering financial advice concerning the investments of the trust estate.

12. No change of name of any corporation or financial institution serving as Trustee hereunder shall affect its appointment and capacity as Trustee hereunder.

    Any domestic corporation into which it may merge or with which it may be consolidated, or any domestic corporation resulting from any merger or consolidation to which it may be a party, shall be its successor hereunder without the execution or filing of any additional instrument or the performance of any further act.

13. Each Trustee hereunder (whether originally designated herein or appointed as successor) shall have the right to resign at any time by giving thirty (30) days written notice to that effect to the current income beneficiary (or beneficiaries) of the trust.

    Thereafter, such beneficiary (or a majority of such beneficiaries) who shall at the time be at least eighteen (18) years of age shall have the right within such thirty (30) day period to appoint a successor Trustee, subject to the provisions hereinabove, and shall notify the resigning Trustee of such appointment.

    In the event that a corporation or financial institution shall be appointed as successor Trustee hereunder, such successor Trustee shall be a domestic trust company or bank qualified to act as such, possessing trust powers.

    In the event the current income beneficiary (or beneficiaries) shall fail to designate a successor Trustee within the time specified, the then-acting Trustee shall appoint a successor Trustee as herein provided.

14. No successor Trustee shall be liable or responsible in any way for any

341

actions or defaults of any predecessor Trustee, nor for any loss or expense from or occasioned by anything done or neglected to be done by any predecessor Trustee. Any successor Trustee shall have, from and after its appointment or succession to office hereunder and without any assignment or other action by any person, all the rights, interests, and powers, including discretionary rights and powers, which are by the provisions of this trust agreement granted to and vested in the Trustee named herein.

C. <u>If the Grantor's Spouse is a United States Citizen</u>. The following provisions shall govern the addition, removal and succession of the Trustee, if the Grantor's spouse is a citizen of the United States or becomes a citizen of the United States so as to qualify this trust for the estate tax marital deduction in accordance with Section 2056(d)(4) of the Internal Revenue Code.

1. Notwithstanding the foregoing, if the Grantor's spouse, _____, survives the Grantor and is a citizen of the United States upon the Grantor's death, or becomes a citizen of the United States so as to qualify this trust for the estate tax marital deduction in accordance with Section 2056(d)(4) of the Internal Revenue Code, or any provision successor thereto, said spouse shall serve as sole Trustee of the Marital QTIP Trust established hereinabove.

2. If _____ shall be unable or unwilling to serve in the capacity of Trustee of said Trust for any reason, then the Grantor's _____, _____, of _____, _____, shall serve in _____ stead.

    If _____ shall be unable or unwilling to serve in the capacity of Trustee of said Trust for any reason, then the Grantor's _____, _____, of _____, _____, shall serve in _____ stead.

3. In the event there shall be no successor Trustee who shall be able or willing to serve in the capacity of Trustee, then a majority of the beneficiaries to whom or for whose use the current net income of the trust estate is at the time authorized or required to be paid or applied, either,

    a. acting individually, if then eighteen (18) years of age, or,

    b. by his or her natural parent, or natural guardian, or Court appointed guardian or Court appointed conservator, if then under guardianship or conservatorship,

    shall appoint a successor Trustee.

4. In the event that any beneficiary of the trust, other than the Grantor, shall serve in the capacity of co-Trustee, then the discretionary powers

to determine whether income or principal is to be distributed to said beneficiary or to any person to whom said beneficiary owes an obligation of support shall be exercisable only by the remaining Trustee.

It is the Grantor's intention by this sub-paragraph to prohibit said beneficiary from benefiting himself or herself as beneficiary in any way by the exercise of such discretionary powers vested in the Trustee as a group.

5. In the event that any beneficiary of the trust, other than the Grantor, shall serve in the capacity of sole Trustee and the Trustee has discretionary powers to distribute income or principal to himself, herself, or to any person to whom he or she owes an obligation of support, then such distributions of income or principal shall be exercisable by the sole Trustee. The maximum amount that may be withdrawn annually by each such beneficiary under this sub-paragraph, however, shall not exceed the maximum amount over which an individual may have a power of withdrawal without its lapse in such year being deemed to be a release of such power under Section 2514(e) of the Internal Revenue Code.

6. No change of name of _____ shall affect its appointment and capacity as Trustee hereunder. Any corporation into which it may merge or with which it may be consolidated, or any corporation resulting from any merger or consolidation to which it may be a party, shall be the successor of the Trustee hereunder without the execution or filing of any additional instrument or the performance of any further act.

7. In the event that a corporation or financial institution shall be serving as Trustee hereunder, a majority of the beneficiaries to whom or for whose use the current net income of the trust estate is at the time authorized or required to be paid or applied and who shall at the time be at least eighteen (18) years of age may by a written instrument signed and acknowledged by them and delivered to such corporation or financial institution remove said Trustee and appoint as its successor Trustee, any corporation or financial institution having a trust department capable of rendering financial advice concerning the investments of the trust estate.

8. Each Trustee hereunder (whether originally designated herein or appointed as successor) shall have the right to resign at any time by giving thirty (30) days written notice to that effect to the current income beneficiary (or beneficiaries) of the trust.

Thereafter, such beneficiary (or a majority of such beneficiaries) who shall at the time be at least eighteen (18) years of age shall have the right within such thirty (30) day period to appoint a successor Trustee, subject to the provisions hereinabove, and shall notify the resigning Trustee of such appointment.

In the event that a corporation or financial institution shall be appointed as successor Trustee hereunder, such successor Trustee shall be a trust company or bank qualified to act as such, possessing trust powers.

In the event the current income beneficiary (or beneficiaries) shall fail to designate a successor Trustee within the time specified, the then-acting Trustee shall appoint a successor Trustee as herein provided.

9. No successor Trustee shall be liable or responsible in any way for any actions or defaults of any predecessor Trustee, nor for any loss or expense from or occasioned by anything done or neglected to be done by any predecessor Trustee. Any successor Trustee shall have, from and after its appointment or succession to office hereunder and without any assignment or other action by any person, all the rights, interests, and powers, including discretionary rights and powers, which are by the provisions of this trust agreement granted to and vested in the Trustee named herein.

8. FIDUCIARIES. No person dealing with the Trustee shall be responsible for the application of any money, securities, or other property paid or delivered, and the receipt of the Trustee shall be a full discharge; and no person dealing with the Trustee, and no issuer, transfer agent, or other agent of any issuer of any securities shall be under any obligation to ascertain or inquire into the power of the Trustee to purchase, sell, exchange, transfer, mortgage, pledge, create a security interest in, lease, distribute, or otherwise dispose of or deal with any money, securities, or other property.

The Trustee shall not at any time be held liable for any action taken or not taken, including any action intended to lessen or eliminate the impact of estate or generation-skipping transfer taxes with respect to any generation or beneficiary, whether or not such action is successful in achieving the results sought and without regard to its effect on other beneficiaries in the same or different generations, or for any loss or depreciation in the value of any property in any trust created herein, whether due to an error of judgment or otherwise, where the Trustee has exercised good faith and ordinary diligence in the exercise of its duties.

The Trustee shall receive reasonable compensation for its services in the administration of the trusts created herein, including reimbursement for amounts reasonably expended for bookkeeping services, investment services and advice, and other professional or paraprofessional services. In addition to the compensation herein provided, the Trustee shall receive reasonable compensation for any legal services provided for the benefit of the trust estate, such as handling any litigation involving the trust, preparing state or federal income tax returns, and transferring any real estate.

9.　　PERPETUITIES. All trusts established under this instrument shall be exempt from the application of the rule against perpetuities. This provision is intended to comply with New Hampshire R.S.A. 564:24, and accordingly, the Grantor specifically authorizes the Trustee to sell, mortgage or lease property for any period of time beyond the period that is required for an interest created under this instrument to vest in order to be valid under the rule against perpetuities, as measured by the period defined hereinabove.

The trusts created hereunder shall be perpetual to the fullest extent permitted by the governing law. If any trust created hereunder is deemed to be subject to the law of a jurisdiction (including, but only to the extent applicable to real property) that has a rule against perpetuities or similar rule which limits the period during which property can be held in trust, then such trust (other than a trust created by the exercise of a power of appointment conferred hereunder which exercise commences a new rule against perpetuities period under the law of such jurisdiction) shall terminate in all events upon the expiration of the longest period that property may be held in trust under this trust agreement under the law of such jurisdiction (including any applicable period in gross, such as 21 years, 90 years or 110 years); provided, however, that if the jurisdiction has a rule against perpetuities or similar rule which applies only to certain types of property, such as real property, the provisions of this paragraph shall apply only to such property. If under the law of such jurisdiction the longest period that property may be held in trust may be determined (or alternatively determined) with reference to the death of the last survivor of a group of individuals in being upon the date of this trust agreement, those individuals shall consist of all of the descendants of the Grantor's parents who were in being on the date of this trust agreement. Upon termination of a trust pursuant to the provisions of this paragraph, the trust property shall be transferred, conveyed and paid over to the persons then entitled to receive or have the benefit of the income from the trust in the proportions in which they are entitled thereto, or if their interests are indefinite, then in equal shares.

10.　　SPENDTHRIFT PROVISION. Except as herein otherwise provided, the interest of any beneficiary hereunder, either as to income or principal, shall not be anticipated, alienated or in any other manner assigned or pledged or promised by such beneficiary, and shall not be reached by, or be subject to, any legal, equitable or other process, including any bankruptcy or divorce proceeding, or be subject to the interference or control of creditors or others in any way or manner, and all payments to, or the interest of, any beneficiary shall be free from the control or claim of any parent or spouse or former spouse or any other third party. Moreover, no power of appointment or power of withdrawal shall be subject to involuntary exercise. Provided, however, this spendthrift provision shall not restrict the exercise of a disclaimer or the exercise of a power of appointment or withdrawal right granted by this trust agreement. This provision is intended to be a material provision of this trust and any other trust established hereunder.

11.   TAX PROVISION.

A. Upon the Grantor's death, the trust estate shall not be charged with the payment of any estate, inheritance, legacy, death taxes or duties of any nature (state or federal), or any interest or penalty thereon, except to the extent that the other assets in the Grantor's estate (excluding any assets which may be exempted from the payment of such taxes by the last will of the Grantor) shall be insufficient to discharge such taxes, interest or penalties or shall be insufficiently liquid to satisfy the same.

The Trustee may rely conclusively upon written certification from the executor of the Grantor's estate, or if no probate administration of the Grantor's estate is required under applicable law, upon request of the person or persons nominated as executor under the Grantor's will or upon any other evidence, as to the existence of such insufficiency and the amount thereof; provided, however, that the Trustee shall not pay any additional tax imposed under Section 2032A or 2057 of the Internal Revenue Code or any generation-skipping transfer taxes imposed under Chapter 13 of the Internal Revenue Code imposed by reason of the Grantor's death.

If the Trustee shall be required to pay any such taxes, they shall be charged against the principal of the trust estate as an expense without apportionment.

Provided, that in the event that no probate administration of the Grantor's estate is required under applicable law, the Trustee shall have all the powers and authority given the executor under the Grantor's will in relation to such taxes, including all elections and allocation of the generation-skipping transfer tax exemption under Section 2631 of the Internal Revenue Code.

B. If the Grantor's spouse survives the Grantor, upon any taxable distribution from the Qualified Domestic Trust during the lifetime of the Grantor's spouse, or upon said spouse's death, or in the event the Qualified Domestic Trust ceases to qualify as such, the Trustee shall pay the full amount of any estate taxes, and any interest or penalties thereon, which may be imposed with respect to such event, out of such distribution.

12.   DEBTS AND EXPENSES. The trust estate shall not be charged with the payment of legal debts of the Grantor's estate, funeral expenses or expenses of administration of the Grantor's estate except to the extent that the other assets in the Grantor's estate shall be insufficient to discharge such debts and expenses, or shall be insufficiently liquid to satisfy the same. The Trustee may rely conclusively upon written certification from the executor of the Grantor's estate, or if no probate administration of the Grantor's estate is required under applicable law,

upon request of the person or persons nominated as executor under the Grantor's will, or upon any other evidence, as to the existence of such insufficiency and the amount thereof. If the Trustee shall be required to pay any such debts and expenses, the same shall be treated as debts and expenses of the trust estate (to the extent the assets of the Grantor's estate are insufficient to satisfy the same) or as loans to the Grantor's estate (to the extent the liquid assets of the Grantor's estate are insufficient to satisfy the same) if any such debts and expenses are deducted for federal estate tax purposes in computing the value of the Grantor's taxable estate under Section 2053 of the Internal Revenue Code.

If any such debts and expenses are either not so deducted or deductible under Section 2053 of the Internal Revenue Code, however, the same shall be charged against the principal of the trust estate as an expense without apportionment.

This provision shall confer no rights upon anyone except the executor of the Grantor's estate.

13. <u>SURVIVAL REQUIREMENT</u>. No person shall be deemed to have survived the Grantor, or any other person or event under the terms of this trust, unless such person survives the end of the period commencing with the close of the calendar day of the Grantor's death, the death of such other person or on which such event occurs, and ending with the close of the thirtieth (30th) calendar day thereafter.

14. <u>DISTRIBUTIONS TO MINORS</u>. In any case where property or funds become distributable to a minor, then the Trustee shall have the additional power to distribute the same in any one or more of the following ways: (1) by distribution directly to the minor; (2) by distribution to the legal guardian of the minor; (3) by distribution to a parent, relative or friend of the minor for the minor's support in reasonable comfort, education and maintenance in health; (4) by applying the same directly for the minor's support in reasonable comfort, education and maintenance in health; (5) by depositing the same in a bank account in the name of the minor or by transferring property to or purchasing property in the name of a custodian for his or her benefit under a Uniform Law relating to transfers or gifts to minors; or (6) by holding the same hereunder in trust or in custody for the minor's support in reasonable comfort, education and maintenance in health and by distributing the remainder thereof to the minor upon coming of age or otherwise to the minor's estate in case of the death of the minor. The receipt of the person to whom property or funds are actually distributed in accordance with any of the foregoing provisions shall fully discharge the Trustee from further accountability therefor.

15. <u>GOVERNING LAW AND SITUS</u>. The Grantor declares that this agreement and the trust created hereby shall be construed and administered under the laws of the State of New Hampshire, that the validity and effect of this agreement and of this trust shall be determined in accordance with the laws of that State.

Further, the trust shall be under the jurisdiction of the courts of the State of New

Hampshire and the Trustee shall voluntarily enter a general appearance in any legal action relating to an accounting of the trust or a declaratory judgment interpreting this trust agreement. The Trustee shall not be chargeable in any court other than one of the courts of that State.

[OPTIONAL] However, the Trustee, at any time and from time to time, in its discretion, may, (1) remove all or part of the trust estate and hold and administer the same in any other jurisdiction where the Trustee shall be then located, (2) change the situs of administration of any trust from one jurisdiction to another jurisdiction; and (3) elect that the law of such other jurisdiction shall thereafter govern the trust to such extent as may be necessary and appropriate, and to amend the administrative provisions of the trust as the Trustee deems appropriate to ensure compliance and compatibility with such law, whereupon the courts of such other jurisdiction shall have the power to effectuate the purposes of this trust agreement to such extent. The determination of the Trustee as to any such removal of assets or change of situs or governing law shall be conclusive and binding on all persons interested in such trust.

16.   AMENDMENT AND REVOCATION. The Grantor reserves the right at any time or from time to time without the consent of any person and without notice to any person other than the Trustee to revoke or modify the trust hereby created, in whole or in part, to change the beneficiaries hereof, or to withdraw the whole or any part of the trust estate by filing notice of such revocation, modification, change, or withdrawal with the Trustee; provided, however, that the terms of this agreement may not be modified by the Grantor in such manner as to increase the obligations or alter the rates of the commissions of the Trustee without its written consent.

The Trustee is authorized and directed at any time and from time to time following the death or incapacity of the Grantor, without the consent of any person, to amend or modify the provisions of this trust agreement in order to qualify the Qualified Domestic Trust of the Marital Share for the federal estate tax marital deduction under Section 2056A of the Internal Revenue Code upon written notice of such amendment or modification to all beneficiaries to whom or to whose use the current net income of the trust estate is at the time authorized or required to be paid or applied, and who shall at the time be at least eighteen (18) years of age. Any such amendment or modification shall be effective, to the extent permitted by law, as if signed by the Grantor prior to the Grantor's death or incapacity.

17.   DEFINITIONS. Whenever used in this trust agreement, the words "child," "children," or "issue" are intended to include not only persons who are descendants by blood, but also persons and issue of persons who have been adopted according to law prior to their attaining the age of eighteen (18) years.

References to the "Internal Revenue Code" or "Code" or to provisions thereof are to the Internal Revenue Code of 1986, as amended at the time in question. References to the "Treasury Regulations," "Regulations" and "Regs." are to the

Treasury Regulations under the Code. If, by the time in question, a particular provision of the Code has been renumbered, or the Code has been superseded by a subsequent federal tax law, the reference shall be deemed to be to the renumbered provision or the corresponding provision of the subsequent law, unless to do so would clearly be contrary to the Grantor's intent as expressed in this Trust Agreement, and a similar rule shall apply to references to the Regulations.

Masculine, feminine and neuter pronouns shall each include all genders, and the singular shall include the plural and vice versa, where the context or facts so admit.

The captions and paragraph headings of this trust agreement are inserted only as a matter of convenience and for reference and in no way define, limit or describe the scope or intent of this agreement, nor in any way affect this agreement.

Whenever used in this trust agreement, the word "hardship" shall refer to distributions from the Qualified Domestic Trust to the Grantor's surviving spouse which are exempt from tax in accordance with Section 2056A(b)(3)(B) of the Internal Revenue Code of 1986, and the regulations thereunder, or any provision successor thereto.

Whenever used in this trust agreement, the words "individual citizen of the United States" shall refer to an individual citizen of the United States with a tax home, as defined in Section 911(d)(3) of the Internal Revenue Code of 1986, or any provision successor thereto, in the United States.

Whenever used in this trust agreement, the term "domestic corporation" shall refer to that term as defined in Section 20.2056A2(c) of Proposed Treasury Regulations, or any provision successor thereto.

18. <u>EXECUTION</u>. This trust agreement, and any amendments hereto, shall be effective when executed by the Grantor, notwithstanding that the signature of the Trustee is provided for, the Trustee's signature being intended to denote the acceptance of the Trustee to serve in that capacity only.

This trust agreement may be executed in any number of counterparts with the same effect as if all of the parties had signed the same document. All counterparts shall be construed together and shall constitute one agreement.

_____   _____
Witness   _____ , Grantor
_____   _____
Witness   _____ , Trustee

STATE OF NEW HAMPSHIRE
COUNTY OF _____

The foregoing instrument was acknowledged before me on _____, 2009 by _____.

Notary Public/Justice of the Peace
My Commission Expires:
(Seal)

Page 892: Add new Forms 71 and 72 after Form 70 in the text:

FORM 71   Ethics Committee Opinion #2008-09/1: Drafting Lawyer Acting as Fiduciary for Client

New Hampshire Bar Association
Ethics Committee Opinion #2008-09/1

Drafting Lawyer Acting as Fiduciary for Client
May 13, 2009

RULE REFERENCES:

*Rule 1.1(b)	*Rule 1.7(b)
*Rule 1.4(a)(2)	*Rule 1.7(b)(4)
*Rule 1.4(b)	*Rule 1.8
*Rule 1.6	*Rule 1.8(a)
*Rule 1.7	*Rule 2.1

SUBJECTS:

*Adverse Effect on Professional Judgment	*Conflict of Interests
*Adverse Representation	*Consultation
*Attorney-Client Relationship	*Estates
*Business Activities	*Harsh Reality Test
*Client Communications	*Independent Judgment
*Competence	*Fees
*Confidentiality	*Probate
	*Wills

ANNOTATIONS:

When drafting various estate planning documents, New Hampshire attorneys are frequently requested by their clients to act in one or more fiduciary roles. The drafting attorney may, at the request of the client, be inserted as a fiduciary in the document or documents being drafted by that attorney, provided that: (1) there has been adequate disclosure of information to the client, as required under Rule 1.4; and (2) the attorney makes a determination as to whether the personal interest of the attorney in being a fiduciary would require compliance with Rule 1.7(b) and that the attorney may continue to exercise independent professional judgment in recommending to the client the best choices for fiduciaries under Rule 2.1. In order to document compliance with these Rules, it would be the best practice for the attorney to confirm in writing the "informed consent" of the client to the selection of the drafting attorney as the named fiduciary.

It is ethically impermissible for an attorney to name that attorney, by default, or require the client to appoint the attorney as a fiduciary, in a document drafted by that attorney.

In the event the drafting attorney actively advertises and solicits clients to consider using the attorney as a nominated fiduciary in documents drafted by the attorney, the relationship that results from such advertisement and solicitation may constitute a "business transaction with the client" and thereby requires compliance with the more stringent Rule 1.8(a).

I.   QUESTIONS PRESENTED:

1. May a lawyer who is drafting a will or other estate planning documents, identify the lawyer as the named executor or other fiduciary in the documents, at the request of the client?
2. May a lawyer identify himself or herself, by default, as the executor or other fiduciary in a client's estate planning documents?
3. May a lawyer solicit and/or require clients to identify the lawyer as a fiduciary in estate planning documents being prepared by the lawyer?

II.   Introduction. It has been common practice for estate planning attorneys in New Hampshire to act as executors, guardians, trustees, administrators and attorneys-in-fact for clients. This is not surprising when considering the role an attorney plays as a trusted advisor, and the complexity and volume of New Hampshire statutes and regulations that are applicable to fiduciaries, and the administration of estates and trusts. However, the selection of appropriate persons or entities to act as a fiduciary is one of the most important decisions a client makes during the estate planning process.

This Committee's Formal Opinion #1987-88/9 ("Prior Opinion") addressed the restrictions on an attorney's ability to act as both the attorney and a fiduciary for the client, and the fees that may be ethically charged by the attorney in both capacities. Subsequent to the Prior Opinion, New Hampshire's Supreme Court adopted a total revision of New Hampshire's *Rules of Professional Responsibility* (where applicable "Rules" or "Rule"); *see,* Order dated July 25, 2007. While the new Rules applicable to the questions posed above are very similar to those that were in effect when the Prior Opinion was adopted, there were significant changes pertaining to what is required for "informed consent" and the necessity that a client's informed consent be confirmed in writing with respect to potential Rule 1.7 conflicts. Accordingly, this Opinion will examine the questions raised above in the context of the new Rules. Unlike the Prior Opinion, however, this Opinion will **not** address the issue of what fees may be reasonably charged by the drafting attorney, when later acting as a fiduciary resulting from a designation in the document prepared by the attorney; while the Prior Opinion will still be useful, there have been significant changes that impact such fee issues. [1]

For the purposes of this Opinion, references to the "attorney" or "lawyer" shall be deemed to include all members of the attorney's law firm as well as the law firm. The term "fiduciary," includes the following roles typically involved in estate planning documents: (a) an executor, (b) a trustee, (c) an Agent named under either a financial durable power of attorney or health care power of attorney in an Advance Directive, (d) a guardian designated under a Nomination of Guardian pursuant to RSA 464-A:10,II, or (e) a designated agent under a Declaration of Final Arrangements pursuant to RSA 290:17, I. The same ethical analysis would apply regardless of whether the attorney is named as the primary acting fiduciary or as an alternate or successor fiduciary.

III. Attorney Becoming a Designated Fiduciary at the Client's Request.

When an attorney has a long-standing relationship with the client or the client's family, and is a trusted friend and professional, it is not uncommon for the client to request that the attorney serve in one or more fiduciary capacities in the client's estate planning documents. In fact, it is not unusual for clients to believe, incorrectly, that they **must** name an attorney as the executor or trustee. However, the designation of the attorney as a fiduciary raises potential conflicts of interest, along with certain other ethical questions. The ABA's Formal Opinion No. 02-426 ("ABA Opinion") provides a comprehensive analysis of this issue, under ABA's current Model Rules (upon which the New Hampshire Rules are based in large part).

A.   *Requisite Competency.* No matter how a client may initiate the request, before the attorney can begin drafting a document that names the attorney as a fiduciary, the attorney must first have the requisite knowledge and experience to be able to satisfy the Competence requirements of Rule 1.1(b). Given the increasing complexity of the rules and procedures

---

[1] With respect to the executor and administrator fiduciary role, subject to the jurisdiction of the Probate Court, there has been a significant change resulting from *In Re Estate of Rolfe*, 136 N.H. 294 (1992). Also, in the event the estate planning process involves flat fee charges, the drafting attorney need be mindful of the change in Rule 1.15(d) requiring that withdrawal of client funds may occur "only as fees are earned or expenses incurred"; see *New Hampshire Comment* for Rule 1.15.

involved in estate and trust practice and administration, this initial ethical inquiry should not be taken lightly by the attorney. [2]

    B.   *Discussion of Options.* When a client asks an attorney to serve in the role of fiduciary, the attorney must comply with Rule 1.4(a)(2) and Rule 1.4(b). [3] The attorney must frankly discuss all available options pertaining to the selection of fiduciaries for the client's documents, and during this discussion may disclose to the client the attorney's availability to serve as the fiduciary, ABA Opinion, at pages 2-3. The attorney and client should discuss whether or not the client's goals will be better served with the attorney serving as a fiduciary rather than the client's family, friends or a professional fiduciary, and the relative skills and experience each may have to assist in the performance of the fiduciary's duties. The discussion should include a disclosure that the professional fiduciary is typically fully bonded, and whether or not an attorney who will act as a fiduciary will be covered by errors and omissions insurance. The attorney should specifically discuss the relative costs of having the attorney or others serve as a fiduciary, as well as how the attorney will charge for the fiduciary services, depending upon the expected complexity or simplicity of the plan and the client's family's dynamics. "When the client is considering appointment of the lawyer as a fiduciary, the lawyer must inform the client that the lawyer will receive compensation for serving as fiduciary, whether the amount is subject

---

[2] The minimum requirements for legal competence under Rule 1.1(b) include:
        (1) specific knowledge about the field of law in which the lawyer practices;
        (2) performance of the techniques of practice with skill;
        (3) identification of areas beyond the lawyer's competence and bringing those areas to the client's attention;
        (4) proper preparation; and
        (5) attention to details and schedules necessary to assure that the matter undertaken is completed with no avoidable harm to the client's interest."

[3] Rule 1.4. Client Communications provides as follows:
  (a) A lawyer shall:
      (1) promptly inform the client of any decision or circumstance with respect to which the client's informed consent is required by these Rules;
      (2) reasonably consult with the client about the means by which the client's objectives are to be accomplished;
      (3) keep the client reasonably informed about the status of the matter.
      (4) Promptly comply with reasonable requests for information; and
      (5) consult with the client about any relevant limitation on the lawyer's conduct when the lawyer knows that the client expects assistance not permitted by the Rules of Professional Conduct or other law.
  (b) A lawyer shall explain the legal and practical aspects of a matter and alternative courses of action to the extent that such explanation is reasonably necessary to permit the client to make informed decisions regarding the representation.

to statutory limits or court approval, and how the compensation will be calculated and approved." ABA Opinion, page 4. Discussing the option of appointing the attorney as a co-trustee, along with a family member, to assist with the growing technical complexities of trust administration, may also be warranted. The discussion should also address the fact that appointed professional fiduciaries, family members, or friends, as well as the named attorney, may retain an attorney to advise and assist them, as needed, to properly perform their fiduciary duties.

    C.   *Independent Professional Judgment.* During the initial discussion with the client pertaining to the fiduciary selection process, the attorney must not "allow his potential self-interest [in serving as a fiduciary] to interfere with his exercise of independent professional judgment in recommending to the client the best choices for fiduciaries." *ABA Opinion*, at page 3. *See also* Rule 2.1. [4] The attorney's discussion must also address possible limitations that could result from the attorney serving as fiduciary. For example: if later faced with the client's potential incapacity and/or involuntary placement, the attorney will be unable to serve as the client's attorney and may become an adverse witness, potentially placing the attorney and client at odds over the issue. Similarly, the attorney will probably also be unable to represent the proponent of the document in question in any proceeding adjudicating the capacity of the client. Clarifications or corrections of scrivener's errors in the relevant documents may also become problematic.

    D.   *Conflict of Interest.* After considering Rule 1.7, the drafting attorney must evaluate whether the attorney's appointment as a fiduciary in a document drafted by the attorney, at the voluntary choice of the client, presents "a significant risk that the representation of ....[the client] will be materially limited ... by a personal interest of the lawyer", and therefore triggers application of Rule 1.7. [5] The attorney who is named as a fiduciary in the document is clearly

---

[4] Rule 2.1., "Advisor" provides as follows:
    "In representing a client, a lawyer shall exercise independent professional judgment and render candid advice. In rendering advice, a lawyer may refer not only to law but to other considerations such as moral, economic, social and political factors that may be relevant to the client's situation."
[5] Rule 1.7., "Conflicts of Interest" provides as follows:
    (a) Except as provided in paragraph (b), a lawyer shall not represent a client if the representation involves a concurrent conflict of interest. A concurrent conflict of interest exists if:
        (1) the representation of one client will be directly adverse to another client; or

Ethics Opinion #2008-9/1:
Drafting Lawyer Acting as Fiduciary for Client

acquiring a possible and lucrative financial interest in that client's future estate or trust. This Committee, however, does not reach the conclusion that a "concurrent conflict of interest" under Rule 1.7(a) always exists in these situations that would trigger having to confirm the client's informed consent in writing, as provided in Rule 1.7(b). Instructive on this issue is the following excerpt under the header "Appointment of Scrivener as Fiduciary", ACTEC Commentaries on the Model Rules of Professional Conduct (4th Ed., 2006), at page 95:

> "As a general proposition, lawyers should be permitted to assist adequately informed clients who wish to appoint their lawyers as fiduciaries. Accordingly, a lawyer should be free to prepare a document that appoints the lawyer to a fiduciary office so long as the client is properly informed, the appointment does not violate the conflict of interest rules of MRPC 1.7, and *the appointment is not the product of undue influence or improper solicitation by the lawyer*. [emphasis added]"

Similarly, the ABA Comment 8, to Rule 1.8. while implying that being named as a fiduciary does not constitute a "business transaction with the client" under Rule 1.8, nevertheless cautions that the situation may require a conflicts disclosure under Rule 1.7. [6] There is some confusion now caused by the Ethics Committee Comment to Rule 1.8, which states in part that "[i]n New Hampshire, Rule 1.8(a) applies to a lawyer's advice as to, or preparation of, an instrument designating or appointing a lawyer ... as executor, trustee or other fiduciary position ...." The Committee notes that this statement is erroneous and may simply be the result of a

---

(2) there is a significant risk that the representation of one or more clients will be materially limited by the lawyer's responsibilities to another client, a former client or a third person or by a personal interest of the lawyer.

    (b) Notwithstanding the existence of a concurrent conflict of interest under paragraph (a), a lawyer may represent a client if:

        (1) the lawyer reasonably believes that the lawyer will be able to provide competent and diligent representation to each affected client;

        (2) the representation is not prohibited by law;

        (3) the representation does not involve the assertion of a claim by one client against another client represented by the lawyer in the same litigation or other proceeding before a tribunal; and

        (4)each affected client gives informed consent, confirmed in writing.

[6] Comment 8 of the ABA Model Rules, Rule 1.8, provides as follows:

"[8] This Rule [Rule 1.8] does not prohibit a lawyer from seeking to have the lawyer or a partner or associate of the lawyer named as executor of the client's estate or to another potentially lucrative fiduciary position. Nevertheless, such appointments will be subject to the general conflict of interest provision in Rule 1.7 when there is a significant risk that the lawyer's interest in obtaining the appointment will materially limit the lawyer's independent professional judgment in advising the client concerning the choice of an executor or other fiduciary. In obtaining the client's informed consent to the conflict, the lawyer should advise the client concerning the nature and extent of the lawyer's financial interest in the appointment, as well as the availability of alternative candidates for the position."

scrivener's error (which should have read "Rule 1.8(a) *may* apply"). The Committee is in the process of revising this Comment in a manner consistent with this Opinion.

There may also be other circumstances that further complicate this ethical analysis. As an example, situations where the attorney represents other family members will add additional potential conflicts that must also be considered. This is accentuated in family situations where the client is seeking to intentionally disinherit another family member who is also a client of the drafting attorney; this may, in certain situations, well prevent the attorney from ethically accepting being named a fiduciary, especially if for confidentiality reasons the attorney is prohibited from obtaining required informed consent by multiple clients. For example, ABA Formal Opinion 05-434 discusses the implications of the attorney drafting a will for one client that disinherits a beneficiary whom the lawyer also represents on unrelated matters, concluding while generally there would be no prohibition, there may be other circumstances that could trigger a prohibited conflict of interest. Ethical dilemmas faced in the representation of multiple family members was also addressed in ABA Formal Opinion 02-428, discussing issues surrounding representation of a testator at the request of and paid for by an intended beneficiary who is a client of the attorney, that concludes that the Rules "do not prohibit multiple representation of family legal interests as long as the lawyer's independent professional judgment is maintained, the lawyer complies with the rules on client confidences, and any conflicts of interest are resolved under the applicable rules." The drafting attorney, therefore, must be extremely vigilant and properly examine all potential other conflicts that may impact upon this fiduciary selection issue.

The attorney must be mindful that a Rule 1.7 analysis will typically only take place, in hindsight, after something has gone dreadfully wrong, and that the facts will be viewed objectively by other disinterested lawyers. Illustrative of such a possible retroactive review of the attorney's actions is New Hampshire's application of its "harsh reality test" *after* an attorney has determined that it is appropriate to request a client's consent to a conflict of interest under Rule 1.7(b).

"[I]f a disinterested lawyer were to look back at the inception of this representation once something goes wrong, would that lawyer seriously question the wisdom of the first attorney's requesting the client's consent to this representation *or question whether there had been full disclosure to the client prior to obtaining the consent.* If this 'harsh reality test' may not be readily satisfied by the inquiring attorney, the inquiring attorney and other members of the inquiring attorney's firm should decline representation ..." [emphasis supplied]. New Hampshire Comment to Rule 1.7

Written confirmation of the client's informed consent of a concurrent conflict of interest under Rule 1.7(b)(4) is not required under all circumstances when documents name the drafting attorney as a fiduciary. Clearly, however, the better practice would be for the drafting attorney to always provide such written confirmation of the client's decision. The written confirmation should document the disclosures and discussions mandated under Rule 1.4. and, if applicable, Rule 1.7, and the client's selection of the attorney to act as fiduciary. See Rule 1.0(c) for a definition of "informed consent".[7]

    E.   *Confidentiality.* The attorney must analyze and discuss with the client the effect that Rule 1.6. ("Confidentiality of Information") may have upon the attorney, when acting in the fiduciary capacity as appointed in the client's documents. [8] The client must understand that the attorney may intentionally or inadvertently use or rely upon intimate details relating to the creation of estate planning documents that would not be available to other fiduciaries during the

---

[7] "Informed Consent" as defined under Rule 1.0 (e) "denotes the agreement by a person to a proposed course of conduct [nominating the client's attorney to act as a fiduciary in the client's document] after the lawyer has communicated adequate information and explanation about the material risks of and reasonably available alternatives to the proposed course of conduct." If a client's informed consent is confirmed in writing, it should include the substance of that discussion regarding fiduciary choices, and the ultimate selection by the client of the attorney, as is required under Rule 1.4, and discussed above.

[8] Rule 1.6., "Confidentiality of Information" provides as follows:

    (a) A lawyer shall not reveal information relating to the representation of a client unless the client gives informed consent, the disclosure is impliedly authorized in order to carry out the representation, or the disclosure is permitted by paragraph (b).

    (b) A lawyer may reveal such information to the extent the lawyer reasonably believes necessary:

        (1) to prevent reasonably certain death or substantial bodily harm or to prevent the client from committing a criminal act that the lawyer believes is likely to result in substantial injury to the financial interests or property of another; or

        (2) to secure legal advice about the lawyer's compliance with these Rules; or

        (3) to establish a claim or defense on behalf of the lawyer in controversy between the lawyer and the client, to establish a defense to a criminal charge or civil claim against the lawyer based upon conduct in which the client was involved, or to respond to allegations in any proceeding concerning the lawyer's representation of the client; or

        (4) to comply with other law or a court order.

Ethics Opinion #2008-9/1:
Drafting Lawyer Acting as Fiduciary for Client

estate or trust administration process. If there is a will contest or a question as to either the interpretation of the document drafted by the attorney/fiduciary or the intent of the client, the drafting attorney may be the primary witness, and may be precluded from handling any litigation involving the particular document or the estate. While having the intimate knowledge and confidential information of the client may aid considerably in the ultimate realization of client objectives, there may be situations where it could possibly complicate the fiduciary's role. Further complicating the issue is that the fiduciary has the authority to waive attorney-client privilege, thereby giving the attorney/fiduciary the power to waive the privilege with respect to the client's communications with the attorney.

IV.   Drafting Documents Naming the Drafting Attorney as the "Default" Fiduciary. The second question presented involves the "default" designation of the attorney to serve as a fiduciary in the documents drafted by the attorney. This question presumes that this practice occurs **prior** to there being any discussion with the client concerning the designation of appropriate fiduciaries, or should the attorney require the client to use the attorney as a fiduciary. Based upon the above discussions, this Committee concludes that such a "default" designation is ethically prohibited under the current Rules. The Committee also believes that this practice could not be properly "cured" by subsequent client discussions and disclosure.

V.   Drafting Attorney Soliciting Use of Fiduciary Services. The third and final question presented, involves the active solicitation of the client to use the services of the attorney as a fiduciary in one or more of the client's estate planning documents. All of the ethical disclosure requirements previously reviewed apply. This question raises the additional question of whether or not the law firm's active solicitation of fiduciary services creates a "business interest" that would also trigger the application of a Rule 1.8 disclosure. The ABA Opinion specifically allows the lawyer "to disclose his own availability to serve as a fiduciary" when discussing fiduciary selection options (at page 3). This question, however, presumes a greater level of solicitation of services by the drafting attorney. Such a determination will depend upon the specific facts involved in any given situation. For example, if the lawyer (1) advertises fiduciary services, and (2) actively solicits its clients consider selecting the lawyer as the fiduciary in the documents drafted by the lawyer, it would be difficult to argue that such solicitation does not

Page 9 of 11

transform the fiduciary selection by the client into a "business transaction with a client." If such practice is determined to involve a "business transaction with a client", then compliance with Rule 1.8 (a) would be required.[9] The more stringent Rule 1.8(a) conflict compliance requires (1) informed consent in writing *that must be signed by the client*; and (2), that the client must be advised in writing by the attorney "of the desirability of seeking and is given a reasonable opportunity to seek the advice of independent legal counsel on the transaction". The attorney is further cautioned that, in certain circumstances involving concurrent conflicts of interest, the attorney may need to comply simultaneously with **both** Rule 1.8(a) and Rule 1.7(b).

It is beyond the scope of this Opinion as to whether or not, and/or how the law firm may ethically establish a fiduciary services law-related business separate and apart from its legal practice, in compliance with Rule 5.7, "Responsibilities Regarding Law-Related Services."

VI. Summary.

When drafting various estate planning documents, New Hampshire attorneys are frequently requested by their clients to act in one or more fiduciary roles. The drafting attorney may, at the request of the client, be inserted as a fiduciary in the document or documents being drafted by that attorney, provided that: (1) there has been adequate disclosure of information to the client, as required under Rule 1.4; and (2) the attorney makes a determination as to whether the personal interest of the attorney in being a fiduciary would require compliance with Rule 1.7(b). In order to document compliance with these Rules, it would be the best practice for the attorney to confirm in writing the "informed consent" of the client to the selection of the drafting attorney as the named fiduciary.

---

[9] Rule 1.8(a) provides as follows:

    (a)   A lawyer shall not enter into a business transaction with a client or knowingly acquire an ownership, possessory, security or other pecuniary interest adverse to a client unless:

        (1) the transaction and terms on which the lawyer acquires the interest are fair and reasonable to the client and are fully disclosed and transmitted in writing in a manner that can be reasonably understood by the client;

        (2) the client is advised in writing of the desirability of seeking and is given a reasonable opportunity to seek the advice of independent legal counsel on the transaction; and

        (3) the client gives informed consent, in a writing signed by the client, to the essential terms of the transaction and the lawyer's role in the transaction, including whether the lawyer is representing the client in the transaction.

It is ethically impermissible for an attorney to name that attorney, by default, or require the client to appoint the attorney as a fiduciary, in a document drafted by that attorney.

In the event the drafting attorney actively advertises and solicits clients to consider using the attorney as a nominated fiduciary in documents drafted by the attorney, the relationship that results from such advertisement and solicitation may constitute a "business transaction with the client" and thereby requires compliance with the more stringent Rule 1.8(a).

Ethics Opinion #2008-9/1:
Drafting Lawyer Acting as Fiduciary for Client

FORM 72   *In re* Estate of Geraldine W. Webber

THE STATE OF NEW HAMPSHIRE

STRAFFORD COUNTY   TRUST DOCKET
                                                  7TH CIRCUIT COURT
                                                  PROBATE DIVISION

GERALDINE W. WEBBER REVOCABLE LIVING TRUST

318-2013-EQ-00694

IN RE: ESTATE OF GERALDINE W. WEBBER

318-2012-ET-01509

<u>ORDER ON PETITION TO SET ASIDE THE GERALDINE W. WEBBER REVOCABLE
TRUST DATED MAY 2, 2012; MOTION TO RE-EXAMINE PROBATE WILL; AND
ORAL MOTION TO ADMIT AUDIO RECORDING</u>

In this consolidated action, <u>see</u> No. 318-2013-EQ-00694 (Index #1) (Order granting

Prayer B); No. 318-2012-ET-01509 (Index #29) (Order granting Prayer A),[1] Memorial

Sloan-Kettering Cancer Center and Shriners' Hospital for Children (the "Hospitals") has

filed a *Petition to Set Aside the Geraldine W. Webber Revocable Trust Dated May 2,
2012* (Index #1)("Petition"), seeking invalidation of the trust (the "2012 Trust"), and a

Motion to Re-Examine Probate Will (Estate Case Index #29)("Motion to Re-Examine"),

asking for disallowance of the Will of Geraldine W. Webber dated May 2, 2012 (the

"2012 Will"), and allowance of her February 5, 2009 Will (the "2009 Will"), together with

a codicil to it dated February 19, 2009 and a "Bequest List" dated November 19, 2009.

---

[1] When necessary to refer to one matter alone, the Court will denote case number 318-2013-EQ-00694 as
the "Equity Case" and case number 318-2012-ET-01509 as the "Estate Case." However, for simplicity's
sake in this Order, it will refer to the index numbers in the equity case only unless otherwise indicated.

1

See *Statement in Support of Motion to Re-Examine Probate Will In Solemn Form* at 14 (Estate Case Index #29).

Petitioners Barbara L. Wardwell, Betsy A. Lodge, Renee Currie, and Joanne B. Peterson (the "Wardwell Petitioners"), later joined the *Petition* and *Motion*, see Equity Case Index #2; Estate Case Index #34, as have Brett W. Webber, see Equity Case Index #15; Estate Case Index #41, and Michael Williams, see Equity Case Index #9; Estate Case Index #35 (collectively, with the Hospitals, the "Petitioners"). Both the *Petition* and *Motion* seek to set aside the 2012 Trust and 2012 Will (collectively the "2012 Estate Planning Documents") claiming that: (1) Geraldine W. Webber ("Ms. Webber") lacked capacity to execute the 2012 Estate Planning Documents; and/or (2) they were the product of undue influence exerted on her by then Portsmouth Police Officer Aaron Goodwin ("Officer Goodwin").[2] Those concerns were tried before this Court over a period of ten-days, during which the Hospitals sought admission of an audio-recording taken during the course of a purported Portsmouth Police Department investigation. See *Memorandum of Law Concerning RSA 516:36, II* (Index #101). Admission was seasonably objected to by: (1) Officer Goodwin, see *Memorandum re: Admissibility of Portsmouth Police Department's Internal Affairs Investigation Recording* (Index #102); (2) Gary W. Holmes, Trustee of the 2012 Trust and Executor of the 2012 Will (the "Fiduciary"); and (3) the City of Portsmouth Police Department.

For the reasons set forth below, the Court GRANTS the *Petition* having determined that the 2012 Estate Planning Documents are rendered invalid as the product of undue influence. Petitions alleging undue influence almost universally present difficult and

---

[2] For convenience, the Court will refer to Aaron Goodwin generically as "Officer Goodwin" because his official position at the Portsmouth Police Department changed during the pendency of this case.

2

close cases for adjudication. This application is no different. Officer Goodwin, the primary distributee of the 2012 Estate Planning Documents, stood in a confidential relationship with Ms. Webber. That so, the Fiduciary and Aaron Goodwin, as proponents of the Estate Planning Documents (collectively, the "Proponents"), bear the burden of demonstrating that they were not the fruit of undue influence. The Court rules that they have not satisfied their burden. Thus, the 2012 Estate Planning Documents are declared void.

The *Motion to Re-Examine* (Estate Case Index #29) is GRANTED IN PART. The request to disallow the 2012 Will on the basis of undue influence is GRANTED, id. Prayer D, and the request to order proof in solemn form is DENIED AS MOOT. See id. Prayer B. The Court DEFERS ruling on Prayer E of the *Motion to Re-Examine* pending further proceedings in relation to: (1) appointment of a successor to Attorney Gary Holmes given invalidation of the 2012 Will nominating him executor; and (2) consideration of whether another alternative testamentary instrument may be admitted into probate in its stead. Finally, because it grants the relief requested regarding the invalidity of the 2012 Estate Planning Documents owing to undue influence, the Court DENIES AS MOOT, the Petitioners' request to set them aside on the basis of lack of capacity[3] and the oral motion to admit the audio-recording.

I.   **Applicable Law**

A. *Undue Influence*

As mentioned earlier, the Petitioners maintain that the 2012 Estate Planning Documents should be set aside by this Court because they resulted from undue

_____

[3] As discussed infra, lack of capacity, under long established standards for legal capacity, poses an even closer question.

3

influence exerted on Ms. Webber by Officer Goodwin over the last two years of her life.

See generally, Bartis v. Bartis, 107 N.H. 34, 37 (1966)(will); RSA 564-B:4-406 (trusts).

"Undue influence" has repeatedly been described in this jurisdiction as:

> the use of such appliances and influences as take away the
> free will of the testator, and substitute another's will for his,
> so that in effect the instrument is not the expression of the
> wishes of the testator in the disposition of the property, but of
> the wishes of another. But, where no fraud or deception is
> practiced, mere persuasion will not invalidate a will on the
> ground of undue influence. On the contrary, a testator may
> properly receive the advice, opinions, and arguments of
> others, and if, after all such advice, opinions, and arguments,
> the testator is not controlled by them to the extent of
> surrendering his free agency and yielding his own judgment
> or will, then there is no such undue influence as is required
> to be proved to avoid the will.

Albee v. Osgood, 79 N.H. 89, 92 (1918). The influence exerted must amount "to force

and coercion, destroying free agency, and not merely the influence of affection, or

merely the desire of gratifying another; but it must appear that the will was obtained by

this coercion." Bartlett v. McKay, 80 N.H. 574, 574-75 (1923)(quotations omitted).

Mere kindness and/or affection, id., or desire to gratify another, Albee, 79 N.H. at 92,

whatever the motives of the influencer, cf. In re Estate of West, 522 A.2d 1256, 1265

(Del. 1987), is not sufficient to support a finding of undue influence. Id. However,

"importunity that could not be resisted," Albee, 79 N.H. at 92, or documents procured

"for the sake of peace," Gaffney v. Coffey, 81 N.H. 300, 304 (1924), have been

determined to equate to "force or fear" sufficient to support a conclusion that undue

influence was exerted upon a testatrix or settlor. Bartis, 107 N.H. at 37. Consistent with

these guideposts, Connecticut courts have explained that "pressure" in the context of

undue influence is "[p]ressure, of whatever character, whether acting on the fears or

4

hopes, if so exerted as to overpower volition without convincing the judgment, is a species of constraint under which no will can be made . . . . though no force was either used or threatened." In re Hobbes, 47 A. 678, 680 (Conn. 1900).

Although the established test to prove undue influence appears rigorous, New Hampshire case law recognizes that undue influence, by its nature, is fact dependent. See In re Estate of Cass, 143 N.H. 57, 61 (1998). "Generally, a court considers all the circumstances surrounding a disposition, including the relationship between the parties, the physical and mental condition of the donor, the reasonableness and nature of the disposition, and the personalities of the parties." Id. (quotations omitted). Although a finding of incapacity is also not required to conclude that dispositions were the product of undue influence, cf. Gaffney, 81 N.H. at 301, 306, it has been long recognized that "manifestly less influence is required to dominate a weak mind than to control a strong one." Harvey v. Provandie, 83 N.H. 236, 240 (1928); cf. Patten v. Cilley, 67 N.H. 520, 528 (1894)(quality of mind a material fact). The level of dependency on the influencer is a factor to consider; as "[e]xperience has shown that in the great majority of cases transactions are not fair and honest in which a person procures a gift from one who is dependent upon him or in some way under his control." Edgerly v. Edgerly, 73 N.H. 407, 408 (1905). As one court observed (and many others have quoted) undue influence:

> may result from more subtle conduct designed to create irresistible ascendency by imperceptible means. . . . The nature of . . . undue influence is such that [it] often work[s] in veiled and secret ways. The power of a strong will over an irresolute character or one weakened by disease, overindulgence or age may be manifest although not shown by gross or palpable instrumentalities. Undue influence may be inferred from the nature of the testamentary provisions

5

> accompanied by questionable conditions . . . . . When the
> donor is enfeebled by age or disease, although not reaching
> to unsoundness of mind, and the relation between the
> parties is fiduciary or intimate, the transaction ordinarily is
> subject to careful scrutiny. . . . Age, weakness and disease
> are always important factors. Relations of intimacy,
> confidence and affection in combination with other
> circumstances are entitled to weight.

Neill v. Brackett, 126 N.E. 93, 94 (Mass. 1920). As such, undue influence may be

shown where "there is substantial evidence not only of opportunity and ability, but of

design and accomplishment." Harvey, 83 N.H. at 240; Loveren v. Eaton, 80 N.H. 62, 64

(1921)(evidence showed opportunity and ability, but not accomplishment); Albee, 79

N.H. at 92 (opportunity does not equate with accomplishment); 36 Am. Jur. Proof of

Facts 2d Undue Influence in Execution of Will §2 (elements of undue influence); cf.

O'Rourke v. Hunter, 848 N.E.2d 382, 392-93 (Mass. 2006)("Four considerations are

usually present in a case of undue influence: that an (1) unnatural disposition has been

made (2) by a person susceptible to undue influence to the advantage of someone (3)

with an opportunity to exercise undue influence and (4) who in fact has used that

opportunity to procure the contested disposition through improper means." (quotations

omitted)). In conducting this analysis, courts have long been entitled to rely on the

testimony of lay witnesses concerning the mental capacity of a testator/settlor who knew

and actually observed the individual's susceptibility to another's influence. See, e.g.,

Pattee v. Whitcomb, 72 N.H. 249, 251 (1903); relying on Hardy, 56 N.H. at 241, 244,

248. Further, undue influence may be demonstrated by circumstantial evidence. See,

e.g., Patten, 67 N.H. at 558.

6

The Court now turns to the evidentiary burdens, and "whether [and, if so, when they lie] with the proponent of the will or the allegator of undue influence." Albee, 79 N.H. at 91. In New Hampshire, "the law presumes the absence of undue influence upon proof of the voluntary, formal execution of the will by a competent testator and that, *in the absence of circumstances arousing suspicion*, the proponent of the will is not required to offer express affirmative proof of the absence of undue influence." Id. (emphasis added). This "presumption of fact, which excuses such offers of proof, however, neither extinguishes the original issue nor shifts the burden of proof to the contestant. It simply suspends the requirement of further proof of the voluntary character of the testator's act until it is called in question, if at all, by the submission of *substantial evidence* of undue influence by the contestant." Gaffney, 81 N.H. at 306-07 (emphasis added).

Where a distributee/beneficiary is acting in a "fiduciary capacity" or is in a "confidential relationship" with the testatrix/grantor, he has "the burden of proving an absence of undue influence. This [rule is] based upon the inference of undue influence which arises in cases in which the beneficiary of a transfer holds a position of trust and confidence with the party making the transfer." Archer v. Dow, 126 N.H. 24, 28 (1985)(inter vivos transfer); relying on Edgerly, 73 N.H. at 408-09 ("[W]henever it appears that the donor was dependent upon or under the control of the donee, and that the latter took an active part in procuring the gift, it may be inferred that the gift was procured by undue influence." (will contest)); see, e.g., Patten, 67 N.H. at 528-29 ("*inferences of fact* may be drawn against a confidential agent in cases like this; but there is no *presumption of law* against the agent")(emphasis added); In re Estate of

7

Sharis, 990 N.E.2d 98, 102 (Mass. App. Ct. 2013)(grandson with power of attorney had "burden to prove that the will was not the product of his undue influence").[4]

"The term 'fiduciary or confidential relation' is a comprehensive one and exists wherever influence has been acquired and abused or confidence has been reposed and betrayed." Cornwell v. Cornwell, 116 N.H. 205, 209 (1976)(quotations omitted). A "confidential relationship" is found where "between two persons . . . one has gained the confidence of the other and purports to act or advise with the other's interest in mind. It is particularly likely to exist where there is a family relationship or one of friendship." Id. (quotations, brackets, and ellipses omitted). A confidential relationship has been found supported where an individual "was dependent upon [another] for transportation, banking services, the preparation of checks, and the payment of bills." Archer, 126 N.H. at 28.

It remains unclear to this Court, however, whether, in the instance of a confidential relationship, benefit, and resulting inference of undue influence, the quantum of proof necessary to demonstrate an absence of undue influence is elevated.[5] See generally 25 Am. Jur. 2d Duress and Undue Influence Weight and Sufficiency of Evidence §42 (noting split in jurisdictions over whether standard is preponderance, clear and convincing, or beyond a reasonable doubt). The law in New Hampshire is ambiguous at best. The New Hampshire Supreme Court, in a case whose facts could have supported a finding of confidential relationship, but did not include such a ruling, Gaffney, 81 N.H.

---

[4] Interestingly, some jurisdictions, unlike it seems New Hampshire, distinguish between inter-vivos transfers and will contests. See Matter of Estate of Todd, 585 N.W. 2d 273, 277 (Iowa 1998) overruled in part by Jackson v. Schrader, 676 N.W. 2d 599, 605 (2003); but cf. Burkhalter v. Burkhalter, 841 N.W. 2d 93, 100 (Iowa 2013)("if a confidential relationship existed between the testator and the putative beneficiary, the burden shifted to the recipient to establish by clear and convincing proof that the advantage was procured without undue influence")(quotations omitted).

[5] The Court requested briefing from the parties, but only the Fiduciary, see Index #103, and Hospitals, see Index #104, responded.

at 303-04 (observing that testatrix was dependent upon the influencer and he was her "advisor and counselor"), noted, inter alia, "if the jury should find upon a consideration of the conflicting testimony upon this issue that a condition of even balance of the evidence has been reached, the proponent of the will has failed to maintain the ultimate burden of proof which is his from the beginning to the end of the trial." Id. at 307; cf. Estate of Washburn, 141 N.H. at 663 (where testamentary capacity is contested, proponent maintains burden to demonstrate capacity throughout the proceeding, he is aided, however, by presumption of capacity, if contestant rebuts presumption, then proponent must persuade court, by a preponderance, of requisite capacity). This would appear to support a determination that the evidentiary measure of persuasiveness required of the will/trust proponent where there is a confidential relation is by a preponderance. It is uncertain, however, whether the Gaffney court even considered the inference of undue influence specifically arising from a confidential relation described by the Archer/ Edgerly courts, as the court first required the will contestant to offer "substantial evidence of undue influence." Gaffney, 81 N.H. at 303. Archer, 126 N.H. at 28, appears to indicate that in order to generate an inference of undue influence, the contestant need only show that the individual was: (1) a beneficiary and (2) "holds a position of trust and confidence." [6]

The Hospitals, parties potentially benefiting from an elevated quantum of proof, state that where there is a confidential relationship, the absence of undue influence merely must be shown by a preponderance of the evidence. *Memorandum of Law Concerning*

---

[6] The Court also takes account of the Archer court's specific affirmation of the trial court's ruling that as a result of the inference, the influencer has "the burden of proving *an absence* of undue influence." Id. In a matter concerning testamentary capacity, however, see Estate of Washburn, 141 N.H. at 662, the court was careful to note that if the presumption of capacity is rebutted, the will proponent was not required "to prove a negative – that the testatrix did not lack capacity." Id. at 663.

9

Burden of Proof at 4 (Index #104). A review of case law from other jurisdictions reveals a deep split.[7] *See generally* In re Last Will and Testament of Melson, 711 A.2d 783, 786-88 (Del. 1998)(in a case where beneficiary drafted the will, discussing split across jurisdictions regarding the application of burdens, and, by a divided court, adopts preponderance standard); *cf.* Burkhalter, 841 N.W. 2d at 101-106 (evaluating split over quantum of proof where no fiduciary relationship is involved). As one court noted in a case involving the applicable standard of proof in the absence of a fiduciary relationship:

> the courts have never been consistent in their definitions of the term, nor in the judicial tests used to evaluate proof of undue influence. The difficulty with the notion of undue influence in the context of a will is illustrated by the question of the appropriate standard of proof required to prevail on a claim. On the one hand, undue influence seems like a relative of fraud, which generally requires a heightened standard of proof. On the other hand, undue influence can occur without a material misrepresentation or omission, which makes it analogous to ordinary civil causes of action at law where a preponderance-of-the-evidence standard prevails.

Burkhalter, 841 N.W. 2d at 97 (quotations, brackets, and citations omitted).

Some jurisdictions impose a higher "clear and convincing" standard where there is a confidential or fiduciary relationship, noting that this standard "ensures that the law will protect those who cannot protect themselves." In re Jane Tiffany Living Trust 2001, U/A/D Nov. 5, 2001, 177 P.3d 1060, 1063 (Nev. 2008); *see generally* In re Estate of Bethurem, 313 P.3d 237 (Nev. 2013)(discussing quantum of proof to rebut undue influence where confidential relationship shown and lower standard to demonstrate

---

[7] The Delaware Supreme Court aptly noted that determination of the appropriate burden and quantum of proof "is complicated by the failure of the courts to clearly elucidate the sense in which they have used such terms as 'presumption,' 'inference,' 'burden of proof,' and the like." In re Last Will and Testament of Melson, 711 A.2d at 787 (quotations omitted). As such, the Court, when discussing precedent from other jurisdictions, uses the nomenclature chosen by that court (often "presumption"), recognizing, however, that the New Hampshire Supreme Court specifically decided that a confidential relationship and benefit creates an *inference* of undue influence. *See* Patten, 67 N.H. at 528-29.

10

undue influence in the absence of a presumption); <u>Berkowitz v. Berkowitz</u>, 162 A.2d

709, 711 (Conn. 1960)("clear preponderance"). Others have determined that where a

beneficiary assists in drafting *or procuring* a will, a presumption of undue influence

arises and this presumption must be rebutted beyond a reasonable doubt. <u>See</u>, <u>e.g.</u>,

<u>Looney v. Estate of Wade</u>, 839 S.W. 2d 531, 533-34 (Ark. 1992) Still others put a finer

point on the issue, and recognize that while ordinarily the quantum of proof needed to

rebut the presumption of undue influence where a non-family member is in a position of

confidence is elevated, the law will not create a presumption where the confidential

relationship involves children who are recognized to be the natural object of one's

bounty. <u>See</u>, <u>e.g.</u>, <u>Berkowitz</u>, 162 A.2d at 711.

The Court has considered the issue and is inclined to agree with those courts that

impose a clear and convincing standard. This Court has presided over many cases

involving claims of undue influence. Of them, numerous, if not the majority, have

concerned influence exerted over individuals rendered vulnerable by age or physical

decline, living in the shadows of society. By its nature undue influence by a confidante

is often unseen and nearly undetectable to the outside world. <u>See generally</u> <u>Neill</u>, 126

N.E. at 94. This concern must be balanced against recognition of the right of each

person to determine the objects of their bounty free from community comment and/or

judgment. As such, it strikes this Court that the best rule is one imposing a higher level

of proof to rebut an inference of undue influence after a challenger first demonstrates a

confidential relation and benefit conferred. In the matter at hand, however, given the

uncertainty of New Hampshire law, the deep split across jurisdictions, and, perhaps

most importantly, the apparent concession by the Hospitals that where an inference of

11

undue influence arises, the absence of undue influence must be demonstrated by a preponderance of the evidence, the Court has decided to follow the wise path tread by a sister Florida court. In Hack v. Janes, 878 So.2d 440 (Dist. Ct. App. Fla. 2004), the District Court of Appeal of Florida, was confronted with uncertainty concerning the "question of the quantum of proof the proponent of a will must produce to overcome the presumption of undue influence." Id. at 444. The Hack court rightly observed that while sound policy arguments could be made for imposing a clear and convincing standard, in the absence of clear direction by the Legislature (or presumably here, New Hampshire judicial precedent), it is best to apply the "generally accepted burden of proof in civil matters." Id. In this instance, the Court will apply New Hampshire's generally accepted quantum of proof in civil matters, preponderance of the evidence, see also RSA 464-A:26-a,V (burden for testamentary gifts of ward); Estate of Washburn, 141 N.H. at 660 (after presumption of competency rebutted, respondent must prove capacity by a preponderance), to the burden to disprove the absence of undue influence where a contestant has demonstrated: (1) a confidential relationship and (2) a benefit conferred.

B. *Capacity*

Although as noted supra, analysis of undue influence and testamentary capacity are often closely intertwined, absence of capacity can itself be an independent basis for invalidating a testamentary instrument. See, e.g., Perkins v. Perkins, 39 N.H. 163 (1859). The standard for establishing testamentary capacity is that the testator at the time of making a will:

> must have been able to understand the nature of the act she was doing, to recollect the property she wished to dispose of and understand its general nature, to bear in mind those who were then her nearest relatives as such, and to make an

12

> election upon whom and how she would bestow the property
> by her will; that she must have had the ability, the mental
> power or capacity to do this; that if she had, the law
> regarded her as of sufficient mental capacity to make the will
> . . . .

In re Estate of Washburn, 141 N.H. at 661 (quotations omitted); cf. Boardman v.

Woodman, 47 N.H. 120, 122, 140 (1866) (upholding a jury instruction with this standard)

overruled on other grounds by Hardy v. Merrill, 56 N.H. 227, 234-52 (1875). The law

also has long recognized that capacity is judged at the time of execution, see Hardy, 56

N.H. at 243 ("The question of testamentary capacity is in strictness limited to a very brief

period of time – the few minutes occupied by the attestation of the will."), thus, where a

"testatrix was under delusion, but the will and its provisions were not in any way the

offspring or result of the delusion, and were not connected with or influenced by it, then

she was of sane mind to make the will . . . ." Boardman, 47 N.H. at 140 (quotations

omitted); see e.g., In re Estate of Washburn, 141 N.H. at 661-62. By statute, the

standard for determining capacity to execute a trust is the same as a will. See RSA

564-B:6-601. Thus, this Court, when determining whether Ms. Webber possessed

sufficient capacity to execute the 2012 Estate Planning Documents, must inquire: "1)

whether [she] possessed testamentary capacity to execute a will; and 2) if [she] had

such capacity, whether the will is the offspring of a delusion or was created during a

lucid interval." In re Estate of Washburn, 141 N.H. at 662. Again, courts are permitted

to consider lay witness testimony concerning the mental capacity of a testator/settlor by

those who knew and actually observed the individual. See, e.g., Pattee v. Whitcomb,

72 N.H. 249, 252 (1903), relying on Hardy, 56 N.H. at 241, 244, 248.

13

Important to this case is the distinction between legal incapacity, medical incapacity and, in ancient parlance, "moral [incapacity]". See, e.g., Boardman, 47 N.H. at 138-39. Legal incapacity occurs when a testatrix is unable to understand the nature of the act undertaken, recollect her assets and their nature, know her relations, and elect to whom and how her property should be distributed. Id. at 122, 140; In re Estate of Washburn, 141 N.H. at 661. Medical incapacity includes both legal incapacity and an inability to make judgments about whether certain choices are "sensible" under certain societal norms. Boardman, 47 N.H. at 138-39. "Moral" incapacity was long ago defined as a "disordered state of the affections, or moral powers of the mind." Id. at 139. The law, however, has long recognized that "it is difficult to see how in a will case it would be practicable to administer the law or do justice according to law if moral [incapacity] were held sufficient to avoid a will." Id. Hence, lack of testamentary capacity will not be used by courts to "disturb those numerous testamentary dispositions of property which are made by those whose . . . affections may not run in the same channel with those of their neighbors."[8] Id. Rather, this Court chooses to follow the long recognized thesis that

> [w]e all have likes and dislikes among our acquaintances and even among our relatives, and, it may be, among the members of our own families, for which we might not be able to give an intelligible reason, or one that would be satisfactory to another person, who did not see with our eyes

---

[8] Therefore, this Court's ruling is not colored by the May-December nature of Ms. Webber's friendship with Officer Goodwin. Although it believes that our community lives in a more enlightened and less judgmental era than the Boardman Court in 1866, it has decided to discuss and reflect on legal versus moral incapacity given the sometimes judgmental undertones it perceived from certain witnesses in this case. Put another way, the law of testamentary capacity both in 1866 and 2015 does not take into account whether Mrs. Webber's affections or habits ran "in the same channel with those of the [community]." Rather, courts must discern whether, under the legal standards set forth supra, the 2012 Estate Planning Documents are valid. That said, this Court was impressed with the respectful nature of the presentations of counsel for all litigants in this matter and their exhibited respect for the dignity of Ms. Webber.

14

and hear with our ears, and the operation of whose mind
might not be like ours in every essential particular, and yet
are we all insane because we dislike somebody that some
one else likes, and because we make a will according to
these peculiarities of our views, must it be set aside? . . .
But so long as the law allows a man to do what he will with
his own, he may exercise his individual privilege of having
preferences and prejudices as between friends and relatives
and even children, without his being called on to give any
reason further.

Id.

"In New Hampshire, the burden of proving testamentary capacity in will contests

remains on the proponent of the will throughout the proceeding." In re Estate of

Washburn, 141 N.H. at 662. However, the will's proponent "may safely rely upon the

presumption of the law that all men are sane until some evidence to the contrary is

offered." Perkins, 39 N.H. at 170; accord In re Estate of Washburn, 141 N.H. at 662.

Thus, "[a] will proponent need not introduce any evidence upon the issue of the

testatrix's capacity until a will contestant first rebuts the presumption by offering

evidence of incapacity." In re Estate of Washburn, 141 N.H. at 663. "This burden

remains upon [the will/trust proponent] till the close of the trial." Perkins, 39 N.H. at 171.

As such, "once the presumption is rebutted, the proponent merely retains the initial

burden of proving due execution. The proponent must persuade the trial court, by a

preponderance of all the evidence presented, that the testatrix possessed the requisite

capacity to make the will." In re Estate of Washburn, 141 N.H. at 663.

II. Facts

The Court now proceeds with its findings of the pertinent facts based on the

evidence adduced over the course of the ten-day trial. First, however, mention must be

made that all parties of record assented to a procedural stipulation by the Hospitals that,

15

with respect to the 2012 Will, independent proof in solemn form pursuant to RSA 552:7

of the technical requirements for will execution established under RSA 551:2,[9] is waived

as unnecessary given the alternative consolidated proof within the context of the

substantive will challenge on grounds of undue influence and lack of testamentary

capacity under the *Motion to Re-Examine* and *Petition*. See *Assented —To Motion*

Regarding Pretrial Procedure (Index #94).

A. *Geraldine Webber*

The Court's recitation of facts begins, most appropriately, with Ms. Webber and her

physical, mental, and environmental conditions between 2010 and 2012. By all

accounts of those who knew her for many years, and those who met her during the

waning years of her life, she was a rather eccentric, outspoken, "unfiltered" and funny

person who sometimes expressed herself with rather colorful, and often overtly sexual,

language and mannerisms. She was born in Portsmouth in 1918, see Pet.'s Exh. 76,

returned to Portsmouth later in life and lived alone for many years in a sizeable home

with river frontage at 36 Shaw Road. It is undisputed that by the end of her life on

December 11, 2012, just short of her 94th birthday, id., she was a wealthy woman with

liquid assets, personal investments, and real estate worth over two million dollars. She

had been married twice (widowed once and divorced once) and had earlier lost her only

child, Bruce Webber, to cancer. She had only one grandchild, Brett Webber, who

apparently suffers from one or more disabilities and lives in Massachusetts.

---

[9] RSA 551:2 provides: "To be valid, a will or codicil to a will shall: I. Be made by a testator qualifying under RSA 551:1; and II. Be in writing; and III. Be signed by the testator, or by some person at his or her express direction in his or her presence; and IV. Be signed by 2 or more credible witnesses, who shall, at the request of the testator and in the testator's presence, attest to the testator's signature."

16

Many witnesses whose testimony the Court found credible,[10] and had occasion to observe Ms. Webber's behavior in her last years, testified to a noticeable cognitive decline. Her longtime landscaper, Jeremy L. Bernier stated that he provided services to her for fifteen years and that during the last two years of her life, he noted that she was "slipping." She would miss paying bills and repeat herself in conversation. He noticed that after conversing with her for ten-to-fifteen minutes, he would sense that she did not recognize him although he had been regularly providing landscaping and handyman work for her for well over a decade. Mr. Bernier began requiring payment by check so that he would have a record to show her when she disputed whether a bill had been paid. One time, during 2010 or 2011, Ms. Webber called Mr. Bernier and asked him to remove a tree. The following day, he followed her instruction, after which he received

---

[10] Due to its often contentious nature, cases involving undue influence are particularly difficult, and as such, the credibility of witnesses is a very important component of any court's determination. In this matter, the Court found the testimony of Dr. Ira Schwartz, her longtime physician, Jeremy Bernier, her long-time landscaper, Ray Pasquale, who rented a boat slip from Ms. Webber for several years, and Joanne Gile and Jay Gibson, long-time bank employees of the Piscataqua Savings Bank, particularly credible on facts they testified to and to their observations regarding her mental state. The Court also credits, to a lesser extent, given what it perceives as their profession-driven inquiries of more finite dimension into the circumstances and mental state of Ms. Webber during their respective engagements, the testimony of Dr. John Hopkins, Nancy Euchner, and Attorney David Mulhern. While it has no cause to question the truthfulness of the testimony of Attorneys Boesch and McGee, their even more abbreviated exposure to Ms. Webber further diminishes the import of their testimony.

The Court also finds that various aides hired after January 2011 largely testified credibly, however, their lack of familiarity with her medical history diminishes the weight given to their testimony. It does not place great confidence in the testimony of the witnesses to the document signings, because of their at times selective testimony, in some instances professed non-recall of highly unusual, indeed conspicuously irregular to the norm, commentary and gestures of Ms. Webber, or lack of preparatory knowledge of her medical history. Due to their often evasive and contradictory statements, it gives little credence to the testimony of various present and former non-party employees of the Portsmouth Police Department. It found the testimony of Attorney James Ritzo, Officer Goodwin, and Attorney Gary Holmes to be often defensively self-serving and at most critical points implausible. As such, it has accorded weight only in those instances when independently corroborated by credible testimony of others or documentary evidence. Similarly, the Court found the testimony of Dr. David Bourne to be remarkably one-sided. He never met Ms. Webber and only interviewed the will/trust proponents. Little weight is allocated to his testimony. Cf. Fenlon v. Thayer, 127 N.H. 702, 708 (1986)("Whether an expert is a 'hired gun' or one whose opinions have greater foundation of objectivity is an issue to be . . . considered by the [fact-finder]"). The remaining witness testimony is accorded no special weight, although the Court is grateful for their time and service in testifying to the best of their abilities and knowledge.

17

an angry call from Ms. Webber accusing him of removing the tree without her authority. Although he agreed that she had some "good days," toward the final days of her life there were more "bad days" (i.e.: days when she was clearly impaired). However, even those "good days" were far worse in terms of apparent impairment than his observations of her mental state during the 2004 to 2006 timeframe.

Ray Pasquale, a boater who rented a slip on Ms. Webber's dock every summer from April/May 2007 to September 2012, testified to significant deterioration in her mental faculties in 2011 and 2012. He stated that her memory in 2011 was "really bad" and by the summer of 2012 she was "even worse." Near the end of her life, he began mailing rental payments to her out of concern that if he handed them to her they would be misplaced and he would be accused of failing to make payment.[11]

Finally, Joanne Gile, an employee for over twenty-nine years at Piscataqua Savings Bank who had known Ms. Webber since 1987/1988, offered that towards the end of her life, Gile became concerned about certain inappropriate or random comments Ms. Webber would make. Although for many years Ms. Webber was "sharp" and cognizant of many details of her finances,[12] noticeably beginning in 2011, she became less concerned and thoughtful. She lost the keys to her safe deposit box and would hide significant amounts of money in her home. The banker testified to instances of confusion and stated she observed that Ms. Webber appeared lonely and would call her during work hours just to "chit-chat." Finally, Ms. Gile, joined by a customer service

---

[11] He further testified that if Ms. Webber was his mother, he would have admitted her to a nursing home for full-time care. Although the Court does not credit this statement as evidence that full-time care was appropriate, it is reflective of Mr. Pasquale's observations regarding Ms. Webber's cognitive health at the time.

[12] Indeed, before her mental faculties started to fail, Ms. Webber carefully managed her money at the bank and aggressively sought the best rates available.

18

representative at the bank, contacted the state Bureau of Elderly and Adult Services ("BEAS") in November 2012 to voice her concerns about Ms. Webber's vulnerability to financial exploitation due to her advancing mental and physical decline.[13] Ms. Gile reported that in her many years at the bank, this was her first call to BEAS regarding a bank customer.

The documentary medical evidence and the testimony of Ms. Webber's long-time physician, Dr. Ira Schwartz, comport with the view that her cognitive abilities had been in decline for a number of years before her death. He was also concerned about her ability to properly care for herself. Dr. Schwartz was Ms. Webber's primary physician for over twenty years. His records and testimony indicate that she suffered from cognitive impairment beginning at least by 2008 – four years prior to execution of the 2012 Estate Planning Documents. That year, he administered a "mini-mental status exam", the results of which indicated mild cognitive impairment. He represented that the exam was administered after Ms. Webber expressed her own concerns about her cognitive abilities and visiting nurses had noted confusion during their visits. He also discerned that her cognitive issues did not later improve over-time.

Dr. Schwartz further testified that in February 2011, a psychiatric evaluation was ordered after Ms. Webber was admitted to the hospital but did not demonstrate an understanding of the nature of her physical issues. Pet.'s Exh. 44. His discharge notes dated February 26, 2011 reflect that although she lived alone and engaged in social activities with friends, "[w]e have known for quite some time that she has cognitive

---

[13] The Court similarly credits testimony presented by Jay Gibson, former president of Piscataqua Savings Bank, who had less frequent contact with her than Joanne Gile. He detected, based on those encounters, that while he found Ms. Webber "pretty sharp" in February 2011, he also had concerns about her vulnerability to exploitation by her former Attorney James Ritzo and, "perhaps anyone."

19

impairment." Pet.'s Exh. 46. The psychological evaluation was conducted by Dr. Simon

Eisen on February 24, 2011. Pet.'s Exh. 44. Dr. Eisen opined that Ms. Webber did not

understand the nature of her condition; she required constant prompting, displayed mild

paranoia and very poor judgment regarding management of her medical condition. He

diagnosed her with "[d]ementia, mild, most likely Alzheimer's type," and recommended

that "a guardian be applied for to help with both her financial and medical affairs." Id.

Although Dr. Schwartz testified that he did not agree that a guardianship was necessary

at that point, he did agree that she could not make informed medical decisions and he

remembered that at the time, she had significant cognitive deficits and dementia. His

memory is bolstered by records inclusive of: (1) his written note of March 8, 2011,

reflecting his observation that Ms. Webber has "memory issues" and is able to remain

living at home "with the help of a power of attorney, someone who transports her, and

someone who comes in and cleans and cooks for her"; Pet.'s Exh. 49; and (2)

observations made by a wound care doctor on March 10, 2011 "questioning her

cognitive abilities." Pet.'s Exh. 50.[14]

    In August 2011, Dr. Schwartz directed that his staff place a call to BEAS to express

his concerns about Ms. Webber's ability to manage and understand her medical

conditions and that she was refusing to allow visits from social workers. Pet.'s Exh. 53.

He contacted "protective services" again in February 2012 expressing his opinion that

Ms. Webber "needs protection" as she appeared to forget what she had been told

---

[14] Although on cross examination, the will proponents tried to press the point that Ms. Webber's mental health may have been compromised as a result of some temporary medical issues surrounding her hospital admission in February 2011, the Court notes that Dr. Schwartz testified very consistently about his concerns regarding her mental state in 2011 and his growing concern as time went on. Indeed, what is clear from her medical records is that at least by February 2011, a full fourteen months before the 2012 Estate Planning Documents were executed, Ms. Webber displayed significant cognitive issues.

20

regarding the nature of injuries that had sent her to the emergency room just prior to their meeting. Id. He called "protective services" again in March 2012 expressing concern about whether her in-home care was properly supervised and opining that at this time, she had "severe dementia." Id. He phoned yet again in late April 2012 to express concern. Id. He gave unchallenged testimony that in his forty-one years as a physician, he contacted BEAS less than ten times in total. He became frustrated by the failure of BEAS to satisfactorily respond to his entreaties concerning Ms. Webber.

Finally, the Court credits Dr. Schwartz's testimony about inquiries made by Attorney David Mulhern in April 2011, see generally Pet.'s Exh. 51, regarding Ms. Webber's capacity to execute a will. Dr. Schwartz testified that he made two calls to Attorney Mulhern, each time indicating that he could not attest to her competency. Similarly, he testified that during a February 2012 meeting with Attorney Gary Holmes, see Pet.'s Exh. 54, in which they discussed Ms. Webber's mental status and ability to sign legal documents, he declared her incapable of having sufficient insight to sign such documentation.

Although there were other notes in the record by medical providers who did not see Ms. Webber regularly indicating less severe cognitive issues, Dr. Schwartz testified consistently and credibly about his serious concerns about her ability to understand legal documents at the end of her life, in particular shortly before or at the time of the execution of the 2012 Estate Planning Documents. After acknowledging that he is not a lawyer and may have a different understanding of legal capacity, he expressed that this belief was premised on his examinations of her and that he had seen her as unable to understand complex issues, her own medical problems, and her ever-declining

21

cognitive impairment. He testified that if Attorney Gary Holmes had asked him if Ms. Webber was capable of understanding a will signing, or put another way, if she was mentally capable of executing a will, he would have replied, "no."

A March 2012 report filed by Dr. John Hopkins, engaged at the behest of BEAS to undertake a "consultation on [her] mental status and . . . her capacity to take care of her personal and estate affairs." Pet.'s Exh. 55. Although the Court gives less weight to this report than those of her long term caregivers because Dr. Hopkins met Ms. Webber only once, it is noted for its consistency with them. He spoke of having conducted assessments for BEAS five-to-six times a year for between twenty and thirty years. He reported that Mrs. Webber was friendly and had "seemingly good recall of people, places and things in general." Id. However, he also observed her to be "professionally suspicious," noted that "her recall of recent events and her time frame for injuries, hospitalization and rehab care at home are definitely off" and her memory lapses were "apparent." Id. He reported that she made accusations of "things being stolen," financial exploitation, the commission of other nefarious acts or of being essentially up to no good, against individuals he identified as being her former attorney James Ritzo and Officer Goodwin. He further expressed that although "[i]t is not my place to suggest . . . that this is an old woman with dementia and paranoia," he could

> confidently report to BEAS that Geraldine Webber has cognitive impairment, significant medical challenges and, in the current living situation, is very much at risk for self harm by neglect and unintentional errors in judgment about how to take care of herself.
>
> On a related dimension, her need for help along many dimensions makes her a very vulnerable target for exploitation of several types.

22

<u>Id.</u> He concluded his report by noting that: "she deserves even more combined security of the protection of her person as well as her estate." <u>Id.</u>

The Court divines from the trial record and testimony that because of her physical and mental decline, the naturally spirited Ms. Webber became increasingly dependent upon friends, neighbors, and hired professionals in the final years of her life before meeting Officer Goodwin. Mrs. Wardwell, for many years before Ms. Webber befriended Officer Goodwin, drove her weekly to medical appointments, lunch, and shopping. Landscaper Bernier testified that Ms. Webber would often call seeking assistance with in-home plumbing and heating concerns, even assistance finding her television remote control. Neighbor John C. Connors testified she would call for assistance with small tasks, likewise among them retrieval of her remote control. Both Mr. Connors and Ms. Wardwell testified to a near stable-full of friends and a housekeeper who maintained weekly contact with Ms. Webber, giving her assistance with daily tasks and affording socialization. Worthy of note, by 2011, Ms. Webber maintained a flip double-paged date calendar in which she commonly recorded meaningful daily visits and/or events. <u>See</u> Fid.'s Exhs. DDD & EEE. When friends or assistants would call, she would typically record the contact on her calendar. One housekeeper testified that she would record the time of a following week's visit in the calendar to help Ms. Webber remember the time and date of the next housekeeping appointment.

There was also credible testimony elicited that Ms. Webber became more suspicious and fearful during her waning years. Dr. Eisner found evidence of mild paranoia; however, Dr. Schwartz disputed whether she was paranoid. As such, the Court finds

23

that at the very least she was suspicious and fearful. Her longtime friend, petitioner

Barbara Wardwell told that she would not enter Ms. Webber's home for fear of being

accused of stealing. Neighbor John Connors testified that beginning in early 2010 Ms.

Webber reported to him on multiple occasions that she thought there were prowlers in

the neighborhood, though none of her other neighbors noticed anything amiss. There

also was testimony by more than one witness that Ms. Webber appeared particularly

concerned about what she suspected was gang activity, led by a relative of her last

husband, targeting her home for a possible home invasion. It was never clear to the

Court, however, whether that fear was real or imagined.

After Ms. Webber lost her ability to drive, her long-time attorney, James Ritzo, began

assisting with her banking and testified at trial that he visited her home at least twice

weekly to attend to minor household, as well as official legal tasks, and bill paying. This

was inferentially supported by banker Gile who testified that she was aware Attorney

Ritzo provided both legal and non-legal support to Ms. Webber and that she was

dependent and relied upon him.

Attorney Ritzo had provided legal services to Ms. Webber for many years and had

drafted, or at times arranged for another attorney to prepare, a series of simple wills and

codicils for her beginning as early as 2004. See Pet.'s Exh. 1. In the February 2004

will, he was nominated to serve as a co-executor, there were small legacies to a few

close friends and one to establish a scholarship at Braintree High School. Conditioned

on his survival of her, Ms. Webber's former husband was given a forfeitable right under

an included testamentary trust to life use and occupancy of her home and some

income, in addition to her tangible personal property and some stock, outright. It further

24

specified that on her former husband's death or forfeiture of his rights to receipt of the trust income and use and occupancy of the home, the testamentary trust would terminate, with its remaining assets distributable among three charities, as well as the Portsmouth Police and Fire Departments for use in the purchase of safety equipment. Her grandson, Brett Webber, was not named, though her late son and Brett's father, Bruce Webber, was referenced in the provision establishing a scholarship at Braintree High. See Pet.'s Exh. 1(A).

Ms. Webber's former husband was removed as an object of her bounty in a subsequent 2006 will. See Pet.'s Exh. 1(B). Instead, small to modest legacies were made to friends and for funding the Braintree High School scholarship: her assets were directed to be liquidated, with the residue distributable to five charities, again in addition to the Portsmouth Police and Fire Departments for use in purchasing safety equipment, in what is incongruously stated to be one-fifth shares each. Attorney Ritzo was once more nominated executor, but this time also bestowed "five (5%) per cent of [her] gross estate for services as [her] Executor."[15] Id. As with the 2004 will, grandson, Brett Webber, was not mentioned in the 2006 will iteration, while his father was anew in the provision establishing the scholarship at Braintree High. Id.

---

[15] The Court makes no ruling regarding the ethical propriety of this, and subsequent provisions for Attorney Ritzo in later wills, as it is beyond the scope of this case. However, it pauses to mention that it has grave concerns based on the quality of the wills and the propriety of the provisions giving Attorney Ritzo an ever-greater share of the gross value of the estate. It is also deeply concerned about other possible ethical lapses as well, including: (1) testimony of John Connors indicating a possible violation of the attorney-client privilege between Ms. Webber and Attorney Ritzo; (2) a letter/"bill" sent to Ms. Webber on August 10, 2012 containing overt threats; (3) his eventual admission that he had conversations with Attorney Gary Holmes and Attorney Ralph Holmes that failure to pay this "bill" would result in litigation to set aside the 2012 Estate Planning Documents; and (4) signing checks purporting to be the act of Ms. Webber, without indication that it was done pursuant to a power of attorney until questioned by bank employees. The Court is without jurisdiction, however, and it would be inappropriate in the context of this matter, to make substantive rulings in address of its concerns.

25

In June 2007, a similar will was executed, including a provision for liquidation of all her assets, but this time naming Brett Webber as a legatee, and including new legacies to her former husband and others. A list of charitable organizations and the Portsmouth Police and Fire Departments were designated to split the residue of the estate.[16] See Pet.'s Exh. 1(C). In this will, Attorney Ritzo and another co-executor, each were slated to receive 2.5% of the gross value of the estate "for serving as Co-Executors." In addition, Attorney Ritzo was to be given 5% of the gross value of the estate "for services as [Ms. Webber's] [a]ttorney." Id. Another will was executed two months later in August 2007, substantially akin in form to the last, but with a slightly different clause for gifted legacies, among them one distributable to Brett Webber. Pet.'s Exh. 1(D). Compensation for Attorney Ritzo remained the same as the provisions in the former June 2007 will. Id.

Another comparable will, with a further slight modification of the gifting of legacies not omitting one to Brett Webber, was executed in January 2008. See Pet.'s Exh. 1(E). In this version, inter alia, Attorney Ritzo was directed, for services as co-executor, to "set [his] own fees for this service." In addition, he was granted 5% of the value of the gross estate for other services rendered. The will further directed that only Attorney Ritzo "shall serve[] [a]s my attorney and administrator, and probate [sic] my Estate . . ." Id.

Yet another will was executed in July 2008, with another changed recital of legacies to individuals including Brett Webber, but the same compensation provisions for Attorney Ritzo set out in the previous January 2008 will. See Pet.'s Exh. 1(F). A

---

[16] The Court notes that it is not clear from the exhibit whether five or six charities each receive 1/5 of the residue, because while six are recited each is allotted a 1/5 share. Id.

26

substantially similar will was executed in October 2008 with still an additional altered gifting of legacies, inclusive of a legacy to Brett Webber. See Pet.'s Exh. 1(G). It recites once again that Attorney Ritzo was allowed to "set [his] own fees" for serving as co-executor, but was now granted a supplemental 5% of the gross estate "for his past services." Id.

On February 5, 2009, a further will was executed. See Pet.'s Exh. 1(H); Pet.'s Exh. 2. In this instrument, the residuary distributees remained the same as the prior October 2008 instrument, but a listing of legacies to individuals was separately appended under a document bearing the same date and purported signature of Ms. Webber alone, captioned: "BEQUEST LIST TO BE INCORPORATED INTO MY LAST WILL AND TESTAMENT." Again, Brett Webber is among those to receive a legacy. Id. While Attorney Ritzo was to be to be compensated by the same self-determined fee set out in the wills of January, July and October 2008 for acting as co-executor, his fee for past services rose to 5% of the gross estate plus Ms. Webber's automobile. Id. A codicil executed some 14 days later, on February 19, 2009, amended the February 5th version to direct that her automobile be sold with the proceeds derived added to her "gross estate". See Pet.'s Exh. 2.

After the February codicil, any changes to the will were apparently designed and/or intended to be made by what might be seen as endeavored codicils including a substantially similar, but still distinct, "BEQUEST LIST TO BE INCORPORATED INTO MY LAST WILL AND TESTAMENT." See Pet.'s Exh. 2.[17] The "Bequest List," bearing a date of November 17, 2009 and the signature of Ms. Webber only — thus possibly

---

[17] The Court notes that the legacy list appended to the February 2009 Will in Petitioners' Exhibit 1(H) is unsigned and differs from the one appended to the copy of the February 2009 Will in Petitioners' Exhibit 2. That legacy list bears the same date as the will, February 5, 2009, and signature of Ms. Webber.

27

failing as a proper amendment to her will, see RSA 551:2, or as incorporated into it by

reference given its presumptive non-existence on the date of the will's execution, see

Hastings v. Bridge, 86 N.H. 247, 249 (1933) — bore some altered legacies, but still

included a legacy to Brett Webber. See Pet.'s Exh. 2. Another slightly different

"Bequest List" represented at trial by the parties to have been dated April 14, 2010,[18]

Fid.'s Exh. PP(7), also bearing only by Ms. Webber's signature, and still another

unsigned list with handwritten adjustments, Fid.'s Exh. PP(8), prepared in December,

2010, were introduced into evidence; however, owing to the noted deficiencies of

execution and/or recited dates, appear never to have gained legal efficacy.

By 2010, Ms. Webber began to voice distrust of Attorney Ritzo. She accused him of

failing to pay for a couch he may or may not have "purchased" from her. As far as the

Court can discern, this accusation was never substantiated. In July 2010, Attorney

Ritzo, as part of his practice to conduct banking services for Ms. Webber, arrived at her

bank and presented a number of checks totaling $7,953.60. See Pet.'s Exh. 8. He

sought to deposit $3,187.50 and take cash totaling $4,766.10. Id. Bank employees

noticed that two checks were presented purporting to be signed by Ms. Webber, but

were in fact signed by Attorney Ritzo. The Bank did not have authorizations on file from

Ms. Webber allowing Attorney Ritzo to "cash checks and withdraw funds." Id. Bank

employees called Ms. Webber, who at first denied signing any power of attorney form;

however, Attorney Ritzo returned to the bank with such a document signed four years

earlier. Id. The bank president, Jay Gibson, spoke with Ms. Webber, who confirmed

that while the attorney returned with the proper amount of cash and that she was aware

of the transaction, she was very insistent that she did not want any person to act under

---

[18] The date is illegible on the submitted exhibit.

28

a power of attorney, including Attorney Ritzo. Mr. Gibson testified that he understood that in the end, Ritzo had acted according to Ms. Webber's instructions.

Ms. Webber seemingly perseverated about the July 2010 bank incident and continued to increasingly accuse Attorney Ritzo of criminal acts through execution of the 2012 Estate Planning Documents. The video of the document execution reveals an almost obsessive distrust of, indeed even disdain for, him. As discussed more fully infra, the BEAS, with assistance from the Portsmouth Police Department, investigated Attorney Ritzo. He was ordered not to have further contact with Ms. Webber beginning in February 2011, see Pet.'s Exh. 69, and he appears to have complied. An August 2012 letter from the Attorney General's Office later cleared him of any criminal wrongdoing. Pet.'s Exh. 70.

B. *Ms. Webber and Aaron Goodwin*

Within months of the banking incident involving Attorney Ritzo, Ms. Webber met Officer Goodwin. In October 2010, Officer Goodwin arrived at Ms. Webber's home as part of an investigation into suspicious activity in the area. She invited him into her home and engaged in conversation. Officer Goodwin very quickly became a regular visitor at her home, and soon was "stopping by" multiple times a week. His cell phone records, which do not include calls placed from landlines at the police department, document 832 calls between them during an approximately 24 month period from October 25, 2010 to November 4, 2012.[19] See Pet.'s Exh. 3.

It is safe to say that Ms. Webber became very fond of, and perhaps even likely smitten with, Officer Goodwin. Attorney Ritzo testified that by November of 2010, she had informed him of her desire to leave everything to Officer Goodwin in her will. Her

---

[19] The majority of these calls were placed by Officer Goodwin.

29

personal calendars/diaries for 2011 and 2012, see Fid.'s Exhs. DDD & EEE, are full of references attesting to her "love" – Aaron Goodwin – and reflecting a certain excitement when documenting the fact that he had called, visited or was planning a visit.[20] There was also testimony that she stated he was sent by God as she was despairing over perceived threats from potential robbers and/or Attorney Ritzo. Shortly after meeting him, she confided in long-time friends and neighbors that she found Officer Goodwin attractive and was "in love."[21]

Officer Goodwin very quickly became a central figure in Ms. Webber's life. He arranged for her to meet with Chief David (Lou) Ferland[22] and Captain Michael Schwartz of the Portsmouth Police Department to facilitate an investigation into her allegations of financial exploitation by Attorney Ritzo. Joan Gile testified that she first met Officer Goodwin when he brought Ms. Webber to the bank in January 2011 to make a deposit. She also testified that in July 2011 he assisted Ms. Webber to have her safe deposit box drilled and replaced, and entered the vault with her as she inspected the contents of the box. He was given a key to her house. He became increasingly in charge of her medical care, by at least early 2011. Medical records indicate that by January 2011, he became the "contact person" for her care. See Fid.'s Exh. CCC(A).

---

[20] The Court briefly notes that it rejects claims by Officer Goodwin and some others that she loved Officer Goodwin "like a son." Without going into detail, there are enough highly sexual or romantic notations in the diaries and sexual references about Officer Goodwin in the videotape to dispossess the Court of the notion that the genesis of her affection was predominantly of a parental nature. Although many testified that she was known to use crude and often inappropriate language, sometimes for attention-getting purposes, the sheer volume of her romantic/sexual comments, along with the fact that some of them were kept in a personal diary, suggests that they were not written for attention and that she did not view Officer Goodwin as solely a "second son."

[21] The Court also notes that when one neighbor told Attorney John P. McGee that Ms. Webber stated Officer Goodwin was going to leave his wife for her, Attorney McGee concluded, after spending time with Ms. Webber, that this comment was in jest.

[22] For convenience, the Court refers to the police department witnesses by their titles at the time of the events in question.

30

One entry in her medical records seems to indicate that he was assisting with dispensing her medication as early as February 24, 2011. Pet.'s Exh. 45.

As discussed more fully infra, he sought out, and actively procured either personally or through his attorney, Justin Nadeau, a series of attorneys to draft her 2012 Estate Planning Documents naming him primary recipient of Ms. Webber's assets. Finally, as some members of her former support system became estranged from her, Officer Goodwin arranged for replacement assistance through various service providers. He also took her out for cocktails and meals and at least once to a casino in Connecticut to gamble. Toward the very end of her life, he arranged for a friend having a background in "wholesale vintage clothing and antiques," as well as hospice care, to visit twice weekly with Ms. Webber.

In December 2010, Ms. Webber gave Officer Goodwin some small gifts for his children in appreciation for his attention. Officer Goodwin testified that he called her on Christmas Eve 2010, roughly two months after first meeting her, and during the ensuing conversation she told him she wanted to leave her home to him when she died. Over time, the breadth of her generosity expanded, so that by the time she met with the first attorney procured for her by Officer Goodwin in February 2011, he was also going to receive the contents of her home; later that year her generosity toward him was further increased to include grants of stock and her car. The Fiduciary's notes from April 16, 2012, made in preparation of a meeting with her shortly before the final documents were drafted, pegs an approximate value of her estate at $2,250,000; of that figure, Officer Goodwin was to receive assets valued at approximately $2,000,000, astonishingly after only knowing Ms. Webber for eighteen (18) months. See Fid.'s Exh. JJ. It is also of

31

import that in all the prior wills offered as evidence in this case, no other beneficiary, including long-time friends who had themselves provided companionship and support, her grandson, and even a former husband with whom she briefly reconciled, were to receive such generous beneficence. See Fid.'s Exh. PP. That said, the Court is mindful that from December 2010 when she first offered to leave her home to Officer Goodwin until May 2012 when the 2012 Estate Planning Documents were executed, Ms. Webber consistently voiced a desire to benefit Officer Goodwin in her will.

C. *Portsmouth Police Department*

The Court pauses briefly to make certain findings concerning both Officer Goodwin's interaction with, and the "investigation" conducted by, the Portsmouth Police Department with respect to his relationship with Ms. Webber. It makes these findings only to the extent relevant to determination of the issues before it.

There was significant conflicting and sometimes vague testimony regarding what was known, and when, within the Portsmouth Police Department about the nature of Ms. Webber's testamentary plans for Officer Goodwin, how often he was visiting with her, the extent to which he was telephoning or visiting her during work hours, and the nature of the directives given to him regarding his continued relationship with her. For example, Officer Goodwin testified that he told Chief Lou Ferland about a potential post-mortem gifting to him of Ms. Webber's house on January 4th, a claim Chief Ferland denied on the witness stand. Officer Goodwin claims, rather vaguely, that he informed Captain Corey MacDonald about the potential gifting in early-or-mid January. However, Captain MacDonald's January 17, 2011 report, Pet.'s Exh. 62, makes no mention of it and Captain MacDonald testified at trial that as of January 17th he had no knowledge of

32

it. Although some of this testimony was ancillary to the questions before the Court, it does impact the Court's assessment of the credibility of witnesses, including, Officer Goodwin.

The Court was impressed, though not in a positive fashion, by the apparent lack of concern within the department about the potential for exploitation of Ms. Webber by department employees.[23] Concern appeared only to center on: (1) a financial exploitation investigation of Attorney Ritzo; and (2) making sure that Officer Goodwin was not observed visiting Ms. Webber during work hours.[24] The Court was struck by an email sent to Officer Goodwin by Captain MacDonald, in December 2011 after Ms. Webber sent a box of chocolates to the department as a thank you for police assistance when she fell down at her home. In that email, Captain MacDonald writes to Officer Goodwin: "How come you get the house and we just get chocolates?" Pet.'s Exh. 68. This is striking given that the department, including Captain Michael Schwartz and Police Chief Ferland specifically, had been involved in investigating concerns about financial exploitation of Ms. Webber by Attorney Ritzo. Indeed, all agree that Chief Ferland met with Ms. Webber in January 2011 to discuss a potential investigation of the attorney. Department personnel testifying at trial each appeared aware of the Ritzo investigation. It is not apparent from the record, therefore, that any concern regarding the potential vulnerability of Ms. Webber to exploitation by one of their own was ever seriously considered, let alone truly investigated by the department.[25] Whether this

---

[23] The Court notes that Officer Michael Schwartz was named as a beneficiary of a $25,000 distribution from the 2012 Trust. Fid.'s Exh. B, §5.13. He has since disclaimed it.

[24] It did not appear to extend to personal phone calls during work hours, as cell phone records show numerous calls made by Officer Goodwin to Ms. Webber during this time. Pet.'s Exh. 3. As such, a reasonable inference can be made that official concern extended to appearances only.

[25] Based upon documents before this Court, Ms. Webber's home was worth approximately $750,000. By comparison, the department was concerned that Attorney Ritzo was to take 11.5% of what they estimated

33

amounted to acts of omission or commission is not before this Court, and will not be

decided by it. However, it does cast a shadow on department officials' credibility and

reduces the evidentiary weight given to police witnesses.

The Court was presented evidence of, and is cognizant that, an "internal

investigation" was conducted by Detective Frank Warchol in response to allegations

proffered by Attorney Ritzo and possibly others[26] against Officer Goodwin concerning

his potential financial exploitation of Ms. Webber. Detective Warchol testified he was

told by Chief Ferland to ask, and indeed asked, Officer Goodwin only one question

during that February 14, 2011 interview – essentially whether a written report by

Goodwin to the Chief dated January 10, 2011, see Pet.'s Exh. 59, was complete or

should be amended and/or supplemented. Both Detective Warchol and Officer

Goodwin[27] admitted that Detective Warchol's inquiry was limited to whether the earlier

report was complete, and that Officer Goodwin indicated, in some fashion, that it was.

Remarkably, this January 10th memorandum, while mentioning gifts of limited value,

completely omits any mention that Ms. Webber, by the date of the memo, wanted to

leave her house to Officer Goodwin.[28] Neither Officer Goodwin nor Detective Warchol

---

to be a $2,000,000 estate. See Pet.'s Exhs. 60 & 62. By the Court's modest calculation, as of January 2011, Officer Goodwin's potential gift from a woman he had only known a few months was over three times as large as the feared excessive compensation to Attorney Ritzo.

[26] An email from Captain Schwartz dated the same day as the internal investigation interview indicates that Detective Warchol was briefed, prior to the interview, that Ms. Webber's former daughter-in-law was alleging financial exploitation against "a detective." See Pet.'s Exh. 66.

[27] Although Officer Goodwin initially had a relatively selective memory of these events, he did finally admit that he told Detective Warchol that his January 10th memo was complete and he had nothing to add.

[28] This document, see Pet.'s Exh. 59, which is the only independently verifiable record standing in the face of contradictory testimony across the Portsmouth Police Department's "chain of command", however, states on page one that it is "a summary of mostly phone and some person-to-person conversations with Ms. Webber in the weeks and months following my first meeting with her." Entries dated December 29, 2010 and January 3, 2011 completely omit any mention of the potential home gifting first mentioned by Ms. Webber on December 24th. Id. Similarly, a January 17, 2011 memo written by Captain MacDonald to Captain Schwartz likewise only mentions small gifts from Ms. Webber to Officer Goodwin's children and omits her offer to leave him her home. Pet.'s Exh. 62. Captain MacDonald testified that at that time, he

ever supplemented, or asked to supplement, the memorandum. The former testified unconvincingly that no mention was made because he was told that the subject of the memo was Attorney Ritzo and that valuable gifts were being brought up a separate "chain of command." The Court has a very difficult time with this explanation as Officer Goodwin testified that he was given notice about the internal investigation concerning a complaint involving a proposed will/bequest by Ms. Webber.

Here, the Court again pauses to reflect, albeit not in a positive light, on the apparent lack of concern within the department that Officer Goodwin was actively procuring legal counsel for Ms. Webber. Any concern appears centered on ensuring that Captain Corey MacDonald, a member of the New Hampshire Bar, not provide legal services in this matter. The Court disbelieves the claim by more than one police witness, including Goodwin, that Officer Goodwin was actively procuring counsel at the *direction* of the Attorney General's Office. There is no independent documentary evidence to support this explanation. Although it is true that the Attorney General's Office advised Ms. Webber, during a February 1, 2011 meeting that she should hire a lawyer to redraft the Ritzo generated wills, see Exh. ZZ(1), it discerns no specific direction that Officer Goodwin take the lead. See id. Also, it appears from that same transcript that Ms. Webber states at least three separate times that Officer Goodwin had already begun efforts to procure a lawyer for Ms. Webber before the February 1, 2011 meeting. Finally, Joan Gile testified that in January 2011, Officer Goodwin asked her if she could recommend an attorney for Ms. Webber.

---

did not know about this potential gifting. As noted supra Officer Goodwin testified, rather vaguely, that he informed Captain MacDonald in early-to-mid January, whereas Captain MacDonald states he was informed after the 17th. This rather self-serving memorandum was likewise never supplemented with information regarding the potential gift to Officer Goodwin.

35

The Court, after due consideration, could write pages of observations regarding the sometimes self-serving and dubious, often contradictory, testimony by Detective Warchol, Officer Goodwin, Chief Ferland, Captain MacDonald, and Captain Schwartz. These witnesses also displayed an unusual measure of selective memory regarding the events at hand. As such, it finds much of the testimony unhelpful to the matter decided today and indeed reflects adversely on this Court's assessment of the overall credibility of Officer Goodwin.

D. *Ms. Webber's 2012 Estate Planning Documents*

Beginning in early 2011, Officer Goodwin began to seek out counsel to draft a new set of estate planning documents for Ms. Webber. As mentioned supra he approached Joan Gile for advice on new counsel in January. Captain MacDonald testified that in late February/early March, he advised Officer Goodwin to contact Attorney Sally Mulhern.

Attorney David Mulhern, a law partner with Sally Mulhern, disclosed that he was contacted by Officer Goodwin about drafting an estate plan sometime prior to his first visit with Ms. Webber at her home on February 8, 2011. See Pet.'s Exh. 14. During his first meeting with Ms. Webber, he particularly remembers her professed anger with, and repeated derogatory commentary regarding, Attorney Ritzo. This perseveration on her long-standing attorney gave him pause.

When he met with her again on February 17, 2011, with her accountant Bill MacDonald, he became concerned about her capacity as she wildly inflated the value of her home. So much so, that he declined to be agent on a power of attorney because of it. He also was alarmed by her statement that she was not going to provide for Brett

36

Webber in her estate because she had arranged to make him a beneficiary of a certificate of deposit (CD) at her bank. Mulhern contacted the bank, and learned that Brett was not a beneficiary of the CD.[29]

Attorney Mulhern testified that after his two meetings with Ms. Webber, he concluded that he needed to conduct a deeper inquiry into her mental health and the circumstances surrounding her proposed estate plans. His concern was driven by a number of factors, including: (1) Officer Goodwin had initiated the referral; (2) Ms. Webber, although he described her as a forceful eccentric old woman, was elderly and in poor health; (3) her new plan included large dispositions to a police officer she had only recently met; (4) she was cavalier about not providing for her sole heir whom he knew to have disabilities and/or special needs; and (5) she did not understand the value of her assets.

Attorney Mulhern met with Officer Goodwin and accountant MacDonald on March 1, 2011 to discuss his concerns. He later sought out Ms. Webber's medical records and learned, for the first time, of her dementia diagnosis. He sent a letter to Dr. Schwartz, see Pet.'s Exh. 16, setting forth his interpretation of New Hampshire's law on testamentary capacity, and requesting "your professional judgment regarding Ms. Webber's capacity to execute a will." Id. As discussed supra, Dr. Schwartz replied via voicemail on April 8, 2011. A transcription of that voicemail, states: "I cannot attest to her competency. I can give you more details why, plus other information you may find relevant. There is no way in the world I am going to be able to say this eccentric woman is competent." Pet.'s Exh. 17.

---

[29] This comports with testimony by Joan Gile.

37

By May 2011, Attorney Mulhern decided that he could not move forward with drafting

a traditional estate plan for Ms. Webber. He was careful to state at trial that his

reticence was not a judgment about capacity, but rather reflected a concern about

drafting an enforceable plan. In a letter to her dated May 9, 2011, he opined that "it is

clear to me that serious professional questions have arisen about your testamentary

capacity . . . [and] any Will you signed would be highly subject to legal challenge, . . .

[that] might well be successful." Pet.'s Exh. 20. This letter also notified Ms. Webber of

her mistaken belief that Brett Webber was a beneficiary of a CD at the bank. Id.

Attorney Mulhern's letter suggested initiating a process to allow for court oversight and

have a "guardian-initiated estate plan prepared" on her behalf. Id. The lawyer testified

that Ms. Webber was not happy with his plan,[30] and he later learned she had hired or

was planning to hire new counsel.

On May 3, 2011, Ms. Webber contacted Attorney William S. Boesch. Pet.'s Exh 25.

She informed him that she had obtained his number from Officer Goodwin. In their first

conversation, she seemed to indicate that she was calling about problems with buoys

on her dock. He informed her that buoys were not his specialty. She called back on

May 9th, indicating for the first time that she would like to draft a new estate plan. Id. At

their first meeting on May 23rd, Ms. Webber at first was focused on buoys, but later

turned her attention to estate plans. She gave him a copy of a prior will, spoke of her

affection for Officer Goodwin and her displeasure with Attorney Ritzo. She shared her

letter from Attorney Mulhern, of which Attorney Boesch took note.

---

[30] Ms. Webber later referred to Attorney Mulhern as a "thief and a robber" when meeting with a third
lawyer, Attorney John P. McGee.

38

Attorney Boesch eventually spoke with Attorney Mulhern about his concerns. Attorney Boesch offered that after that discussion, he concluded that his concerns were not as acute and though Ms. Webber was lonely, she was lucid, articulate and clear about wanting to benefit Officer Goodwin. He did concede, however, that at that point he had not seen her medical records and had only met with her one time. Attorney Boesch's relationship with Ms. Webber abruptly ended when, after returning from a two week vacation, he learned she had hired Attorney Gary Holmes.

Before Ms. Webber hired Attorney Gary Holmes, she met with one more lawyer, Attorney John P. McGee, who reached out to Ms. Webber after being contacted by Officer Goodwin's attorney, Justin Nadeau. Attorney McGee met with Ms. Webber on August 18th. He testified that she showed him a copy of a 2008 will, but seemed uninterested in reviewing it, instead, stating she just wanted to give Officer Goodwin her house, car, and "things." As he went through the list, he noticed that Ms. Webber was confused about her former daughter-in-law, Joanne Peterson, whom she repeatedly called "Shirley." She expressed unhappiness with Attorney Ritzo, called Attorney Mulhern a "thief" and "robber", and did not recall Attorney Boesch by name. She voiced suspicions about her long-time accountant, Bill MacDonald. At first, when discussing her family, she appeared to initially forget about grandson Brett Webber. He also noted that although Ms. Webber appeared relatively "with-it" at first, she began to "fade" after a half-hour. Her understanding about the value of her assets was not clear. See Pet.'s Exh. 33

His notes about that meeting drafted a day later, see id., indicate that "[a]ll in all, I have to say I was thinking of Probate Court intervention before she could do a Will."

39

Attorney McGee decided not to work on the case after discovering, upon leaving her home, that his friend and client, John Connors, allegedly had been reported by Ms. Webber to the Portsmouth Police Department. He sent a letter to Ms. Webber declining representation on the basis of that conflict. Pet.'s Exh. 34. He testified that he spoke with Attorney Nadeau, advising him to "be careful" and declined to refer other attorneys to Attorney Nadeau as possible counsel to Ms. Webber.

Finally, Ms. Webber engaged the Fiduciary to draft what eventually became the 2012 Estate Planning Documents. The Fiduciary was contacted by Attorney Nadeau on August 25, 2011, and the documents were not executed until almost nine months later. The Fiduciary held between eight and ten meetings with Ms. Webber in her home prior to execution of the documents. See Fid.'s Exhs. G (summary prepared for trial); & H (calendar entries). The Fiduciary's notes indicate that although certain individual post-mortem gifts changed over this time, those to Officer Goodwin of her home and contents remained a constant, her car and "1/3 Aaron" for the residue were added in February 2012, see Fid's Exh. CC, and by March 2012, valuable stocks "that Aaron wanted" were entered. See Fid.'s Exh. HH-1.

Before the Court discusses in greater detail the factual background of this relationship, it halts to underscore the Fiduciary's consistent emphasis in his testimony that he took a "slow, cautious, approach," see Fid.'s Exh. G (summary of meetings prepared for litigation), and did not decide to draft an estate plan for final execution until the end, or nearly the end, of his "process." He also testified that while engaging in an on-going evaluation of Ms. Webber's cognitive abilities, he never questioned her capacity.[31] After careful consideration and review of the documentary evidence, trial

testimony and importantly a video of the execution of the Estate Planning Documents,

the Court reluctantly discerns, from the totality of the evidence presented at trial, that

the "cautious approach" was as much, if not more, an endeavor to bolster sustainability

of the documents under uncertain or problematic circumstances than a bona fide probe

or search for confirmation pertaining to the propriety or impropriety of their execution

and efficacy. In a similar vein, the "process" might well have reflected as much his

reluctance to finalize documents as an ongoing attempt to uncover or document facts

supportive of their ultimate validity, while turning a blind eye to information that might

have shed further enlightenment. It reaches that conclusion after considering, inter alia,

as discussed in greater detail infra: (1) that the Fiduciary, despite concerns voiced by

Dr. Schwartz[32] and his own hired expert, Nurse Practitioner Nancy Euchner ("N.P.

Euchner"), calling Ms. Webber's mental state into question, personally administered his

own mini-mental status exam from a form taken from the internet, rather than engaging

an independent expert; (2) he never reviewed her medical records before the

---

[31] At the end of the Fiduciary's testimony, the Court queried the Fiduciary about his statement at trial that he never questioned Ms. Webber's capacity between September 2011 and May 2012. In light of his confidence, the Court asked something to the effect of whether those documents might have been signed well prior to May 2, 2012. Though he answered by appearing to stand firm on his employment of "the process", when more narrowly asked whether he would have proceeded without delay to have the documents executed if he received word that Ms. Webber had been diagnosed by her doctor as having stage 4 cancer and only days to two weeks to live, he unhesitatingly and unequivocally stated that he would have done so. Given the risks of delay given Ms. Webber's age and precarious health condition, this reinforces, by logical and rationale inference, the Court's perception that "the process" was engaged largely, if not solely, to aid sustainability of the documents if later attacked, via a veneer of calculated and deliberate process. The Court further takes note that in earlier testimony, the Fiduciary stated he did not make a final decision about capacity until May 2, 2012, even though he had her execute powers of attorney in October 2011. As such, it remains at best unclear when or if he actually attained full confidence in her capacity and whether the powers of attorney were valid.
[32] The Court in particular notes as remarkable the Fiduciary's testimony that when he met with Dr. Schwartz in February 2012 he did not remember asking Dr. Schwartz directly whether Ms. Webber was competent to sign legal documents. Nor did he prepare for this meeting by reviewing Dr. Schwartz's medical records or the file of a prior attorney made available to him, who had concluded that Ms. Webber should not execute documents without a guardian.

41

documents were executed; (3) he took the unusual step of engaging lawyers as witnesses, but did not share key medical/psychological information of which he was aware with those witnesses before the documents' execution; (4) a review of the videotape of the 2012 Estate Planning Documents' execution demonstrates that he acted in a manner that discouraged, or with relative ease deflected, Ms. Webber's attention away from certain changes requested or responding to certain questions she posed during the signing, evincing a purposeful desire, if not design, that day to have the documents signed as prepared[33]; (5) that with regard to the assets in particular, he asked numerous, and at times a series of, leading questions to Ms. Webber at the May 2nd document execution -- to which she merely concurred without manifesting any substantive or self-initiated thoughtful engagement or response; (6) he did not follow-up after learning that Dr. Hopkins, the gerontologist hired by the BEAS, visited Ms. Webber weeks before execution of the documents and was concerned about the potential for, or her vulnerability to, exploitation; and (7) he did not obtain and review copies of a psychological evaluation of Ms. Webber conducted on February 24, 2011 that raised serious concerns about her mental state.[34] In addition, he did not, despite a process of considerable and uncommon duration, execute an engagement letter until the Estate Planning Documents were signed in May 2012, despite his own claim that she became his client in September 2011. Finally, the documented fact that the 2012 Will states that "I have no children" and fails to name Brett Webber, see Fid.'s Exh. A, provoking a

---

[33] In point of fact, the relative ease apparent from the video with which the Fiduciary was able to keep Ms. Webber on task and dissuade her from making such changes in the Estate Planning Documents as she voiced wanting, strikes the Court as markedly inconsistent with his testimonial description of her as a decisive person, clear on what she wanted, hard to take advantage of and strong-willed, as well as his expressed disbelief that "anyone could persuade her to do what she did not want to do."
[34] Indeed, the Court is unsettled as much by what he did not do, in terms of serious investigation into her capacity and failure at signing to honor Ms. Webber's wishes, as what he in fact did.

42

potential pretermitted heir assertion, see generally RSA 551:10; In re Estate of Treloar, 151 N.H. 460 (2004), belies the avowed aim of the slow and *cautious* approach advanced by the Fiduciary.

The Court's view of the "process" is further colored by Fiduciary's Exhibit OO, which is labelled as "Undated – Gary Holmes' notes" and appears to be a "to do" list. Although undated, it can be reasonably inferred as drafted toward the beginning of the process as one notation indicates that the Fiduciary contemplates "[m]aybe" using Nancy Euchner, having Ms. Webber sign releases, and obtaining originals of the will and medical reports. Supportive of the Court's assessment of the purpose of the "process" advanced by the Fiduciary are notations on the "to-do" list to: "keep Aaron away," "do [a] video," "do a preliminary oral test for video," and "use knowledg[e]able volunteers." Id.

As noted supra, the Fiduciary was contacted by Attorney Nadeau on August 25, 2011, looking to make a referral of the Webber estate planning concerns. The Fiduciary's notes indicate he was told that the matter involved Ms. Webber and a Portsmouth police officer. He was made aware that Attorney Mulhern believed "she is not competent" but that Officer Goodwin "says she is very competent." Fid.'s Exh. K. This phone call was not Attorney Nadeau's only contact on behalf of Officer Goodwin. The Fiduciary's records indicate follow-up calls from Attorney Nadeau in February 2012. See Fid.'s Exhs. EE & FF. Attorney Nadeau also sent letter on October 18, 2011.[35] stating that he "represents Mr. Aaron Goodwin" and seeking information about Ms.

---

[35] Although the letter is dated October 18, 2012, testimony at trial indicated that this was a typo, as the letter was actually sent in 2011.

43

Webber's estate planning "so that I may update my client as to the current status of this matter." Fid.'s Exh. T.

The Fiduciary met with Ms. Webber on September 9, 2011. See Fid.'s Exh. M. He testified that he found her engaged and interested and that she discussed her desire to give Officer Goodwin her home. He added that they discussed, in general terms, the structure of an estate plan. Over the course of his two-day testimony, each time the Fiduciary testified about his interactions with Ms. Webber, he stated that she was engaged, demonstrated little or no confusion, knew her assets and family,[36] and expressed a desire to benefit Officer Goodwin.

Three days after meeting Ms. Webber for the first time, the Fiduciary called Officer Goodwin. Fid.'s Exh. N. During this call, he recorded Officer Goodwin's recitation of his history with Ms. Webber, her conflicts with Attorney Ritzo, Ms. Webber's mental state, and attempts to procure counsel. The Fiduciary's notes of that telephone call are striking to the extent that Officer Goodwin shades unfavorable information, for example, claiming Attorney Mulhern was fired for taking too long and lack of attentiveness. There appears to be no mention of Attorney Mulhern's suggestion that they seek court oversight. Officer Goodwin apparently told the Fiduciary that Ms. Webber was "very competent"[37] and was only confused when she was outside her home, a proposition to some degree contradicted by the fact that competency concerns voiced by Attorney Mulhern arose from in-home meetings with Ms. Webber. Medical records indicating concerns of Dr. Schwartz and Dr. Eisen were dismissed as the product of unusual upset

---

[36] The Court notes the contrast between this claimed complete clarity and the testimony of her former lawyers.
[37] It is unclear from the notes and the fiduciary's testimony whether this was Officer Goodwin's impression or that of his father.

44

caused by hospitalization. He did not inform the Fiduciary of the dementia diagnosis. The Fiduciary testified that during this conversation, he found Officer Goodwin to be trustworthy. The Fiduciary, however, never sought to confirm the allegations against Attorney Ritzo, nor himself ever obtained and read the medical records referenced by Officer Goodwin.

He met again with Ms. Webber on September 15th, and after a conversation about her fear that Attorney Ritzo would use the 2006 power of attorney, she signed a revocation of that document. See Fid.'s Exh. O.

The Fiduciary engaged the services of N.P. Euchner, a geriatric nurse practitioner with thirty-seven-years-experience, to evaluate Ms. Webber and offer an opinion on Ms. Webber's competency. The Fiduciary and N.P. Euchner met with Ms. Webber on September 19, 2011 and then N.P. Euchner had a follow-up visit alone. See Fid.'s Exhs. P, Q & S. After the first visit, she reported that Ms. Webber seemed alert, engaged, and "fiercely independent." N.P. Euchner noted a particular fondness for Officer Goodwin. See Fid.'s Exh. Q. The Fiduciary's notes of a telephone call with N.P. Euchner reflect the following comments: "Presents a difficult case! Aaron may be on thin ice!" Fid.'s Exh. P.[38] It also indicates that there were concerns about Ms. Webber's short term memory and "process/perception of information." Id.

N.P. Euchner's notes after a second visit indicate that at she had some difficulty obtaining a medical records release because Ms. Webber was "unwilling to sign a form authorizing me to speak with . . . her doctor without giving it more thought and possibly speaking with Aaron." Fid.'s Exh. S. After finally obtaining some medical records, N.P.

---

[38] N.P. Euchner has no memory of saying this, but agreed it sounded like something she could have said.

45

Euchner observed that "[t]he records indicate that there has been cognitive impairment for some time, but the clinicians still feel she can live at home alone with the help she has." Id. She also noted that:

> Dr. Schwartz knows his client well. I am not in a position to really make a recommendation on her capacity to sign new documents since she won't let me assess her fully. I recommend that Gary speak with Dr. Schwartz directly about the questions at hand.

Id. She shared this information with the Fiduciary during a phone call on October 26th. Fid.'s Exh. U. By letter dated December 22, 2011 and phone call that same day, N.P. Euchner terminated her engagement with the Fiduciary, again suggesting that he contact Dr. Schwartz. Fid.'s Exhs. Y & Z. At trial, N.P. Euchner stated that Dr. Schwartz, having had a long-term relationship with Ms. Webber was in the best position to assess her cognitive ability and that she knew him to be fair and balanced.

The Fiduciary met with Dr. Schwartz in February 2012. Before the meeting, he prepared a list of possible subjects to discuss, see Fid.'s Exh. BB, and then filled it in later. The Fiduciary testified that he did not, however, despite having releases from Ms. Webber, see Fid.'s Exh. X(2), read either Dr. Schwartz's medical files or Dr. Eisen's report prior to meeting with Dr. Schwartz. (Indeed, he testified that he never read them before execution of the documents.)

Dr. Schwartz testified that he told the Fiduciary that Ms. Webber lacked the insight to sign legal documents based on his observations that she was unable to understand complex issues and medical issues, she lacked insight and that medically she was impaired to an extent that she could not make appropriate decisions. The Fiduciary's notes reflect only "poor" next to line item "awareness" and "poor" next to line item

46

"memory." Next to line item "capability"[39] it appears to note: "not adequate evaluation." He also makes note that a "psychiatrist determined her to be incompetent to go home . . . she didn't want to go 'that moment'." See Fid.'s Exh. BB. At trial, the Fiduciary claimed that he discounted the "psychiatrist's" evaluation as pertaining only to "that moment" and it applied only to her ability to make medical decisions. Remarkably, the Fiduciary testified that he did not remember if he asked Dr. Schwartz directly whether, in the doctor's opinion, Ms. Webber had testamentary capacity.[40] He also testified that he decided to continue his "slow, cautious approach" because he had yet to decide if Ms. Webber had capacity.[41] As earlier noted, however, he later also testified that at no time did he perceive her as lacking capacity.

Instead of obtaining and reading medical records and/or hiring an independent expert who would opine on Ms. Webber's mental capacity given that N. P. Euchner had declined to do so, the Fiduciary administered, himself, a form of a mini-mental exam,[42] a "competency questionnaire" and a "close your eyes" diagram, see Fid.'s Exhs. HH(2)-(3), on March 27, 2012. He brought his paralegal, Irene Ray, with him to make notes of the results. See Fid.'s Exh. HH(1).

The Fiduciary's records indicate that a few weeks later, on April 9, 2012, he had a series of phone conversations with Deborah Gendron of BEAS. In the first conversation, see Fid.'s Exh. II, Ms. Gendron indicated that she and a BEAS

---

[39] Notably, the Fiduciary's line items do not include "competent" or "capacity."

[40] Medical evidence discussed supra shows that within the next month, Dr. Schwartz either authorized, or directly called, protective services at least three times with concerns about exploitation of Ms. Webber and that she suffered from "severe dementia." As such, the Court is inclined to believe Dr. Schwartz's version of what transpired at the meeting.

[41] However, he did prepare, and present for execution on December 8, 2011, powers of attorney, indicating he had previously made some sort of decision regarding capacity. See Fid.'s Exh. X(1).

[42] The source of this exam is unclear. The Fiduciary testified to both having gotten it from the internet and then having no memory of where he obtained it. The form notes that it is "[p]rovided by the Alzheimer's Drug Therapy Initiative for physician use." See Fid.'s Exh. HH(3).

47

gerontologist[43] had visited Ms. Webber as part of an investigation of whether Ms. Webber was the victim of financial exploitation. She stated that Dr. Schwartz had opined that Ms. Webber suffered from "significant dementia." He was told that the gerontologist's report noted concerns that she was vulnerable, had cognitive impairment, and was isolated. The Fiduciary never reviewed the report or reached out to the gerontologist because he did not consider it something he needed to do as part of his "cautious, careful process."

Ms. Ray's notes indicate that at the March 27th meeting, the Fiduciary and she sought to confirm a list of distributions. See Fid.'s Exh. HH(1). This confirmation followed a pattern employed by the Fiduciary in that he would prepare a chart or list of assets and distributions for Ms. Webber to review before meeting her at her home. See Fid.'s Exh. HH(3). Upon inquiry by the Court, the Fiduciary clarified that these lists were based on prior wills as a template, to which Ms. Webber made changes. The Fiduciary testified that on April 16, 2012, he brought a detailed list of assets and distributions to Ms. Webber for review. See Fid.'s Exh. JJ. He first testified that he felt that he was impressed by her continuing knowledge of the value of her assets. However, upon further inquiry of the Court, it became apparent that he prepared the value designations in advance and presented them to her. He did not ask her if they were accurate, but rather, reviewed them and she agreed. Similarly, he testified that after he presented her with a chart outlining the estate plan he had developed over time, see Fid.'s Exh. KK(2), on April 26, 2012, he observed that she did not express or demonstrate confusion about her assets and distributions. He then concluded that he had completed his "careful, cautious process" and scheduled the appointment for executing the Estate Planning

---

[43] Dr. John Hopkins. See supra.

48

Documents. It is not apparent, however, to the Court how much of this final plan was organically derived from Ms. Webber, or instead involved a process of presentation and assent based on a pre-existing template and prepared asset values.[44] Significantly, during a February 1, 2011 meeting with representatives of the Attorney General's Office, Ms. Webber states that she is reluctant to immediately revoke (i.e.: "rip up") a prior will, despite her desire to remove the provisions granting fees to Attorney Ritzo, because she did not remember the details of her other gifting and "need[s] [a prior will] to see to whom I've left money". Fid.'s Exh. ZZ(1) at 103.

On May 2, 2012, the Fiduciary, his paralegal, Irene Ray, and two former paralegals, now Attorney Jesse Krall, and Attorney Jennifer Hoover, arrived at Ms. Webber's home for the document signing. The Fiduciary also brought along a videographer. See Fid.'s Exh. D. Officer Goodwin did not attend the signing. The Court has reviewed the video taken on May 2, 2012 and makes the following observations about the documents' execution:

- Ms. Webber appears happy and sociable. She makes a number of sexual gestures and comments regarding Officer Goodwin despite his claim that she loved him like a son. Ms. Webber also flirts with the Fiduciary; however, because there was extensive testimony that this was her manner, this behavior does not cause concern about her capacity. It does, however, call into question the general credibility of any witnesses claiming that Ms. Webber's affection for Officer Goodwin was purely maternal.

---

[44] This distinction did not concern the Court until after it viewed the video of the Estate Planning Documents' execution, see Fid.'s Exh. D, and noted the leading nature of the Fiduciary's questions and dismissal of Ms. Webber's attempts to make changes.

49

- Ms. Webber claims that she was offered $3 million for an unremarkable decorative painting hanging on a wall.

- The Fiduciary appears dismissive of certain requests, either ignoring them or telling Ms. Webber it can be dealt with at another time including: (1) a distribution to a kind gentleman whom she wished to favor; and (2) multiple requests that both Officer Goodwin and the Fiduciary be joint agents on the power of attorney documents. In one instance, that related to a residuary distribution to a charitable organization affording residence for children, Ms. Webber instructs the Fiduciary that the distribution was not to be for the general benefit of the organization itself or a girl, but for a "worthy young man" or "boy" only, which the Fiduciary wrongly confirms he had done but had not.[45]. Trial testimony and documentary evidence on file indicates that Ms. Webber's estate plans were never amended to honor these requests, despite assurances given of follow-up by the Fiduciary.

- Despite Ms. Webber's attempts to insist that a distribution be made to a kind gentleman, including the reasonable request that it be added to the 2012 Trust by hand, she acquiesces to Attorney Holmes after his insistence that it would be against his practice, calling into question whether the distribution list accurately or truly reflected Ms. Webber's intentions.

- She does not mention Brett Webber at all during the proceeding.

- Late in the video, after execution of the 2012 Trust, Ms. Webber displays confusion and a lack of understanding of the documents she just executed and needs prompting by Attorney Holmes.

---

[45] In Article Five, Section 5.06 of the 2012 Trust a non-residuary $25,000 is given to the charity, Chase Home for Children, "to be used for a Scholarship Fund for a deserving young man"; however, the residuary distribution of concern is recited in Article Six, Section 6.06 and reflects that it is "to be used for [the charity's] general charitable purposes." See Fid.'s Exh. B.

50

- She makes fairly irrational and disturbing statements that she wanted to suffer physical pain during the death process.

- She makes statements that Attorney Ritzo had stolen from her and he should be shot.

- The interview is riddled with leading questions, and this, combined with the document preparation discussed supra, calls into question whether Ms. Webber reasonably knew how much or what she was leaving whom and the value of her assets, rendering her actual unprompted self-awareness of dubious prospect.

The witnesses to the signing, Attorneys Hoover and Krall and Ms. Ray, all testified that in their opinion, Ms. Webber had the requisite capacity to sign the documents. Ms. Ray, who had met Ms. Webber in March 2012, agreed that questions asked regarding Ms. Webber's assets were leading, and that the documents were signed without changes requested by Ms. Webber. Attorney Hoover, who had worked as a paralegal for the Fiduciary for eleven years, testified as well that she felt Ms. Webber possessed the requisite capacity to execute the documents. Unlike Ms. Ray, however, she did not have a clear memory of the red flags noted supra. She also admitted that she was not aware of concerns voiced by Ms. Webber's physician or her medical history. Finally, Attorney Krall, who also had worked for the Fiduciary as a paralegal before entering private practice, similarly testified that she had no concerns on May 2nd about Ms. Webber's capacity. She was not aware, however, that Ms. Webber had been diagnosed with cognitive impairment and/or dementia. She also displayed a rather selective memory of events that day.

51

Ms. Webber's health began to decline precipitously in the fall of 2012. No further changes were made to the 2012 Estate Planning Documents. She passed away in her home on December 11, 2012.

III.   Analysis

A. *Undue Influence*

The Court, for the reasons set forth more fully below, concludes that the 2012 Estate Planning Documents must be invalidated as the product of undue influence exerted by Officer Goodwin. As stated earlier, evaluation of a claim of undue influence is by its very nature a difficult task. This Court reaches its decision only after careful consideration of: the totality of the trial testimony; extensive documentary evidence; Ms. Webber's medical history; the video of her executing the 2012 Estate Planning Documents; Officer Goodwin's standing as a police officer and the control he exercised over most details of Ms. Webber's life; the "process" engaged in by the Fiduciary resulting in execution of the documents; and the common law governing undue influence, as well as all applicable inferences when there is a confidential relationship.

In sum, as has been found, it is uncontroverted that Officer Goodwin stood in a confidential relationship with Ms. Webber, procured legal counsel for her for the purposes preparation and execution of the Estate Planning Documents, and was the beneficiary of the vast majority of lifetime assets accumulated by a ninety (93) year-old woman he had only known the final twenty-six (26) months of her life. Because of these undisputed facts, Officer Goodwin and the Fiduciary, as Proponents of the 2012 Estate Planning Documents, had the minimal burden of demonstrating by a preponderance of the evidence that those documents were not the product of undue influence. The Court

52

concludes, given Ms. Webber's age and weakened mental condition, Officer Goodwin's

standing as a police officer, the nature of extraordinary gifting to someone relatively new

to her life, and her dependence upon Officer Goodwin for love, attention and valuable

life supports, that the Proponents have failed to rebut the inference of undue influence

rendering the Estate Planning Documents invalid. To put it another way, the

Proponents have failed to demonstrate the absence "not only of opportunity and ability,

but of design and accomplishment." Harvey, 83 N.H. at 240.

    The analysis begins with a presumption of the absence of undue influence. See,

e.g., Albee, 79 N.H. at 91. This presumption arises only "upon proof of the voluntary,

formal execution of the will by a competent testator and . . . *in the absence of*

circumstances arousing suspicion . . . ." Id. It is suspended, however, when contestants

of an estate plan show there is "substantial evidence" of undue influence. Gaffney, 81

N.H. at 307. Here, the contestants offered substantial proof of Ms. Webber's failing

mental capacity and growing fear and paranoia; cf. Harvey, 83 N.H. at 240, her

dependence upon Officer Goodwin and the control he exerted over her life, Edgerly, 73

N.H. at 408, and the unusual circumstance of her largesse in conferring a lifetime of

assets to a relatively new, unrelated person in her life. Neill, 126 N.E. at 94.

    Put another way, the Petitioners offered substantial proof of "opportunity and ability"

as well as "design and accomplishment[.]" Harvey, 83 N.H. at 240, and thus are seen as

having sufficiently rebutted the presumption of validity. As more than one medical

professional, long-time acquaintances and banker Gile testified, Ms. Webber was

vulnerable given her growing confusion, inability to make sound judgments, and

tendency toward fear and suspicion. Officer Goodwin, by his initial introduction as a

53

police officer,[46] and rapid installation as her close friend, confidante, quasi-protector, and point-person for medical care, had the ability to exert influence, even if not overt in the nature of force or threats, but by acting upon her fears and hopes. See In re Hobbes, 47 A. at 680. Certainly, the contestants offered proof of design as Officer Goodwin, as early as January 2011, actively sought to procure legal counsel for Ms. Webber either directly or through his surrogate, Attorney Justin Nadeau. Finally, the contestants offered substantial proof of accomplishment as the estate plans were drawn up, serious medical/mental health concerns were seemingly ignored, and a process was implemented to a pre-determined end by the Fiduciary.

As has been found, Officer Goodwin was in a confidential relationship with Ms. Webber. A confidential relationship exists where one has "gained the confidence of the other and purports to act or advise with the other's interest in mind." Cornwell, 116 N.H. at 209. Although it could be argued that Officer Goodwin's official status is sufficient to support a finding of confidential relation, the record also shows that Ms. Webber relied upon "her friend" Officer Goodwin to arrange medical and life supports, in addition to obtaining legal counsel. Officer Goodwin presented himself as acting in the best interests of Ms. Webber by calling her multiple times per week, taking her to restaurants and at least one casino, acting as her contact person for medical care, and arranging for in-home services when Ms. Webber's former support system no longer was available. Ms. Webber gave him a key to her home. When procuring counsel for Ms. Webber, he presented himself as a friend who was assisting her to replace estate documents

---

[46] During trial, Officer Goodwin and members of the Portsmouth Police Department offered testimony that after January 2011, his relationship was one of a friend instead of a police officer. Even assuming that this bifurcation of roles was clear in Ms. Webber's mind, by the time he began acting as her "friend" he had already begun to exert significant control over, and become a central figure in, her life.

54

drafted by Attorney Ritzo. Indeed, with the one exception of her expressed distrust of Officer Goodwin to Dr. Hopkins, referenced earlier, there was overwhelming evidence that to Ms. Webber, Officer Goodwin was her "love," a trusted companion, and even perhaps sent by God to protect her from outside threats.

It cannot be disputed that Officer Goodwin was a beneficiary, indeed the primary distributee, of the 2012 Estate Planning Documents; and having found that he stood in a confidential relationship with Ms. Webber, and actively assisted in procuring the documents, an inference arises that they were the product of undue influence. Edgerly, 73 N.H. at 408-09; Archer, 126 N.H. at 28. The documents can only be declared valid, therefore, if the proponents prove an absence of undue influence. Archer, 126 N.H. at 28. As discussed at length supra, proof must be established by a preponderance of the evidence.

After considering "all the circumstances surrounding a disposition, including the relationship between the parties, the physical and mental condition of the donor, the reasonableness and nature of the disposition, and the personalities of the parties," In re Estate of Cass, 143 N.H. at 61 (quotations omitted), the Court concludes that the Proponents have failed to rebut the inference of undue influence. This case is difficult because, like many such cases, undue influence is "not shown by gross or palpable instrumentalities" such as overt threats, rather, evaluation of the presence or absence of undue influence must be derived from the circumstances of the devise or grant. Neill, 126 N.E. at 94. The Court's task is made immeasurably more formidable given that the precise point or moment that one's free will is destroyed or subjugated to another's

55

control or coercion is rarely, if ever, discernable to the judicial eye owing to its imperceptible progression to full maturity.

In addition to the common law inference of undue influence, several facts elicited at trial provide substantial evidence of opportunity, ability, design and accomplishment and thus independently favor a determination of undue influence. Importantly, Dr. Schwartz testified that her age, cognitive deficits, and poor judgment made her vulnerable or susceptible to undue influence despite her feisty and unfiltered demeanor. Others voiced this concern as well. Ms. Webber had become particularly suspicious, fearful of being robbed, lived alone, and despite many hired and friendly helpers, was lonely, -- in particular it appears to the Court, for male companionship. Officer Goodwin provided security and very quickly after they met, became a critical lifeline to medical and other life supports. Although she, before meeting Officer Goodwin, had a long, and often shifting, list of intended post-mortem gifts to friends and helpers, there is no evidence that she ever desired to benefit another in such a generous manner. Indeed, even her former husband, Douglas Miller, received only a life estate in her home (subject to conditions including that it could be revoked if he lived with another woman or his children), some stock, and some monthly income from her investments. See Pet.'s Exh. 1(A). No provision ultimately was made for Brett Webber. Simply put, the uncharacteristic generosity to a relatively new friend to whom she became emotionally and physically dependent made the devise/grants to Officer Goodwin strikingly unnatural, in particular when compared to prior planned dispositions when Ms. Webber was in stronger mental and physical health, and less dependent or under the control of

56

any one person. It is these special circumstances that lead the Court to conclude that the common law inference of undue influence has not been disproved.[47]

In addition, the Court holds that the Proponents of the 2012 Estate Planning Documents' have not overcome the inference that Officer Goodwin, by design, carried out through the Fiduciary, accomplished execution of documents reflecting his will and not the free unfettered agency of Ms. Webber. Officer Goodwin actively sought out counsel for Ms. Webber. Although it was Attorney Nadeau who ultimately contacted the Fiduciary, the Court cannot ignore the hand of Officer Goodwin, in particular given Attorney Nadeau's letters to the fiduciary seeking updates on behalf of his client, and thus applying subtle pressure on the Fiduciary to complete the "process." Design can also be inferred by Officer Goodwin's failure to update his January 10, 2011 memo during Detective Warchol's investigation to reflect that: (1) Ms. Webber had informed him that she would be leaving him her home and contents; and (2) he had begun a process to procure legal counsel to draft documents including such a generous devise. Finally, it is curious that Attorney Mulhern was dismissed after suggesting court intervention, which naturally would have increased independent scrutiny on whether the intended gifting to Officer Goodwin might be indeed the product of an unfettered will. The Court is not at all persuaded that he was dismissed for lack of attentiveness or diligence and it specifically does not credit Officer Goodwin's testimony that Ms. Webber of her own volition initiated his dismissal.

---

[47] The Court is not unmindful of the difficulty that the common law may place on proponents advocating the validity of legal documents where there is a confidential relationship, however, that onus could have been avoided had they acted on the advice of Attorney Mulhern and sought probate court oversight given the unusual circumstances of this case.

57

Accomplishment was effected through choice of counsel who ever-so-slowly marched toward final execution without reading key medical reports, and, in the face of experts who could not (N. P. Euchner) or would not (Dr. Schwartz) attest to Ms. Webber's competency, administered his own mental status exam.[48] As noted supra, the Court is particularly unsettled by the Fiduciary's offhand dismissal of requests by Ms. Webber during the videoed document execution, casting further shade on the question of whether Ms. Webber's independent will was being effectuated. Again, Officer Goodwin's participation in the choice of counsel and then oversight through his lawyer is indicative of accomplishment and casts doubt on whose will was driving execution of an estate plan with such generosity bestowed on him.

In rebuttal, the Proponents offered testimony of Officer Goodwin that he was only helping Ms. Webber accomplish what she wanted and that he only agreed to accept millions of dollars of assets to make her happy. Again, given his often evasive, sometimes dubious testimony and often selective memory, the Court cannot give credit to Officer Goodwin's recounting of facts without independent verification.[49] Similarly, the Court does not give substantial weight to the Fiduciary's testimony on this matter in light of his own clouded credibility borne of the process he effected and his own often selective and sometimes self-serving memory.

Although all agree, and the video demonstrates, that Ms. Webber possessed a vivacious, funny, irreverent, and lively personality, those traits do not logically offer sufficient support to overcome an inference of undue influence, particularly in the face of

---

[48] The Court does not intend to create a requirement that counsel hire expert evaluators in every case, however, where there are serious concerns about capacity, practitioners should tread with great care.
[49] There was testimony that Ms. Webber consistently voiced a desire to benefit Officer Goodwin. Though the Court does not doubt the truth that she made such declarations, it is suspect, however, that the idea and insistence was truly autonomous and not that of Officer Goodwin.

58

those facts indicative of undue influence discussed <u>supra</u>. Moreover, viewing the video, the Court was struck by how easily she submitted to Attorney Holmes' rejection of her desire, stated multiple times, to have co-agents on the power of attorney and add a distribution to a man whom she wished to favor with a gift. In that regard one might reasonably deduce that her will was also subjugated to the desire/convenience of Attorney Holmes.

Finally, the Court rejects the Fiduciary's contention, without citation or other support, that "[n]either case law not public policy supports shifting the burden of proof to a neutral trustee representing the interests of innocent beneficiaries to prove that a challenged trust was established without undue influence." *Trustee's Memorandum on the Burden of Proof* at 1 (Index #103). Case law has always been clear – the burden of proving the validity of either a will or trust is *always on the proponent* of that document, although in most circumstances a presumption of validity assists with this burden. See e.g. <u>Estate of Washburn</u>, 141 N.H. at 663; <u>Gaffney</u>, 81 N.H. at 306-07. A confidential relationship and beneficial grant or devise simply creates an inference of undue influence which must be overcome before a document can be deemed valid. <u>See</u>, e.g., <u>Edgerly</u>, 73 N.H. at 406-09. In the case of both the presumption of validity or inference of undue influence, the focus of the law is, appropriately, on *due execution* as without it, a document is void *ab initio*. The alleged neutrality of a proponent, or composition of the other members of a beneficiary pool, is simply not the foundation of inquiry. The Court is empathetic to those entities and/or persons who, through invalidation of the 2012 Estate Planning Documents, will have their distributions invalidated.[50] However, it has

---

[50] The Court observes that in other contexts, courts have not hesitated to invalidate will and trusts improperly executed without accounting for "innocent beneficiaries."

long been the law that a party who is a proponent of a legal document carries the ultimate burden to demonstrate its validity.

Moreover, there are also strong policy arguments against adoption of the Fiduciary's view. Namely, such a policy would allow an improper influencer to insulate nefarious acts by ensuring that there are one or more gift provisions made to innocent parties.[51]

B. *Capacity*

Given the Court's decision that the 2012 Estate Planning Documents must be invalidated as the result of undue influence, it need not decide whether Ms. Webber lacked the requisite capacity on May 2, 2012. As noted supra, the law requires: (1) understanding of the nature of the act; (2) a recollection of property and its nature; (3) recollection of the nearest relatives or natural objects of her bounty; and (4) ability to make elections as to disposition. See, e.g., In re Estate of Washburn, 141 N.H. at 661. Although the Court has deep concern about her overall mental health, even pre-dating her introduction to Officer Goodwin, though often seemingly confused, Ms. Webber does indeed appear in the video, at the time of execution, to understand that she is signing a testamentary document and trust that include post-mortem gifting. See Boardman, 47 N.H. at 140 (even if testator is under a delusion, if it clears at the time of execution, a will is valid).

The Court observes however, that it remains unconvinced that Ms. Webber, given her dementia, confusion, and lack of judgment, history of exaggerated statements about the value of her home, and a claim of value of a painting, was able to recollect her

---

[51] The Fiduciary also asserts that the case should be dismissed as it should have been brought as a petition for constructive trust. That vehicle, however, is a remedy when there has been an asset transfer. Cf. Hopwood v. Pickett 145 N.H. 207, 208-09 (2000). It is "based upon principles of restitution, to prevent unjust enrichment of one person at the expense of another. Cornwell, 116 N.H. at 208-09. That is not this case.

60

property and its nature to the extent the law requires. In addition, evidence presented at trial suggests that without prompting by the Fiduciary and copies of prior wills, she was largely unable to independently and accurately self-recall and rationally understand the requisite nature of her property.

Similarly, it is unclear to the Court whether, or the extent to which, Ms. Webber had the contemporary capacity to bear in mind Brett Webber and the nature of her gifts, or lack thereof, for his benefit. As Attorney Mulhern testified, she was consistently mistaken about the existence of a certificate of deposit held for his benefit.

Finally, as it concerns the fourth element requiring the ability to make an election and bestow property, the Court is particularly troubled by actions in the video where the Fiduciary effectively ignores Ms. Webber's direction, on multiple occasions, to include a distribution to a certain helpful young man and honor her insistence that the one distribution to a charity benefit only a worthy young man or boy. Thus, although her ability to bestow property may not be the product of a delusion, her inability to prevail upon the Fiduciary to amend her distributions may well reflect some level of incapacity.

Determination of capacity presents a closer question for this Court. The Petitioners, in particular by introduction of Ms. Webber's medical records, the testimony of Dr. Schwartz, Joan Gile, Jeremy Bernier, Raymond Pasquale and N.P. Euchner, raised serious doubts about Ms. Webber's mental state such that the common law presumption of capacity was rebutted. In re Estate of Washburn, 141 N.H. at 663. Had the Court been called upon to render a decision on capacity, concerns about elements three through four, however, may have been sufficient to support a ruling that the

61

Proponents of the 2012 Will and 2012 Trust failed to carry their burden of showing, by a preponderance of the evidence, testamentary capacity. Id.

IV. Orders

As the Court is satisfied that it has sufficiently set out the facts and applicable law essential to support its rulings on appeal, the parties' respective requests for findings of fact and rulings of law are granted so far as consistent with the narrative facts, rulings and law set out within. Any of their requests that are inconsistent, either expressly or by necessary implication, are denied or determined otherwise unnecessary. See Crown Paper Co. v. City of Berlin, 142 N.H. 563, 571 (1997).

In accordance with the above findings and rulings, the Court enters the following orders:

- The *Petition to Set Aside the Geraldine W. Webber Revocable Trust Dated May 2, 2012* (Index #1) is GRANTED.

- The Court GRANTS Prayer D of the *Motion to Re-Examine* (Estate Case Index #29), and the request to order proof in solemn form is DENIED AS MOOT. See id. Prayer B.

- The Court DEFERS ruling on Prayer E of the *Motion to Re-Examine* pending further proceedings in relation to: (1) appointment of a successor fiduciary to Attorney Gary Holmes given the invalidation of the 2012 Will nominating him; and (2) consideration of another prior testamentary instrument to be submitted for admission into probate.

62

- The Clerk is DIRECTED to assign a post-trial status conference for **September 21, 2015** at 9:30 a.m. and parties and/or counsel (with authority to act on behalf of their client(s) in their absence) are ORDERED to attend.

- The Court DENIES AS MOOT the Hospital's request to set aside the 2012 Estate Planning Documents on the basis of lack of capacity.

- The oral motion to admit an audio-recording of Captain Warchol's interview with Officer Goodwin is DENIED AS MOOT.

SO ORDERED

Dated: August 20, 2015

_____

Gary R. Cassavechia, Judge

63